# Writing into the Future

NEW AMERICAN POETRIES FROM *THE DIAL* TO THE DIGITAL

ALAN GOLDING

The University of Alabama Press
*Tuscaloosa*

The University of Alabama Press
Tuscaloosa, Alabama 35487–0380
uapress.ua.edu



Typeface: Warnock Pro, Takota and Avenir

Cover image: Detail of *Annunciation* by Laurie Doctor,
12 × 12 in., oil on wood; www.lauriedoctor.com
Cover design: David Nees

Cataloging-in-Publication data is available from the Library of Congress.
ISBN: 978-0-8173-6049-8
E-ISBN: 978-0-8173-9411-0

For Lisa, at last and always

and for Chase and Jordan

# Contents

# Acknowledgments

Any work like this, produced over a number of years, emerges from, and perhaps belongs to, a community of colleagues, peers, and friends. For everything from local insights to samizdat publications to decades-long conversations, I am grateful to Donald Allen, Bruce Andrews, Jane Augustine, Jessica Burstein, Tom Byers, Michael Davidson, Johanna Drucker, Rachel Blau DuPlessis, Andrew Epstein, Norman Finkelstein, Harry Gilonis, Lisa Gitelman, Paul Griner, Carla Harryman, Burton Hatlen, Michael Heller, Aaron Jaffe, Kevin Killian, Tony Lopez, Peter Middleton, Cristanne Miller, David Moody, Harryette Mullen, Peter Nicholls, Aldon Nielsen, Marjorie Perloff, Stephen Rodefer, Joan Retallack, Mark Scroggins, Tim Shaner, Ron Silliman, Brian Kim Stefans, John Taggart, Robert von Hallberg, Barrett Watten, Beth Willey, and Tyrone Williams. Particular thanks to Bruce Andrews for supplying me with a wide range of his hard-to-get early texts. Much gratitude also to my two readers Stephen Fredman and Bob Perelman, who provoked valuable re-assessment and re-organization.

I also owe a lasting debt of gratitude to Charles Bernstein and Hank Lazer, who first encouraged this volume, continued to do so, and remained patient with me beyond all reason. The team at the University of Alabama Press brought the project to fruition: Pete Beatty, Jon Berry, and Dan Waterman. Thanks to Susan Harris for her simultaneously expert and friendly proofreading.

My thanks to the University of Louisville for the sabbatical that enabled completion of the project, and to Dean Kimberly Kempf-Leonard in particular for an important final nudge.

Artist and poetry lover Laurie Doctor generously granted me use of her rich and layered work for the cover art. I encourage readers to explore that work further at www.lauriedoctor.com.

My dear friends, readers, and editorial coconspirators Lynn Keller and Dee Morris deserve a special mention: our regular and often daily contact over decades has kept me learning, kept me thinking, and often kept me going. It's hard to imagine my professional and personal life without them.

My wife Lisa and my sons Chase and Jordan have lived with, laughed about, and needled me about my labyrinthine processes for longer, I'm sure, than they care to think about. This book is for them.

# Introduction

A few months into George Oppen's return to poetry after a twenty-five-year hiatus, and while Donald Allen was editing his epochal anthology *The New American Poetry 1945–1960,* Oppen proposes in an early 1959 letter that "a poem has got to be written into the future. I don't mean something about the admiration of posterity . . . but simply that it's something that is not the past" (*Selected Letters* 22). At the same time, Oppen's version of "Make It New" has behind it a certain skepticism about the avant-garde vividly captured in a daybook comment:

> "avant garde": I have no liking for the word and no need of it One does not need the word, it is obvious enough that there is little use in repeating what has been adequately said before. . . .
>
> "avant-garde"—the distinction between the avant garde and anything I could wish to be is the distinction between writing stylishly and the attempt to say with lucidity some part of what has not been said—but to be anti-avant garde is what? to write Yeats over again? ("Selections" 2)

But if Oppen equated the avant-garde with the merely fashionable ("writing stylishly"), it was the perceived codification of an exploratory poetry into a movement that he finally resisted: the term, "the word," not the impulse behind it. That impulse is foundational to Oppen's sense of poetry: "To say . . . some part of what has not been said," for "there is little use in repeating" either Yeats or anyone else. No: "A poem has got to be written into the future," into the unknown.

A selection of essays from across my career, *Writing into the Future: New American Poetries from "The Dial" to the Digital* treats poetic formations and individual writers within a continuum of innovative poetics that moves from experimental modernism through the Objectivists to the New American poetry, Language writing, and beyond. A central thread running through the chapters is a long-standing interest in how various versions of the "new" have been constructed, received, extended, recycled, resisted, and reanimated in American poetry since modernism, at the level of collective practice (the "contexts" of chapters 1–4) and individual practice (the "texts" of chapters 5–13). Thus the title concept, "writing into the future," extends but gestures beyond Oppen's usage toward a number of interrelated processes: the poetic production of innovative, culturally oppositional work; poets' efforts (via supportive group networks, magazines, anthologies) to facilitate that work's entrance into the social and literary histories both of their own moment and of the future; avant-garde ambition and the blurring of the binary oppositions on which historically it has often rested; questions of canonicity; questions of continuity, transmission, filiation, and conflict within and between group formations and particular poets; and questions of textual, cultural, and institutional politics.

"Writing into the future," that is, encodes matters of both production and reception. The essays gathered here represent the two main methodological emphases of my critical work, literary history and close reading. I operate on the premise that both are equally necessary (though not sufficient) for an adequately nuanced understanding of US poetry since modernism and, indeed, of any literary text or period. "Always historicize," as Fredric Jameson influentially insisted. While the loosely chronological organization, from modernist magazines to digital poetics, does not involve a developmental argument, it does respect historical priority and implicitly values a historically informed perspective. I've always been drawn to formally and thematically exploratory or resistant poetry, work that enacts an oppositional or investigative cultural politics in its forms and that resists, in the process, the hegemonic definitions of "poetry" operative in its own moment and, just as often, the very category of "poetry" itself. On this point, it is no accident that, among my central subjects, Bruce Andrews and Susan Howe came to poetry from other arts and that Oppen did not write a poem for twenty-five years after the publication of his first book. Rachel Blau DuPlessis writes, "The only poem for our time is something that refuses poetry" (*Blue Studios* 197): that about covers it. DuPlessis's concept of "sociopoesis, or the analysis of poetry by helixed social and aesthetic concerns" (*Blue Studios* 2), or what she terms the "social philology" of her *Genders, Races and Religious Cultures in Modern American Poetry*, both capture what I have usually tried to do in my critical work: connect the formal with the social, the aesthetic with the ideological, at the level of textual detail.

While the bulk of this collection concerns innovative poetries in the decades (more or less) 1950–2010, I begin with a modernist case study. My opening chapter foregrounds the tension between a cleanly polemical, strongly articulated, and ambitious set of notions around the "new" among certain modernist writers and the much messier and contingent circulation of those notions into and in the public sphere through the medium of magazines. Widely acknowledged as crucial, if very different, periodicals in the formation of modernism, with *The Little Review* also offering a model for the experimental little magazines of the 1950s, 1960s, and 1970s, *The Dial* and *The Little Review* in the 1920s represented radically different outlets for the modernist "new," outlets that held different attitudes toward innovation as an intrinsic value but that cooperated ambivalently to advance it through an uneasy combination, in Ezra Pound's words, of "lunacy" (in *The Little Review*) and "stodge" (in *The Dial*). Chapter 1 revisits this germinal moment in the promotion, circulation, or publicizing of the poetic new, one marked both by radical ambition and persistent negotiation and one that anticipates some of the dynamics in the anthologies that I discuss in chapters 2–4.

In particular, various forms of the fraught negotiation, compromise, conflict, and consolidation that marks *The Dial–Little Review* relationship underlie these anthologies and their surrounding contexts. If chapter 1 is concerned with part of the process by which modernism became Modernism, chapter 2 considers how new American poetry in the 1950s became *The New American Poetry*, using archival research to consider the editorial construction of the anthology and how strongly claims to newness were internally contested among the parties embracing them. Claims to newness may well develop their own lineage, evident in the attempt to use anthologies to re-create the originary New American moment and to perpetuate or advance the tradition erected on it, in a risky ratio of stultification to advancement (chapter 3). And in any literary historical moment, these claims for emergent cultural formations occur or erupt in the context of residual/dominant formations that we need to understand if we wish to understand that moment more fully (chapter 4). Thus, these chapters use anthologies in various ways to map the contexts in which the innovative poetics discussed in the remainder of the book emerge. To speak of "innovative" poetics with reference to the late millennium begs the question "'innovative' in relation to what?," and in chapter 4, I analyze the network of mainstream anthologies in the last quarter of the twentieth century that sustained and consolidated the very real poetic hegemony against which Language writing and other post–New American experimental practices continued to emerge—a network of narrow, exclusive, and widely repeated set of assumptions about poetry that generally claimed merely a neutral representativeness and inclusiveness for itself.

Following on these chapters, the turn to close readings that I take can usefully be framed through Gerald Bruns's 2018 book *Interruptions*.

Bruns begins with a reminder of "Friedrich Schlegel's inaugural theory and practice of the fragment as an assertion of the autonomy of words, their freedom from rule-governed hierarchies" (ix). In the same spirit, he moves on to Friedrich's brother, August Wilhelm, who asserted in 1798 (the year of the first edition of *Lyrical Ballads*) that "'it is necessary not to treat language in poetry as a mere instrument of the understanding'" (qtd. in Bruns 1). The fragment, autonomy, the freedom of words, anti-instrumentalism, an "'imperative [that] demands the mixing of all poetic genres'" (6)—the Schlegels seem to anticipate the twentieth- and twentieth-first centuries' art of the fragment. This "'feeling for fragments,'" in Bruns's reading, "allows one to think serially, or maybe one should say *ironically*, free from the law of noncontradiction or of any principle of subordination" (6–7). Summarizing Friedrich Schlegel, Bruns argues "irony does not subsume the many into one but instead arranges them as singularities in a series, whence dialogue displaces dialectic" (2). (The reference to "singularities" will resonate for readers of Susan Howe.) While this form of dialogue is particularly important to the work of George Oppen that I discuss in chapter 5, most of the poets whom I treat here work with some version of the paratactically organized fragment, often in serial form: Oppen, Robert Creeley, Howe, Rachel Blau DuPlessis, Andrews, and William Carlos Williams and the Language poets harking back to his earlier generically hybrid work. We are used now to think of the "fragment" as a whole in itself, rather than as a broken and incomplete part of some larger whole, and as such, it resists hermeneutic assimilation into such a whole: "A fragment, whatever its internal arrangement, is not part of any hermeneutical circle, which is, after all, made of links rather than breaks" (13). Again, then, the fragment lends itself to paratactic rather than hypotactic organization—seriality, a seemingly discontinuous use of page space, breaks, not links—and "*parataxis* foregrounds the 'between': the break, pause, swerve, or stammer that materializes the word in a space (or interminability) of its own" (18).

The bulk of my readings (chapters 5–13) return to four overlapping concerns or features of experimental poetries since the mid-twentieth century: three constitutive formal features suggested in Bruns's analysis—-seriality or serial form, the material text, page space and the visual layout of the page, features that can be comprehended under the general rubric of a materialist poetics—and the frequent intersection of these with questions of gender. Permutations of these categories, that is, can be used to define much of what we mean by "innovative" or "alternative" poetics post–World War II. At the same time, my reading of that period involves multiple overlapping chronologies and histories, and relevant lineages extend back to the troubled one of Ezra Pound and the somewhat less troubled one of William Carlos Williams, active participants in *The Dial–Little Review* debates, then foundational figures for *The New American Poetry*, and, in Williams's case, finally a poet of the 1970s and beyond through the 1970 reissue of the 1923 *Spring and All* (previously unavailable in its complete form outside of a Rare Books room) and other 1920s work.

Oppen has been a crucial poet for a number of writers in what we can call "an Objectivist continuum" (Davidson, *Ghostlier Demarcations* 23) and a related "neo-Objectivist branch" (DuPlessis and Quartermain 3). (I am inclined to add the term "post–New American.") In moving from more literary historical discussions of "contexts" to a greater emphasis on readings or "texts," then, I begin with influential experiments in serial form by Oppen and Creeley and move to Oppen's late-career experiments with page space and syntax (in a sense, seriality at the level of the word and phrase). The particular stakes for women writers of a materialist poetics are central in the subsequent four chapters on DuPlessis and Howe. I read DuPlessis's *Drafts* in a post-Objectivist context, as DuPlessis builds a serially organized long poem on Objectivist premises and simultaneously works through and against the gendered history of modernist epic. Just as Oppen's use of serial form resists canonical models of the modernist long poem, so too does *Drafts*, in particular the example of one inaugural figure in Objectivist poetics, Pound. While Howe also typically composes in series or sequences, I emphasize page layout in my two chapters on her work: radical experiments with the design of the page as a textually embodied feminist poetics that extends its critique to "centers" and spurious authorities of all kinds: patriarchal, national, colonial, literary.

Bruce Andrews, the subject of chapter 11, is a limit case for the poetics of the material text, particularly in the creolizing of genre and the visual experimentation that enact his career-long suspicion of "poetry." To consider one of the roots of this materialist poetics, I then turn to the aforementioned reissue of Williams's 1920s work as source and model for Language writing and other contemporaneous innovative poetics. The idea of the "two Dr. Williams" enables us to consider the cultural dynamics of late twentieth century poetry from a number of angles: if the poets of chapter 4's mainstream anthologies read the "scenic" Williams of direct presentation and everyday speech, Language poets read the hybridizing, genre-mixing Williams of the late 1910s and 1920s. And finally, chapter 13 considers how the page-based materiality of Language writing might extend into the digital realm and complicate digital definitions of "materiality" and the material text.

"I sometimes think the Leaves is only a language experiment—that it is an attempt to give the spirit, the body, the man, new words" (Whitman, *American Primer* vii): to recall Whitman's late remark about his life's work is to recall that much US poetry since Emerson, Whitman, and Dickinson has its roots in the idea of a "language experiment."[1] Joan Retallack begins her 2007 essay "What Is Experimental Poetry and Why Do We Need It?" with some "linked propositions with several implications:

> a) There is the shock of alterity. Or should be.
> b) There is the pleasure of alterity. Or should be.
> c) We humans with all our conversational structures have yet to invite enough alterity in.
> d) Experiment is conversation with an interrogative dynamic. Its consequential structures turn on paying attention to what happens when well-designed questions are directed to things we sense but don't really know. These things cannot be known by merely examining our own minds."

The shock and pleasure of alterity, a certain ethical idealism (what "should be"), paying attention, "an interrogative dynamic" embodied in "structures" designed to explore "things we sense but don't really know" and to push us beyond mere introspection: these are some of the central values of a poetry written into the future, of what Marjorie Perloff calls, in the title of her study, the "21st-century modernism" that extends through the twentieth century into the present.

# Writing into the Future

# I

# Contexts

# 1

# *The Dial, The Little Review,* and the Dialogics of the Modernist "New"

"Make it new"; "no good poetry is ever written in a manner twenty years old"; "nothing is good save the new"; "it is the new form, for however great a period of time it may remain a mere irritant—that moulds consciousness to the necessary amplitude for holding it."[1] Taken together, these statements constitute a familiar mantra for experimental American modernism, for the "experimental" is intimately connected to this foundational category of modernist poetics, the "new." In beginning with these well-known aphorisms, I operate with a formalist definition of the new or experimental, which means that I do not treat what one might call the social new (the New Woman, the New Negro, often linked with the experimental though it was) or the new of the marketplace (fashion, novelty, technological progress, and the advertising thereof). Indeed, experimental modernist craft set itself against the alienated labor and mass production of urban-technological modernity, of emergent Taylorism. I also begin with writers imagining a future (or possible futures) for poetry, in a way nicely encapsulated by a little-known archival feature of Mina Loy's 1914 poem-essay "Aphorisms on Futurism." On a printed leaf of her essay (from the little magazine *Camera Work*), Loy penciled in "modern" and "Modernism" as substitutions for every use of "future" and "Futurism."[2] Preserving the rhetorical extremity that we recognize as quintessentially Futurist, Loy's projected revisions, then, yield exhortations, warnings, or "Aphorisms on Modernism" like "DIE in the Past / Live in the Modern" or "THE Modern is limitless." If "YOU prefer to observe the past on which your eyes are already opened," "the past a trail of insidious reactions" or "turbid stream of accepted facts" that "you" know how to read, the new "language of the Modern" is barely assimilable in its unfamiliarity, force, and power: "Form hurtling against itself is thrown beyond the synopsis of vision."[3] But if this "language" and "new form" is to "[mould] consciousness" or create the conditions for its reception, it needs to circulate in arenas more mundane than Loy's visionary but abstract limitless future. If the modern is synonymous with writing into the future in Loy's privately revised text, that writing also depends on editing into the future—the complications of which, in the pages of modernist magazines, are the subject of my first chapter.

Thinking that he had lost the chance to publish *The Waste Land,* which he had not yet actually seen, Scofield Thayer, joint owner and editor of *The Dial,* wrote to his staff in March 1922 that "'if Eliot's long poem was anything like Pound's Cantos, perhaps we are unwillingly blessed'" in losing it (qtd. in Joost, *Scofield Thayer* 160). Accepting the poem subsequently under pressure from his partner James Sibley Watson and his Paris correspondent, Pound did not improve Thayer's opinion of it. In October 1922, the month of *The Waste Land*'s publication, he wrote to his prospective new managing editor Alyse Gregory: "'I feel forced to refrain in the future from publishing such matter as the silly cantos of Ezra Pound and as the very disappointing "Waste Land" and I should like to secure for The Dial the work of such recognized American authors as Edith Wharton'" (qtd. in Joost, *Scofield Thayer* 111).[4] Thayer was about to preside over a turning point in the institutionalization of Anglo-American modernism and in the positioning of his own magazine within that institution. Under the circumstances, these hardly sound like words calculated to make *The Dial* one of the most influential literary reviews ever published in America.

Yet the aesthetic conservatism implied in Thayer's choice of examples—Wharton over Pound and Eliot—was, paradoxically, necessary to *The Dial*'s promotion of aesthetic revolution. Already an established magazine, under Thayer and Watson *The Dial* put experimental modernist work in a context that made it more palatable to a general audience. Meanwhile, *The Little Review* (1914–29), a contemporary of *The Dial* (1920–29) and perhaps the quintessential little magazine, provided a first outlet and encouragement for much of that experiment.[5] While some initial comparison and contrast will be useful, I do not want to retread too much of that well-worn ground. Rather, I propose that by emphasizing the relationship between these two equally important, though very different, magazines, we can better understand how together they helped promote an experimental modernist poetics and thus shape one version of an emerging modern American poetry canon. (I stress "one version" of a possible modernist canon because both magazines show themselves either largely ignorant of or uninterested in the Harlem Renaissance; in the female popular modernism of, say, Millay, Wylie, or Teasdale; and, except for *The Little Re-*

*view*'s politically engaged teen years, the various leftist poetries in active circulation at the time.) The relationship between *The Dial* and *The Little Review* also demonstrates how, in its rapprochement with a mainstream publishing outlet, early twentieth-century American avant-gardism bears a very different relationship to its mainstream contemporaries from that of the European movements on which canonical theories of the avant-garde rest. As Andreas Huyssen puts it, "the cultural politics of 20th-century avantgardism would have been meaningless (if not regressive) in the United States where 'high art' was still struggling hard to gain wider legitimacy and to be taken seriously by the public" (167). Thus we need to theorize the relationship between the avant-garde and modernism differently for the American scene—to think in terms of avant-garde tendencies, impulses, or moments rather than movements. Mainly, however, I want to propose here a historically based model for considering how the shaping of taste by modernist magazines is a collective project, not a matter of the atomized influence of single publications. Such a model complicates the center-margin oppositions that have often driven our thinking about the reception of innovative poetries, and blurs some of the binaries proposed in an influential theory of the avant-garde like Peter Bürger's by suggesting how *The Dial* and *The Little Review* needed each other to accomplish their cultural work. This is not to deny that some magazines have a longer-lasting and deeper impact than others. It is to assert, however, that even those magazines—like individual canonical authors—have their meaning and effect not in isolation but in relation to others.

Historians of modernist magazines have consistently linked *The Dial* and *The Little Review*, usually to contrast them, and apologists for both magazines have used the example of one to excoriate the other as it suits them. A long-standing and successful magazine of literature, politics, and the arts, under Thayer and Watson *The Dial* shifted its orientation more exclusively toward literature and cultural coverage. Nicholas Joost describes this *Dial* in terms often reserved for the high modernist artwork, defining it as a "disciplined and ordered artifact" in opposition to *The Little Review*'s "glittering, and occasionally silly, hodgepodge" that failed to offer anything "more than self-expression" (*Scofield Thayer* 102). On the other hand, Gorham Munson, who had kicked off his little magazine *Secession* in spring 1922 with a critique of *The Dial*, subsequently contrasted *The Dial* and *The Little Review* to the latter's advantage under the title "How to Run a Little Magazine": "*The Little Review* came out for years, cheaply printed on cheap paper, relying solely upon the interest of its contents; to many young writers it was during those years far more thrilling than the expensively printed *Dial*, which after all was not serializing *Ulysses*"

(4). More neutral is Richard Sieburth, who constructs the difference between the magazines as one between modernism and the avant-garde. As Sieburth puts it, "the opposition . . . between a modernism based on the autonomization of art and an avant-garde praxis based (as Peter Bürger defines it) on the radical questioning of art as an institution is neatly illustrated by Pound's simultaneous affiliation . . . with the mandarin *Dial* on the one hand and the partisan, anarchistic *Little Review* on the other" (7). Sieburth stresses about *The Dial* "the role it played in establishing what has since become the official academic canon of modernism. Its tables of contents now read like the standard syllabus of Modern Masters" (5). Given that some of *The Dial*'s closest descendants are academic publications, and critical as much as literary ones (*Hound and Horn, Symposium, Southern Review,* and the *Kenyon, Hudson, Partisan,* and *Sewanee Reviews*), the terms "official academic" and "syllabus" are particularly revealing here of the direction that *The Dial*'s influence would take.

These oppositions are familiar enough, and genuine, but they mask the crucial component of interdependence between the magazines. John Timberman Newcomb writes of this dynamic among little magazines when he describes Wallace Stevens's relationship to *Others* and *Poetry. Poetry*'s "solidly established position" meant for Stevens "a relatively wide audience and the possibility of a long-term critical advocacy"; *Others* "offered Stevens the editorial approval to extend his innovative wings, giving him notoriety as an intriguing mystery man" (*Wallace Stevens* 32–33). What Newcomb elsewhere calls "the often mutually beneficially dialectical tension between magazines such as these" applies exactly to *The Dial* and *The Little Review* ("*Others*" 258).

To understand their simultaneously conflicted and complementary relationship, it will help to review briefly the clear differences between *The Dial* and *The Little Review.* Although *The Little Review* enjoyed a greater longevity (fifteen years) than most publications of its kind, it had all the characteristics of the classic little magazine; indeed, it came to define (starting with its name) what the very term "little magazine" meant. Coedited by Margaret Anderson and Jane Heap, it was programmatically noncommercial, lived constantly on the edge of bankruptcy, could not pay its contributors, and—relative to *The Dial*—had a small circulation of never more than two thousand and probably closer to one thousand.[6] It was politically engaged, in its explicit and enthusiastic embrace of feminist and anarchist principles.[7] Its tone and stance were vigorously avant-garde, and its audience mostly one already committed to the value of artistic innovation, even while its lively correspondence section courted controversy about the magazine's own contents in a way that *The Dial* never did. And it quickly came to see its primary audience as other artists, dubbing itself (in a new epigraph proposed by Pound in 1917) the magazine "read by those who write the others." In a characteristically avant-gardist move, then, *The Little Review* sought to influence the art of the future—to influence production as well as reception.

*The Dial*, by contrast, took a more cautious or muted tone, generally avoiding political controversy and any evidence of the kind of internal debate that often marked *The Little Review*. Its intended audience was the interested, informed general reader rather than the specialist or initiate of the avant-garde, its goal to extend the audience for modernist art by reaching potentially sympathetic but as yet unconverted readers—to influence reception.[8] It paid contributors and, backed by Thayer's and Watson's personal wealth, remained financially stable even as it lost money.[9] And in ways important for my argument here, it consciously saw itself as engaged in dissemination as much as discovery.

Despite these differences, the magazines started out as complements rather than as rivals. In fact, *The Little Review* even had offices in the same Chicago building as the pre-Thayer *Dial* for a year, and Margaret Anderson learned some of her editorial trade as an assistant to that magazine and by working in the *Dial* bookshop. Although *The Little Review* campaigned more explicitly and energetically, and was more committed to innovation for its own sake, both propagandized in favor of modernist art. *The Dial* even supported *The Little Review* in various tangible and intangible ways. In its April 1920 issue *The Dial* gave *The Little Review* a full-page ad that the smaller magazine could not have afforded itself; soon thereafter, its purchase of an ad in the July–August 1920 *Little Review* helped revenue. On several occasions Watson gave money to *The Little Review* that kept it afloat. And in giving Pound its 1927 award for service to American letters, bringing him back into its fold of authors at Marianne Moore's behest after years of estrangement, *The Dial* generously acknowledged his contributions as foreign editor of *The Little Review*, saying that he helped make it "the most interesting magazine of a quarter century" ([Watson], "Announcement" 89).[10] The magazines shared numerous contributors (of the thirty-four *Little Review* contributors named in its 1920 *Dial* ad, nineteen had also published in *The Dial*), as *The Dial* did with other avant-garde little magazines such as Alfred Kreymborg's *Others*;[11] they shared Pound's influence at crucial points in their lives as he negotiated between the more mainstream modernism and the aggressive avant-gardism that the two magazines represented; they shared the typical modernist sense of schism between high and popular culture, in a way that separates *The Little Review* from a European avant-gardism (otherwise well represented in its pages) bent on reconnecting those realms. When *The Dial* praised William Carlos Williams, in giving him its 1926 award, for "'Service not to that Juggernaut, the Reading Public,'" but "service rather to the Imaginative Individual, to him who is in our world always the Marooned Individual," it sounded surprisingly like *The Little Review*, which announced itself in the epigraph of its early years as "Making No Compromise With The Public Taste."[12] And finally, perhaps appropriately, they expired in the same year, sharing an obituary in the September 1929 issue of *Poetry* (although *The Little Review* had functionally ended with its last-but-one issue of 1926).

This combination of similarities, overlaps, and differences led to a relationship both mutually sustaining and conflicted—though the sense of conflict derived more from the embattled *Little Review* side. Early in the magazines' relationship, *The Little Review* came to see *The Dial* as stealing its ideas and contributors. In its first year, for instance, *The Little Review* had started a "New York Letter," a "London Letter," a theater section, and a section of short book reviews, all of which showed up in only slightly different forms in *The Dial*.[13] *The Little Review* started to criticize *The Dial* in its September–October 1920 issue, when the "new" *Dial* was less than a year old; in its own view, *The Little Review* published first the kind of work for which *The Dial* later got all the credit. One *Little Review* subscriber wrote (assuming the letter quoted is not a fiction) complaining of *The Dial*, "'Why in the name of literature do they start a magazine at this date and follow directly in your footsteps. Can't they do any pioneering of their own?'" (qtd. in Heap, "Loyalty" 93). Jane Heap responded drily by remarking "we have had this called to our attention many times," and fueled the fire further by calling *The Dial* "a de-alcoholized version of *The Little Review*," linking *The Dial* with the repressive temperance politics of Prohibition (93).[14]

This very complaint, however, helps clarify the developing relationship between the two magazines—a relationship between two kinds of publication, the avant-garde little magazine and the more mainstream literary review, both of which played their part in the advancement of innovative modernist poetries. *The Dial* came late as an apologist for modernist poetry insofar as by the end of 1919, when Thayer and Watson took it over, most of the poets that it began to publish had already published elsewhere—though we should recall that the pre-1919 *Dial* was not primarily a magazine of the arts. The single significant exception was Cummings. By 1919, for example, *Poetry* alone had published Pound, Eliot, Stevens, Moore, H.D., Lawrence, Sandburg, Bodenheim, Lindsay, and Lowell. *The Little Review* had published all of these too, along with Williams, Stein,

Loy, Crane, Kreymborg, and Masters. At the same time, Thayer and Watson did publish most of these poets, many of whom had not yet established their reputations, in their first two years as editors. Its circulation and resources helped *The Dial* canonize what *The Little Review* helped to discover, and thus in some sense *The Little Review* exercised its influence through *The Dial.*

From the beginning, *The Dial* saw itself as consciously entering and engaging the processes of canon making and institutionalization. Watson observes in the "Comment" for August 1920 that "the engines for accelerating and predisposing favourable opinion are grown remarkably in our time. The dynamics of reputation are a serious study, the mechanism for creating fame is always in smooth and certain motion" (217).[15] One historian of the magazine, William Wasserstrom, describes *The Dial* in Arnoldian terms as "a magazine whose chief function was to provide a center, train an audience, and acquire a public for the arts" (79). It fulfilled this function successfully enough that through its efforts "what had seemed shatteringly novel in 1920 was acceptably orthodox in 1929" (Joost, *Scofield Thayer* 23). Acceptable orthodoxy is hardly the deliberate goal of any avant-garde, but it is usually a risk the avant-garde runs and often the fate it suffers. When Pound admonished Williams to submit more work to *The Dial* and "crowd . . . out" Amy Lowell, he revealed an innovative poetry's paradoxical ambition to become the art of the future by occupying an institutional center (and outflanking a powerful female competitor in the process); Pound wanted to establish an experimental poetics by mediating it through a mainstream magazine (*Letters* 159). In turn, the successful canonization through a mainstream journal of the movement that it promoted severely reduced the raison d'être of a little magazine like *The Little Review*; its apologias for the new carried the threat of its own demise.

*The Dial* exercised its influence, then, by acting as "mediator between the avant-garde and the general reader," occupying a middle ground "between the arts magazine and the general publication" (Wasserstrom 134; True 13). And the magazine itself articulated this position on its own behalf. The first "Comment" section of the new *Dial*, for March 1920, claimed the cultural politics of the little magazine: a magazine "ought to print, with some regularity, either such work as would otherwise have to wait years for publication, or such as would not be acceptable elsewhere." But then an important qualifier was added: these pieces should be combined with less "'impossible'" ones "in the interest of completeness" (408). In the interest of completeness, then, *The Dial* would both represent and soften the edge of the forceful avant-gardism reflected in *The Little Review*'s unattributed 1922 self-description (apparently authored by Jane Heap) as

"AN ADVANCING POINT TOWARD WHICH THE 'ADVANCE GUARD' IS ALWAYS ADVANCING" ("Full of Weapons!" 33).

*The Dial* maintained this position as late as Watson's "Comment" for September 1927. Watson here distinguished two types of literary magazine. The first type, of which *The Little Review* would be an example, was the little magazine edited by its own contributors and existing mainly for the writer's sake, to support new work. As Watson puts it, "magazines of this type are often more immediately encouraging to interesting new writers, not to mention movements, than magazines like THE DIAL." The second type of magazine, like *The Dial*, "pretends to general interest" and must therefore remain more oriented toward an imagined general reader. Watson rather sarcastically concludes that "many writers will continue to appear first in small 'group magazines.' Our business is to furnish a not too scattered public for what they write well" (270).[16] To put this another way, *The Little Review* brought writers together, made them aware of each other, gave them an outlet, and thus contributed significantly toward making "modernism"—whatever exactly we might mean by that—a movement. *The Dial* made its contribution in publicizing that movement by drawing attention to its supposedly best products. From the magazine's point of view, then, Marianne Moore—acting and then full editor in the years 1925–29—seemed the quintessential *Dial* poet. In citing her for the 1924 *Dial* award, Thayer described her poetry in terms that may say more about his own editorial orientation than Moore's writing: it was designed for "the informed literary middle-of-the-road" ("Announcement" 90), a poetry that, in William Wasserstrom's comment on the award, received Thayer's approbation because it "reconciled the rewards of experiment with the comforts of custom" (113).[17]

T. S. Eliot's career illustrates concretely how the two kinds of magazine that *The Little Review* and *The Dial* represented worked almost symbiotically to shape the reception of modernist experiment. *The Little Review* played an important role in Eliot's early career by publishing him and keeping him encouraged. The magazine published four of his poems in July 1917, four more in September 1918—more, if less distinguished, work in poetry than *The Dial* ever published—and promoted the slim volume *Prufrock and Other Observations* via sixteen separate references to it between 1916 and 1919. Further, these eight *Little Review* poems made up two-thirds of Eliot's second book, the 1920 *Poems*. In a letter for the magazine's final issue in 1929, Eliot wrote that in the late 1910s, "*The Little Review* was the only periodical in America which would accept my work, and indeed the only periodical there in which I cared to appear" (380).

It is Eliot's association with *The Dial*, however, that demonstrates the power of an influential magazine to promote successfully a still relatively unknown poet. In Wasserstrom's accurate summary, "by December 1922, when Eliot resigned his post as London correspondent, Thayer and Watson had published ten separate items . . . , given him *The Dial* Award, printed reviews of his work by Miss Moore, Cummings, and Edmund Wilson, and in space reserved for the editor's own comment, pronounced him the exemplary modern poet and critic" (173n5)—all within two years. The *Dial* management also arranged with Boni and Liveright for book publication of *The Waste Land* on December 15, 1922, on the heels of the poem's appearance in the November 1922 *Dial* and the October 1922 *Criterion*; and they contracted to buy 350 copies. With the visibility that *The Dial* brought *The Waste Land*, the book's first edition of one thousand quickly sold out, necessitating a second run of a thousand copies.[18] This promotion was reinforced in other magazines: in December 1922, Gilbert Seldes, a member of *The Dial*'s staff, published an essay in *The Nation* praising Eliot and explaining the form of *The Waste Land*, and in the space of eight months between June 1923 and February 1924, *Vanity Fair* reprinted a batch of earlier Eliot poems and carried three articles *by* Eliot and an article *on* him (by Clive Bell). He quickly became enough of a celebrity to be praised in *Vogue* in 1924 and slammed in the first issue of *Time* in 1923.[19]

*The Dial* thus played a crucial role in the canonization of one particular cornerstone of high modernism, and in the institutionalization of a previously coterie poetics, but a role still best understood in relation to other magazines. Analyzing *The Waste Land*'s publication in marketing and institutional terms, Lawrence Rainey argues that it "marked the crucial moment in the transition of modernism from a minority culture to one supported by an important institutional and financial apparatus, . . . from a literature of an exiguous elite to a position of prestigious dominance" (91). Rainey presents the triangle of possible outlets that Eliot considered or negotiated with as a triangle of mass culture (*Vanity Fair*), the avant-garde (*The Little Review*), and high culture (*The Dial*). In particular, *The Dial* was in conscious competition with *Vanity Fair* for the rights to the poem.[20] For *The Dial, The Waste Land* would represent a key investment in the emerging commodity known as modernism: as Rainey puts it, "what they had decided to purchase was less a specific poem, more a bid for discursive hegemony" (88). In this argument, canonization is synonymous with assimilation into the very market economy that high modernism claims to resist, with the three journals simply occupying different points "within a shared spectrum of marketing and consumption" (99).

Rainey's move to unify a wide range of cultural activity under the umbrella term "market" offers a suggestive blurring of boundaries among avant-garde, high, and mass culture. At the same time, however, publication in *The Dial* constituted a particular choice within the nexus that actually helped to reinforce those boundaries. To argue, as Rainey does, that "*The Dial* . . . differed from the *Little Review* and *Vanity Fair* in its tone of high seriousness and gravity, not in substantive ideology" (95) is to miss the fact that the different magazines' relation to capital is *itself* an ideological difference inseparable from their aesthetic stances; Thayer's family money that bankrolled *The Dial gave* it a wealthy patron that (with the partial exception of John Quinn's financial contributions during the Pound years) *The Little Review* never had. Mark Morrisson, in *The Public Face of Modernism*, lays out *The Little Review*'s use of the techniques and rhetoric of commercial mass culture in the interests of audience building. But this imbrication in advertising techniques (which could equally be seen as techniques of the machine aesthetic later endorsed by Jane Heap) seems largely a formal one.[21] The magazine did not use these commercial tropes for commercial purposes (or at least did not do so successfully), and advertisers themselves seem quickly to have noticed the conflict between their goals and *The Little Review*'s contents and cultural politics. *The Little Review* both expressed and ironized its own desire for advertising revenue when the June–July 1915 issue ran seven pages of small notices suggesting what businesses might have advertised there—businesses unlikely to be attracted to a venue that foregrounded the anarchist Emma Goldman or that ran a partially blank issue in September 1916 due to an alleged lack of quality submissions.

In 1923, three events symbolically coincided: the Baroness Elsa von Freytag-Loringhoven, the German Dadaist whom *The Little Review* had published extensively, returned to Europe; Margaret Anderson relinquished *The Little Review*'s editorship and moved to Paris; and a handful of Eliot's earlier poems were reprinted in *Vanity Fair* as part of a larger project of framing Eliot's work for the magazine's readership. As I've already noted, Rainey reads *The Waste Land*'s publication and reception as the culmination of an always immanent *con*vergence of avant-garde high and mass culture. I would suggest, however, that Eliot's success in 1922–23 and Anderson's move to Paris mark both the crowning achievement of the first stage of modernist poetry and the end of modernism's kinship with the avant-garde. It is the point at which a previously more connected modernism and avant-garde (connections reflected in the multiple affiliations of many writers) diverge, the point at which modernism becomes Modernism. The early *Little Review* had been part of a historical moment "when a revolution in poetry seemed naturally to entail commitment to social change, when all the arts were in ferment and aesthetic innovations were politically inflected" (Nelson 230). Eliot's reception in *The Dial* and *Vanity Fair*, one can speculate, symbolized the end of that moment, at least for Margaret Anderson.

Canon making involves more than saturating a corner of the market with a given poetic product, of course, as *The Dial* did with Eliot (and as it did with Moore to a lesser extent, in five consecutive issues from January to May 1925 that primed readers for the announcement of her appointment as acting editor in June 1925). Both *The Dial* and *The Little Review* contributed to the formation of a modernist poetic canon in various ways that are probably familiar enough not to need detailing: by providing a mutually supportive network or community, by offering the encouragement that comes with having a regular outlet for one's work, by supplying a forum in which poets could act as critics and write about and support each other's work, and by placing poets in editorial or correspondence positions that gave them control over or input into what poetry got published and praised.[22] Yet another way in which magazines can indirectly shape canons in poetry is by affecting the kind of work that emerging poets write—by influencing poetic production. This happened in the case of Hart Crane, and it is fitting that he got his start in *The Little Review*, which more than *The Dial* presented itself as a magazine for other artists, "The Magazine That Is Read By Those Who Write The Others." In this view, it was the little magazine's function as much to generate further writing and put writers into dialogue as it was to spread the word or proselytize to some not-yet-available audience. Early influences on Crane were *Ulysses*, the prose of Wyndham Lewis, and the poetry of Pound, Yeats, and the French moderns, all of which he read or read about in *The Little Review*. Later, however, he was powerfully affected by the Watson translations of Rimbaud's *Illuminations* and *A Season in Hell* that he read in *The Dial* in 1920, and by his reading of *The Waste Land* there in 1922 (his disappointment with *The Waste Land*, which he found "so damned dead" [105], being part of what drove him to write *The Bridge*).

This list of Crane's influences is notable for the mixture of American and European names, and indeed both *The Dial* and *The Little Review* were internationalist in their thrust, open equally to work from both sides of the Atlantic. *The Dial*, however, tended to neglect European avant-garde movements such as Dada and surrealism, with which such *Dial* contributors as Pound, Williams, and Stein were well acquainted. Consistent with the respective magazines' aesthetics, *The Dial* tended to publish work from the European mainstream and *The Little Review* from the European avant-gardes—as illustrated by the fact that *The Little Review* carried more work by von Freytag-Loringhoven than any other publication, along with early concrete and sound poems by Baader and Huelsenbeck, and work by Tzara, Picabia, and Arp, to name only a few associated with various avant-gardisms. Even though *The Dial* was often accused of supporting older European writers at the expense of younger Americans, both it and *The Little Review* can be said to have constructed a transatlantic axis for modernism from their New York base (*The Little Review* moved from Chicago to New York with its March 1917 issue), creating an additional center for the movement outside of European capitals.[23] Together, they did much to advance a cosmopolitan American modernism, pushing writers of an internationalist bias like Pound, Eliot, Crane, and Stevens over the democratic or popular modernism of nativists like Lindsay, Sandburg, and Masters.

This latter group had in fact been well represented in both magazines until the arrival of Pound on the *Little Review* scene and Eliot at *The Dial*. They had been among the earliest contributors to *The Little Review*, after Margaret Anderson had met them in Chicago as part of the Jackson Park art scene associated with Floyd Dell and Margery Currey.[24] But the conflict between a national and an international poetry that both magazines' pages enacted actually concerned questions of craft and originality—definitions of "the modern" or the meaningfully new in art—as much as nationality. In *The Little Review* for September 1918, Edgar Jepson reprinted a condensed version of his essay from the *English Review* called "The Western School," arguing against the claim that Lindsay, Masters, and Frost represented a new, genuinely indigenous poetry. He did not deny that these writers were *echt* American. He denied that they were any good. According to Jepson, Lindsay wrote "rank bad, jingling verse"; Masters "bad, bald, prosy prose"; and Frost "maundering dribble" (6–7). Jepson's alternative model for craft and innovation was Eliot, whose poems appeared alongside his essay and in contrast to whom the other poets "create no new diction, no new idiom. They create nothing" (8).[25]

Pound, always well attuned to the zeitgeist, knew that *The Little Review*'s readers were likely to be almost obsessively committed to newness, prone to dismiss work even five years old. He himself agreed with Jepson's negative diagnosis of Frost, Masters, and Lindsay, as he wrote in a May 1918 letter to Jepson following the essay's original publication in England: "Frost, Masters, Lindsay . . . are dead as mutton so far as the *L. R.* reader is concerned. The *L. R.* reader in America, anyhow, has had all he can stand of that lot. He knows what their stuff looks like etc. Masters we have said farewell to. Frost sinks of his own weight. Lindsay we have parodied" (*Letters* 135). In this letter, Pound both prophesies accurately the future hierarchy of a long-dominant version of the modernist canon and notes how that canon was starting to be composed of contributors to, and proposed by readers of, avant-garde little magazines: "Mi credo, Masters, Frost, Lindsay are out of the Wild Young American gaze already. Williams, Loy, Moore, and the worser phenomena of *Others*, to say nothing of the highly autochthonous Amy [Lowell] (all over the bloody shop) are much more in the 'news'" (135–36).[26]

While Pound saw *The Little Review* as an organ of the 1918 avant-garde, however, he did not, looking back, regard it as concerned with newness alone. During the magazine's lifetime, he was not always kind in his comments on the magazine's quality, but in retrospect, he found in *The Little Review* a commitment to "the best" that, in a 1940 letter, he contrasts deliberately with what he sees as *The Dial*'s more superficial commitments. (In framing the difference as one of editorial policy, Pound finesses the fact that the magazines held radically differing definitions of "the best," and a shifting relationship to the very concept.) He writes:

> No editor in America, save Margaret Anderson, ever felt the need of, or responsibility for, getting the best writers concentrated—i.e., brought together in an American periodical. . . . *The Dial* might fool the casual observer; but its policy was *not* to get the best work or best writers. It got some. But Thayer aimed at names, wanted European celebrities and spent vast sums getting their left-overs. (*Letters* 346)

In a related critique, he explicitly contrasts the editorial risks taken by *The Little Review* with *The Dial*'s centrism. Recommending in 1920 that Joyce submit something to *The Dial*, he tells his impecunious friend that "it wont be as much fun as the L. R." but at least it pays (*Pound/Joyce* 164). A few days later he writes: "The Dial will never print 'Ulysses.' The Dial will never be any real fun" (166). Certainly, it is hard to imagine *The Dial* running an issue with thirteen blank pages to confront readers with the paucity of available artwork or carrying critical commentary under the title "Bla-Bla-Bla." Through such moves, *The Little Review* modeled for later little magazine editors a particular tone, attitude, or ethos.[27]

In contrast to *The Little Review*'s emphasis on newness, some of *The Dial*'s harshest critics come from among its most consistent poetic contributors, who, fairly or not, perceived it as resistant to artistic innovation. Although both published many of the same poets, they were perceived very differently by those poets, who often seemed to object as much to *The Dial*'s ethos as to its contents. Not surprisingly, *The Dial* was at its liveliest and best while Pound exercised some influence on its editorial policy and gathering of material, between April 1920 and April 1923—a period during which, as G. A. M. Janssens puts it, "Pound's influence strengthened [*The Dial*'s] family resemblance to *The Little Review*" (53). But Thayer's resistance to innovative American material gave even Pound—surely no literary nationalist—cause to complain as early as April 1921, when he wrote to Moore thus: "I have tried for a year to get Thayer to print—i.e., at least get—an article on younger American writers. No use" (*Letters* 168). In a 1928 letter to Louis Zukofsky, Williams describes *The Dial* as "about as dead as a last-year's birds' nest" and celebrates Zukofsky's appearance in the magazine with the gleeful if paradoxical claim that Zukofsky's work represents "another nail in the *Dial* coffin" (Williams and Zukofsky 547, 5). He had written to Kenneth Burke in 1924 that *The Dial*'s "only use now, as far as I can see," was to give away its money, and he was pleased enough to receive the *Dial* award himself (*Selected Letters* 62).[28] In the same year, he complained to Pound that "I myself feel so disgusted with *The Dial* for its halfhearted ways that I am almost ready to agree with anyone concerning its worthlessness" (103). By November 1922, the month of *The Waste Land,* Crane writes to Gorham Munson that "*The Dial* seems to have abandoned all interest in publishing American things, or anything, in fact, that comes to them unheralded by years of established reputation" (*Letters* 103). "It is plain," he writes to Allen Tate in February 1923, "that their interest in helping American letters is very incidental. Note the predominance given to translations of the older generation of Germans, etc., who have absolutely nothing to give us but a certain ante-bellum 'refinement'" (124). He voiced essentially the same objection in an August 1927 letter to Yvor Winters: "'The decrepit old wind bag goes wheezing along month after month with dear old Schnitzler and Mann the main bellows-workers'" (qtd. in Parkinson 102).[29]

*The Dial* thus came to be criticized on two related scores, its perceived reluctance to support American writing and experimental writing. In 1923, for instance, Henry Seidel Canby accused *The Dial* of trying to institute "'another age of Longfellow,'" of encouraging American writers to follow English models (qtd. in [Seldes] 637).[30] In 1927, Watson had to respond to a similar complaint from *The New Republic,* that *The Dial* had "'not encouraged a single interesting new American writer since 1920'" (qtd. in [Watson], "Comment" [1927] 269). From *The Dial*'s point of view, however, it simply resisted use of the local or national as a criterion of critical judgment. When the magazine announced Eliot's winning the 1922 *Dial* award, for instance, despite Thayer's misgivings about *The Waste Land,* it praised Eliot for not pleading the "'localism' which . . . takes so much of American writing out of the field of comparison with European letters and . . . requires for American writers a special standard of judgment'" (qtd. in [Seldes], "Comment" [1922] 686).[31] This context gives added weight to Williams's notorious complaint that, just when American little magazines were approaching "a new art form . . . rooted in the locality which should give it fruit," "out of the blue *The Dial* brought out *The Waste Land* and all our hilarity ended" (*Autobiography* 172). To Williams, *The Dial* was responsible for obstructing—when it should be facilitating—an emergent American modernism represented by little magazines, to the point where "by 1925 it had alienated many of the people whom the editors admired most," and "pleased its European public . . . but perplexed people at home" (Wasserstrom 88, 92).

*The Dial*'s critics, however, remained willing to publish there. In May 1920, soon after the controversial "Nausicaa" episode of *Ulysses* had appeared in the April *Little Review*, Pound wrote to James Joyce encouraging him to submit any work outside of *Ulysses* to *The Dial* (which would not risk the clash with postal authorities over the Comstock Act likely to ensue from publishing anything from *Ulysses*).[32] Pound's challenge was this: in soliciting *The Dial*, he and Joyce would "have stodge instead of lunacy (as on L. R.) to contend with" (*Pound/Joyce* 164). "Lunacy" and "stodge": not especially nuanced theoretical terms, and finally perhaps a rather extreme binary, but Pound's formulation does capture something of the tensions that occupy me here. Like many of his peers, Pound published in both places. He realized the necessity of combining lunacy and stodge if his version of modernist poetry—one rooted in avant-garde practice—was to occupy a central position on the American literary stage. And as we move into the post–World War period in the next three chapters, the relationship or negotiations between "lunacy," or the emergent, and "stodge," or the dominant/residual, and the internal divisions within each, will be a recurring theme in the reception of new American poetries.

# 2

## *The New American Poetry* Revisited, Again

In terms of its defining "anti-academic" role in the 1960s anthology wars, its impact on later collections and editors, its importance for later poets, and its central place in most readings and structurings of postwar literary history, Donald Allen's *The New American Poetry* (1960) is generally considered the single most influential poetry anthology of the post–World War II period. A high percentage of the largely unknown Black Mountain, New York School, San Francisco Renaissance, Beat, and other poets whom Allen introduced to a broader reading public went on to significant writing careers, and many have become widely read, taught, anthologized, honored, and commented upon. As regards writing practice, *The New American Poetry*, more than any other anthology, helped promote and canonize ideas of field composition based on Charles Olson's "Projective Verse," a (re)definition of poetic form as immanent and processual, a poetics of dailiness and of the personal (as distinct from the confessional), and a poetry of humor and play (as distinct from wit). It is *the* anthology, in short, that marked the early postmodern turn, in Charles Altieri's still-useful terms, "from symbolist thought to immanence."[1] It has retained enough staying power as an anthological touchstone for alternative poetries that, as I discuss in chapter 3, editors of avant-garde anthologies continued to invoke it as a model over thirty years after its publication. Meanwhile, its 1999 reprinting (with a new Allen afterword) by the University of California Press—that rarest of fates for an earlier poetry anthology—and its ongoing reassessment via anniversary conferences and scholarly work in progress stand as further testimony to its historical importance and continuing relevance.[2]

But how did we get *The New American Poetry*? The process of editing poetry anthologies is still rarely discussed in concrete detail, even while it is assumed to be a highly contingent one.[3] It is also a social process. Initiated and completed as an individual labor of love (Allen typed the whole manuscript himself), *The New American Poetry* also reveals a good deal about the possible role of poets, and the networks to which they belong, in compiling an influential anthology. The collection is as much the product of multiple, interacting poetic communities and affiliations, of correspondence among contributors and editor, as it is the work of an individual editor himself. In this sense, *The New American Poetry* is very much a communal construction or shared enterprise.

*The New American Poetry,* then, provides a revealing case study of the contingencies involved in producing what has become a canonical anthology. Such contingencies can be divided into two kinds, those of construction and of reception. The former includes all the variables that affect the evolving ambitions, contents, and organization of the anthology: the resistance (in this case, Robert Duncan) or input (Charles Olson) of major contributors; the differences and conflicts among groups and individuals represented, particularly relevant to an anthology structured around hypostatized poetic communities; the background of cultural debate out of which the anthology emerges (the embattled relationship between a so-called "academic" and alternative poetics); the race and gender politics of the anthology's moment (which, while not thoroughly determining, are still more likely than not to shape the text). The latter includes reviews, popular and critical reception, reception among other poets, and classroom use. While I pay some attention later in this chapter to the contingencies of *The New American Poetry*'s reception by discussing early reviews and debates over the question of the "academic," I devote myself mainly to the process of the anthology's construction. My governing question is this: How did *The New American Poetry,* this venerable institution of alternative poetics, come to take the form that it finally did? How did this version of the "new" acquire its public shape?

One irony of *The New American Poetry*'s central place in recent literary history is that Allen's ambitions for the anthology (like its scale in relation to later, comparable texts) were quite modest, out of all proportion to the text's eventual impact. In a July 18, 1958, letter to Cid Corman, Allen writes of his plans to devote "320 pages [rather than the final 362] to the poetry" of "about 25 poets" (the final total is 44) in a book "to be of interest for a couple of years—then to be replaced by another view."[4] Initially, he seems to have planned a series of anthologies, one every few years. In an August 29, 1961, letter, Paul Blackburn makes recommendations to Allen for a revised edition of *The New American Poetry.* (That revision did not materialize until *The Postmoderns* in 1982). Other correspondence from the period reveals this to be the standard description that Allen circulated to prospective contributors. He apparently had no plans at this time for the "Statements on Poetics" section that became one of the means by which his poets announced their differences from a theory-phobic mainstream.[5] He also mulled over the volume that eventually became *The Poetics of the New American Poetry* (1973), however, and this plan may well underlie the "Statements on Poetics" in *The New American Poetry*, that section, then, a kind of stop-gap measure or minivolume in the absence of a full, independent book.

So much for Allen's original ambitions. What about his evolving sense of the anthology's contents and organization? Fairly late in the editorial process, Allen still had a conception of *The New American Poetry* significantly different from its final form. When he mailed a contract and descriptive form letter to Robin Blaser and Charles Olson on September 24, 1958, he hoped for a 1959 publication. He still planned to devote around three hundred pages to the work of "25 to 30 poets," with a brief preface, biographical notes, and headshots of the poets. As regards organization, "the arrangement of the poems will be alphabetical by name of author, I think" (Maud 47). The working title was still, as it had been from the beginning, *Anthology of Modern American Poetry (1948 to 1958–59)*.[6] In terms of presentation, then, here Allen had in mind a much more conventional anthology than he finally produced, something paradoxically closer in format to later, more mainstream collections.[7]

Soon after this communication with Blaser, and still thinking the book only a few months away from publication, Allen sent Robert Creeley a tentative list of contents—one that featured no women poets except Denise Levertov and that did not mention a number of the San Francisco poets whose work he finally used. His "maybe" category at this point contained both eventual exclusions (Theodore Enslin, William Bronk) and inclusions (Bruce Boyd, Blaser), and he asked for Creeley's help in making the Larry Eigner selections. Creeley's October 8, 1958, reply adds another spice to the potpourri: "What about Jonathan Williams?" One year later, in September 8, 1959, letters to Creeley and Charles Olson, Allen is still vacillating on whether to provide historical context by including post-1945 work from an older, high modernist generation and a middle generation of Louis Zukofsky, Kenneth Rexroth, Paul Goodman, and perhaps Kenneth Patchen.[8] A number of writers whom he includes here in a general "new poets" group end up placed elsewhere in the anthology, while Creeley, in his September 11, 1959, response, proposes dropping Goodman and suggests that "Bronk is marginal, more Stevens than anything" (although seven months earlier he had recommended Bronk).

Also at issue for Allen was the use of longer poems or excerpted sequences, about which he vacillated considerably. He frequently states in his correspondence that he will not use longer pieces; as late as October

15, 1959, he writes to Duncan that "I've not included *Howl,* nor other very long poems, and have avoided taking excerpts from long poems, with the exception of two of the Maximus letters." In a draft paragraph finally cut from his preface, however, he argues that "one prominent feature of the period is the recreated long poem," with Duncan's *The Venice Poem* (1948) "the first sustained achievement." Among other longer poems, Olson's "The Kingfishers" (though hardly in the category of what we would now call "the long poem") "remains one of the starting posts for the course" (a phrasing that actually derived from an October 3, 1959, Olson letter to Allen) and "Howl" "has already assumed the status of *The Waste Land* for our age"—claims that eventually showed up, in revised form, on the jacket blurb. This unpublished paragraph reminds us of how many longer poems *The New American Poetry* does indeed include or excerpt. In it, Allen mentions Duncan's "Poem Beginning with a Line from Pindar," and work by Jack Spicer, Gregory Corso, Frank O'Hara, Stuart Perkoff, Gary Snyder, Edward Marshall, and Michael McClure; one could add Ginsberg's "Kaddish" and selections by Jack Kerouac, Kenneth Koch, and Ray Bremser. In the cases of Marshall, Spicer, and Kerouac, the poets' sole representations are from a long poem or excerpted sequence. This use of longer poems or excerpts (running up to eleven pages in the cases of Snyder and Marshall) is both consistent with the anthology's promotion of a poetics of exploratory process and contrasts vividly with the emphasis on the self-contained artifacts of Donald Hall, Robert Pack, and Louis Simpson's rival *New Poets of England and America,* where the only selection that stretches to four of that text's smaller pages is extracts from W. D. Snodgrass's *Heart's Needle.*

On November 6, 1959, Allen writes to Olson that he had just delivered the anthology to the printer, but with "a couple of items, chiefly Duncan's statement on poetics still to come." His thinking about the contents seems to have been in process up to the last minute. On October 29, 1959, one week before delivering the manuscript, Allen tells Duncan that "I've had a long visit with Sanders Russell" and "I plan to include him in the collection." Russell never made the cut, however. Further changes in the contents—changes of poems, though not of names—did in fact take place even in the late stage of page proofs. In this stage, Allen dropped poems by Duncan, O'Hara, James Broughton, Richard Duerden, Philip Lamantia, Peter Orlovsky, and Kirby Doyle; he also added a poem written as late as December 12, 1959, O'Hara's "Hotel Transylvanie," and he apparently changed his choice of Helen Adam's work in response to a December 23, 1959, letter from Duncan pushing her "I Love My Love."[9] He made structural changes such as removing Gilbert Sorrentino from the Black Mountain section of the anthology and inserting Ebbe Borregaard into the San Francisco Renaissance section. He also changed the order of numerous poets' selections to reflect the chronological order of composition, apparently in response to late information from his contributors. Responding to page proofs on December 27, 1959, for instance, Olson writes, "the only significant change is the dates of composition. Which wld shift the order of the 'Harrison' to before the Satyrs if you wanted to maintain it" (Maud 67).[10]

One of the most influential figures in the final product, Olson was also crucial to the editing of *The New American Poetry,* and his advice played a significant role in the conceptualizing and shaping of the anthology. The Olson-Allen correspondence, which contains numerous mentions of Allen's visits to Olson's home in Gloucester, suggests that much of their discussion of the anthology took place in person.[11] After one visit, for instance, Allen writes on June 3, 1959, to thank Olson "for that great carrying gift of a plan for the anthology" (Maud 52).[12] On August 14, 1959, he is still pondering the problem of organization, the twin issues of how to group his contemporaries and whether to include an earlier generation of writers. A September 9, 1959, letter to Olson reveals his continuing ambivalence about contents and organization. Here, he considers an organization that implies a rather different historical argument from that which he finally used: a brief modernist section followed by a section of midcentury "continuers"—a section that he quickly came to see, however, as "pretty meaningless" (Maud 58–59). (One can only speculate how much an appearance in *The New American Poetry* might have advanced the serious reception of Louis Zukofsky's work.) He did know, however, the poets whom he wanted to represent most thoroughly, and the space allocation would also involve "in many cases with minor poets and greener ones, only 1 or 2 poems" (58). Allen wanted simultaneously to promote particular individual poets and some particular conceptions of poetics. The latter goal is presumably what impelled him to include poets about whom he had reservations—Richard Duerden, for instance, whom he describes in an October 6, 1959, letter to Olson as "very intriguing" but also characterized by a "programmatic half truth . . . bought ready packaged from Duncan" and sometimes by a "glossy period newness look." More than many reviewers allowed, Allen was sensitive to the differences between a more superficial and a deeper sense of the "new" among his poets, and many of those whom he cut when he revised the anthology as *The Postmoderns* (1982) were those whom he had included only ambivalently in *The New American Poetry.*[13]

In the fall of 1959, Olson's own epoch-defining section of the anthology was also very much in process. After consultation with Olson, Allen finally used only five of the ten poems that he had proposed in an August 26, 1959, letter. At one point he expected to exclude one of the defining documents of American postmodernism, writing on September 5, 1959, that "I admit to an abiding love for ["The Kingfishers"] and wish I could use it, but believe you prefer ["To Gerhardt, There, Among Europe's Things . . ."] in this context—right?" Wrong, apparently, since Olson responds on October 3, 1959, that "if you continue to want to add ["The Kingfishers"] please above all do DO: for me it is like the starting post" (Maud 62). Thus "The Kingfishers" leads off *The New American Poetry* and "To Gerhardt" does not appear. The influential presence of Olson's statements on poetics similarly required a last-minute shift in Allen's editorial thinking. In the same letter in which he discusses use of "The Kingfishers," he asks Olson, "Should I print your letter to Elaine [Feinstein], or take a section out of ['Projective Verse?']" Acknowledging the latter option as "impossible," he finally used both documents in their entirety.

Olson responded immediately to Allen's queries about the representation of earlier generations, writing on September 12, 1959, that "I wldn't myself add either of those two units: either the 'aunties' or the grandpas" (Maud 59).[14] For Olson, the anthology's point was not to trace genealogies but to suggest connections among contemporary writers and to propose a break into the postmodern: "In fact those connections strike me as smudging the point: 1950 on," with the "change of discourse" that period brought (60). As he continues in this letter, "<u>any</u> chronology—other than the watershed of the 1948–1950 break over—loses, and leaves the picture only further scattered: yr anthology ought to be the decisive defining factor, that American writing went into a new gear, which is what it is now running on" (61). So, Olson advised, "Don't drag in those other gooks of the past—& present solely because they hang around (don't die![])" (61) Olson saw *The New American Poetry* as self-validating, especially given its appendix on poetics; "relations" with earlier writers would be self-evident, he thought, and should not be explicitly invoked for the sake of "shoring or helping" the book (61–62). Openly indebted to modernist precursors, and actively in conversation with those still alive, Olson sought to foreground a changed (post-1945) sense of poetics, to foreground rupture over continuity.

Only a few months before publication, then, the contents and form of *The New American Poetry* were by no means entirely in place. Most significantly, in an October 15, 1959, letter, Allen was still trying to get one central figure, Robert Duncan, who had backed out a year earlier, to contribute to the anthology, now called *The New American Poetry, 1948?–*

*1960*. (The year 1948 is the date of Duncan's *The Venice Poem*, which both Allen and Blaser thought a defining product of an emerging New American poetics [Blaser 6].) Duncan was not just a key contributor to *The New American Poetry*, however, but also, through his correspondence, a key figure in its shaping. (During his period of supposed noninvolvement, he had passed on suggestions through Creeley and Blaser.) Allen's first recorded mention of the project to him came in a July 8, 1958, invitation. Duncan responds, on July 12, 1958, that "where an anthology is not edited by a poet for a poet's particular purposes I have doubts" but agrees to participate, making numerous recommendations for inclusions. This idea of the poet-edited anthology, and particularly the issue of purpose, goes a long way toward explaining Duncan's year-long withdrawal from the project and his last-minute return to it. While Allen wrote to Duncan on July 17, 1958, that "I hope to show you as one of the major poets of the decade," only four days later Duncan backed out, claiming a lack of trust in Allen as an editor and protesting that "nowhere do you give any idea what it is you think the anthology will show. . . . The appeal is so sheerly to my vanity; and there is no key as to what other value might be realized." Echoing his letters to Allen, Duncan expresses to Blaser on August 28, 1958, suspicion of any editor who was not a poet: "The outrage with Don is the same as with the idear [*sic*] of some damnd non-poet . . . teaching or arbitrating the art" (Duncan, "Letters" 128).[15] One surprising result of this demand that an anthology "be edited from such a center that makes it authentic" was that, at least in August 1958, Duncan found himself less sympathetic to Allen's proposal than to Allen's antagonist in the anthology wars, Donald Hall, Robert Pack, and Louis Simpson's *New Poets of England and America*:

> The Donald Hall/Louis Simpson anthology defines an area of contemporary practice because its editors are poets vitally concerned that such an area exist; they create it and are responsible for it. It is authentic not only can we trust what they include; but we can trust that what they exclude is a definition too. (128)

Duncan's initial objections to *The New American Poetry* also rested on his view of literary careerism and the canonizing thrust of anthologies. That is, he rejected a venture that he saw as dominated by aspirations toward taste making, career building, influence, and representation of a period—all of which, at least in retrospect, *The New American Poetry* could lay claim to. He dismissed the very principle of gathering what Blaser had apparently called the "'extensively published and most influential among the poets who are to be taken seriously'" (126)—even if he was one of those poets. "In the whole given realm of cultural development, publishing and career of writing my spirit shrivels," he writes (127). Duncan turns his back on the critical categories that tend to drive anthologizing, hoping, paradoxically, to reach a point where "no one devising such a proposition of the most important and influential poets will dream of me" (128).

These reservations about what we would now call the canonizing enterprise connect to Duncan's sense of himself as a coterie poet (presumably with a coterie audience), a sense that made him wary of how his work might be used: "If by any means I could prevent . . . false readers from ever having access to my work to make of it the guts of whatever new poetry I would do so" (126). As Creeley explains in an August 17, 1959, letter to Allen, Duncan "does not seem to want his work ever used as an 'example' unless he can clearly control the terms of the representation." Duncan also preferred to control the means of his work's consumption, as he writes with regard to the book that eventually became *The Opening of the Field*: "I want to govern who will be able to buy a copy and have some idea of their reasons for reading" (127).

Duncan's distaste for Allen's project at this stage (August 1958) was emphatic, to say the least. He comments to Blaser on "the idiocy and evil of this damnd anthology"—"yesterday I was still shaking with my hatred of it" (126–28). Allen was finally able to persuade Duncan of his seriousness of purpose, however, and Duncan was willing to return to the fold once "he found you were scholarly," as Blaser reports to Allen in a January 14, 1960, letter. (As I argue later, "scholarly" meant something very different from "academic" for Duncan.) Duncan himself said in 1971 that "I was refusing to be in the anthology because I *hate* anthologies, and not until I saw a table of contents did I consent to be in it" (Ginsberg, *Allen Verbatim* 132). But the text's contents, which Allen laid out only when he approached Duncan the second time, were hardly Duncan's only basis for dissent. In a 1985 interview, he recalls his first response to Allen's plans: "I did not want to be in the sort of circus where the polar bear is brought in right after the monkey is brought in right after the—and that's the way all anthologies were. Actually it would be the polar bear then the pole cat, because they'd be alphabetical" (Duncan, "In Interview" 84). Organization was the issue as much as content, with Duncan "refusing to be in the anthology unless it had an organization on historical [not alphabetical] principles" (84).[16]

Duncan's concerns with, and relief over, the anthology's purpose and coherence, its revelation of a network of related poetries, emerged vividly in an unpublished June 12, 1960, letter to the *San Francisco Chronicle.* Duncan responds to accusations of cliquishness made in a review of *The New American Poetry*:

> These movements were created in living associations, a complex of meaningful relationships over years, before they became so defined. They were not . . . a matter of Mr. Allen's arrangement. No amount of arrangement . . . can make Kaufman seem to have done the work, have been the creative spirit that Corso was and is, in the creation of the "Beat" vision.

While generally defending Allen's groupings, however, Duncan denies the existence of a San Francisco Renaissance, calling the term

> a band-wagon slogan or a grab-bag. What common concerns or views of the nature of poetry are there? What, other than a mistake, groups Brother Antoninus and James Broughton, Lawrence Ferlinghetti and Jack Spicer, together as a movement, or even as what is called now a "scene"? Here alone there may be some question of a clique, for it is social ties and local reputations that dictate what San Francisco is—not shared principles or common works. . . . "The San Francisco Renaissance" is a misnomer, a term that misleads us from showing meaningful orders.[17]

Terms such as "clique" and "gang" arose so often in early reviews of *The New American Poetry* that it is worth pausing to suggest some distinctions on the issue.[18] Before the idea of *The New American Poetry* was ever proposed, Duncan had made an important distinction between the regional and the coterie poet, a distinction that helps clarify his observations on the nature of a "movement." He writes to Blaser on June 8, 1957, that "it's just that by some damnd incident of geography I am so solidly placed in region, and not in coterie. And I'm a coterie poet not a regional one" ("Letters" 106).[19] This position explains his insistence to Allen in an October 26, 1959, letter that he belonged to the Black Mountain section of the anthology, not the San Francisco section. He rightly describes the anthology as an aesthetic extension of the magazines in which these poets published: "It *is* ORIGIN and then BLACK MOUNTAIN REVIEW that makes your group #1 [Olson, Duncan, Creeley] and group #2 [other Black Mountaineers] all one group—and I belong there for my mature work."[20]

Duncan's sense of distance from any such thing as a "San Francisco Renaissance" extended to the Beats. On February 7, 1959, he writes to Olson: "The effect of Ginsberg's campaign is as damaging to the cause of a sound concept of what a poem is as is the academe's literature. // Where the conventional and the unconventional are one force [Ginsberg supplying what most English professors believe would happen if you kicked over the traces]" ("Eleven Letters" 104). From within the New American ranks, then, Duncan anticipated the same critique of the Beats proposed by many mainstream reviewers and later commentators: that they merely offered a kind of reactive or inverted mirror image of that which they resisted, in a binary opposition the two halves of which were mutually determining. (He even anticipated these reviewers' language by referring to "Ginsberg and *gang*" [104; emphasis added].) By contrast, Duncan thinks himself anomalous in the San Francisco context for being concerned with "FORM, critical structure . . . while the pariah generation shootz the joy-juice into their frantic nerves and stands on their hands for the daily press" (104). Similarly, in a July 2, 1959, letter to Blaser, he describes himself as "isolated by my demand for 'form' from the fashions of the day" ("Letters" 131) and critiques what he saw as Beat-related poets' verbosity, overbearing reading style, and limited conceptions of poetry. For Duncan, the coterie poet, a shared poetics was far more significant than a shared cultural activism.

Duncan, then, felt a striking sense of generational and aesthetic difference between himself and many other San Francisco poets, a sense of himself as a senior poet in relation to others whom he included in the general category of "the young," "les jeunes," such as Michael McClure and Richard Duerden. One finds in Duncan's letters from the mid- to late 1950s a persistent effort to define or articulate his relation to particular aspects of the work of John Wieners, Helen Adam, Madeline Gleason, McClure, James Broughton, and Duerden, doing so on the basis of aesthetics rather than "these aberrations of the social scene—where any attention to what is being done in writing is avoided by reversion to personalities" ("Letters" 109). In September 1957, he mentions to Robin Blaser how "Olson left here with some outrage at the insolence of the young, that they rejected any demand for coming to grips with a larger struggle than their own environs" (111). Along similar lines, Olson wrote to Cid Corman on January 2, 1958, after a visit to San Francisco, that "Ginzy I find very lively, but they are all so dull and *social*" (G. Evans 155). For both Olson and Duncan, the term "social" meant not so much "politically engaged" as "cliquish" and "self-involved."

Duncan's and Olson's comments suggest plenty of differences (and even conflict) among Allen's poets, differences that reinforced and yet also went beyond whatever one might infer from the evidence of the text itself. In seeking to represent both a nexus of poetics and a nexus of "scenes,"

Allen faced the conflict between aesthetic and social criteria for anthologizing that had bedeviled anthologists of American poetry since the early nineteenth century and that continued to manifest itself into the late twentieth century in such alleged "oppositions" as that between experimental and identitarian poetics.[21] Part of *The New American Poetry*'s ongoing interest for literary historians is precisely that it provides a conflicted rather than homogeneous picture not of "the" postwar avant-garde but of multiple avant-garde communities. No matter how tentative an anthology's organization is intended to be, it is likely to become reified, as *The New American Poetry*'s did, in the minds of reviewers. But Allen's "groups" turn out to be more internally unstable than they were often perceived to be.

Not the least interesting instance of dissent is Allen's reprinting the very "Pages from a Notebook" of Duncan's that had aroused Olson to public disagreement in his own essay "Against Wisdom as Such." To take just a few other of various possible examples of internal difference, in an August 11, 1959, letter to Creeley Allen writes that "when I was working on the San Francisco issue [of *Evergreen Review*,] [Duncan] refused to be in it if I included any of Gregory Corso"—this despite Duncan's subsequent insistence on Corso's importance to "the creation of the 'Beat' vision." Ginsberg remarks in an (April?) 1958 letter to Allen that he does not know Duncan's work well and that he "never much cared for F Antoninus. Nor Brought[o]n, Blaser, & others you like"; he even expresses some ambivalence about Ferlinghetti. Blaser's own critique of Madeline Gleason and James Broughton in correspondence with Allen involves terms like "awful," "incompetent," "uninteresting," "boring," "provincial," and the catch-all "bad," and in a letter to Allen of January 14, 1960, he also alludes to disagreements over the work of another contributor, John Wieners's *The Hotel Wentley Poems*.[22] While Duncan acted as a conduit for Black Mountain materials in the San Francisco community (although James Broughton had actually introduced him to "Projective Verse"), response there to Olson involved, in Blaser's words, widespread "consternation" and "dismissals," along with "Spicer's I'll-think-about-it-twice approach, and my confusion" (Blaser 6). Spicer's thinking about it twice, moreover, produced an emphatic rejection of Olson's poetics. As Duncan writes to Allen on June 13, 1960, "later Spicer did *not* read Origin, rejected all ideas and possible directions from the work of Olson, and then Creeley and Denise [Levertov]."

Such examples of internal dissent within *The New American Poetry* extend in numerous directions. Duncan observed in 1971, "My relationship with the New York school has been very difficult—O'Hara was absolutely intolerant of my existence" (Ginsberg, *Allen Verbatim* 135). The roots of this relationship went back to the late 1950s. Donald Allen writes that

> when I published Frank O'Hara's "In Memory of My Feelings" etc. in ER, Duncan wrote O'Hara a most condescending letter, rather like elderly royalty acknowledging the existence of a mere commoner. Frank showed me the letter and asked how he should answer. I tried to explain Duncan a little to him, but in the end Frank never replied. (letter to the author, October 9, 1996)

Animosities between New York poets and Spicer ran both ways. O'Hara and Ashbery disliked both Spicer's person and his work. In a July 15, 1959, letter to Jasper Johns, O'Hara wrote of Spicer, "he always disappoints me," and Joe LeSueur observes "Frank represented a very urbane and (to Jack, I believe) a campy kind of poetry, or maybe he felt it was a little effete, I'm not sure; but I do remember Jack not much liking Frank's work . . . And Frank, though he could see that Jack had talent, wasn't very attracted to his poetry" (qtd. in Ellingham and Killian 65). According to Landis Everson, Spicer called Ashbery "'a faggot poet'" and referred to his first book as "'Thumb Twees'"; Blaser corroborates the reference in a 1990 letter to Kevin Killian (qtd. in Ellingham and Killian 65, 75). Meanwhile, only a few months after *The New American Poetry*'s publication, in a September 1960 letter James Schuyler describes the initiation of the New York School little magazine *Locus Solus* as a critical response to the anthology: "Part of [*Locus Solus*'] unstated objective is as a riposte at The New American Poetry, which has so thoroughly misrepresented so many of us—not completely, but the implications of context are rather overwhelming" (qtd. in Herd, *John Ashbery* 52).

As with any ongoing cultural conversation, we need not think of all these positions as being permanently staked out by their proponents nor of the personal differences as carved in stone. Ginsberg, for instance, maintained significant friendships with Duncan and Olson. Nevertheless, Michael Davidson is right to point out how the 1965 Berkeley Poetry Conference, which brought together San Francisco Renaissance and Black Mountain poets in their third key gathering (after *The New American Poetry* itself and the 1963 Vancouver conference), "expos[ed] some of the lesions that had developed" not only in aesthetics but "around matters of power and authority within the poetry community itself" (*San Francisco Renaissance* 204). These lesions were always immanent, and imminent. No wonder Allen wrote to Blaser on August 16, 1959, that "editing an antho is very different from the tactics required of mag editor; now I fight to keep clear of all the politics, to see it whole." One goal of his much-debated, and constantly changing, organization was to minimize these differences—to create, as he puts it in an August 11, 1959, letter to Creeley, "a tentative arrangement which would have some meaning *and also avoid pointless confrontations*" (my emphasis).

While I've concentrated in the last few pages on poetic, social, and personal differences among Allen's New American poets, the text draws much of its force and coherence from its focus on demographically narrow or fairly homogeneous writing communities. That focus, however, can also be seen to contribute to the anthology's race and gender lacunae. At the time of the anthology's publication, Amiri Baraka (then LeRoi Jones) was publishing many of the New American poets in his magazine *Yugen*, about which he cheerfully admits "if it seems like a coterie—well, it turns out to be that way" ("Interview" 319). In his *Autobiography* (or at least that of Jones), Baraka observes that by the time of *The New American Poetry* and editing *Yugen*, his "social focus had gotten much whiter," and he "sincerely had no ax to grind but the whole of new poetry" (157, 159). He did not particularly promote Black poets, despite publishing a number of them alongside the white Americans in *Yugen*. A few years later, however, and after his politically life-changing July 1960 visit to Cuba, Baraka uses the idea of the "club" to comment on the racial homogeneity of *The New American Poetry*:

> American poetry, &c. anthologies are like memberships in the same ofay suburban social clubs of the walkaround world. We are poets from different sources, finally, for different reasons. Only LeRoi Jones in New American Poetry, 1945–60. *The* Negro! Whose poetry, then, only a reflection of what the rest of that E-X-C-L-U-S-I-V-E club was doing. You mean there was no other poetry, you mean there were no other spooks, &c. I pass. (*Raise Race* 25)

Aldon Nielsen's *Black Chant* and his coedited anthology with Lauri Ramey, *Every Goodbye Ain't Gone*, should effectively dispel any notion that the racial contours of *The New American Poetry* simply reflect the fact that there were no black poets to be included—that, in Baraka's ironic phrasing, "there were no other spooks."[23] A number of the poets whom Nielsen and Ramey resurrected and who appeared in *Yugen* would not look out of place in *The New American Poetry*: Tom Postell, Oliver Pitcher, A. B. Spellman (for whose 1965 volume, *The Beautiful Days*, Frank O'Hara wrote an introduction).[24] In the 1950s, Harold Carrington, who spent much of his young adult life in jail before his 1964 death, corresponded with various New American poets (including Baraka), read their work, and shared a cellblock and conversation on poetics (and possibly collaborated) with Allen contributor Ray Bremser. Russell Atkins had been editing and publishing in the avant-garde little magazine *Free Lance* throughout the decade. Despite Baraka's subsequent acknowledgment of his own immersion in a predominantly white poetic milieu, it remains an odd feature of *The New American Poetry* that he did not apprise Allen of the work of more black writers—or perhaps he did, and Allen did not take to their poetry. It is also striking that Allen himself did not find more such writers, given the overlaps between their work and some of his own contributors, his habit of seeking out new poets through correspondence, and the undeniable editorial diligence that Baraka himself praises: "[Allen] worked meticulously, and he went to great pains to investigate the poetic scene, inquiring after new poets, buying all the magazines, going to all the poetry readings and events manqué. (He had found me through *Yugen*)" (*Autobiography* 160).

I don't want to fall into a glib anachronism on these complex social questions: "How poorly Allen did with women and minorities in contrast to the enlightened present." At issue here are the ideological limitations of a historical and political moment as much as those of an individual editor. But at the very least it would be surprising if Allen did not know of the work of Steven Jonas, Bob Kaufman, Clarence Major, and perhaps Ted Joans. Major and Jonas were active correspondents of Baraka's in the late 1950s (Nielsen 166). I assume that Allen knew, or knew of, Jonas and Kaufman through his close connections with the Boston and San Francisco poetry scenes; his archive even contains a very brief correspondence with Jonas. As Nielsen notes, Jonas was a close associate of Spicer and Blaser during their time in Boston and apparently read with them and John Wieners. In a June 18, 1959, letter to Olson, Allen mentions sending the poet a copy of Kaufman's magazine *Beatitude*, generated "in a plan hatched with Allen Ginsberg and others" (Nielsen 166). Meanwhile, Joans had been active in Greenwich Village since the early 1950s, appeared in an anthology almost exactly contemporary with Allen's (Elias Wilentz's *The Beat Scene*), and had read with and known Ginsberg since at least 1958. Ginsberg does not mention Joans, however, in his correspondence with Allen on *The New American Poetry*.

The fact that Allen's contacts lay within predominantly white male networks also does not entirely explain the absence of women writers such as Joanne Kyger (with whom he was in touch, and who complained of her exclusion) or of Diane di Prima, who had published with Jones's Totem

Press and in *Yugen*.[25] These poets are hardly more negligible than some of their male peers who were included, and both went on to more sustained poetic careers than many of those peers. Kyger writes to Allen on August 31, 1959, "Don't you like *my* poetry? Frankly, I think it's more interesting tha[n] Kirby Doyle's and at least three other people that I know. However, perhaps you aren't interested in interesting poetry." Duncan's remarks on the Spicer circle, meanwhile, suggest the possibility that Allen was influenced by Kyger's exclusion from that group's sense of poetry. Duncan says that "Joanne Kyger was read out in these same years . . . although I think most of that seemed to have been coming from some spiff that [Stan] Persky and Blaser had with the idea of Joanne. Yet Jack [Spicer] was cooperative with it" (qtd. in Ellingham 68).[26] Di Prima had published her first chapbook with Totem in 1958; among the authors of the sixteen total chapbooks that Totem published, di Prima is one of only two (the other is Max Finstein) not to appear in *The New American Poetry*. (Jones had recommended di Prima's work, somewhat ambivalently, in a May 15, 1959, letter to Allen: "Sturdy, but sometimes overly-mannered pieces. But always interesting.") Di Prima notes her persistent structural exclusion from public events featuring her male associates. Regarding "some kind of poetry conference at Wagner College," "spearheaded" by Ginsberg and also featuring Jones, "Joel Oppenheimer and a few of the others," di Prima writes "I had of course not been asked. . . . I was often not asked to literary events, though I published with everyone in the usual places, worked side-by-side with the men putting out the magazines and books, read here and there with them on the East Side or in the Village. As a woman, I was invisible. I took that as a matter of course" (*Recollections* 237–38). This cultural invisibility left di Prima unsurprised at her exclusion from *The New American Poetry*, an exclusion for which she recalls Allen coming up with a social, rather than literary or aesthetic, explanation or excuse: "He had been, he told me . . . , requested by Hettie Jones to leave me out. Because of my ongoing affair with LeRoi" (238)—something that, in a later letter, Allen denies saying. Like Kyger, di Prima was convinced of the value of the work she had submitted. As she puts it in a 2001 interview, "I think I should have been in that anthology" because "I knew [my work] was as strong as anything in Roi's early work that was going in from that *Preface to a Twenty-Volume Suicide Note* [Baraka's first book]." She is left raising a compelling concrete and theoretical question: "Given the fact that me and Roi and Hettie, we were all basically in one position of misbehaving—how does it happen that the woman gets left out of the anthology?" ("In Conversation").[27]

Furthermore, an anthology dominated by Olson—the phallocentrism of whose poetics has received quite extensive commentary in recent years—was likely to be heavy on homosociality.[28] On this point, Michael Davidson provides a useful term for understanding some of Allen's exclusions when he argues for "compulsory homosociality" as a defining feature of two of the milieus that dominate *The New American Poetry*, those of the Spicer circle and Black Mountain College. (Davidson expands his argument, in passing, to the Beats and others.) He suggests that women's relative "absence in these groups was a structural necessity for the liberation of a new, male subject" (*Guys Like Us* 30); by extension, their absence from *The New American Poetry* enacts a similar "structural necessity."[29] Meanwhile, where Davidson focuses specifically on the homosociality of the New American scenes, Rachel Blau DuPlessis argues more generally that homosociality and "hyperactive gender binaries seem to be one major ideology of the institution called 'poetry'" (*Blue Studios* 93), perpetuated alike in more mainstream (her example is Allen Grossman) and more alternative (Olson) theorizing on poetics. The unacknowledged function of the phallic and homosocial language of "Projective Verse" was to "(re) claim poetry for masculine discourse, making poetry safe for men to enter, making poetry a serious discourse of aroused, exploratory manhood" via the essay's "gender-exclusionary subtext" (84).

Reading *The New American Poetry* from this perspective serves as a reminder that its aesthetic critique does not extend quite as broadly into cultural critique as has often been claimed, at least in the area of gender. The cluster of alternative poetics that makes up *The New American Poetry*—especially insofar as it is presented under the sign of Olson and "Projective Verse"—is marked by a gender conservatism that we now recognize as historically a part of much avant-garde practice, that conflicts with its aesthetic radicalism, and that actually maintains certain received features of the poetic. As DuPlessis puts it, "Olson's is not a poetics that undermines the poetic compact of male mastery. Those positioned as 'not-men' are dismissed, and the speaking female is missing" (*Blue Studios* 86).[30] In other words, if the poetics underlying *The New American Poetry* are heavily gendered male, those poetics require for their sustenance the exclusion or minimal presence of women writers in a representative anthology.[31] When Allen told Robin Blaser of his effort "to keep clear of all the politics," he was referring to the interpersonal and group politics that I describe earlier in this chapter. But as it will for any editor, a broader politics still inscribed itself and contributed to the shaping of his text.

Allen engaged a broader *cultural* politics, of course, in his now-notorious sally against the "academic verse" of Hall, Pack, and Simpson's *New Poets of England and America* (a text never actually named at any point in Allen's book), the position summarized in the widely quoted assertion from his preface that the various poetries that he has gathered share "one common characteristic: a total rejection of all those qualities typical of academic verse" (Allen, *New American Poetry* xi). This comes close to being the single most repeated and debated assertion in all of postwar American poetics. As one unpacks Allen's claim, however, the term "academic" tends to become muddied, as do the distinctions between targets that are finally not easily separable: Allen's poets tend variously to oppose the academic criticism of their moment, the poetry written under the aegis of that criticism (often, but not always, by teacher-poets in mainstream academic institutions), the larger institutional structures of academe, and the intellectualism associated with academic pursuits. Any reconstruction of the processes behind *The New American Poetry*, then, should involve some scrutiny of the term "academic" and of the context in which the "othering" of this term became crucial to the identity formation of 1950s poetic avant-gardes. The New American critique of the academic is best contextualized as part of a period anxiety over the academicizing of poetry that can actually be seen among the *New Poets* poets as well as the *New American* poets—an anxiety handled differently, however, on each side.

We can see Allen's conception of the "academic" evolving through his reader reports for Grove Press during the years preceding *The New American Poetry*, reports that consistently invoked "the academy" in negative terms. The literary values driving the anthology were already in place in Allen's November 24, 1957, report on Edwin Honig's submission of the manuscript *Poems* (or, *Owners of Their Faces*):

> Honig has no native talent for poetry at all. He is another of our teacher poets, who wants very much to be a poet and works hard grinding out poetry. . . . His poetry is little more than a collection of cleverly contrived effects imitated after other better poets. He has nothing whatever to say, that I can see anyway, and he says it in an artificially complicated way that makes one feel he's essentially irresponsible as a writer.

Similarly, about Albert Cook's submission, "Chiaroscuro and Other Poems," Allen writes in a July 13, 1958, report that "these are conventional poems of the forties-fifties type, they are the kind of poems encouraged by professors and taught in most of our schools."[32]

Especially to the point are Allen's critiques of submissions to Grove from poets eventually included in *New Poets of England and America*, critiques that help flesh out what he had in mind by the term "academic."

Donald Finkel's manuscript "The Clothing's New Emperor" (poems from which make up Finkel's section in Hall, Pack, and Simpson) is "tasteless and derivative," "mechanical, insipid stuff," and "despite his use of elaborate verse forms, even the villanelle figures here, his verse tends to be prosy, 'literary' in the worst sense, imitative." Another "one of our teacher poets," Finkel "derives his themes entirely from other books; and one wonders in the end just why he does bother to write poetry." In Allen's view, then, one could be a professor poet without literally being a professor. The work of another Hall, Pack, and Simpson contributor, Thom Gunn's *The Sense of Movement*, already published in England by Faber, gets by with a slightly less withering critique: "Unfortunately, like his colleagues [in English poetry], his verse is not very modern; he writes the prevalent kind of fixed form verse and expends most of his ingenuity in working out rime schemes" (which Allen admits he does "fairly effectively"). Regarding what Allen calls, using Olson's term, Gunn's "stance," "he's only got the 'hell' of sexual desire and callow ruminations on history and such to offer," so that finally "I don't feel Gunn's book is worth publishing here." (It was soon published by a university press, Chicago, in 1957.)

Allen was not necessarily kinder to his own eventual contributors, among whom, as I've said, he certainly made distinctions. Reporting on Paul Carroll's manuscript *De Medici Slot Machine* on November 26, 1958, he writes that "on the whole Carroll's verse is better than that of the academic poets, but as a poet he must be rated in the second or third rank, below some 15 (I'd guess) of his contemporaries." Of Brother Antoninus's *The Crooked Lines of God*, "the only rugged & original religious poetry being written in America today," he also says that "I find myself frequently embarrassed by these poems. Some seem quite uninteresting to me as poems." In an August 11, 1959, letter to Creeley, Allen writes without enthusiasm that "a little of Helen Adam and of James Broughton is all right," implying that "a little" is also quite enough. Allen's inclusion of these writers suggests both that his commitment to his project overrode his reservations about individual contributors' work and that he considered his anthology a gathering not only of poets and scenes but of poems, since he picked individual strong poems by those he considered lesser writers.

Allen knew that the *New Poets* collection had already partly defined his territory for him, writing in his September 1958 form description of *The New American Poetry* that "the academic poets of the decade are well enough represented in the Meridian Books anthology edited by Donald Hall, and others, and I do not plan to include their work in the anthology I am compiling" (Maud 47). Allen's response to the "academic" involves not just one specific anthology that provides a convenient target, however, but the increasing institutionalization—or academicizing—of "Creative Writing." His well-known repudiation of "academic verse" brings to a head an already well-established discourse, manifested among other places in Kenneth Rexroth's 1957 essay "Disengagement: The Art of the Beat Generation." Through a now-familiar tirade against the "Reactionary Generation" of New Critical poet-critics "dominant in backwater American colleges," against the "blight of poetic professors" and workshop writers read only by each other, against "mainstream" magazines and that ever-convenient antagonist, the Iowa Writers' Program, Rexroth builds to the claim that the San Francisco Renaissance is "characterized by total rejection of the official high-brow culture" (182–92)—a phrasing prophetic of Allen's preface.[33]

Conversely, when Robert Pack defends the academy as the ideal site for poetry's production and consumption in 1962, against "literary cliques" and "the incestuous pages of little magazines" ("Introduction" 182), he does not merely respond to Allen but reiterates a position that had been proposed for some years. In a 1958 talk, Delmore Schwartz had praised *The New Poets of England and America* in contrast to "the San Francisco Howlers" for a "professional competence" reinforced by many of them being teachers of literature (44–47). September 1955 had brought the first volume of a serial anthology of student writers, *New Campus Writers*, and the preface to the second volume in this series, from the same year as *New Poets of England and America*, both anticipates Pack's position and wishfully revises the literary history of its own moment: "It is now clear that the Bohemias of yesterday have pretty much disappeared. Our academic communities . . . have become the principal focus of the arts. Ask the young writer why he comes to the university, he answers, 'Where else can I go?'" (Miller and Jerome v).[34]

If *The New American Poetry* offered an aggressively anti-academic response to such arguments, some writers in *New Poets* also engaged in their own satires on the academy, seeking to separate themselves from "scholars" and suggesting ambivalence about their own academic affiliations. In Snodgrass's well-known "April Inventory," the teacher-poet congratulates himself that "In one whole year I haven't learned / A blessed thing they pay you for," that "I haven't read one book about / A book or memorized one plot," aligning himself with the values of nature, the erotic, and the intuitive against a world where "the solid scholars / Get the degrees, the jobs, the dollars. // And smile above their starchy collars" (297–98). Reed Whittemore's "A Treasure" is a trunk of papers "awaiting the tireless hunter, the scholar, the drudge / Now on his way on a generous grant" (316). In a way that James Breslin (1–22) argues is characteristic of their generation, the American *New Poets* thematized fears of their own slightness. Thus, Whittemore writes of producing mere exercises, "a kind of verse / Neither major nor minor but merely (an old kind) doodle," something that "might be likened to those / Hobbies with hammers and drills / Practiced in all the best basements" ("A Week of Doodle" 317–18).

Divisions within *The New American Poetry* complicate the issue of the "academic" further. On the one hand, a now-familiar negative construction of the "academic" pervades Allen's "Statements of Poetics" section, in observations by Ginsberg, James Schuyler, Jones, and Duncan. From Ginsberg: "I hear ghostly Academics in Limbo screeching about form" and "a word on Academies; poetry has been attacked by an ignorant & frightened bunch of bores who don't understand how it's made, & the trouble with these creeps is they wouldn't know Poetry if it came up and buggered them in broad daylight" ("Notes" 415, 417). Schuyler comments on the "blinders-on regression" of "the campus dry-heads who wishfully descend tum-ti-tumming from Yeats out of Graves with a big kiss for Mother England" (418). Jones: "The diluted formalism of the academy (the formal culture of the U.S.) is anaemic & fraught with incompetence & unreality" ("'How You Sound??'" 425). Duncan imagines a utopian moment "when poetry no longer furnishes the gentleman's library with its elegance or the English professor with his livelihood" ("Pages" 402). Meanwhile, the biographical statements contain numerous claims to autodidacticism and, almost proudly, to unfinished degrees. On the other hand, many of the poets were clearly interested in pursuing alternative definitions of or possibilities for an "academy." Often, they objected not to learning but to its institutional forms—forms experienced, in many cases, while earning Ivy League, private college, and distinguished state university degrees. Some relocated a positive notion of the academy in a person rather than an institution. Thus, Creeley describes Olson's letters as "a practical 'college' of stimulus and information" ("Olson & Others" 409), and Philip Whalen writes, "I do not put down the academy but have assumed its function in my own person, and in the strictest sense of the word—academy—a walking grove of trees" (420). Poets such as Duncan and Olson were self-consciously learned, "scholars," a term that, unlike Snodgrass, they were careful to distinguish from "academics."

The example of Jack Spicer further reveals that *The New American Poetry* does not entirely represent the complexity of its own contributors' thinking on the "academic." Spicer's letter to Robin Blaser, collected in *Admonitions*, that contains the famously dismissive phrase "the English Department of the spirit," defines that term as "that great quagmire that lurks at the bottom of all of us" (Spicer 163). Rather than an external and easily located “enemy,” the academy stands metonymically for an internalized set of constraints operating on all New American poets. More specifically, the negative lesson of the English Department for Spicer's generation was that it preached the doctrine of the single, self-contained poem: “I learned this from the English Department . . . and it ruined ten years of my poetry.” At this point (1958), Spicer claimed that he wished to preserve only “Imaginary Elegies” and *After Lorca* (both of which Allen excerpts), writing to Blaser in his apparent role as anthological go-between, “don't send the box of old poetry to Don Allen” (Spicer 163).[35] Yet, just as Spicer records in this letter a change in his thinking in the direction of serial poems, so in the first *Admonitions* letter, to Joe Dunn, he shows himself rethinking the relationship of poetry (“celestial mechanics”) to criticism (“terrestrial mechanics”). A flat opposition no longer obtains: “Muses do exist, but now I know that they are not afraid to dirty their hands with explication—that they are patient with truth and commentary as long as it doesn't get into the poem” (157). Poetry and the academy remained in ambivalent but not entirely exclusive relation to each other for Spicer.

In fact, within months of Allen's anti-academic anthology, Spicer and Blaser came up in spring 1960 with the idea of forming an academy. “White Rabbit College” was apparently to be modeled on Black Mountain; Blaser conceived of it as “Black Mountain College in Exile,” and he and Spicer sought to enlist the services of Duncan, Whalen, the painters Harry Jacobus and Jess, and the composer Pauline Oliveiros. Though Spicer, the Berkeley linguistics graduate, had devoutly resisted all things academic, he found himself disturbed by the anti-intellectualism of his younger peers. Writing to Duncan of George Stanley and Ebbe Borregaard's resistance to learning about modern French poetry and mythology respectively, he remarks, “I quote the reaction of the two most educated members of that generation then I remember how we learned and listened from Kantorowicz and weep” (qtd. in Ellingham and Killian 192–93).

The instability of such categories as the “anti-academic” illustrates one of my main concerns in this chapter: the contingencies and impurities that make up both the editing and the reception of a now-canonical anthology of “new” work. *The New American Poetry* offers a valuable case study in the fortuitousness of the anthologizing process; such a study seems particularly instructive when, decades after its publication, Allen's collection continued to be treated in some scholarship as something of a monolithic construction. Into the 1980s and 1990s, readers still defined *The New American Poetry* in terms that uncannily repeated early responses to the text, terms that constituted what one might call the “negative mirror” critique. In this critique, a number of early reviewers accuse *The New American Po-*

*etry* of lacking any positive identity beyond its claims to oppositionality or of perpetuating the academicism it claims to resist, as they list excluded poets (that familiar trope of the anthology reviewer) in a way that, rhetorically, functions to deny or resist Allen's polemical point in the anthology.[36] Thus John Robert Colombo writes that "the criterion of inclusion is a negative one" (85), and Karl Shapiro finds in the "self-styled literary Underground," which he would apparently have liked to defend, "only a negative version of culture poetry" (27).[37] Firing back in the anthology wars via a barely disguised critique of *The New American Poetry* (metonymically represented by the Beats and "Howl"), Robert Pack argues that "the personality that is constitutionally grounded in opposition—sentimentalism in reverse—has a facile subject in hand, and lightly finds fluency in complaint. The shriek [or howl] against the world adds no wisdom to what is obvious" (182). Among later critics, Daniel Hoffman asserts that Allen's poets "share little but their rebellion against the period style of the fifties" (497); Vernon Shetley finds in them "an antiacademic opposition that had shaped itself as a mirror image of the academic formalism it was rejecting" (*After the Death* 14); Walter Kalaidjian writes of "the collection's oppositional *dependence* on the very traditions it repudiated" (7).[38] In the "negative mirror" critique, all resistance becomes merely reactive, shaped by its opposite, and indeed the critique itself can function as a way of denying cultural resistance any seriousness. While this set of claims has some substance to it, to exercise this co-optive logic in the present would seriously understate the undeniable historical impact of *The New American Poetry*; underplay the genuine differences between the traditions upon which Allen and Hall, Pack, and Simpson drew; and overlook the kinds of internal difference that I have laid out here. To trace those differences and to unpack the editorial process behind Allen's anthology should lead us to reshape and complicate the critical story that we tell about *The New American Poetry* and the literary historical moment it catalyzes.[39]

## Coda: One New American Moment— David Ossman's *The Sullen Art*

It was one of those moments where one turns out to have participated in, and even helped shape, a significant literary history without necessarily planning to do so. A precocious young California transplant to New York graduated from Columbia University in 1958 and walked into a revolution in American poetry. David Ossman was born on December 6, 1936. When he interviewed emergent American poets for WBAI radio in New York from early 1960 to 1961, he was only twenty-three to twenty-four years old, in some cases talking to emergent poets not much older than himself, and learning as he went. Subsequently better known as a founder of the counter-culture comedy group Firesign Theatre, in 1960–61 Ossman was an engaged participant-observer in the scene that he documented: he read with Jerome Rothenberg and Robert Kelly, he met Rochelle Owens at a poetry reading, his first book of poetry was published by one of his interviewees, Margaret Randall. And the book that originally gathered these important early interviews, *The Sullen Art* (1963), was published from within that community, by Ted and Eli Wilentz's Corinth Books, publisher of LeRoi Jones, Diane di Prima, Edward Dorn, and others. The expanded 2016 reissue, now titled *The Sullen Art: Recording the Revolution in American Poetry,* allows us to reimagine the New American moment from within a scene that featured a number of Donald Allen's poets but that was much more capacious than the anthology and that implicitly offers a broader, and even occasionally competing, definition of what a "New American Poetry" might mean. The internal differences that I've discussed in *The New American Poetry* and its larger nexus, and that have sometimes been occluded in its reception, are nicely encapsulated in *The Sullen Art.*

In the contemporary era of the interview—facilitated by email, which both brings thoroughness and nuance to the proceedings but reduces irreverence, spontaneity, and surprise—it is hard even to find a poet, emergent or established, who does not have an interview published somewhere. Not so in the early 1960s, and the original *Sullen Art* features the first published interviews with a number of significant poets who were unlikely to get a hearing anywhere else. That 1963 edition was a characteristic small press production, modest in scale, featuring fourteen interviews and a brief introduction across ninety-five pages. The 2016 expanded edition adds various forms of apparatus, but more importantly, it doubles the number of interviews from the original fourteen to twenty-eight, and there are more in the archive, which contains interviews with forty-four poets.[40] The full *Sullen Art* archive at the University of Toledo includes interviews with British fellow travelers such as Charles Tomlinson and Gael Turnbull, writers who were close to inclusion in *The New American Poetry* (Judson Jerome, Gene Frumkin), and unlikely outliers who were themselves very different from each other such as Michael Benedikt and Lewis Turco. But more generally, what does the collection as a whole now offer? Today the interviews no longer serve their once-introductory function for what Ossman "considered a pretty un-hip listening audience" (*Sullen Art* [2016] 13), and their brevity—they were mostly thirty minutes long and often included the poet reading his/her work—makes them a rather sparse resource for someone interested in a developed discussion of an individual's poetics. If the questions sometimes seem basic to insiders, they are also well-informed, sometimes challenging, and specific to the writer being addressed, and we should consider that Ossman brought this work, with only a few minutes airtime available, to a general public largely unaware of any new or "alternative" American poetry outside of "Howl" and a general set of stereotyped and inaccurate notions about "Beats" or "Beatniks." What Ossman's opening up of the archive does offer is a rich collective portrait of a moment in American literary history the implications of which are still being lived and written out. If no one interview is a major statement, the cumulative conversation is a crucial and often entertaining contribution to the historical record and to our understanding of a cultural and literary moment in the process of its formation. Himself "openly curious . . . as to what was going on in contemporary writing, what was in fact new about it" (13), Ossman simultaneously anticipated, engaged, and pushed back against New American poetics at the time of its public emergence.

Like any document of a particular literary moment, Ossman's germinal collection of interviews contains some names now largely lost to literary history: C. V. J. Anderson, for instance, who published no books of poetry after the 1961 *A Litany for Dragons*, or Tuli Kupferberg, whom more people will know as a cofounder of the Fugs than as a poet and editor and the character who is represented as jumping off the Brooklyn Bridge in Ginsberg's "Howl." But a genuinely thorough and textured literary history needs to pay attention to its minor figures; as T. S. Eliot (perhaps an odd name to conjure here) observed early in his career, "the main current . . . does not at all flow invariably through the most distinguished reputations" ("Tradition" 51). At the same time, the original book was remarkably prescient in that all of the people included went on to significant careers in ways that could not have been anticipated at the time, and even the expanded edition largely represents a group of then-emergent writers.

Pervaded by the rhetoric of the anthology wars that marks its moment, *The Sullen Art* situates itself emphatically, but still with a nice sense of nuance and complexity, on *The New American Poetry* side of things. It's worth noting, however, that only ten of the twenty-eight poets (and eight of the original fourteen) interviewed for the 2016 volume appeared in that anthology. Ossman operated not narrowly within a *New American Poetry* framework but more within a larger New American nexus, matrix, or network of associated poets. The official release date for *The New American Poetry* was May 29, 1960; Ossman conducted his earliest interviews in the spring of 1960, before the anthology was even in the world, and had completed ten of them by summer 1960. Those interviews represent a snapshot of the poetry scene at the very moment when it was congealing into movements, when apparently sharp distinctions were being fiercely articulated. The fault lines that complicated such tidy binaries as those of the anthology wars—like the fact that Allen Ginsberg first met Michael McClure at a party for W. H. Auden—are always of interest, of course, and *The Sullen Art* both reflects and partly resists these oppositions. In this context, it's appropriate that Ossman's questions return consistently to the issues of club, clique, school, movement (various terms are used) that persistently arose in critiques of *The New American Poetry* and that I address in this chapter. His original May 1962 introduction raises the issue explicitly: even as he acknowledges that "the community of these new poets is small and in contact directly or by correspondence" and "bears little or no relation to the academic communities in which most other poets find themselves writing," nevertheless, "it is too bad that American poetry today appears to fall into two distinct camps" (*Sullen Art* [1963] 8). It is often hard to say whether Ossman is registering his own skepticism or ventriloquizing what he imagined to be the skepticism of his audience. He asks LeRoi Jones about publishing "one of the three or four 'clique' magazines around today" (*Sullen Art* [2016] 89); he asks Michael McClure about the "clubbiness" of his new journal project (156). He resisted emphatically the idea of "a single 'avant-garde' clique . . . in opposition to what has been variously called 'The Academy' and 'The Establishment' when many of them [have] been teachers" and "would readily admit the talents of others who are called their opposition" (*Sullen Art* [1963] 8). In a prescient question in early 1961, he asks Paul Carroll "Don't you think the 'New American Poetry' is on its way to becoming the 'New American Academy'?" (*Sullen Art* [2016] 37).

I already quoted Robert Pack inveighing in 1962 against "literary cliques" in "the incestuous pages of little magazines," and we immediately recognize such remarks as part of anthology wars rhetoric. But this concern also marked, as a point of internal difference, the "New American" side of things and saturates *The Sullen Art*. Robert Creeley—at this stage in his career one of the more energetic critics of mainstream poetics around—says, "I have a little hesitation about the question of 'schools,'" while, speaking from the other "side" as a Hall, Pack, and Simpson participant and Yale Younger Poet whose work was changing radically, W. S. Merwin says (perhaps disingenuously), "I don't know what either 'school' is supposed to consist of, but I don't think I've ever been a part of either" (*Sullen Art* [2016] 51, 248). In the newly published interviews, although Rochelle Owens considers the presence of schools "invigorating" (150) and does not question it, Margaret Randall specifically feels no connection with "any group"

(99); Armand Schwerner tactfully sidesteps questions about the Deep Image "movement" or "school"; Jack Micheline insists that "I've got my own school and that's me" and that "I'm not interested in schools, I'm interested in my poetry" (165); Barbara Moraff admits to publishing under a pseudonym to avoid being labeled a Beat because "I don't see myself in any 'school' or in any group at all" (171); and C. V. J. Anderson says that *The New American Poetry* "is derisively referred to in the underground cellars and such of Greenwich Village and North Beach as the 'club book'" (189), despite its demonstrable internal tensions.[41]

The relationship between individual and group, movement, or community has often bedeviled American poets. It is a recurring dynamic in the mainstream anthologies that I discuss in chapter 4. Ossman's conviction of the artist's essentially solitary practice stands in interesting tension with the sense of an already established sociopoetic network projected in many of the interviews, in parts of his own original introduction, and in Allen's anthology. In the 1946 Dylan Thomas poem from which he takes his title, "my craft or sullen art" is "exercised in the still night / When only the moon rages / And the lovers lie abed"; the poet "labours by singing light" in solitude (142). Ossman concludes his introduction with the assertion that "these poets, and all poets, despite their contacts with the world, are ultimately alone. One creates, after all, by one's self" (*Sullen Art* [1963] 9). Yet in many of the *Sullen Art* interviews, one sees a highly self-conscious historicizing going on, as one after another writer offers a minimap of what has come to be called New American poetics. Despite a certain "mutual admiration society" quality to the interviews, this accounting of the moment is not always positive. Seams show, just as they do when we look into *The New American Poetry* archive. Robert Bly, always good for some cranky divergence from popular opinion, says that the work associated with the New American poetry "is old-fashioned. The way they put together a poem is basically the way a poem was put together in the nineteenth century" (*Sullen Art* [2016] 136); "our poetry . . . has tended to become too barren" (136) and "is in a poor state relative to poetries in other languages" (138). John Logan, who appears in the second edition of *New Poets of England and America,* well after his spring 1960 *Sullen Art* interview, puts welcome pressure on the abuse or overuse of the term "academic" (244–45). Gilbert Sorrentino lambastes the Beats, "whose ideas and aesthetics I have no truck with whatsoever" (235), for ego-obsessed "neo-Romantic . . . burble" (233). Indeed, a number of the writers show the desire to distance themselves from the Beats, from Sorrentino to Clayton Eshleman's "the 'Beats' don't have enough control, really, to satisfy me" (240). The status of the Beats, and the definition and boundaries of the term, was quite contested here, appropriately so when *The New American Poetry* was widely misread as a Beat anthology. They are a pervasive background presence in a book that, of the best-known figures, only represents Ginsberg, and even C. V. J. Anderson, one short-term editor of *Beatitude*, shows an entertainingly irreverent distance from the very scene that he was most deeply involved in.

*The Sullen Art* moves, then, within a New American nexus but with both notable additions (Logan, Merwin) and absences (Olson, O'Hara and the rest of the New York school, the major Beat names outside of Ginsberg). Unsurprisingly, the racial and gender lacunae of the period perpetuated themselves in the interviews (though Ossman's interviewing five women out of the twenty-eight writers represented here, and seven in the total archive, was an improvement on *The New American Poetry*). To some extent, one assumes, *The Sullen Art* was always a highly contingent project, its contents tentatively proposing a new canon but also shaped by the material question of whoever happened to be living in or visiting New York at the time and whose presence Ossman's many contacts alerted him to. For instance, while the absence of New York school poets raises contemporary eyebrows, and while in Ossman's view they were "somehow too 'uptown'" (*Sullen Art* [2016] 13) for an interviewer's tastes shaped in a Greenwich Village and Lower East Side environment, it was also the case that John Ashbery was living in Paris—along with, though not *with*, Gregory Corso—and the reticent James Schuyler would have seemed an unlikely interview candidate.[42]

If *The Sullen Art* constituted its own kind of introduction to alternative US poetics, we can note some further, not necessarily predictable, points of particular interest. Translation was a recurring theme, interestingly so for a nexus that sometimes claimed a kind of American exceptionalism for itself. The translators here include some of the most significant poet-translators of the period: Rexroth, Blackburn, Randall, Rothenberg, Bly, Eshleman, Merwin. In only two interviews does the term *avant-garde* come up in the poet's comments, with Rexroth and Kupferberg, and even Rexroth uses it somewhat ironically. Despite Allen's use of it in his preface to *The New American Poetry*, despite Ossman's using it as an organizing category (for Jackson Mac Low, Owens, and McClure) in the 2016 edition, and despite interviews turning repeatedly to the felt poetic differences of the moment, it is simply not a crucial part of the *Sullen Art* discourse. As Allen had decided not to do in his anthology, Ossman begins with an elder statesman, Kenneth Rexroth, spokesperson and apologist for much of the new work. The first of many in the book to complicate boundaries at the very moment they were in the process of forming, Rexroth says, only partly tongue-in-cheek, "I've never understood why I'm a member of the avant-garde. I write more or less like Allen Tate thinks he writes—like the great Greeks and Romans and the Chinese" (*Sullen Art* [2016] 25)—though the results are clearly different. Otherwise, we find repeated and fascinatingly failed attempts by its supposed practitioners to define Deep Image, an emergent poetics "making no appearance . . . in *The New American Poetry*" (13) because it had not emerged as a coherent tendency by the time of Allen's editing. Beyond first interviews, we also encounter first—or at least very early—discussions of topics that became central to experimental poetics. One great contribution of the expanded edition is Jackson Mac Low's discussion of chance and indeterminacy, surely one of the first commentaries on that topic in a poetics context. Ossman asks of *The New American Poetry* "where was Jackson Mac Low and the way-way-out voices of other artist-composer-performer-Happenings-makers? John Cage was behind a lot of it" (13). If it had appeared even just one year later, *The New American Poetry* might have been a very different book. Only a few years later still, Ossman himself had moved on, and he describes the Firesign Theatre as a way "to communicate with avant-garde poetry fans" outside of "the narrowly self-centered culture that had become the world of poetics for the later Sixties" (15). But through the interviews that preceded his disillusionment, the expanded *Sullen Art* both richly supplements the archive and legacy of the New American poetry and provides an opportunity to revisit, reanimate, and rethink it from multiple perspectives within its own contested moment.

# 3

## New, Newer, and Newest American Poetries

KOALA—To survive you have to be willing to do anything. Anthologies! That's where the money really is, or might be. At least so I imagine from my fuzzy animal distance. Reprint the material! Dominate the gene pool! Rise like Godzilla and make them read you for fucking ever!

—Bob Perelman, "*The Manchurian Candidate*: A Remake," in *The Future of Memory*

By the mid-1990s the avant-garde, we were told, was, at least in theory, dead, the impulses behind Allen's *The New American Poetry* no longer relevant. Meanwhile, the poetic "mainstream" was supposedly becoming so diverse and democratically inclusive as to be unlocatable, unrecognizable as a mainstream. This same historical moment, however, with its purported all-inclusiveness that would render the notion of an avant-garde meaningless, brought the publication of five self-consciously avant-garde anthologies of American poetry within a few years of each other: Eliot Weinberger's *American Poetry since 1950: Innovators and Outsiders* (1993); Douglas Messerli's *From the Other Side of the Century: A New American Poetry, 1960–1990*; Paul Hoover's *Postmodern American Poetry: A Norton Anthology*; Dennis Barone and Peter Ganick's *The Art of Practice: 45 Contemporary Poets* (all 1994); and Joseph Donahue, Edward Foster, and Leonard Schwartz's *Primary Trouble: An Anthology of Contemporary American Poetry* (1996).[1] This intensive anthologizing of experimental writing was one of the more notable social developments in US poetry at the end of the twentieth century. What especially interests me about this situation, and in these texts specifically, is the apparent reemergence of a version of the late 1950s and early 1960s anthology wars, as anthology editors once again unapologetically used terms like *avant-garde, center, mainstream*, and so on, and rebranded, historicized, and re-presented what Harold Rosenberg once called (in the title of a 1959 book, a year before Donald Allen's landmark *The New American Poetry*) "the tradition of the new."

What version(s) of the "new" circulated in these texts? Did the return of anthology wars rhetoric represent merely the flogging of a dead socio-aesthetic horse? Jed Rasula, for one, argues that it did. He finds Weinberger and J. D. McClatchy, editor of *The Vintage Book of Contemporary American Poetry* (1990), for instance, "waging a massively retrospective combat" centered on "nostalgic invocations of the 1960 anthology wars, with the editors cavorting about in period dress like history buffs reenacting the battle of Gettysburg" (*American Poetry Wax Museum* 449).[2] He argues that Weinberger, McClatchy, and Messerli anachronistically "perpetuate the sectarianism that was manifest" in *The New American Poetry*'s oppositionality and display "a nostalgia predicated on a 'recuperation' of New American poetic dissidents, but the logic is flawed because they've come too late to get in on the fruits of first acclaim" (461). Rasula has a point here; 1993 is a long way from 1960. But apparently Civil War reenactment dies hard, in poetry as in other areas of US culture. If this debate was so outdated, why did its rhetoric return to anthologies of innovative poetry in the mid-1990s? What function did that rhetoric serve in the later historical moment? Aside from maintaining a good deal of historically descriptive power, it was used by contemporary editors to further and articulate the development or construction of a *New American Poetry* tradition derived from Allen's influential 1960 anthology. The construction of that tradition of the new via further anthologies—especially the rhetoric or self-presentation of these texts, rather than their structure, contents, and so forth—is my subject in this chapter.[3] Weinberger and his fellow anthologists argue less about the state of the (mid-1990s) poetic present and future (though those issues are at stake too) and more about competing versions of literary history and poetic legacy: Weinberger says of *American Poetry since 1950* that "it was intended to be an historical anthology, and not particularly a representation of 'what's happening now.' . . . I thought I was merely offering a reading of certain poets from a certain line in a certain period" ("Conversation"). Hoover sees his anthology similarly as a historical corrective: on the *Norton Anthology of Modern Poetry*, he comments, "When the second edition came out in 1988, I was surprised to see some of my favorite poets . . . being dropped from the canon, thereby from literary history. I decided that something needed to be done to correct the situation" ("Interview").[4] From this point of view, the apparently retrospective quality of these editors' arguments can be seen not as anachronistic sentimentality but rather precisely to the point.[5]

Rasula is right to note the limitations of the center-margin model that shapes both my chosen anthologies, in their different ways, and to some extent my analysis of them. One obvious limitation is the risk of a too-easy and falsely stable binarism. Weinberger and Hoover, for instance, both tend to assume that mainstream poetic practice and ideology is monolithic and that "we" know it when we see it. As Hank Lazer observes, however, this reduction of poetic variety to an allegedly monolithic mainstream is itself a "rhetorical straw man of the (similarly multiple) avant-garde" (*Opposing Poetries* 1:136). Nevertheless, if we think of "center," "mainstream," and "margin" as cultural and even psychological locations that are in process rather than fixed, these misleadingly topographical metaphors can retain some analytic usefulness. If I seem both to suggest the inadequacy of a center-margin model and also depend on it for understanding patterns in a particular set of anthologies, my point is that this model had grown more complex in the late twentieth century rather than collapsing completely. Further, in defense of these texts, a cluster of alternative anthologies, demanding more attention than isolated collections, could more effectively counter an otherwise pervasive anthological inattention to innovative work. With reference to the Hoover, Weinberger, and Messerli anthologies, Steve Evans suggests that "the near-simultaneity of their appearance and the many points of overlap between them raises the possibility of interpreting them as a single text comprised of partially reinforcing, partially interfering patterns" ("Anthslide"). Meanwhile, the discrepancy between the level of scholarly attention to Language writing and most anthologists' bypassing of it in the mid-1990s meant that commentary on that writing was often more widely available than the writing itself—hardly a set of conditions in which the tensions driving avant-garde oppositionality have been happily dissolved.[6] But with experimental poetries suddenly anthologized in such bulk, not only such inattention but also aesthetic tokenism—the mainstream inclusion of some aesthetically challenging work as a marker for that which can be ignored literally as long as it is represented symbolically—also became much harder to defend.

Among the editors of these anthologies, Weinberger and Hoover especially applied a center-margin model in their representations of post–World War II American poetry, in a way that openly derived from Allen's *New American Poetry*. Weinberger begins his preface: "For decades American poetry has been divided into two camps." He rightly describes the relationship between these "ruling and opposition parties" as "full of defections, unaligned members, splinter parties, internecine disputes and ideas stolen across the aisle" (*American Poetry* xi). Nonetheless, his governing metaphor explicitly invites a replay of the old anthology wars. Thus,

Weinberger's concluding historical essay on the post–World War II period consistently pits the avant-garde against the Establishment, uppercase E and all, "bands of rebels" against "middle-brow" producers of "Official Verse Culture" (397). Again echoing Allen, he also pits the avant-garde against the academy, although this move later becomes problematic when he wants to make "avant-garde" and "academic" synonymous for the purpose of critiquing Language poetry (406).[7]

A similar rhetoric of avant-gardism pervades Paul Hoover's introduction to his *Postmodern American Poetry,* a rhetoric that itself can be seen as one defining feature of the particular anthological tradition deriving from *The New American Poetry.* His intention to extend or respond to *The New American Poetry* emerged explicitly in a 1995 interview: "My idea was to create a definite but also wide-ranging and inclusive collection beginning with Charles Olson in 1950. . . . Olson was also the starting point for Donald Allen's *New American Poetry: 1945–1960.* This had been the standard, but now it has become outdated" ("Interview"). Hoover explicitly makes the "postmodern" of his title synonymous with "avant-garde": "Postmodernist poetry is the avant-garde poetry of our time" (*Postmodern American Poetry* [1994] xxv)—a debatable equation, perhaps, but I am less concerned here with the equation's accuracy, and more with the fact that Hoover made it.[8] He frames his introduction with assertions of the continued relevance and vitality, aesthetic and political, of avant-garde practice: "This anthology shows that avant-garde poetry endures in its resistance to mainstream ideology" (xxv), he notes early on, and ends by dismissing those critics who argue "unpersuasively that 'innovation no longer seems possible, or even desirable'" (xxxix). In fact, Hoover operates on a thoroughly progressive model of avant-garde writing, a model that seems driven by a certain anxiety: "The poetry now being produced is as strong as, and arguably stronger than, that produced by earlier vanguards" (xxxix).

As a widely circulated and academically adopted Norton publication aspiring to avant-garde status, *Postmodern American Poetry* complicated any debate over center and margin even as it occupied a particular position within that debate. But Hoover barely touches on the institutionalization of the avant-garde that his anthology could be seen to represent (though he does address the issue in the 2013 2nd edition). Nor, although he mentions it, does he respond to Frederic Jameson's implication that the "postmodern" is synonymous with "mainstream," or at least can be seen as a symptom, rather than a critique, of mainstream ideology—the opposite position from Hoover's own. For Hoover, as I've said, postmodernism was "an ongoing process of resistance to mainstream ideology," employing "a wide variety of oppositional strategies" (*Postmodern* [1994] xxvi, xxvii).[9] Thus, he organized his introduction around familiar contrasts: on the one hand, using terms such as "postmodern," "avant-garde," "oppositional," "transgressive," "resistance," "revolt," and on the other, "centrist," "mainstream," "bourgeois self," terms that mirror Weinberger's sense of "camps," his "opposition," "outsiders," and "ruling party." Not surprisingly, given this terminology, the minihistory of post–World War II American poetry that Hoover provides has a familiar founding moment: "In analyzing American poetry after 1945, it is traditional to point to the so-called battle of the anthologies" (xxviii), Hoover argues, and even goes on to contrast the "model poet" of each side in that battle.[10]

Continuing this familiar set of oppositions, Donahue, Foster, and Schwartz's *Primary Trouble* gathers, in the words of Leonard Schwartz's introduction, "writers associated with the 'avant-garde' or 'anti-academic' segment or 'experimental wing' of American poetry"—though Schwartz admits these as "labels that most in the end will find inconclusive" (1). The text "seeks to elevate a certain poetics into view against the mainstream poetics that might obscure it" (3). In the words of the book's jacket, and in an echo of Donald Allen's well-known preface, we have here "poetry outside academic and conservative traditions," including work from "younger generations of poets influenced but unnostalgic about the work represented in Donald Allen's seminal anthology *The New American Poetry*" (1). (The editors also follow Allen in concluding with a section of statements on poetics.)

The relationship to New American traditions in *Primary Trouble* turns out, not surprisingly, to be a complex and ambivalent one, however. More specifically, for Schwartz as for some other editors, Language writing—itself a movement with a multifaceted and contestatory relationship to New American sources—becomes the site where an editor seeks to work through these complexities, to test the connection between *The New American Poetry* and contemporary claims to avant-garde status. Schwartz suggests three main, and often overlapping, areas of practice on which *Primary Trouble* draws. The first includes those poets just mentioned, working in a processual poetics traceable to *The New American Poetry* and earlier. A second group includes next-generation poets associated with or influenced by the New York school. And a third includes "poets who share some of the formal concerns of, and even may be affiliated in part with, the L=A=N=G=U=A=G=E project" (2). As we shall see later with Ganick and Barone's *The Art of Practice, Primary Trouble* manifests an ambivalent desire (at least as expressed in the editorial introduction) simultaneously to affiliate with and dissociate from Language writing, especially in representing younger avant-garde writers. Schwartz acknowledges that some of the *Primary Trouble* poets share certain interests with Language writing, "without on the other hand sharing in that school's agenda for poetic hegemony" (2). Repeating this accusation elsewhere, Schwartz refers to "the hegemonic mode of experimental formalism known as language poetry" (3), stressing also the alleged absence of erotic "pleasure" in that work. As with Weinberger, then, we again find the editor of an avant-garde anthology accusing one avant-garde group of a desire for "poetic hegemony." (Meanwhile, within the text, Robert Kelly gently echoes Schwartz's skepticism in his exposition of a meditative, self-questioning poetics "similar to, and . . . perhaps more efficacious than, the project of de-referencing language" ["Spirit" 451] theorized in his view by Steve McCaffery and Bruce Andrews.) Thus the old argument that the margin merely wants to become the center gets played out within the alleged margin's own circles, as part of the late twentieth-century avant-garde's attempt at anthological self-definition.

What sense of the "margin" and of New American anthological tradition operates in Douglas Messerli's *From the Other Side of the Century*? His volume had been brewing, Messerli notes, since 1984, and in this sense it is the project that his 1987 *"Language" Poetries* interrupted and wanted to be. As his anthology's Other, Messerli puts forward "the academized bastion of the *Norton Anthology of Modern Poetry*" (31)—interestingly, at a point in time when Norton was publishing one of the two texts, Hoover's, that competed with Messerli for a similar textbook market.[11] He, too, begins his editorial introduction, then, by implicitly invoking the anthology wars between Allen and Hall, Pack, and Simpson's "academized" *New Poets of England and America*. Though Messerli generally leaves unanswered his own question as to "the role of anthologies in general," he does claim that "no major volume has served our own generation" (31) as *The New American Poetry* served Allen's, and implicitly presents his own text to perform that service.

Messerli was not alone among this group of editors in perhaps trying too hard to replicate the impact of *The New American Poetry* under different historical circumstances that make it impossible to do so. Marjorie Perloff argues that these mid-1990s post-Allen anthologies of innovative poetics are characterized by two recurrent features: belatedness and buttressing. They suffer from a kind of anxiety of lateness in relation to *The New American Poetry*, that is; and they serve to buttress an already established tradition rather than exploring new avenues.[12] This view helps put any claims to newness in perspective. At the same time, however, it provides only a partial description of these anthologies' projects. For

Weinberger, Hoover, and Messerli, unlike Allen, were engaged not just in presenting new work but in historicizing its precedents. Thus, buttressing involved far more than the mere repetition that Perloff seems to imply; it involved maintenance and preservation, yes, but also rearticulation, addition, and critique. Taken as a group, and allowing for differences in editorial emphasis, these collections go beyond a buttressing of *The New American Poetry* in numerous ways: in their revival and representation of the Objectivists (in Weinberger and Messerli); in their use of generically hybrid texts; in their use of visual texts; and in their representation of an experimental women's writing, especially in Dennis Barone and Peter Ganick's intergenerational *The Art of Practice*, the only one of the group that is fully gender-equitable.[13]

*The Art of Practice* both furthers and complicates the construction of a New American anthological tradition, as it simultaneously extends New American poetic practice and critiques its predecessor anthologies. This is one sense in which it can be seen as an anthology of "post-Language" poetries.[14] While *Practice*'s forty-five poets is close in number to Allen's forty-four, the earlier text does not seem to be a model. Rather, in the editors' words, "the impetus for this anthology was two [other] previous ones," Ron Silliman's *In the American Tree* and Messerli's *Language Poetries* (Barone and Ganick xiv). There are deliberately no overlaps with either of these collections. At the same time, Barone and Ganick share with Allen, Silliman, Hoover, and Messerli a sense of resistance to the institutionalized poetics of their own historical moment: they construct an anthology "opposed to the so-called natural free verse poem," on the assumption that "poetry is not the place for expression of common or authentic voice" (xiv, xiii). (The fact that *The New American Poetry* helped promulgate a poetics that, in the form of the much-maligned workshop or scenic lyric, became a later version of the "academic"—that the collection generated both its own tradition and that tradition's antithesis—is the subject for another essay.)[15]

While Barone and Ganick describe their organization as "somewhat democratic (not chaotic or autocratic)" (xv), it is hard to tell exactly what these terms mean in context. Beyond local appropriate juxtapositions, such as placing the work of *Big Allis* coeditors Jessica Grim and Melanie Neilson side by side, the principle of organization remains largely submerged.[16] A "democratic" organization does show up, however, in the refusal to elevate any one poet or group of poets to accrediting or originary status. Indeed, *Practice* begins and ends with antiauthoritarian tropes. In an implied critique of the Allen-Weinberger-Hoover privileging of the notoriously phallocentric Olson and of US writing, this anthology of North American writing begins with a Canadian woman poet and editor, Susan Clark, and ends with a then barely published younger Canadian poet and editor, Louis Cabri. The editors appear as the second and penultimate selections: close to (but, importantly, not actually) framing the collection but still not pretending disingenuously to merge or hide.

In one sense, however, Silliman becomes an accrediting figure in the text, by having the last word (an afterword) and historicizing the collection. Reversing the anthology's title in his afterword, "The Practice of Art," Silliman places *Practice* in the New American Poetry tradition without precisely connecting it to Allen's anthology. He describes the collection as "a survey of the broader horizon of the progressive tradition in North American poetry," and on this basis differentiates it from his own and Messerli's first anthology, which did not "set out to represent the big picture of what we might think of as Post-New American Poetry" (372, 371). Silliman stresses that "it's essential to recognize what this book is not: *In the American Tree: The Out-takes* or *Language Poetries: The Next Generation*" (371).[17] If "margin and center have shifted over the past decade," that shift has occurred partly within the margin itself, in the form of "a critique by example of a narrowly configured (and macho) language poetry" (372). Thus a "critical response to language poetry becomes an unspoken unifying principle of *Practice*" (375). This critique is precisely what the notion of buttressing cannot accommodate. At the same time, in this consciously historicizing and canonizing afterword (one-half of a framing context that also consists of the editors' more aesthetically oriented introduction), Silliman devotes much of his argument to constructing a New American lineage. He argues that "*Practice*'s passionate relationship to the New American Poetry of the 1950s and '60s may be more visible than that of the *Tree* only because of the lower level of militancy in editorial focus"—more visible, note, but not more genuine. Then he turns to a specific example from *Practice* to reinforce this construction of a lineage: "[Norman] Fischer's work . . . offers the quintessential evidence for the argument that language poetry (so-called) embodies a direct extension of the New Americans, albeit an extension that transforms and problematizes its own understanding of what came before" (374).

Repeating his gesture from *In the American Tree,* where his list of exclusions is longer than his list of inclusions, Silliman goes on to name ninety-three writers who could have been included in *The Art of Practice.* He concludes, collating inclusions and exclusions across both texts, "that more than 160 North American poets are actively and usefully involved in the avant-garde tradition of writing is in itself a stunning thought" (377). Stunning indeed, though not in an entirely benign sense. This statistic has various possible implications. From one point of view, such numbers make the avant-garde robustly unassimilable simply because of its size. From another, they intensify, even necessitate, the tendency to reify the avant-garde in the work of a selected handful of writers. By the time of these anthologies there was already a substantial history to the critical trope that invoked "so-called" Language writing and then "explained" the label by trotting out a list of paradigmatic names, at least one of which was always utterly inappropriate: "The so-called Language poets, such as. . . ." From yet another perspective, the idea of an avant-garde becomes meaningless once it refers to at least 160 writers in a single historical moment (and remember, Silliman collates actual and potential inclusions only for two texts). That avant-garde is close to the size of its mainstream Other.

If we are to see these anthologies of innovative writing, and this 1990s literary moment, as engaged in the ongoing construction of a New American poetry tradition, what kind of consensus on that tradition do they achieve? Despite the different purposes, criteria, and to some extent periods covered by Hoover, Weinberger, and Messerli (to turn to the more historically inclusive collections), 16 poets appear in all 3 texts. Of 287 selections from these 16 writers, however, not a single *selection* appears in all 3 anthologies. Further, out of that 287, only 9 poems overlap between even 2 of the anthologies. The closest these texts come to consensus is that they each reprint sections (though different ones) from Clark Coolidge's *At Egypt*. Also, regarding the writers they agree on, there is only one writer of color, Amiri Baraka, and one woman, Susan Howe. Is this fruitful difference? Is it tradition as heterology? Is it sensible marketing strategy, with each anthology seeking to differentiate itself as it covers somewhat similar ground? Or is it incoherence? Given such differences, what might the notion of a New American tradition mean, and to what extent does it perpetuate the exclusions of Allen's original anthology?

These questions relate to others: to what extent (if at all) do such terms as "margin," "avant-garde," "mainstream" remain critically viable, especially when they resist precise definition? How will we continue to negotiate aesthetic and sociocultural definitions of the "marginal" that are frequently at odds with each other? For readers in the third decade of the millennium, such questions register very differently against the backdrop both of contemporary social realities and ongoing debates about race and the avant-garde.[18] Problematic as these terms remain, however, for late twentieth-century anthology editors they played a significant role in constructing genealogies for particular areas of American poetry and in continuing to think through the ongoing reception of the "new" (both the once-new and the recently new). Lyn Hejinian acknowledges how these anthologies complicate relations between "mainstream" and "margin":

> My career's ended up so much better than anything I would have dreamed could possibly happen, that I could never complain about being excluded. So much good has happened. I don't have any justification for being pissed off. As we're looking at the end of this century and these huge anthologies that are coming out, this correspondence [among poets] with complaints about being marginalized is going to look pretty ludicrous. The language poets, for example, are being taught all over the place. It's not maybe the mainstreaming of the work, but it's not by any stretch marginal. ("Eternal Repository" 21)

From one point of view, "these huge anthologies" do indeed render complaints about marginality a little silly. They may mark the point at which the mainstream-margin distinction finally breaks down, given—whatever the editors' individual intentions—the institutionalization of the avant-garde that they represent. But they may also represent less a mainstreaming, as Hejinian said, than one resting point in an ongoing upstream swim against the dominant currents.

In what appears to be Norton's sequel to the Hoover anthology, *American Hybrid: A Norton Anthology of New Poetry* (2009), coeditor Cole Swensen actually begins her introduction in the historical and conceptual territory of this chapter, setting the moment of the New American poetry and of Robert Lowell's raw versus cooked distinction next to Weinberger's statement, quoted above, about American poetry's "two camps." "Were the poetic landscapes of 1960 and 1993 as similar as these two statements might imply? And where are we in relation to them today, at the end of the first decade of the new millennium?" (xvii), Swensen asks. She answers that "this anthology springs from the conviction that the model of binary oppositions is no longer the most accurate one"—*American Hybrid* takes us beyond "the two-camp model" (xvii), just as, along similar lines, Claudia Rankine and Juliana Spahr's *American Women Poets in the 21st Century* (2002) "begins a dialogue between the two often falsely separated poetries of language and lyric" (Spahr 11).[19] Swensen's coeditor David St. John frames the hybridizing breakdown of poetic oppositions even more energetically, arguing that "the notion of the 'poetic school' is an anachronism, an archaic critical artifact of times long gone by" and "the poetic activities of the poets here in *American Hybrid* have helped to erase the boundaries of poetic schools and leveled out many assumed hierarchies" (xxviii).

Swensen claims that one main difference between the mid-1990s and 1960 "was that binary opposition was beginning to break down, notwithstanding three major anthologies designed around it" (xx)—presumably the collections that I've been discussing by Hoover, Weinberger, and Messerli. While "the tension between experiment and convention had begun to break down" (Swensen xxii), the 1999 reprinting of *The New American Poetry* and the public events and scholarly work focused on the collection's 2010 fiftieth anniversary suggest an ongoing lively interest in the work and texts it put before us.[20] *American Hybrid* represented a significant transition, but hardly a tidy one: four years after it came out, its publisher brought out the revised second edition of the anthology, Hoover's *Postmodern American Poetry*, that *American Hybrid* aspired to supersede, and in his preface Hoover explicitly sets his own collection against the premises of *American Hybrid*. "The two-camp model" is indeed no longer viable, but its passing has been more a process of erosion, dispersion, and multiplication than a clean break, and examining the post–New American anthological tradition provides one way to understand the history and dynamics of that process.

# 4

# Poetry Anthologies and the Idea of the "Mainstream"

"There's nothing that can be called a mainstream movement in our poetry—or an avant garde"; "there is no need for any anthology to choose sides" (Field xli; McClatchy, "Introduction" xxi). These two statements from editors of American poetry anthologies, the first by Edward Field in 1979, the second by J. D. McClatchy in 1990 (and repeated in his 2003 second edition), summarize one widely shared "poetic positioning," to use Christopher Beach's term, of their period. But for all the alleged inclusiveness that would destabilize ideas of "mainstream" and "margin"—the watchwords for anthology editors in the new millennium are terms like "hybrid" and "synthesis"—a mainstream in late twentieth-century American poetry can indeed be located and described.[1] This mainstream reveals itself especially at those points where its existence is most energetically denied or its inclusiveness most energetically touted, and those points include anthologies. Critics such as Beach and Jed Rasula have offered cogent analyses of the mainstream's characteristics and operations by attending to synecdochic texts: for Beach, Dave Smith and David Bottoms's *The Morrow Anthology of Younger American Poets*, and for Rasula, *The Morrow Anthology* and McClatchy's *Vintage Book of Contemporary American Poetry*.[2] In this chapter, however, I want to move beyond the synecdochic or symptomatic and examine patterns of editorial rhetoric and self-representation across the range of anthologies from which Beach and Rasula chose their particular examples: the survey-style collections of recent (or in a few cases, of post–World War II) American poetry, designed for the college creative writing and literature classroom, that appeared mostly from trade and university presses in the 1970s, 1980s, and into the 1990s.

Although boundaries between "center" or "mainstream" and "margin" had become more porous during this period than in the times, say, of the early 1960s anthology wars, we can still derive from these collections a reliable picture of a dominant aesthetic ideology, especially at those points where ideology and its conflicts are denied. Reading in these anthologies, that is, makes it possible to construct a picture of the period's aesthetic center based on a broad range of examples. In turn, understanding more precisely this dominant poetic formation helps us also to understand more precisely the impetus behind emergent alternative ones, especially Language writing and various post-Language formations. While I do not examine here the relationship between general editorial claims and the contents of individual texts—an important factor in assessing any anthology fairly—analyzing the rhetoric of such anthologies still provides a concrete example of the circulation of poetic value within the period and an instructive case study in cultural politics.[3] It involves reading anthologies as cultural artifacts, products of a particular cultural formation—and a hardy one too, given that many of the collections that I discuss, including one published as early as 1969, remain in print.[4] Obscured by editorial assertions of its benignly amorphous inclusiveness, nevertheless some kind of mainstream in late twentieth-century American poetry recognizably flowed on. We're familiar with the oft-repeated formal characteristics of the mainstream lyric poem that dominated the period; we tend to think less about the mechanics and effects of its social circulation and maintenance.

These mainstream surveys typically project a bogus tolerance, a denial that "sides" have to be taken when in fact they always already have been. As Eliot Weinberger points out in the introduction to his openly avant-gardist anthology *American Poetry since 1950,* what he calls (from the poetic "outsider's" point of view) ruling-party rhetoric "insists there is no ruling party, and thus no opposition" (xi). Whether or not one agrees that Weinberger's view rests on a "disabling nostalgia" for a time of clearly locatable poetic dissidence (Rasula, *American Poetry Wax Museum* 461)—an issue that I address in chapter 3—the denial to which Weinberger points does evade the social and the institutional factors that shape editorial decisions and ultimately canons. It pervades, for instance, McClatchy's introduction to his *Vintage Book of Contemporary American Poetry,* the beginning of which I cite in my opening sentence: "There is no need for any anthology to choose sides." In a contradictory move, McClatchy lists historical examples of "sniper fire from the poets themselves" but then dismisses such conflicts as "merely sibling rivalries and territorial imperatives." He claims to separate the purity of poets from the tainted interests of readers and critics: "Though angry ideologies have been built of such flimsy stuff, it's usually done not by poets but by their dull readers" ("Introduction" xxi).

Given the role of twentieth-century poets and poet-critics in debates that have been simultaneously, and inseparably, both literary and ideological, this stance is both disingenuous and not even close to historically accurate. Belatedly perpetuating the separation of the aesthetic or private and the social in terms derived from Harold Bloom, McClatchy argues that only weak poets are concerned with superficial issues of social conflict; strong poets work privately, "alone with their art," their apparent differences mystically reconciled by subterranean, nonideological "streams of sympathy and influence" that unite them under the surface "landscape of trends and schools and movements" ("Introduction" xxx, xxii).[5] Not surprisingly, the assertion that a deeper inclusiveness has really existed all along works to deflect more ideologically charged writing. That is, claims to a false pluralism help suppress or deflect emergent poetries that are part of a real pluralism (socially, if not always aesthetically): "Of the claims made that new literary movements—black, feminist, gay—have emerged, it would be better to say that new audiences have developed; weaker poets play to them, stronger poets . . . attend to their art and work to complicate the issues" ("Introduction" xxviii).[6]

Like McClatchy, William Heyen in *The Generation of 2000* (1984) is baffled by the idea of an "enemy" in poetry but immediately dismisses "quasi-surrealist[s]," "dadaists," "faddists," "stand-up comics," and "aestheticians tripletalking ethereal voices"—quite a long list of "enemies" (xx–xxi). Daniel Halpern is equally eager to argue that the camps and groups of 1950–65 no longer apply but less than eager to include much of the poetry that stems from them, either of the formally traditional or more innovative variety—this in the context of an allegedly heterogeneous collection offered as *The* (not *An*) *American Poetry Anthology* (1975) (xxxi–xxxii). In Ronald Wallace's *Vital Signs: Contemporary American Poetry from the University Presses* (1989), too, we find the common conjunction of three points: explicit commitment to a mainstream aesthetics, claims to "richness and diversity" in representation, and the denial of "warring 'schools'" (xix). Like McClatchy, Wallace collapses difference in the image of a "great ongoing dialogue" among poets, just as Heyen links his denial of opposition to his aim "to reach that level where 'the most divergent intelligences' . . . may come together" (Wallace xix; Heyen xx).

This rejection of the highly charged term "schools" recurs throughout mainstream anthologies as a constitutive part of their self-definition. Contrary to what Stuart Friebert and David Young argue in their *Longman Anthology of Contemporary American Poetry* (1983), however, "tolerance of one another's ways" and "dislike of schools and dogmas" (xxix) is not an intrinsic generational trait of poets who started publishing between 1950 and 1980 but rather a trait constructed through the editors' representations of that "generation." In effect, an anthology compiled on this basis reinforces an aesthetic ideology that privileges the figure of the individual artist—an issue to which I return later. For one could equally construct a picture of the period precisely in terms of schools, movements, and dogmas—or "networks," "affiliations," "coteries," "principles." Further, the poetic mainstream, despite its wariness of schools, can itself easily be seen as one. Admittedly the creative writing workshop that produced so many of the poets in late twentieth-century mainstream anthologies did not, on the surface, look like a "school." Affiliation with a workshop did not tie the poet to a particular time and place (Black Mountain College in the early mid-1950s, New York or San Francisco at the same time or in the 1970s and early 1980s); it did not suggest an overt coherence of poetic concerns; it did not issue in manifestos or distinctive little magazines. The workshop was not easily identified as a "movement," then—until it issued an anthology. But when it did, uniformity of background and of shared but unstated assumptions worked against the eclecticism and "school-less-ness" that the editors often asserted. Describing a period in which creative writing programs were far less aesthetically diverse than they are now, John Koethe argues that such "programs are not usually 'schools'" in the sense of proposing an explicit and exclusionary poetics. However, he continues, "in the absence of explicitly articulated theoretical principles regarding the nature and purpose of poetry, [these programs] inculcate, by default, a poetics of the 'individual voice' that valorizes authenticity and fidelity to its origins in prepoetic experience or emotion" (70).[7]

The close relationship between creative writing programs and university press publishing further shows how mainstream anthologies can end up representing a de facto "school," or at least a more specific point on the literary political spectrum than they claim. One subset of the mainstream survey, the collection of university press poetry, uses just this institutional conjunction allegedly to "cover" American poetry. As Michael Collier puts it in *The Wesleyan Tradition* (1993), "a program such as Wesleyan's arrived to meet the future publishing needs of university creative writing programs" (xxvi). Both Collier and Ronald Wallace, in *Vital Signs*, see creative writing programs as promoting the decentralization of literary power. The growth of these programs could equally be seen, however, as a relocation of power in an institution (rather than in a place, a handful of critics and reviewers, a magazine). How does this relocation work? Wallace praises the poems in his collection for having survived evaluation by numerous different readers: "The poems included here have been judged excellent by magazine editors, press editors, and reviewers, as well as myself, over a period of time" (xvii). More accurately, however, these poems have been praised at different stages by similar kinds of readers, those within a university poetry publishing network that in the 1970s and 1980s was considerably less diverse in all ways than it is today.[8]

In principle, this structure of mutual reinforcement was not unique, and operated no differently from most kinds of self-authenticating literary network. In practice, however, it was different because it pretended to be neutral, not partisan. Without thinking of this network as monolithic, one can assume some consistency of taste and principle throughout it, especially given Wallace's own acknowledgment of university presses' historical commitment to mainstream poetry and to the dissemination of a period style.[9] Again, as we approach the present, a number of university presses have become increasingly open in their poetry publishing, while operating under severe economic constraints. But in the period under discussion here, as Wallace says, "the trade and university presses tend to preserve the conservative mainstream. There is little radical experimentation, little extreme political poetry, little ethnic dialect, little of the avant-garde, little of the flamboyance associated with the great modernists." Later he adds, "most poets publishing with university and trade presses today reject modes of disruption, discontinuity, inconsistency, erasure, and incoherence" (20, 32).

Like Wallace, Collier relates university press publishing to "the democratization of poetry that was taking place through the creative writing programs in American universities and colleges" (xxii). At the same time, and again like Wallace, Collier admits that historically Wesleyan has stayed "solidly within the mainstream and normative in contemporary American poetry," even while remaining "alive to the widespread possibilities of the newest work being written" (xxv, xxiv)—an aliveness that has been more genuinely evident at Wesleyan over the last twenty years in the expansion of its poetry publications to a formally wide-ranging, cross-generational list of close to two hundred international titles. Jack Myers and Roger Weingarten similarly attribute "pluralism and decentralization of aesthetic-political power" in significant part to creative writing programs (*New American Poets '90s* xv). By constructing a democratized mainstream, its spokespersons could simultaneously claim for it both normative status and "aliveness to the widespread possibilities of the new."

Despite the impossibility of an inclusive or representative anthology for the post–World War II period, many late twentieth-century editors still claim to produce just that. Most such claims occur, however, in mainstream survey anthologies that nearly always exclude aesthetic extremes (from Language writing to New Formalism). While mainstream poetics indeed started to grow more pluralist in the 1980s and 1990s, it is important to realize the limits of that pluralism in the face of editors purporting to offer "eclecticism regarding styles, concerns, and forms" and "a representative array of some of the best and most exciting poetry being written today by young to mid-career poets"; "an enormous range of styles and perspectives"; "an eclectic book," "a gathering . . . of various aesthetics"; "diversity and richness," "heterogeneity . . . of form, attitude, and treatment of content" (Myers and Weingarten *New American Poets 80's* xiv; Myers and Weingarten, *New American Poets of the '90s* xv; Pack, Lea, and Parini v; Heyen xx; Halpern xxix, xxxi). "This book is pluralistic," insists McClatchy ("Introduction" xxvii). Mark Strand asserts that "it is part of the character of American poetry since 1940 to have made friends with everyone. Many different sorts of poetry seem to have existed more or less peacefully" (xiii). Given that Strand was writing in 1969, at a time of intense social conflict over the Vietnam War, one can understand his wishful thinking about peaceful coexistence at home and abroad. But at home especially, that peaceful coexistence is hardly all-embracing; at the end of two intensely active civil rights decades, Strand's ninety-two poets since 1940 include precisely two African Americans. In a rhetoric that uses military metaphor to suppress literary ideological conflict, Strand dismisses the 1950s and 1960s anthology wars as "a brief skirmish" (xiii) rather than as a charged symbolic moment.[10] I do not mean to argue the impossibility of inclusiveness and then indict these editors for not being inclusive. My point is to comment on their baseless claims to breadth and representativeness. Despite Wallace's and Collier's admissions in their collections that university presses tend to stick with "the mainstream and normative," editors will still argue that the products of a single university press distilled into an anthology can provide, in Wesleyan's case, "a definitive record of American poetry written since the late fifties" or, in Pittsburgh's case, "as valid a cross-section of contemporary American poetry as we know" (Collier xxii; Ochester and Oresick xv).

Another feature by which we can recognize the mainstream survey as such is that it foregrounds a contrast between, on the one hand, "poets," and, on the other, "poems" or "poetry." Some sample statements: "Any anthology is finally a gathering of poems rather than of poets"; "it is hoped . . . that more concern will be given the poems than the poets"; "the preface to this book directs the reader's attention to contemporary *poems* and suggests that it is less than useful to consider them chiefly in the light of school or coterie"; "the generation [of 2000] is in the poems themselves, of course, or it is nowhere"; "*Poetry* [magazine] publishes not poets but poems; this surely is what a magazine, or anthology, of verse exists to do"

(McClatchy xxviii; Strand xiv; Leary, "Postscript I" 559; Heyen xix; Hine xlvii).

This proposed emphasis on the poem would seem on the surface to imply a proportionately reduced focus on individual careers. Despite such protestations, however, the editors of mainstream anthologies more often construct texts that privilege the category and identity of the "poet." These editors contradict the pretense of stressing poems over poets by their overwhelming focus on a poetry of the self and by an idealizing of the individual (sometimes reinforced by photo portraits) that connects directly to the widespread mistrust of "movements" and the imagined loss of self that they bring. (This mistrust drives Heyen's remark, in attempting to define the generation of 2000, that "I've needed to feel part of something, not necessarily a 'movement' or 'group' or 'school' with cloned characteristics, but of a community" [xix].) Thus Strand finds a recurrent concern of American poetry since 1940 in "the self, a self defined usually by circumstances that would tend to set it apart," and he notes "the energetic pursuit of an individual manner that would reflect a sense of self-definition" (xiii). McClatchy sees "the hazards of the self as the primary focus" for his poets' work. "All of them have put the private life on public view," he continues, in "the lyric [that] has continued to dominate our poetry" ("Introduction" xxvi, xxviii). Self, individual, the poet: these are the recurring concepts that betray what Jed Rasula calls the mainstream "anxiety of contact, a neurosis that fears collaboration as much as confrontation" (*American Poetry Wax Museum* 466).

In this way anthologies buttress the cult of the individual voice that came to define the center of American poetry in the mid-1970s. In the revealingly titled *Singular Voices* (1985), Stephen Berg gathers "a wealth of original voices. . . . Each poet in this book writes his or her own kind of poem" (ix). Poets in Robert Pack, Sydney Lea, and Jay Parini's *Bread Loaf Anthology of Contemporary American Poetry* (1985) must each have "a well-developed voice" (vi). As I've already observed, Friebert and Young's "primary emphasis is on the poets as individual artists," poets whose "dislike of schools and dogmas [is] concomitantly high" (xxix). Smith and Bottoms's *Morrow Anthology of Younger American Poets* illustrates vividly the felt tension between the claims of representativeness and individuality that shapes the rhetoric of many mainstream survey editors. In the space of a little over one page, Smith and Bottoms assert the "vigorous, rich, and diverse" nature of recent American poetry; paint a generic, composite portrait of the young American poet-professor who produces such diversity; and propose that "the assertion of an individuality" lies at the heart of this composite poet's work (17–18).[11]

Also governing the mainstream survey is an ideology of the unmediated or self-evident that again suppresses the evaluative criteria involved in selection and removes the poetry from the circumstances or site of its production, collection, and consumption: "The work of the poets speaks best for itself" (Myers and Weingarten, *New American Poets 80's* xiv). Such statements echo throughout the introductions to these texts: "The poetry . . . speaks for itself" or "defines its own excellence" (Halpern xxxiii; Ochester and Oresick xvi).[12] Speaking for itself, the poetry apparently just talks its own way into the mainstream anthology. That to anthologize a poem is already in some sense to speak for it rather than have it speak for itself; that even at the time of these texts' publication, "excellence" was widely being discussed as historical, institutional, and contingent rather than self-defining: these are issues that the mainstream editors tend to finesse. Sometimes they seem to do so out of a resistance to "theory" that puts "art" and "theory" at odds: "Editing is an art, and we don't intend to theorize our position" (Ochester and Oresick xvi). This rhetoric extends to anthologies that once looked far more adventurous than they do now, such as Stephen Berg and Robert Mezey's *Naked Poetry* and *The New Naked Poetry*. In *Naked Poetry* (1969) Berg and Mezey assert that the poems "certainly don't need interpreters" and immediately follow this exercise of the self-evidence principle by recording their resistance to theorizing the work in their anthology: "We soon grew bored with our original plan to discuss the theory and practice" of what they call "Open Forms" (xi). In their 1976 revision, *The New Naked Poetry*, this resistance emerges even more strongly, as they invoke the overdetermined opposition between theorist and poet: "In any case, we are not theoreticians. We write the stuff" (xix). This opposition anticipates that inscribed in Smith and Bottoms's figure of the composite individualist poet, "rarely a card-carrying group member, political or aesthetic," who "seems to jog more than to write literary criticism" (19).

The disavowal of conflict and the denial of sides that have already been taken; the related distaste for "schools"; dependence on the creative writing program as a primary site of poetry's production and consumption; untenable claims to eclecticism; the university presses' reinforcement of the "normative"; the alleged privileging of "poems" that conflicts with the actual privileging of "poets" and the reifying of "voice"; an ideology of the unmediated or self-evident: all these features combine to make up the late twentieth-century mainstream survey of American poetry and to maintain the structure of the mainstream anthologizing machinery. As Rae Armantrout puts it in her review of the *Morrow Anthology*, "it is worthwhile to examine claims to naturalness and objectivity carefully to find out what or who is being suppressed" (*Collected Prose* 20). Examining these claims allows us to understand and denaturalize these texts' efforts to claim a center in the guise of decentralization.

Like many critical terms, the term *mainstream* in reference to poetry conflates the social and the aesthetic, describing both a location within a range of publishing, grant-giving, and degree-granting networks and a set of formal features associated with that location. In mainstream anthologies, social and intellectual background, academic training, and aesthetics tend to meet and perpetuate each other. To discuss a poetic mainstream in this way runs some risk of circularity: I choose what I have already decided are mainstream texts in order to generate a pseudoinductive account of mainstream texts. However, the apparent problem of circularity—picking mainstream anthologies as a way of defining the mainstream—is itself a problem within mainstream poetics, where social and formal considerations are hard to separate even as their connectedness is persistently either denied or dismissed as coincidental. To analyze the social and the formal as intimately connected becomes especially necessary when claims about the distinctive aesthetics of individual writers are used to efface or evade the social components of mainstream poetics.

One other possible objection to the kind of analysis that I conduct here is that it risks collapsing distinctions among poets, to whom as readers and critics we owe our attention on a case-by-case basis. From this point of view, the mainstream proves a chimera once one starts to ask how or where given poet X fits, how the work of Y can fairly be reduced to its allegedly "mainstream" features, or how two poets as different as A and B can both meaningfully be described as "mainstream." Almost by definition, attention to individual cases is likely to foreground difference, distinctiveness: this is part of the ground that the mainstream anthology claims for itself. But at the same time, an anthology often puts individual poets and their individual(ized) poems in a context that deindividualizes them while claiming to showcase their uniqueness.[13] The irony of this situation for a poetics of fetishized individualism is especially acute. Furthermore, objections to the notion of a "mainstream" that rest on the distinctiveness of the individual poet can be seen equally not as the refutation of the idea of a mainstream poetics but as a tactical example of it. In other words, the critical strategy of dismissing "mainstream" as a meaningful category by reference to the work of individual poets replicates the strategy among anthology editors of denying similarities among the hardy individualists whose work they gather. Indeed, the mainstream's denial of its own existence as a sociopoetic formation parallels, in Althusser's terms, the workings of ideology, one attribute of which is to maintain its own invisibility in order to do its regulatory work.

The notion of a "mainstream" exists in relation to various other terms within critical discourse that have also been under pressure for some time—"margin," "center," "avant-garde," "experimental," "oppositional," and so forth. Skeptical as one might be of the terms' precise usefulness, in the period under discussion they did continue to provide ways of mapping the poetic field—and for poets, not just for critics. For instance, Language writing arose in the context of—though only partly in response to—a hegemonic poetic ideology of antitheoretical lyric individualism: a setting of "mainstream poetic 'individuality,'" as Charles Bernstein puts it, in which "the prevalent phobias against groups and against critical thinking encouraged us to make our opposing commitments specific and partisan" (*My Way* 249), and a set of socioliterary structures that Bernstein came to name, influentially, Official Verse Culture.[14] Furthermore, these mainstream "phobias" were represented and circulated in anthologies coincident with the planning (1976 on) and eventual founding of *L=A=N=G=U=A=G=E* magazine: in Halpern's *The American Poetry Anthology* (1975), for instance, or Berg and Mezey's *The New Naked Poetry* (1976). Comments from Language writers such as Bob Perelman or Rae Armantrout on a poem like William Stafford's "Traveling in the Dark" reflect a genuine and active cultural conflict, one feature of which was the alleged margin's tendency to claim a deeper, more authentic mainstream status for itself.[15] In his 1978 anthology *A Big Jewish Book,* Jerome Rothenberg argues that "no minor channel, it is the poetic *mainstream* that [one] finds here: magic, myth, & dream; earth, nature, orgy, love; the female presence the Jewish poets named Shekinah" (xxxiv; my emphasis). In *The Postmoderns,* Donald Allen and George Butterick's 1982 updating of Allen's *The New American Poetry,* the editors propose the New Americans as "the dominant force in the American poetic tradition" since World War II: "These are among the most truly authentic, indigenous American writers, following in the mainstream of Emerson and Whitman, Pound and Williams" (9).[16] Reviewing the *Morrow Anthology,* Armantrout argues for the essential marginality of the mainstream that this text claims to represent, a position encapsulated in her title: "Mainstream Marginality."[17]

Meanwhile, from 1975 to 1985 the "workshop lyric" was getting established as mainstream contemporaneously with the development of Language writing, as the period saw not only a rush of anthologies but also a sudden increase in the number of poetry prizes and trade and university press publication series and a dramatic expansion in the credentializing reach of creative writing as an institution. According to D. G. Myers, "between 1971 and 1989 the number of degrees awarded in the field more than tripled—from 345 to 1107" (166).[18] The decades of the creative writing workshop's expansion were also the decades of the anthologies that gathered the writers who had studied or who were teaching in those workshops—ninety-two collections published between 1970 and 1989, according to Jed Rasula, who includes in his count textbooks devoting substantial space to poetry but excludes topic-based and identity-based anthologies (*American Poetry Wax Museum* 485). Given the claims to newness proposed in a number of these collections, it is worth noting that only Halpern's *American Poetry Anthology*—as the first of its kind, the mainstream survey—really served the function of introducing new poets. Sixteen of Halpern's poets received their first anthology appearance in his text. Ten years later, by contrast, the *Morrow Anthology* served more of a retrospective or consolidating function: only 8 of its 103 poets were new to anthologies, as were only 10 of Jack Myers and Roger Weingarten's 65 allegedly "new" poets of the 1980s. In line with these figures, Jonathan Holden reads the *Morrow Anthology* and the Myers and Weingarten collections as what I call "career" anthologies, sequels to Halpern's (which Holden, too, credits for instituting a new mainstream) insofar as they gather poets first appearing in Halpern's text and document their ongoing achievement ("American Poetry" 273).[19] Thus the mainstream anthology, while certainly foregrounding a particular aesthetics, also occupies a crucial place in a self-sustaining sociopoetic network.

Data on academically sponsored poetry readings further illustrate how the anthologies under discussion here functioned as part of a larger network of legitimation. Hank Lazer finds that in the period from 1985 to 1987—which saw the publication of two anthologies of the same poetic generations, the *Morrow Anthology* and Ron Silliman's *In the American Tree*—40 of the 104 *Morrow Anthology* poets delivered academically sponsored readings, while 9 of the 40 *In the American Tree* poets did so—a disparity heightened by the fact that most of these *In the American Tree* readings took place at a single local outlet for these writers, San Francisco State University. (This near 40 percent figure from the *Morrow Anthology* also represents a kind of shared mainstream canon between that anthology and *New American Poets of the 80's*: 37 of Smith and Bottoms's poets reappear among the 65 of Myers and Weingarten's 1980s anthology.) To come at Lazer's data from a different angle, the poets from one single anthology accounted for close to 20 percent of the 400 campus readings that he surveyed. In the face of these data, it is hard to argue with Lazer's view of the period's "academic poetry reading circuit [as] a narrowly constituted prop for the dominant craft of the workshop" and as such "condemned to a non-self-reflective act of formal repetition" (*Opposing Poetries* 1:53–54).[20] The anthologies described here exercised their influence as part of a wider cultural field that tended to sustain the same values via literary histories, interviews, and other, more specifically focused anthologies. In his critical book *The Fate of American Poetry*, for instance, *Morrow Anthology* contributor Jonathan Holden praises that anthology for demonstrating "the depth and strength of the mainstream, 'centrist,' realist mode" (48).[21] In *The Columbia History of American Poetry* (1993), postwar experimental movements such as the New York School, Black Mountain, and Language writing are barely mentioned (and mostly in the context of one essay, by Lynn Keller, who is also the only writer in the book to consider innovative writing by women) and the Objectivists as a group are not mentioned at all. In a remarkable revival of nineteenth-century gentility, Longfellow enjoys a full single-author chapter, while Louis Zukofsky and Charles Olson get a total of four pages combined.[22] Meanwhile, the mainstream workshop lyric gets its own chapter (Gregory Orr's "The Postconfessional Lyric"), as does confessional poetry itself.

This category of the "postconfessional" had already provided the title for a 1989 collection of interviews that, in the words of coeditor Stan Sanvel Rubin, "represents what might be termed the 'mainstream' of American poetry during the seventies and eighties"—which means that "many of [the poets] are included" in Smith and Bottoms's and Heyen's anthologies, have won prizes, "published at least one major book," and appear regularly in "the major journals" (15, 11). (Rubin's invocation of prizes is one of the many places in the mainstream's self-valorization where one sees at work the circular premise that the prizewinners must be the best poets because only the best poets win the prizes.) In turn, those "major journals" have made their own contribution to maintaining the mainstream by producing their own historical anthologies, from *Poems from the "Virginia Quarterly Review," 1925–1967* (1969) up to anthologies from *Poetry* (1978), *Antaeus* (1986), *Georgia Review* (1987), *Ploughshares* (1987), and the *Paris Review* (1990). A comparable category of anthology related both to the magazine and to the university press collection would include those published by university presses to commemorate academic poetry awards—the University of Michigan's *Hopwood Anthology* (1981), the University of Missouri's *Devins Award Poetry Anthology, The Yale Younger Poets Anthology* (both 1998).[23]

As a relational term, *mainstream*, not surprisingly, has been used much more commonly by those who see themselves on the margins of it than by those who might be described as occupying it. Less established poets working in "alternative" modes ended the millennium still turning to the familiar structuring binary as a way of locating themselves socio-poetically. In 1960, Donald Allen made his influential claim that the New American poetry "has shown one common characteristic: a total rejection of all those qualities typical of academic verse" (*New American Poetry* xi).[24] In 1998, Lisa Jarnot prefaced a coedited *Anthology of New (American) Poets* by arguing that "what all these writers share" is, among other things, "their marginalization from mainstream literary culture" (1), suggesting that, both at the levels of editorial rhetoric and aesthetics, versions of this binary retained some force. What can appear from one point of view as a binarized and dated "war of the anthologies" looks different if one views anthologies in toto, as a genre, as a site of ongoing conversation, debate, and struggle over literary and social values. Anthologies and their editors are constantly measuring themselves against their market competition and their predecessors; the texts have their meaning partly in relation to other anthologies. Thus it is unsurprising to find Dennis Barone and Peter Ganick couch the poetics of their *Art of Practice* in the explicitly anti-mainstream terms that I point out in chapter 3: "Poetry is not the place for expression of common or authentic voice," and their anthology is "opposed to the so-called natural free verse poem" (xiii–xiv). Setting one stated criterion of the mainstream anthology against what can often appear as an actual, if unstated, criterion, Barone and Ganick claim that "the poem—not degrees, hobbies—is primary" (xiv). What constitutes "the poem" here, however, is one thing that further separates *The Art of Practice* from more mainstream anthologies. That is, the latter typically preserve the generic stability of the poem, while gatherings like *The Art of Practice* and other experimental anthologies (Douglas Messerli's *From the Other Side of the Century* is a prime example) foreground work that "challenges the rigidity of genre," in Barone and Ganick's words (xiii). Over half the writers in *The Art of Practice* (twenty-five out of forty-five, including seventeen women) are represented partly or wholly by prose, as are thirteen out of sixty-three in Leonard Schwartz, Joseph Donahue, and Edward Foster's *Primary Trouble*, which, as I note in chapter 3, explicitly "seeks to elevate a certain poetics into view against the mainstream poetics that might obscure it" (L. Schwartz 3) even as it complicates the usual binary by expressing considerable ambivalence toward Language writing. In another context, one of the editors (Edward Foster) shows comparable ambivalence about the terms "avant-garde," "experimental," and "alternative" but still situates the poets who interest him "outside the poetic mainstream as defined in standard classroom anthologies and histories of American poetry" (*Postmodern Poetry* vii).[25]

While I have not organized this chapter around particular collections, Smith and Bottoms's *Morrow Anthology* has been widely taken as the most influential and representative anthology of those under discussion. That is, the poetic mainstream became widely noticed as such with the *Morrow Anthology*'s publication. Commenting on the Associated Writing Programs' institutionalization of creative writing, Rasula argues that "while there has been no *official* anthology, the hefty *Morrow Anthology of Younger American Poets* (1985) has, in its fidelity to the workshop mode, preempted the need for one" (*American Poetry Wax Museum* 417).[26] Vernon Shetley shares this judgment, describing the *Morrow Anthology* as "very much an anthology of mainstream poetic practice, the mainstream that flows through the creative writing programs"; as such it is an anthology of a period style, and "canon-formation . . . is at work here" despite the implied claims to representativeness ("Place of Poetry" 434).[27] Smith and Bottoms begin their preface to this representative text with a revealing slippage, as they implicitly compare their situation as editors with "Emerson greeting Whitman at the beginning of a new poetry" (15). If we recall Emerson's actual phrasing, however, he greeted Whitman "at the beginning of a great career" (362). Smith and Bottoms's unspoken conflation of "poetry" and "career" seems as symbolic a moment as any of the forces that drove mainstream American poetry anthologies through the last quarter of the twentieth century. In a collaborative 1988 essay, six then Bay Area Language writers respond to Smith and Bottoms's individualist wariness of a phantasmatic "card-carrying group member." They write, "If such poets avoid 'card-carrying' explicit aesthetics, it may be because they provide an ideology of no ideology, a plausible denial of intention in their work. However, it's easy to read intention in such a project. In these examples, the maintenance of a marginal, isolated individualism is posited as an heroic and transcendent project" (Silliman et al. 264)—a set of comments that captures precisely how the anthologies that I analyze here make up the cultural dominant against which much of the work I discuss in subsequent chapters emerged.

# II

# Texts

# 5

# Serial Form in George Oppen and Robert Creeley

George Oppen has often been discussed as if he were a kind of miniaturist, preoccupied with the small, the particular, the concrete detail. Even sympathetic readers note how modest his ambitions seem, how he writes mostly short poems capturing what he calls "moments of conviction" ("George Oppen" 174), how he pays fiercely focused attention to, in his own words, "the small nouns." Certainly, this view is not wrong, and Oppen himself, both in his poetry and in interviews, does much to invite it. He summarizes his ambitions as follows in "Route": "I have not and never did have any motive of poetry / But to achieve clarity"—"a limited, limiting clarity" of perception applied to what Oppen calls in another poem "the lyric valuables" (*New Collected Poems* 193, 50).[1] In a 1968 interview he said, "All the little nouns are the ones that I like the most: the deer, the sun, and so on" ("George Oppen" 175). In 1980 he explained his characteristic disruptions of syntax thus: "All along I've had a sense that the structure of the sentence closes off the little words. That's where the mysteries are, in the little words. 'The' and 'and' are the greatest mysteries of all" ("Poetry and Politics"38). In "Song, the Winds of Downhill," "the words // *would* *with* *and* take on substantial // meaning handholds footholds // to dig in one's heels" (*New Collected Poems* 220). And "Psalm" contains these often-quoted lines: "The small nouns / Crying faith / In this in which the wild deer / Startle, and stare out" (99).

But despite Oppen's genuine and often-stated faith and interest in "the little words," "the small nouns," it is worth remembering a few things: that he won a Pulitzer for *Of Being Numerous*, a book dominated by the long serial poem of the same title; that this book contains a second serial poem, "Route"; that both *This in Which* and *Seascape: Needle's Eye* contain series ("A Language of New York" and "A Narrative" in the former book, "Some San Francisco Poems" in the latter); that Oppen began his career with a book-length serial poem, *Discrete Series*; and that some of his closest associates and poetic models—Zukofsky, Pound, Williams—did much of their major work in the long poem. I don't want to make a perversely revisionary case for Oppen as a writer of epics. Obviously, he never wrote anything on the scale of *'A,'* the *Cantos*, *Helen in Egypt*, *Paterson*, *The Maximus Poems*, *Iovis*, *Drafts*, or the ongoing multivolume serial project of Nathaniel Mackey. Nevertheless, Laszlo Géfin exaggerates only slightly in claiming that "from the beginning Oppen conceived of poetic creation in the form of series" (63); Marjorie Perloff also remarks that "from the beginning . . . Oppen has displayed a penchant for what we might call a poetic of 'discrete series'" ("'Shape of the Lines'" 223). Most readers now would agree that Oppen did distinguished work in the genre of the serial poem. My point, then, is this: that to overlook Oppen's series *as* series—to ignore *why* Oppen works in this genre—is to misunderstand, by limiting, the nature of his achievement and to overlook a significant part of his impact on contemporary poetics. As Michael Davidson puts it, "it is as though we have focused only on the first word in the title to [Oppen's] first book, *Discrete Series*, to the exclusion of the second. By doing so we have reified the processual—and I would argue dialogical—nature of his thought in an ethos of the hard, objective artifact" (*Ghostlier Demarcations* 71).

One reason that Oppen has been underdiscussed as a writer of serial poems until recently is that for years critics seemed not to know how to read his work in that genre. Except for Joseph Conte's approach in *Unending Design*, where he explicitly theorizes seriality, most critical paradigms for reading the American long poem or sequence in the period of Oppen's return to poetry emphasized epic ambition and either the bardic or personal lyric voice, downplayed questions of serial form, and thus could not accommodate Oppen's work. I have in mind here the approaches proposed by Roy Harvey Pearce in *The Continuity of American Poetry*, by Michael André Bernstein in *The Tale of the Tribe*, by James E. Miller in *The American Quest for a Supreme Fiction*, by Thomas Gardner in *Discovering Ourselves in Whitman*, and by M. L. Rosenthal and Sally Gall in *The Modern Poetic Sequence*. In none of these books, all but one of them written after Oppen had published the bulk of his major work and won the Pulitzer Prize for *Of Being Numerous*, does Oppen make so much as an index appearance (nor do the other Objectivists, beyond Miller's one mention of Zukofsky).[2] Pearce finds in the American long poem "an effort to wrest a hero from history" (133)—an effort on the poet's part to make him or herself into that hero by pursuing through poetry a struggle for "self-identification and self-preservation," what Pearce calls "the epic struggle of modern times" (130). Oppen's series, however, are resolutely nonmythopoeic and nonheroic, and he suspects the ambition and large vision by which Pearce measures the success of the American epic. Michael André Bernstein calls for a similar scale or ambition in his discussion of Pound, Williams, and Olson's "modern verse epics." Bernstein implies in his title and proposes in his book the paradigm of a didactic cultural narrative addressed to the *polis*. This paradigm, however, has no place for Oppen, who is rarely didactic, has a modest sense of audience, and does not write poems "including history" in the same way that Bernstein's poets do.[3]

James Miller sees Whitman as the presence that presides over nearly all American long poems since *Leaves of Grass*. He calls such poems "personal epics" and summarizes their main characteristics as follows. First, "the new epic is written in a 'free' form, with a loose or an open structure, in a style that is familiar, colloquial, common, or earthy." Its action is "interior," frequently a spiritual quest, emphasizing mediation, rumination, contemplation. As regards character, "the hero of the new epic is created out of the poet's self," "an embodiment of his time and place"—a criterion that recalls Pearce. The place setting is the poet's own locale, "and the time is his time, a continuous present." Subject and theme involve implied or direct social criticism, the sketching of an implied ideal order, the seeking and delineation of new myths (34–36). How useful is Miller's paradigm for discussing Oppen? Certainly, Oppen uses "a loose or an open structure." But his style is hardly familiar—he openly disavowed Williams's faith in the vernacular ("Interview" 15)—and while the action of his serial poems may be interior or psychological, Oppen himself is not consistently their focus. He subdues his personal presence and does not use a strong central voice to organize his work in serial forms. And finally, while he may offer social criticism, he is too much the skeptic to offer new myths or resuscitate old ones, as do Eliot, Crane, Williams, Pound, H.D., and Olson (Miller's subjects). As Oppen writes in "Philai Te Kou Philai," "the myths / Have been murderous, // Most murderous" (*New Collected Poems* 98). Not surprisingly, then, since Whitman is the model, Miller's approach works best to describe Whitmanesque long poems or sequences.

The project of connecting American long poems to Whitman continues in Thomas Gardner's argument that "Whitman's creation of a self-portrait out of his indirect embrace of a medium can be used as a model for reading a number of important contemporary long poems" (21) by Berryman, Kinnell, Roethke, Duncan, Ashbery, and Merrill. For Gardner, "it was Whitman who most clearly identified and exploited the distance between an individual voice and the larger world . . . shaped, entered, and drawn from" (1). While Oppen (like many poets) may share Whitman's concern with that distance, he is hardly the kind of poet, one "wrestling with and empowered by the problems of self-rendering" (2), in whom Gardner is most interested and for whom Gardner's approach works best. A late allusion to Whitman, in *Primitive*, suggests that Oppen found his predecessor too self-involved to be an entirely useful model: looking back over his own career, Oppen wonders if he has produced "images // of existence (or song // of myself?)" (*New Collected Poems* 276).[4]

At first glance, Rosenthal and Gall's approach looks more promising. They are interested in lyric sequences, and are Oppen's serial poems not usefully described that way? Certainly, Perloff uses the term in her discussion of "Of Being Numerous." Rosenthal and Gall's late Romantic view of poetry, however, leads them to find in every poetic sequence a series of quasi-confessional lyrics. Following Poe, they see the poetic sequence as simply a series of intense local effects or expressive peaks. They characterize the modern sequence as "intimate, fragmented, self-analytical, open, emotionally volatile," as driven by "a highly subjective impulse of lyrical energy at work" in "the poem's 'speaker' or 'protagonist'" (9). Their least convincing chapters concern those sequences where the sense of a central speaking subject is least stable or those that do not place the poet *in extremis* on center stage, work such as "Notes toward a Supreme Fiction" or *The Maximus Poems*. Like Pearce, Bernstein, and Miller, Rosenthal and Gall do not even mention Oppen's sequences. If they did, it is hard to imagine how they could discuss satisfactorily the work of a writer who does not shape his serial poems around privileged centers of emotional intensity, who defines the self as "what I've seen and not myself" (*New Collected Poems* 56), and who, at a time when confessional poetry was at its peak of popularity, published these lines:

> Soul-searchings, these prescriptions,
>
> Are a medical faddism, an attempt to escape,
> To lose oneself in the self.
>
> The self is no mystery, the mystery is
> That there is something for us to stand on. (159)

As a 1975 letter to Harvey Shapiro suggests, Oppen found confessional poetry (as represented, in Oppen's own example, by Lowell's "Skunk Hour") problematic because "it doesn't tell, it's locked in itself" and fails to acknowledge that which is outside the self, "the force of the given" (*Selected Letters* 313). One year earlier, writing to James Laughlin, Oppen seems to dismiss the confessional in asserting that "weakness is common" (and thus, implicitly, an inadequate basis for a poetics), and that while he himself has "put in the moments of extreme weakness, extreme error," he has stopped short of Lowell's notorious moment of voyeurism in "Skunk Hour": "Not the love-cars" (282).

Conte offers a more useful framework for reading Oppen's serial poems in differentiating the "series" (which he sees as a distinctively postmodern form) from the modernist epic and "neoromantic sequence" (15). In doing so, he opens up considerably the canon of poets discussable under the rubric of the "long poem."[5] Conte proposes a valuable contrast between the discontinuity, incompleteness, and "accumulation" of serial form and the impulse toward "encompassment, summation" and "'totality'" of the modernist epic (37). He then distinguishes between the infinite and the finite series, placing Oppen's *Discrete Series* in the latter category as a work that "emphasizes the separate validity of the individual poems" while the infinite series (Creeley's *Pieces,* Duncan's *Passages,* Blackburn's *Journals*) "emphasizes the continuous process and the multiplicity of poems which find their validity in that process" (130).[6] Conte's tendency to take *Discrete Series* as representative of all Oppen's work in serial form leads him to overlook differences within Oppen's career and thus to propose too sharp a distinction between Oppen and Creeley; later in this chapter I argue for significant similarities between their serial works. Nevertheless, Conte provides one of the more helpful paradigms and terminologies available for distinguishing Oppen's series from the work of his modernist and late modernist contemporaries.[7]

Oppen is temperamentally suspicious of the large claims for poetry, of the expansive tone and form that in various ways characterize the modernist long poem. Not for him the rhetorical stance, derived from Whitman, that leads Jeffrey Walker to coin the term "bardic poem" for the *Cantos, The Bridge, Paterson, Maximus.* As Walker rightly says, "the fundamental enterprise in which [these] modern poems participate is Whitmanesque. And because it is Whitmanesque, it is necessarily suasory as well. Pound, Crane, Williams, and Olson all want to constitute themselves, like Whitman, as an American epic bard," uttering a "polemical call . . . to alter and direct the national will" (xi). In "Route," by contrast, Oppen writes, "If having come so far we shall have / Song // Let it be small enough" (*New Collected Poems* 199). In "West" he waxes incredulous: "'We address the future? ' // Unsure of the times / Unsure I can answer // To myself" (215). These are not the words of a poet likely to write the kind of long poem undertaken by a Zukofsky, a Pound, a Williams, an Olson.[8]

Oppen's skepticism regarding epic claims left him with serious doubts about the longer poems of all these writers, "'the great mish-mashes, the doubtful knowledge of the Pounds, Zukofskys, Olsons'" (qtd. in Nicholls, *George Oppen* 17). Some sample comments: "I can make an awful lot of objections to parts of *'A'*" ; "Pound's ego system, Pound's organization of the world around a character, a kind of masculine energy, is extremely foreign to me"; "I've always had reservations about *Paterson*"; "I don't really like the *Maximus Poems* nor accept them at all" ("George Oppen" 183–184). While place—New York, San Francisco—affects Oppen's poetry, it does not lead him to write an epic identifying with a place as Olson and Williams did. Contrasting himself specifically with these poets, he says, "I have no theory of the need for a locality at all. It would rather frighten me to be too dependent on a locality" ("Interview" 9).[9] From among the works of these twentieth-century writers of long poems, rather, Oppen values the lyric poem or the lyric moment. Of Olson and Pound, for example, he remarks, "I think 'In Cold Hell, In Thicket' is a very fine poem"; "what I really read in Pound are passages and lines. Just about the time I'm beginning to consider Pound an idiot, I come to something like the little wasp in the *Pisan Cantos*, and I know that I'm reading a very great poet" ("George Oppen" 184, 183).[10]

Given these reservations and his own undoubted lyric talent, why did Oppen turn to serial form as often as he did? For Oppen, poetry is a form of thinking, and the serial poem allows him a different, a more extended, and flexible form of thinking than is possible in the lyric.[11] Lyn Hejinian frames the usefulness of seriality for a poetry of thought as follows:

> Serial forms . . . permit one to take the fullest possible advantage of the numerous logics operative in language. These logics provide us with ways of moving from one place to another, they make the connections or linkages that in turn create pathways of thinking, forming patterns of meaning (and sometimes of meaning's excess, incoherence).
>
> The terms of the series are in perpetual relative displacement, in a relationship that may be, and sometimes should be, upsetting, disruptive. Each element in the series recasts all the other elements. In this respect the serial work is dialogic. It is also heuristic. (*Language of Inquiry* 167–68)

As John Taggart puts it, "the series permits any number of variations without forcing new beginnings and without losing sight of the object." It enables Oppen "to *think actively in his poetry*" ("Deep Jewels" 163, 162) without, on the one hand, having to formulate an inclusive philosophical system or, on the other, having to begin over with a kind of self-imposed tabula rasa in each new poem, "'out of poverty / to begin // again'" (*New Collected Poems* 220). As many of his readers have realized, and as one would expect of someone as affected by Marx and Heidegger as he was by most poets, Oppen is a dialectical poet and thinker. The dialectic especially between particular and general, between individual and group, between the One and the Many (as Henry Weinfield, calling on a long-standing philosophical tradition, frames it) always occupied him. Oppen plays out this dialectic in his serial poems—what Rachel Blau DuPlessis calls "the dialectical oscillate of meditation" (*Pitch* 48) in her poetic conversation with Oppen, "Draft 85: Hard Copy"—by foregrounding as a formal problem the relationship between individual piece and whole sequence.

Especially in a poet like Oppen, who pays such insistent attention to discrete particulars, the serial poem has a formal dialectic built into its very structure. Are Oppen's serial poems most usefully seen as a number of discrete pieces added together to make a whole? Or do they represent the remains of single, continuous poems that have been shattered into pieces? Serial organization in Oppen's poetry goes back to his first book, *Discrete Series*, and his comments on that volume emphasize alternately the whole and the part, seriality and discreteness. Oppen's goal in *Discrete Series*, he says, was "to construct meaning, to construct a method of thought from the imagist technique of poetry—from the imagist intensity of vision" ("George Oppen" 174)—to build a larger worldview ("meaning") and an epistemology ("a method of thought") from the brief, closely scrutinized moments characteristic of the Imagist poem. "Intensity" also implies the need to maintain a sharp intellectual and perceptual focus: "One must not come to feel that he has a thousand threads in his hands, / He must somehow see the one thing; / This is the level of art" (*New Collected Poems* 180). L. S. Dembo summarizes Oppen's position by saying, "one can know only particulars and hope to build a meaning from them" (68). Oppen himself further explains his thinking using Williams's dictum "no ideas but in things": "I have always wondered whether that expression didn't apply to the construction of meaning in a poem—. . . that there would be in the poem no ideas but those which could be expressed through the description of things" ("George Oppen" 183).[12]

Oppen tends to talk of his poetic technique in ethical terms and in terms that try to reconcile the claims and limitations of the Imagist poem/moment with the (always unfulfilled) hope for a broader system of thought or belief.[13] Thus, in discussing *Discrete Series*, he conflates terms of form and structure ("construct," "technique") with terms of content and value ("meaning," "intensity of vision"). "Intensity of vision" implies not only clear rendition of the image but also spiritual or moral insight and an emotional response: "The virtue of the mind // Is that emotion // Which causes / To see" (*New Collected Poems* 107), as Oppen writes in "Guest Room." Elsewhere in the interview from which his comments on *Discrete Series* derive, Oppen uses an ethical criterion to explain a formal feature of the book, saying that its disjointed structure results from his perceiving and writing in isolated "moments of conviction" ("George Oppen" 174). The term "conviction" implies what most of Oppen's work makes clear, that he sees his poetry as an effort to formulate an ethic for living. In "Blood from the Stone" he asks, "What do we believe / To live with?" and answers "all / That verse attempts" (*New Collected Poems* 52). He feels that he can formulate that ethic only in "moments of conviction"—that conviction is so fragile and fleeting as to be available only in moments. For Oppen, however, every moment is charged with potential material for poetry, the "thousand threads" from which the poet must select. Hence Oppen speaks of "the moment's // Populace" and "The light, the volume / Of the moment" (43, 46). The richness and value of this material—of *The Materials*, to use one of his book titles—is, I take it, part of what Oppen means he is convinced *of* in his moments of conviction.

In the context of explicating Oppen's sense of the Imagist moment and his effort to weld those moments into larger poetic structures, his gloss on the title *Discrete Series* deserves repeating: "A discrete series is a series of terms each of which is empirically derived, each one of which is empirically true. . . . The poems are a series, yet each is separate" ("George Oppen" 174). Here Oppen stresses not the cumulative effect of the "terms" or poems in his discrete series but their separate, self-contained quality. The construction of meaning involves forging or finding relationships among ideas and things; the very gesture of putting fragments of language into a series invites us to connect them in some way. At the same time, "meaning" remained something more sought after than achieved for a skeptic like Oppen, and something momentary: "meaning's // instant," "meaning / in the instant" (*New Collected Poems* 241, 243). He uses in *Discrete Series* the least "constructed" form of connection possible—seriality, or, in his own words, "Successive / Happenings" (35). Further, he rejects any notions of progression, climax, or organic form in favor of a literal materiality of the page: "Not by growth / But the / Paper, turned, contains / This entire volume" (33). Oppen tries to realize what might seem an unrealizable oxymoron—a long poem based on principles derived from Imagism.[14]

This strategy invites these questions: Do the particular empirical "truths" in fact add up to anything larger? What is the relationship of part to whole, poetically and politically? Characteristically, Oppen explores these questions obliquely rather than answers them and the form of that exploration moves by fits and starts, inconclusively. Seeing things in "moments of conviction," attending to words one by one, breaking up syntax, refusing full predication—when all these familiar Oppen techniques of disjunctiveness come together, inevitably a poem or series of poems will move fitfully. Oppen says he "had trouble with syntax in this undertaking" (referring to "Of Being Numerous") and especially "trouble with verbs" ("George Oppen"174), the part of speech connecting the nouns to which Oppen attends so closely.[15] His refusal of any symmetrical structure and of emphatic closure for the series (a form that, by definition, resists closure), his questioning of traditional modes of connection, at the levels of both sentence and series, help make *Discrete Series* one of the first open-form serial poems. Eric Homberger suggests that *Discrete Series* anticipates later serial poems like Berryman's *Dream Songs* or Lowell's *Notebook* (204). Unlike these poets, however, Oppen does not shape his fragments by using a systematic organization and regular form, like Lowell's chronology and pseudosonnets, or by using the distinctive voice and consistent point of view of an "experiencing subject" like Berryman's "Henry." In fact, Oppen describes the series "Some San Francisco Poems" to Charles Amirkhanian and David Gitin as being "written in violation of my own speech," because "I don't want to be tied to the characteristics of voice" ("Conversation" 24).

The formal dilemma posed in *Discrete Series*, that of the relationship between particular fragment and overall series, functions as an allegory of an epistemological and social dilemma, that of the relationship between individual and community. "Party on Shipboard," the poem of *Discrete Series* that Oppen wrote last and that he says contains the seeds of "Of Being Numerous" ("Oppen on His Poems" 201), deals specifically with this latter relationship. By repetition Oppen connects an individual wave with an individual person: the poem begins, "Wave in the round of the port-hole / Springs, passing,—arm waved." Humanity as a whole, however, is "Like the sea incapable of contact / Save in incidents"; sea and humanity are "Homogeneously automatic" (*New Collected Poems* 15). As Michael Davidson observes, Oppen "decries a nominalist theory of language, where words become separated from acts of speech, generalized into categories for being numerous: the social, the masses, mankind, the people" (*On the Outskirts of Form* 271). Against "this reduced code for the collective" (271), Oppen suggests that our daily experience is not of abstractions like "the sea" and "humanity" but of specific waves and humans. If that is true, Oppen wonders, is "humanity" even a meaningful concept?

When he returned to writing poetry—or began again—after twenty-five years occupied with political activism, a variety of jobs, military service, and avoiding the attentions of HUAC in Mexico, Oppen soon picked up this and other issues raised in *Discrete Series*, even if not exactly where he had left off.[16] *This in Which* (1965) includes the two series "A Language of New York" (an early, short version of "Of Being Numerous," which was itself originally titled "Another Language of New York") and "A Narrative." Again, Oppen uses serial form to give his mind free rein to explore questions of connection: here, between mind and world, inner and outer, word and referent. As in *Discrete Series*, Oppen uses structural discontinuity in "A Narrative" to foreground these questions. One such discontinuity occurs between title and text. *Is* this a narrative poem? Whose narrative? A narrative about what? The title's oblique relationship to the text invites questions about language (is "narrative" a useful term?) and about literary mode (what are the boundaries and characteristics of "narrative"?). The poem has none of the traditional features of narrative: no clear time or place setting, no characters, no plot, no narrative organization based on chronology or any of its variations (like flashback). Narrative, Oppen has said, with its implications of an ordered universe apprehensible in a unified work of art, runs counter to his feeling that poetic form is local and temporary and that meaning is constructed disjunctively out of momentary insights: "Narrative has almost always been unfaceable for me. I have all sorts of doubts about it, and it violates . . . my sense of the poem, the 'moments of conviction'" (Oppen and Oppen 35).[17] The late poem "Animula" suggests that, for Oppen, "narrative" means simply the ongoingness of the material world, what he calls in two poem titles "The Occurrences" (*New Collected Poems* 144, 212) to which the poet must learn to attend: "In the starlight things the things continue / Narrative   their long instruction" (213). If "A Narrative" *is* a narrative, it is one of the mind, grappling with epistemological and ontological problems, renewing its contact with the world, and searching for an adequate language in which to talk about that world.

To pursue this project, "A Narrative" moves between the competing terms of binary opposition. A detailed reading of the poem is not to my purpose here; a few brief examples should suffice to illustrate my point. Within individual parts of the sequence, Oppen often adopts a binary stanza structure: two-line stanzas in section 1 and 2, and within section 2 itself, the word count reversed in the first two stanzas; an alternating two-two-one line pattern in section 3; two four-line stanzas split by a central isolated line in section 5; two four-line stanzas in section 6; and so on. Thematically, section 1 concerns itself with lying, section 2 with truth; the bulk of section 7 consists of two equal stanzas, one on the closed self imaged in the "Serpent, Ouroboros / Whose tail is in his mouth" and the other offering the counterstatement that "What breath there is / In the rib cage we must draw / From the dimensions // Surrounding" (*New Collected Poems* 153).[18] Implied in sections 1 and 2 is yet another dialectically organized theme, the relationship between language and experience, that becomes more explicit in section 9's meditation on "the fallacy / Of words" and section 11's contrary vision of "a substantial language / Of clarity, and of respect" (154, 156). Thus Oppen uses serial form to stretch the thematic and structural limitations of the lyric. As Norman Finkelstein puts it, "A Narrative" is "the thematic center of *This in Which*" and structurally "not a unified whole, but a field in which themes may inform each other to a much greater extent than in any single lyric" (370).

The movement of "A Narrative" reflects Oppen's wrestling with what is for him the always problematic relationship between images, between general propositions, and between image and proposition. While he modifies the method of *Discrete Series* somewhat by linking the discrete parts of "A Narrative" through repetition and variation of theme and image, the links never become predictable. Rarely does Oppen use the same device to link more than two successive sections; in other words, he rarely uses the same device more than twice in a row. And while he may use a consistent stanza pattern within a section, only once (between sections 1 and 2) does he maintain a pattern *between* sections. Any sense of unity or continuity, then, remains local and provisional. Just as Oppen destabilizes almost every statement he makes by questioning it or proposing its opposite, so he destabilizes the possibility of any form that, simply by being maintained, excludes other formal possibilities.

When "A Narrative" was published in 1965, Oppen was already working on "Of Being Numerous." He seems to have had his purpose for this poem consciously in mind from the start: to see "whether or not we can deal with humanity as something which actually does exist . . . whether or not one will consider the concept of humanity to be valid, something that is, or else have to regard it as being simply a word" ("George Oppen" 175). In pursuing this purpose Oppen shows an ambition that he measures, surprisingly, not by the achievement of those poets with whom he is most often associated—Zukofsky, Pound, and Williams—but by that of Eliot. He writes to Andy Meyer, "I haven't, I'm afraid, written a Wasteland, haven't written a decisive expression of a period. I meant not to try in [*This in Which*]. I meant to try in [*Of Being Numerous*]" ("Letters to Andy Meyer" 106).[19] Like Eliot, furthermore, Oppen does not equate this ambition with the need to produce a large-scale work. A significantly less allusive poet than Eliot, he seeks a compression similar to that which Eliot's allusiveness, as I. A. Richards famously remarked, affords *him*: "Allusion in Mr. Eliot's hands is a technical device for compression. 'The Waste Land' is equivalent in content to an epic. Without this device twelve books would have been needed" (290–91).[20]

As Oppen's "decisive expression," "Of Being Numerous" makes explicit the question that *Discrete Series* left implicit: the relation of the individual to the group. It rests on the same methodological assumptions as *Discrete Series,* that one can construct meaning using Imagist technique and that "the test of images can be a test of whether one's thought is valid" ("George Oppen" 175). Despite the general resemblance between *Discrete Series* and "Of Being Numerous," however, Oppen modifies, as he does in "A Narrative," the purely serial organization of his first book. "Of Being Numerous" moves by reversal and contradiction.[21] Oppen uses this technique to make local transitions while resisting any overall systematic form. Thus he enacts in the poem's jagged form the dilemma of the relationship—the tension, sometimes the distance—between the "singular" and the "numerous," between "me" and "them," between "the poet" and "the people." As before, the serial form allows Oppen to probe his subject in greater depth and complexity than would the lyric, which has room for only a limited number of reversals and contradictions.

These reversals and contradictions occur both within and between the sections of "Of Being Numerous." To illustrate the principle briefly, I'll review a few examples of the technique as Oppen uses it between sections. Sections 5–8 make up one thematically important cluster of poems that exhibit a pattern of alternating statements and counterstatements and that shows how "Of Being Numerous," like many of Stevens's longer poems, moves by responding to itself.[22] Section 5 focuses on a stone set in the Brooklyn Bridge and dated "1875" as a metaphor for the isolated consciousness, "Frozen in the moonlight / In the frozen air over the footpath" (*New Collected Poems* 165). Section 6 shifts the topic from isolated consciousness to the enforced community of life in New York: "We are pressed, pressed on each other" (165). Section 7 turns from enforced to chosen community: "We have chosen the meaning / Of being numerous" (166). But immediately section 8 reverses 7 and recalls 6. Section 8—which Oppen thought of as "the center of the poem, its meaning" (*Selected Letters* 111)—concerns "*Amor fati* / The love of fate," "destinies" (*New Collected Poems* 166). If fate is the opposite of choice, suddenly the possibility arises that the choice "of being numerous" is no choice but something as inevitable, as fated, as the passage of time itself, "days // Having only the force / Of days" (167). As David McAleavey puts it, "the problem of 'numerosity' is *how* to be social since one *must* be" ("Clarity and Process" 388).

The pattern of reversals continues in sections 9–14. Via a quotation from a Rachel Blau DuPlessis letter, section 9 raises the question that governs the next few sections, of the poet's relationship to others: "'Whether, as the intensity of seeing increases, one's distance from Them, the people, does not also increase'" (*New Collected Poems* 167). Perhaps it does, but of the "absolute singular" poet in section 10, Oppen says, "The isolated man is dead, his world around him exhausted // And he fails! He fails, that meditative man!" (168). Section 12 offers a vision of a lost pastoral community, concluding that "This will never return, never, / Unless having reached their limits // They will begin over, that is, / Over and over" (170). Section 13 cuts from this country past to an urban present to confirm this skepticism and sense of loss: "Unable to begin / At the beginning, the fortunate / Find everything already here. They are shoppers, / Choosers, judges; . . . And here the brutal / is without issue, a dead end" (170; ellipses in original). Oppen's disgust at these "ghosts that endanger // One's soul" has him ending section 13 with the lines "one may honorably keep // His distance / If he can" (170–71)—a chosen distance rather than one enforced by intensity of vision, just as community was first enforced, then chosen. With section 14, however, Oppen immediately qualifies this statement: "I cannot even now / Altogether disengage myself / From those men // With whom I stood in emplacements . . . // How talk / Distantly of 'The People'" (171).[23]

This pattern of reversal, qualification, and self-interrogation continues throughout the poem. Rachel Blau DuPlessis discusses the pattern well in an early essay in which she describes the "structure of alternatives and the thematic concern for propositions and their negation" in Oppen's work:

> I find that formally his poetry constantly expresses dilemma—in the original sense of that word: di-lemma or two propositions. In the prototypical meditative drama of the poetry, Oppen will hold one position, weigh it, test it out, and then become compelled to consider an opposing proposition, equally true, which counters the first one. ("George Oppen" 63)

This does not mean, however, that Oppen simply hops back and forth between A and not-A. He refuses such a predictable movement, and that refusal has a larger thematic point: that the relationship of one person to another and to the mass, of the "singular" to the "numerous," cannot finally be pinned down. While "Of Being Numerous" contains small clusters of related poems within the larger series in which the reversals and qualifications that I have touched on can be seen, the pattern cannot be used to impose any shape on the work as a whole.[24] As with Oppen's other serial poems, structure in "Of Being Numerous" is temporary and provisional.[25] And along with this emphasis on local rather than overall structure, Oppen does not feel his sequence has to get anywhere. The end of "Of Being Numerous" circles verbally back to its beginning, the dilemma of self and society having been explored rather than resolved. As Oppen puts it, his poem "simply shares the problem" ["Adequate Vision" 21]. Oppen begins and ends with awe before the world. Section 1 begins: "There are things / We live among 'and to see them / Is to know ourselves.' // Occurrence, a part / Of an infinite series, // The sad marvels" (*New Collected Poems* 163). In section 39 (out of 40), we find these lines: "Occurring 'neither for self / Nor for truth' // The sad marvels" (187). And as always, Oppen rejects the grand climax. He ends with a chunk of prose, a letter home by the great poet of numerousness, Whitman, the reader's attention left hanging on one word dangling in white space, "curious . . .'" (188; ellipses in original).

Throughout his work, then, both stylistically and thematically, Oppen foregrounds the problem of connection: of word to word, of word to phrase and sentence, of image to image, of singular to numerous, person to group—and of part to part and part to whole in his poetic series. Oppen's calculated discontinuity in his sequences, the writing of more or less discrete series whose individual pieces sometimes are themselves only part of a sentence, mirrors his breaking up of the sentence to attend to individual words. At both levels the technique creates enforced pauses, draws attention to parts, and throws into question the connection of those parts to each other and to the whole. But is this any different from modernist parataxis, suppressing transitions and using abrupt juxtapositions that force the reader to make his or her own connections? Does the use of a fragmented form to render a fragmented worldview take us beyond *The Waste Land*? I think so, if only because Oppen pushes the technique to such an extreme and because he uses a different *kind* of disjunctiveness, syntactic as well as narrative. Oppen's disjunctiveness is so ubiquitous, from the level of small phrase to the level of forty-page serial poem, that it becomes its own subject. Indeed, if a poet as complex as Oppen can be said to have one central subject, this may be it: exploring the limits of verbal, political, and human connection or relation. Michael Heller, one of Oppen's closest readers, rests a whole essay collection on the premise that "estrangement literarily, politically and philosophically is the salient condition of George Oppen's work" (1). And one way Oppen conducts his exploration of estrangement and connection is through the form and structure of his serial poems.

As I suggest in my opening discussion of approaches to the long poem, serial poem, or sequence, Oppen's work in this mode was neglected for a long time because his work did not fit the available critical paradigms. He is not alone on this point. Decades after Robert Creeley published one of the major postwar experiments in serial organization, *Pieces* (in 1969, the year after *Of Being Numerous*), one could still find poet-critics writing for influential journals and academic presses who did not know what to do with *his* work either. Witness Wyatt Prunty's New Formalist critique of Creeley's "Emaciated Poetry," an attack on Creeley's minimalist line resting on an explicit and almost programmatic nostalgia for a traditional prosody, unproblematized syntax, and the New Critical virtues of wit, irony, ambiguity, and paradox.[26] The Creeley of the serial poems, however, is one of the later poets whom Oppen most clearly anticipates in *his* longer works. Creeley is usually, and rightly, associated with Louis Zukofsky among the Objectivist poets. At the same time, he met Oppen, corresponded with him, and read his poetry enthusiastically. He edited Oppen's *Selected Poems* in 2003 and, tellingly, included the generically ambiguous "Twenty-Six Fragments" both in that volume and in his *Best American Poems of 2002*. Oppen's apparent impact on Creeley's own work in and thinking about serial form—work that itself has affected powerfully many poets of the generations following Creeley's—is one measure of the importance of Oppen's serial poems.[27]

Oppen, in his longer poems, and Creeley, in *Pieces*, confront the same problem—how to write (or construct) a serial poem when one habitually tends toward a poetry of the lyric moment. Commenting on *Pieces* in a 1971 interview, Creeley starts by noting the appeal of Olson and Duncan's longer works, which "gave them a range and a possible density of statement that was very attractive" in contrast to his own habit of "work in a small focus in a very intensive kind of address." The serial form of *Pieces* thus came out of Creeley's desire for an inclusiveness that he felt his own lyric practice did not allow:

> I really had a hunger for something that would give me a far more various emotional state, that is, the ability to enter it. And also I wanted a mode that could include, say, what people understandably might feel are instances of trivia. (*Tales*102)

This shift in Creeley's work also represented a historically influential move in two related ways. First, Creeley offered the example of a liberatory shift in emphasis from the production of "poems" to that of "writing." Robert Grenier, editor of Creeley's *Selected Poems* for Scribner's and simultaneously one of the early practitioners and theorists of what came to be called Language writing, connects his serial work *Sentences* (a box of five hundred rearrangeable small cards each featuring a short phrase) to *Pieces* specifically on the basis of this attention to "writing," to the materials of language. He describes his work as that of a

> generation speaking back (different results from similar premises—a toast, as much of my work to date might be—you'd think there were compatriots & tradition) & demonstrating further workings deriving from precedents in Stein & Zukofsky, particularly correlating to that apparently largely neglected & misunderstood second period of Creeley's development, the stuff in *Pieces* . . . , where the primary interest is language process/energy released by an intensity of perception given closeup to the elements of language (letters, syllables, words) in the process of their self-formation. ("A Packet" 422)

Such a reading of *Pieces* as anticipating certain preoccupations of Language writing is reinforced by numerous comments from Creeley himself: "Words are the material of writing," for instance, or "writing is primarily the experience of language" (*Tales* 59, 103).

The second important effect of Creeley's moving from "poems" to "writing" was that he did so in a way that raised what became increasingly pressing issues of literary evaluation and that in fact questioned the very necessity of evaluation—at a time, moreover, when definitions of the poem as well-wrought urn still dominated much mainstream assessment of poetry and when Creeley might reasonably have been concerned with bolstering the reputation derived from his first two books, *For Love* and *Words*. As he says of *Pieces*, "I wanted to trust writing, I was so damned tired of trusting my own opinion as to whether this was a good piece of poetry or a bad piece of poetry" (*Tales* 102–03). For Creeley, at this time, evaluation—that most basic of canonizing gestures, of inclusion and exclusion—sustained only "the most bleak, scared, spineless subservience . . . to the British core of taste" (113). Hence his praiseful comment on an attitude close to the anticanonizing stance of *Pieces*: "What I respect increasingly in students is the ability to stop encapsulating an attitude towards writing in the sentimental sense of evaluation: this is a good poem, this is a bad poem" (113). The craft-oriented "poet" in *Pieces* may still speak: "My plan is / these little boxes / make sequences." But the "writer" instantly, if wearily, responds: "Lift me / from such I / makes such declaration" (*Collected Poems* 440).

Like Oppen, then, the Creeley of the 1960s and early 1970s breaks down the traditional boundaries of the lyric while simultaneously refusing any overdetermined structure for his series. Creeley's boredom in the mid-1960s "with the tidy containment of clusters of words on single pieces of paper called 'poems'" (*Was That a Real Poem* 103) led him to explore a new sense of what makes a poem. *Pieces* is a series of fragments, often only two or three words long. It is frequently impossible to separate individual poems; in fact, if we look for anything resembling the usual poem (with a title and a visible beginning and end), we'll be lost. The book's form "comes and goes / in a moment" (*Collected Poems* 382), a process continually completing itself but, at least in the sense of having formal poetic closure, never actually completed. Its principle of organization is to chart "the day's / particulars, one to one" (436), its effect cumulative rather than local, each piece—in Oppen's words from the beginning of "Of Being Numerous"—an "occurrence, a part / Of an infinite series" (*New Collected Poems* 163). In *Pieces*, then, Creeley's interest shifts from the discrete poem-as-object to the formal possibilities of the series, of what he called "serialogy"—"the concept of poems as set instances of articulate statement yields to a sense of continuity." He says of *Pieces*, "I wondered what kind of modality would really give me something that could also in a sense continue as a situation of writing, that wouldn't each time contain itself in a singular statement" ("Interview" 186).

From this account of *Pieces*, the areas of kinship with Oppen's serial poems should be clear. Oppen's poetry is always formally and intellectually exploratory, a poetry of open-endedness and process, and his serial poems are especially so. Not surprisingly, this quality has been noticed particularly by poets who have found in Oppen's work a valuable source for their own practice and in Creeley a kind of bridge between the older Objectivists and the present. John Taggart observes that Oppen's poetry "at every point radiates process, often in a jagged hesitating manner, [and] frustrates expectations fed on 'finished' verse"; it stands in "a continual, if quiet, opposition to the whole conception of rhetorical completion" ("George Oppen and the Anthologies" 256). DuPlessis notes how *Discrete Series* and "Of Being Numerous" have no means to achieve closure due to the structure Oppen chose for them: "Both [series/poems] have no end sanctified by tradition or history; nor will a meaningful summary act show the ultimate purpose of the sequence. [Each] series is without an ultimate purpose beyond itself and the dilemmas to which it testifies" ("George Oppen" 72). If the parenthesis and the image of ongoing process ("Successive / Happenings / [the telephone]") with which *Discrete Series* ends were not evidence enough, a 1934 letter makes it clear that Oppen did not want a strong gesture of closure for the book, no "emotional extra-ness"; and "Of Being Numerous," he writes in another letter, "ends with retraction, question, fails, if that's failure, of a conclusion" (*Selected Letters* 372n13, 160). DuPlessis puts the issue this way in a later description of "Of Being Numerous":

> How amazing to have statements opening all over the poem like subatomic events happening. The accidents of perception not solidified to one form of matter but joined to each other by the force of occurring. To have that as structure without poems collapsing into drifts and fragments. ("On the Island" 114)

This sense of structure overlaps with that evident in much of Creeley's work in the 1960s and 1970s. What Denise Levertov said of Oppen in 1963 has since become a commonplace of Creeley criticism: "His poems are essentially of process, not tasteful art-objects" (27).[28]

Like Oppen also, Creeley puts a great deal of weight on the relational units or building blocks of language in his serial poems, on articles, prepositions, conjunctions. Key "little words" in *Pieces* are words like "here" and "there"—words that embody centuries of debate about the relationship between subject and object. Creeley uses the little words to meditate on this relationship: "Here I / am. There / you are" (*Collected Poems* 389). Creeley is drawn to attempt the poetry of presence that, at some point in their careers, most Objectivists have aspired to: Charles Bernstein has explicitly linked Creeley and Oppen on this basis, in describing Oppen's "poetics of participatory, or constructive, presentness" as "akin to Creeley's" (*My Way* 192). As summarized by Burton Hatlen, an Objectivist poetics of presence assumes as its base the three famous Imagist principles first laid out by Pound in the 1913 manifesto "A Few Don'ts." These principles assume in turn "that all the 'meanings' we need are already present in the things of this world"; "that language can render the immediacy of things accurately"; that "language . . . can become translucent" ("Zukofsky, Wittgenstein" 66–67). These assumptions—or these hopes—show up in both Oppen and Creeley, though more so in the older poet, and in complicated form. Oppen's emphasis on "moments of conviction" seems to valorize the present, the immediate. His most frequently quoted poem, "Psalm," celebrates the immediacy of the material world: "That they are there!" (*New Collected Poems* 99). (We might set next to Oppen's phrase Lyn Hejinian's observation from her essay "Strangeness": "When the term *realism* is applied to poetry, it is apt to upset our sense of reality. But it is exactly the strangeness that results from a description of the world given in the terms 'there it is,' 'there it is,' 'there it is' that restores realness to things in the world and separates things from ideology" [*Language of Inquiry* 158]). To conclude the fourth section of the sequence "Route," Oppen lays out this side of his poetics: "The purity of the materials, not theology, but to present the circumstances" (*New Collected Poems* 194). But to begin the section he has already asserted a conflicting pull: "Words cannot be wholly transparent" (194). Finally denying the transparency of even the most apparently straightforward statement, Oppen consistently draws attention to *how* he says something. "The simplest / Words say the grass blade / Hides the blaze / Of a sun / To throw a shadow / In which the bugs crawl / At the roots of the grass" (144)—those first four words mark the difference between a poetics of presence and a poetics concerned with the gap between the world and any statement made about it. Even Oppen's literalizing, superficially a trope of presence that promotes "direct treatment of the thing," paradoxically tends to highlight the circularity of language: "the present / Sun pours in the present" (75); "a child / Stands as a child" (84).

Similarly, Creeley, in his *Pieces* phase, wants to "present the circumstances," to write "not from not / but in in," to find himself insistently "here / here. Here" (*Collected Poems* 388). "Inside / and out," he proposes in *Pieces*, are "impossible / locations" (380). As Charles Altieri puts it, Creeley "is trying in his use of terms like 'here' and 'the' to project the actual dynamic moment of apprehension, the field of energy exchange where self and world meet, before the encounter is translated into the irreconcilable terms of subject and object (the names of objects already imply the division of self and world)" (184). This desire "to project the actual dynamic moment" by foregrounding the smallest units of language comes out in passages like Creeley's first stanza of "'Follow the Drinking Gourd . . .'"—"*Present again / present present / again present / present again*" (*Collected Poems* 392)—or in this passage:

> THE FIRST
> time is
> the first
> time. The
> second
> time think
> again. (433)

This projection of presence comes out in the smallest fragment, like "—it / it—" (391). Here the pronoun "it" merges subject and object because grammatically it can function as either.

The Creeley of *Pieces* remains too self-reflexive a poet, however, to embrace a poetics of presence unambiguously. He knows that one is "never / only here" (391). And one site where both Creeley and Oppen play out issues of presence is the line. Oppen wrote in 1975 that "the purpose of prosody" is "the achievement of meaning and of *presence*"—citing Duncan, "'the feeling of presence, not concept'" (*Selected Prose* 49, 47). Yet his and Creeley's prosodies actually share a remarkable ability to enact both presence and the questioning of it. From one point of view, Creeley's nonlexical line breaks, the breaking of lines across words, and his minimalist line can all be seen to mark his moment-by-moment attentiveness to the act of writing. Similarly, Oppen's short (often one-word) lines, the gaps in his lines and page, his use of sentence fragments, and lack of punctuation—techniques that pervade "Of Being Numerous," for instance, before the more radical fracturing of *Seascape: Needle's Eye* and *Primitive*—draw attention to the care paid to the poem's, even the line's, construction. (Oppen, who produced his poems through a palimpsestic layering of alternative phrasings, employs much more of a constructivist aesthetic than Creeley, who claimed to revise rarely.)

In the context of discussing William Carlos Williams, Hatlen connects such a disjunctive prosody with claims to presence, arguing that "Williams's characteristic syntactic dislocations . . . force us to apprehend the poem phrase by phrase," that "through the line and stanza breaks and the (sometimes parallel, sometimes counterpointed) rhythmic and syntactic shifts, Williams holds our (and his) attention close to the sensory particulars" ("Zukofsky, Wittgenstein" 69). Creeley and Oppen's prosody, however, foregrounds or renders present the materiality of language as much as that of the world. In Louis Zukofsky's well-known term, the Objectivist "particulars" that Creeley cares for are particulars of sound and syntax rather than of sight. Charles Bernstein similarly argues that Oppen's prosody—and here I would extend the point to Creeley—conflicts with, rather than reinforces, the ambition to write a poetry of presence. Thus Oppen's "use of the line break as hinge" (and "the typical Oppen hinge is made by starting a line break with a preposition, commonly 'Of'"), in its "insistence on the constructedness of syntax: the manipulation of words to create rather than describe," conflicts with his commitments to transparence and clarity (*My Way* 193–94).[29] In Oppen, then, prosodic means for refusing fluency reinforce what I call his calculated discontinuity. Meanwhile, in *Pieces*, the disjunctively broken short line that, like a poorly tuned car, "coughing moves with / a jerked energy forward" (*Collected Poems* 383) works against any unreflective immersion in poetic process. In one *Pieces* poem, Creeley writes

Don't say it doesn't rhyme
if you won't read it—nor break the

line in pieces that goes
and goes and goes. (*Collected Poems* 430)

Characteristically, in the moment that Creeley asks his reader to honor this book's seriality, not to "break the line" in *Pieces* "that goes / and goes," he disrupts his own injunction by separating article and noun across a line and stanza break. The poem's prosody pulls against its content; for Creeley, a commitment to process does not equate with any kind of organic seamlessness of effect.

Even what Ron Silliman calls "first phase Objectivism" ("Third Phase Objectivism" 85)—represented by the early work of Oppen, Zukofsky, Reznikoff, Rakosi, Niedecker—contains the seeds of a slow growth away from a poetics of presence. This growth can be seen in Oppen's career in the shift from the more presentational *Discrete Series* to the more philosophically self-conscious later work. As many of his critics have noticed, if the typical Oppen poem contains vestiges of Imagist principles, nevertheless it moves toward thought rather than toward things. The same is true of Creeley. Hence Géfin links Oppen and Creeley on a different, although not contradictory, basis from Bernstein, as the two poets in the Objectivist tradition "for whom language itself posed enormous problems" (63). Creeley's worrying over particles of language, which often seizes vividly an instant of perception, just as often serves to highlight the artifice of language. The inherent metaphoricity of words, their power to turn something into what it is not, the use of verb tenses to compartmentalize time—all these features of language work against the early Objectivist ideal of a poetics of presence. Creeley knows this; so did Oppen.

*Pieces* features this poem:

The sun will set again on
the edge of the sky or whatever

you want to call it. *Out there,*
not here, the sun 'will set,

did set, is *now* setting.'
Hear, goddamnit, hear. (*Collected Poems* 429)

The italics of "*out there*" and "*now*," and the irritable "goddamnit, hear" show merely that the poet doth protest too much, aware that "hear" is "not here" and that he finds himself drawn not to the traditional visual account of sunset but to a grammatical account, the process of sunset as a conjugation of verb tenses. Equally revealing is the self-consciousness of "the edge of the sky or whatever // you want to call it," invoking the word "horizon" by pointing to its absence, a distancing trope akin to Oppen's "the simplest / Words say the grass blade / Hides the blaze / Of a sun." Such wrestling with the conflicting claims of presence and absence in Creeley constitutes perhaps his most important advance on Objectivist poetics because it provides a bridge between the older Objectivists like Oppen and younger writers like the Language poets, for whom the workings of the language system have been a central concern and who have often pursued this concern via experiments in longer or serial forms. Poets such as Charles Bernstein, Robert Grenier, Bruce Andrews, Ron Silliman, Barrett Watten, and Bob Perelman, as well as Taggart and DuPlessis, have written perceptively and sympathetically on both Creeley and the Objectivists, especially on Zukofsky and/or Oppen. I take my conclusion, however, from Oppen, commenting in a letter to his great-niece Eve Haight on the processual poetics that he and Creeley share: "I'm planning to show you Robert Creeley's remark: 'the possible is more important than the perfect'" (*Selected Letters* 201)—a remark that encapsulates the shift from a high modernist ("the perfect") to a postmodernist ("the possible") poetics.[30] One premise underlying the serial experiments of Oppen, Creeley, and those who have followed them is surely this: that the possible *is* more important than the perfect.

# 6

# Place, Space, and "New Syntax" in Oppen's *Seascape: Needle's Eye*

Although George Oppen is not usually thought of as a poet of place like the Olson of *Maximus* or the Williams of *Paterson*, his major work, "Of Being Numerous," is very much a poem of New York, with its origins in Oppen's shorter 1964 serial poem "A Language of New York."[1] Almost a year after completing "Of Being Numerous," for reasons of personal health and safety Oppen moved in December 1966 to San Francisco, the city where he had spent his teenage years and where he would live out the last seventeen years of his life and write his last two books. He began almost immediately, in Rachel Blau DuPlessis's words, to "meditate on the meaning of the two cities in his life and the feeling of such a transition back to the place where his family had lived during his adolescence, and to a place experiencing the end of 1960s hippie activism" ("Introduction" xix).[2] As a move back to the site of bitter familial conflicts and personal abuse, the return to San Francisco seems to have been an ambivalent one for Oppen. He writes to Charles Tomlinson on December 24, 1968, for instance, that in representing "a homecoming to my adolescence," San Francisco "gets under my skin a little, my thin, unfamiliar, adolescent skin" (*Selected Letters* 394n4). By April 26, 1971, he found "San Francisco coloring everything, an obsession I can't break if I wanted to" (404–5n1). This change in environment coincided for Oppen with a rethinking of his poetics and his career that is reflected in his first San Francisco book, *Seascape: Needle's Eye* (1972), the poems of which Oppen started writing soon after his arrival. *Seascape* thus represents a key transition in the work of a major poet. In this chapter, I explore the connections between that transition in Oppen's poetics and his new environment—the connections among place, space, and syntax. What is the relationship between the physical space of San Francisco and the newly intensified attention to syntax, language, and page space of *Seascape*? And what was the process by which Oppen produced these distinctive poems? If, as Michael Heller observes, "Oppen's work is characterized . . . by a powerful, and not well-understood, use of white space, semantic break-up and what looks like fragmentation" (111), then some attempt to understand that use of space better would seem to be called for, particularly in the later work in which it becomes so strikingly visible a component of Oppen's materialist poetics.[3]

Commenting during the San Francisco years on his earliest work, Oppen says, "I had trouble with syntax in this undertaking [*Discrete Series*] and, as a matter of fact, I still have trouble with verbs" ("George Oppen" 174). The syntax of Oppen's late work, of his San Francisco writing—*Seascape*, "Myth of the Blaze," and *Primitive*—is far more fractured and hesitant than the work immediately preceding it and marks a return to a mode close to parts of his first volume, *Discrete Series*.[4] This shift goes hand in hand with a renewed focus on syntax and language as such in *Seascape*. In a 1980 interview, Tom Mandel proposes to Oppen that "From a Phrase of Simone Weil's and Some Words of Hegel," the first poem in *Seascape*, "starts with syntax, declares itself as starting with syntax as subject matter, and fragmentary syntax"; among other things, it does so in its very title ("a phrase," "some words"), as well as in its halting beginning, "in back deep." Oppen agrees that "it's entirely a discussion of syntax" ("Poetry and Politics" 38–39).[5] Thus the volume begins in a move away from the tangibility of the world and toward language, in a poem that in one draft was revealingly titled "Poetics." *Seascape* is framed by prepositions (the book's first two words are the widely spaced "in" and "back," the last word is "of") and begins not just in "a discussion of syntax" but also, and relatedly, with a questioning of Oppen's prior poetics of solidity: "In back deep the jewel / The treasure / No liquid" (*New Collected Poems* 211).[6] In these opening lines, the hardness (though not the brightness) of "jewel" and "treasure" to describe the ocean proves the wrong metaphor and has to be replaced by the more literally accurate, and twice repeated, "liquid." Not coincidentally, the "liquid" of this opening poem resurfaces as a feature of language in the last poem, "Exodus," which begins: "Miracle of the children the brilliant / Children the word / Liquid as woodlands" (234). Oppen builds the poem's whole sound structure around the repetition of the liquid "l." In this fifteen-line poem, "children" or "child" appears seven times, "miracle" four times, "brilliant" or "brilliance" three times, along with "pillar" (twice), "Israel," "adults," "woodlands," and "liquid" itself. In the course of *Seascape*, the liquid materiality of the sea transforms into a liquid materiality of language, the word "children" "liquid as [the word] woodland."

Oppen acknowledges that *Seascape* marks a shift from his well-known emphasis on "the small nouns" to "the question of how they take on substantial meaning. I was talking about language . . . that most complex thing of syntax, of those connections which can't be dealt with outside the poem but that should take on substantial meaning within it" (Oppen and Oppen 47). Completed syntax becomes almost an obstruction for Oppen, a matter of excessive mediation, in his attempt "'to make the words hit bottom, to find words that will lie in bed rock, not suspended in a mesh of syntax'" (qtd. in Nicholls, *George Oppen* 138). As Eleanor Berry puts it, *Seascape* objectifies not the poem itself (which historically had been the Objectivists' first goal) but "the very processes by which language makes and unmakes meaning" (322). In other words, Oppen moves from a poetics of "the small nouns" to a poetics foregrounding that which connects them and that which lies between them on the page, "from the noun-based 'statement' to poems in which shifters, conjunctions, and prepositions would be brought to unusual prominence in an attempt to capture the movement and texture of poetic thinking" (Nicholls, *George Oppen* 128). On the matter of syntax in *Seascape*, "Song, The Winds of Downhill" is rightly taken as a key statement of his later poetics. Appropriately enough, given Oppen's increased preoccupation with white (page) space, it begins with a quotation from Charles Simic's *White*: "'Out of poverty / to begin // again.'"[7] And Oppen goes on to a self-description of a poet "impoverished // of tone of pose that common / wealth // of parlance" to the point where "the words // *would* *with* *and* take on substantial // meaning handholds footholds // to dig in one's heels sliding" (*New Collected Poems* 220). Substantial meaning no longer resides mainly in substantives. Awe before the material world—"The wild deer bedding down—/ That they are there!" in the widely cited words from Oppen's 1965 volume *This in Which* (*New Collected Poems* 99)—has become awe before the materials of language.

This linguistic self-reflexiveness is reinforced by the repetition that is so notable a feature of *Seascape*, as Oppen himself confirms: "I was writing the music and talking about the music" (Oppen and Oppen 48). Often Oppen uses repetition with variation, as a way of refining and adding shades of meaning. But equally often, the tone and effect of the multiple repetitions in *Seascape* is one of querying and testing—repetition as a meditation on Oppen's own use of the word or phrase in question. Do these words really mean anything?[8] Repetition in *Seascape* tracks the process of "seeking a statement," as Oppen puts it in a daybook passage from the period:

To stand still
like the bell buoy    tragedy
become mere shabbiness    so widespread

to stand still
like the bell buoy    tragedy
so wide-
spread

            so wide-
spread the tragedy
mere shabbiness    "seeking a statement" ("Adequate Vision" 19)[9]

"Seeking," not "making," a statement: for the effort at firm statement in *Seascape* is undercut by a hesitantly probing repetition and by the slowing effect of spaces introduced in midline, in such lines as "we believe    we believe" (*New Collected Poems* 229).

Yet despite this apparently constrained vocabulary that out of poverty begins again and again throughout *Seascape*, language itself remains, in one of Oppen's recurrent terms from the book and from his working papers, a "miracle." Most often in Oppen this word refers to the "miracle" of the physical world's sheer existence. In "Exodus," *Seascape*'s closing poem, quoted earlier, it at first refers to the "miracle of the children    the brilliant / Children" (*New Collected Poems* 234) who may offer some faint hope for a nation on the edge and for a human species that, in the preceding poem, has "gone / As far as is possible" (233).[10] Yet Oppen also writes of the "miracle on the small page" that is writing ("Circumstances" 17). ("Animula," the third poem in *Seascape*, evokes the miracle of the word in alluding to St. John of the Cross's "Del Verbo Divino.")[11] If "Of Being Numerous" ends with one quintessentially Oppen-like word (stolen from Whitman) floating in space, "curious," *Seascape* ends similarly on an even more modest, nonlexical word: "Miracle / of" (*New Collected Poems* 188, 234). Those small words, the glue of syntax, the withs, ands, and woulds that "take on substantial // meaning" and offer "handholds    footholds" as a culture slides downhill (220), are compressed into this final "of" to form a large part of the miracle, even as the volume ends looking out into space, toward the horizon of a blank half page and beyond.

At moments like this, Oppen uses page space to reinforce awareness of syntax, in a way that points to another significant shift in his work: a shift toward a far more open visual design, with sentence fragments, phrases, and single words separated or punctuated by generous use of white space on the page. Indeed, space is the primary form of punctuation in *Seascape*, a volume characterized by its overall lack of conventional punctuation. While working on *Seascape*, Oppen wrote one of the only three book reviews that he ever published, discussing a book with a title oddly resonant with his own, Armand Schwerner's 1969 *Seaweed*:

> A number of experimental poems, largely experiments in the isolation of words, a radical exploration, depend on space and the organization of the page which cannot be displayed in brief quotation but achieve in the book a remarkably pure lyricism of word and silence and of skepticism. (*Selected Prose* 40)

(It's worth recalling here how rarely Oppen used the word "experimental" as an honorific.) This passage describes an emerging tendency in Oppen's own work as much as it describes Schwerner's.[12] This new sense of space in Oppen is especially striking if one looks at the original 1972 publication of *Seascape* by Dan Gerber's Sumac Press. The all-white cover of this edition, the open medieval-style lettering of that cover, a nine-by-six page larger than that of the eight-by-five New Directions *Collected Poems* of 1975, a larger font—all these factors highlight further the white space already built into Oppen's poems. It is to Gerber that Oppen comments on his own epistolary style in a way that resonates for just this feature of his later poetry: "I would say something about breaking the words, the sentences, the locutions *open* to make some room for ourselves Here among the subatomic fragments" (*Selected Letters* 227). Visual space, then, is metaphorically a human space, "among the subatomic fragments" of language.

At issue here, then, are the relations among this typographical space, syntax, and geographical space. Late in 1975, Oppen praises the English poet Jonathan Griffin as follows: "The syntax! . . . it restores light and space to poetry" (*Selected Letters* 313). Light and space: two of the predominant geophysical features of San Francisco, along with the wind, in Oppen's experience. "A strong wind, a truly startling light like no where else; if it were an historic city or a capital city, there would be a name for this light" (153), he writes soon after his move, and he was persistently struck by the city's beauty. This environment had particular effects on Oppen's work. In early 1970 Oppen writes to Harvey Shapiro, "My own work thins, is what's happening, thins in the influence of the California skies and the seascape Something happening to the solidity of objects. . . . Well, there we are: This in Which, which I seem to have spoken of before, but the center of the picture changes for me" (403n9). He describes that change in a July 1,

1970, letter as follows: "The N.Y. poem (meaning of course *Numerous*) is intellectual and philosophic; The San Francisco Poems are atmospheric" (210). In *Seascape* the solidity of objects is overshadowed by the no less concrete but certainly less isolatable physical phenomena of light, wind, the waves, oceanic space, the horizon. When Oppen moved to San Francisco, and as his attention to syntax as part of the mechanics of meaning making intensified, he started to put the city's spaces into his lines.

I'm wary of lapsing here into an untenably deterministic argument about the relation between locality and aesthetics—and this about a poet who once said "I have no theory of the need for a locality at all" ("Interview" 9). However, there is some warrant for my position in Oppen's own comments on the connection between place and technique. "The poem is more open," he says in 1975, because San Francisco "is another place [from New York], the spare coast" (23). He explicitly connected the form of his poems from his San Francisco period with the experience and meaning of the horizon, the "needle's eye," seen from the city: "If I'm talking about beyond the horizon, it requires some freedom of, of moving around in the poem" (qtd. in McAleavey, "Oppen" 86). And focused as his San Francisco poems are on what lies beyond the horizon, Oppen is just as concerned in *Seascape* with the limits of vision: "I of course meant the needle horizontally and the closure. . . . It sees the horizon as a sharp line but the line—you can't actually see through it, it's too narrow a line. . . . It is the point at which vision disappears. . . . The point at which it becomes blank" (88). "And one can't be just sharply naming things at that point" (87), he adds, as he has aspired to do in his earlier writing life. In other words, if the needle's eye marks the point at which vision ends or becomes blank—"I watched the bird flying until my eyes became sky" ("Adequate Vision" 19)—it marks the outer limit of Oppen's earlier poetics, and perhaps of one version of an Objectivist poetics, as he questions how "to entrust / To a poetry of statement" (*New Collected Poems* 228).

In terms of its impact on the space of his poems, San Francisco's coastal location may have been as important to Oppen as the city per se. The "historical meaning" of "Some San Francisco Poems" involves for him "this distance, this edge of the country, and the thing beyond or outside the sense of metropolis" (*Selected Letters* 405n1); the "feel of bareness" and of "a coast essentially untouched by literature" (394n4, 405n1) gave San Francisco a radically different meaning from that which New York held for Oppen. This edge is not merely a geographical one: "That beach is the edge of a nation" (*New Collected Poems* 224). The word "nation" in this line carries a different weight from its possible alternatives ("country," "continent"), including the implication, as Hugh Kenner writes, that "the nation had fallen off the edge" (186). From the edge Oppen looked out onto a horizon ("Horizon: Needle's Eye" was one working title for *Seascape*) that seemed to combine the poles of two poetics, "the detail, the objectivism in the sense it was usually understood, and the sky, the unlimited space, the unlimited." In the May 22, 1973, interview with Charles Tomlinson from which these words are cited, Oppen describes the "edge" as "metaphysical": "It's a bare edge of a continent. You come. . . . You stand on a little beach, you can stand on one little rock and look out—if you saw far enough you'd see Honolulu. There's nothing between. It's a bare, bare edge; it's a metaphysical edge" (qtd. in *Selected Letters* 407n1). That "metaphysical edge" resonates with a daybook remark from the period: "To perceive . . . . . . / Is to stand on the edge / . . . . . . . . . . . . . . . . . . to recognize / contingency" (*Selected Prose* 150). Meanwhile, beyond Honolulu, you would see Vietnam, where the young person ended up whom "the nation" sent beyond the needle's eye of San Francisco's Pacific horizon.

In 1963 or 1964 (the letter is undated), before his move, Oppen writes to his niece Diane Meyer: "If one is to move to experience further one needs a syntax, a new syntax A new syntax is a new cadence of disclosure, a new cadence of logic, a new musical cadence A new 'structure of space'" (*Selected Letters* 97). In the context of *Seascape*, what is notable in this comment is the phrase "structure of space" as a description of syntax, space as a way of shaping syntax's "cadence of disclosure"—the latter a definition of syntax to which Oppen returned repeatedly and maintained through his later years. In 1966 he writes to Serge Fauchereau that "the line sense, the line breaks, and the syntax are intended to control the order of disclosure upon which the poem depends" (*Selected Letters* 141); in 1967, already at work on *Seascape*, Oppen calls syntax "the cadence of unfolding" (161).[13] A few years later Oppen claims not to care much about space, at least not about page space. Writing to Meyer again in 1970, he says

> I think I don't care at all about design, pattern across the paper, the canvas, or the poem's surface. . . . I'm not sure I ever visualize anything but depth . . . or a point, a detail so sharply defined that I'm shaken by the implication of space. (220)

This passage contains an interesting contradiction, however: Oppen claims to pay no attention to visual design, but attention to a point or to "depth" (to the vertical) leads him to a response to "space," the horizontal, a response that shows up partly in the very visual design of the page that he allegedly ignores.

Despite such occasional disclaimers, it is clear (beyond the evidence of the poems themselves) that use of page space featured in a good deal of Oppen's thinking about his poetics: "One needs no technique at all except to know what word, what punctuation mark what white space must come next," and "the poem must be shaped, yes, even its form on the paper" ("Circumstances" 15). As he once said, "for me the poem is primarily on the page," not in the mouth or voice (Oppen and Oppen 49), and "the spacing is part of the drama of the poem (visible as much as audible)" ("Selections" 17). Sharon Olds reports Oppen as saying, "'It's probably because I haven't been *trained* to *hear* . . . but I need to see a poem *on the page*'" (78). The fact and idea of space reflected at least two things for Oppen: a meditative or antirhetorical silence of observation and the distance and otherness between observer and observed that are foundational to his poetics. On the first point, he writes, "'Space' in the poem, space on the page: NOT [Olsonian] breath—not manner, when space is not silence, the matrix of silence, it is chatter, noise" ("Philosophy" 216).[14] If in *Seascape* Oppen "begins again" "out of poverty," entering on a new phase of his work in a new city, that beginning is founded equally on a felt conjunction of the ideas of space, distance, and otherness evident in this short untitled poem from his archive:

> each other that little
> distance (how is it
>
> held the poem
> begins
>
> each other that little
> space    how
>
> is it
> grasped the poem
> begins
>
> each other that little
> (how is it grasped) the poem
> begins
>
> each other that little
> distance how is it
>
> grasped the poem
> begins ("Adequate Vision" 7)[15]

As Oppen writes elsewhere in his notes, "Directions of space, of distance give meaning to life," and perhaps to the poem ("Selections" 2).[16]

The question remains of the process by which Oppen wrote space and "a new syntax," "a new cadence of disclosure," into *Seascape*: space as an aspect of syntax, in tension with the connective function insofar as it brings the effects of parataxis into syntaxis by isolating words and phrases. As readers familiar with Oppen's working process will know, he constructed his poems out of journal jottings, whole drafts, letters, transcribed quotations from his reading, and much more.[17] In a sense, Oppen was always writing poems and testing his poetics; he even wrote drafts of letters and revised them. The syntax of *Seascape* is equally constructed, simultaneously sculpted and aired out, its spaces as much a part of the syntax as the words. The book's central ten-poem sequence "Some San Francisco Poems" was written out of "notes and scraps" accumulated since spring 1967; by November 1970 he felt these "bits and pieces" were "adhering finally" (*Selected Letters* 187, 216).[18] In light of Oppen's remark that "the serial poem permits the use of space, of silence" ("Selections" 3), as he enacts the formal dynamics of seriality, of disjunctive relations across gaps, at the syntactic level, what is the process by which the spaces that I've been describing enter *Seascape*, and especially "Some San Francisco Poems?"[19]

Rachel Blau DuPlessis comments on Oppen's editing process as follows:

> After the editing, what was left got linked—one simply linked the genuine material (possibly resequencing it). This was his method—making of every poem a "discrete series" and attenuating or cutting the "argument" or the "logic" or the "development." . . . The proposition was that startling and original logic or sequence would emerge from the editing out of the non-genuine, something quite far from the conventional—from the conventional *anything*. You would confront what you really thought in cutting what was inadequate, generic, or "poetic," and trying to comprehend the rest in whatever form it emerged, as traces, fragments, phrases, as constellations. (*Blue Studios* 191–92)

What does the cutting of "argument," "logic," "development," of the "generic, or 'poetic'" look like in practice? One hardly thinks of Oppen as a producer of what was once called the McPoem, but it is in that mode that much of "Some San Francisco Poems" started.[20] To illustrate Oppen's writing of space into final versions—partially, but I'd stress not completely, a byproduct of his cut-and-paste compositional method—let me offer some examples. Here is the archival poem "For Jo Miles":

> We arrived in our wet clothes
> And I carried the canoe uphill from the shore
> To a ruined shack in the tall grass
> Where a piano stood, the wood splintered,
> The keyboard gone    Mary swept her hand
> Across the strings as I dropped the canoe
> And the thing rang out
>
> Over the rocks and the ocean
> Not my poem.    Steinways'
> Poem.    Not mine    A marvelous object is not
>             the marvel
> of things.    but it rang (*New Collected Poems* 399–400)

In revision, Oppen suppresses the first-person point of view and cuts narrative exposition and narrative details (like "as I dropped the canoe") extraneous to the central action as he adapts this poem for the second half of "o withering seas," San Francisco poem #7. And what gets added is space: three spaces between lines and two internal spaces (as well as two new lines) that are not present in the original:

> Ravishment    devastation    the wood splintered
>
> The keyboard gone in the rank grass swept her hand
> Over the strings and the thing rang out
>
> Over the rocks and the ocean
> Not my poem    Mr. Steinway's
>
> Poem    Not mine    A "marvelous" object
> Is not the marvel of things
>
>             twisting the new
> Mouth    forcing the new
> Tongue    But it rang (*New Collected Poems* 230)

Partly due to these changes, the poem acquires both a historical and a self-reflexive dimension absent from its narrative original. "O withering seas" begins with an invocation to Oppen's local environment to reveal its poetry: "O withering seas / Of the doorstep and local winds unveil // The face of art" (229). It then moves into a moment of self-citation: "*Carpenter, plunge and drip in the sea*" (230) adapts an earlier Oppen poem, "Carpenter's Boat" (128), that foregrounds two recurrent Oppen metaphors, the poet as carpenter (his work during his years of self-exile in Mexico) and the ocean-tossed boat (the Oppens were lifelong sailors) as figure of the human condition. Meanwhile, the closing lines suggest Oppen's awareness of San Francisco's effect in "twisting the new / Mouth  forcing the new / Tongue" of *Seascape*'s poetics, even as the objectified poem is inadequate to the world (it "is not the marvel of things") and the addition of quotation marks around "marvelous" suggests distance from or skepticism about a key term of Oppen's work. Oppen's own oral performance of the poem emphasizes the line breaks on "new" in a way not generally characteristic of his reading style, and visually this newness has to be spoken into the line ending's indeterminate space (including that of the aging Oppen's foreshortened future).[21] The space around the added abstract nouns "ravishment" and "devastation" draws attention to those terms and gives them a historical edge sharpened by the preceding images of "a limited // Consensus unwinding // Its powers / Toward the thread's end // In the record of great blows" (230).

As another illustration of Oppen's creating space in the revision process of *Seascape*, I'll compare some lines from "The Extreme" with what survives of them in "Anniversary Poem," the fourth of "Some San Francisco Poems." First, from "The Extreme":

> Light grows, place becomes larger or deepens, the familiar
> Becomes extreme
>
> That the gate swings shut
> That the wooden latch falls quietly
> In this place, that the grass flows with the slope
> Across the meadow
> In this place to where the great trees stand
>
> Or the familiar joy
> Passing the hardware store
> I remember the tools and the house
> We once built
> And the foundations, the stones and the thin worms
> In the earth
> The scratched metal edge of the shovel
> So like another man's I knew even then I was not very
>   young (*New Collected Poems* 332)

This is the second half of a previously unpublished poem from the late 1960s, and again, it is revealing to notice what gets excised as Oppen adapts this passage into a final structure simultaneously more rigorous and more porous. Fifteen lines become four (and two new lines are added), with narrative, personal memory, explicit response to place, explanation, and all but the barest concrete imagery removed:

> A shovel's scratched edge
> So like any other man's
>
> We are troubled by incredulity
> We are troubled by scratched things
>
> Becoming familiar
> Becoming extreme
>
> Let grief
> Be
> So it be ours (*New Collected Poems* 226)

"Edge" now teeters, appropriately, at the end of a line and on the edge of space, recalling "the edge of a nation" of "'And Their Winter and Night in Disguise'" (224–25). This is a powerful, elliptical music in its short, tight-lipped lines, its almost ritualistic anaphora and isocolon: nuggets of language set in (an ocean of?) space created by the excision of long lines and the simultaneous breaking up and compression of free verse blocks into a number of succinct, phrase-based stanzas. We confront something like Oppen's version of *ostranenie*, "scratched things" becoming simultaneously "familiar" and "extreme" and inducing "incredulity" in the process of poetic reconstruction. Oppen himself agrees with the suggestion of a student who reportedly said, "It looks to me like someone has erased half of the words and it's my job to find out what goes in the missing spaces" ("Poetry and Politics" 39). Perhaps this agreement stems simply from politeness, but it does reflect uncannily on his revision process, a process that suggests his spaces are the result both of erasure and of (re)construction, "built in" as a result of words being "built out."

Finally, along similar lines we can compare the draft poem "There Is (Russian Hill)" with the untitled #6 of "Some San Francisco Poems" (*New Collected Poems* 228). The unpublished poem reads:

> Walking home
> We stood in the dark among trees
> In the city

Looking down on the bay
To the lights
Across rough water

There is a sparkle below us
On the wave tops
It is the town lights
On the liquid waves
In the tide rips
In racing riots

While the dark
At the grass roots
Has silenced the mountainsides

Who dares pity
The pitiful

Who that is alone
Can shut the house door ("Adequate Vision" 15–16)

All that survives in publication is phrases: "The liquid waves / In the tide rips," and a version of the last-but-one stanza, "I dare pity no one" (*New Collected Poems* 229). Yet again Oppen breaks open in revision the familiar structure of a personal narrative leading to a mildly epiphanic conclusion and nugget of wisdom: that narrative is excised, along with, interestingly for this poet of the "this in which," the monofocal concreteness of the original. The poem in which these phrases end up begins concretely enough, the waves "silver as / The needle's eye // Of the horizon" (228). But they quickly become metaphorized as a "net of branches," "swarm," "avalanche" and are linked with the abstractions of epistemological belief ("conviction's // Net of branches") and history ("the horde of events") (228).

In yet another draft, this time of "A Morality Play," Oppen begins

Preface
The play begins with the world

Piety

We who once said
Objectivist

A play exposed and jagged
On the San Francisco hills (*Selected Letters* 395n11)

This draft appears in a letter of spring of 1967. Parts of it survive in two different "San Francisco" poems, "A Morality Play: Preface" and "Anniversary Poem," but I want to emphasize in closing the central phrases. The play still *begins* with the world, the vantage point of the San Francisco Hills. But the poet "who once said / Objectivist," who refused the abstraction "Objectivism," is now more inclined to embrace abstractions as he ponders the "incalculable" spaces beyond the needle's eye horizon that this new vantage point opens up in his mind, in his sentences, and on his pages.[22] This opening up of the syntax and the page in late Oppen is a means simultaneously to respond to his new environment and to track his own developing thinking about the possibilities and limits of poetic statement.

*Segmentivity*, DuPlessis's term for poetry's defining characteristic as developed in essays on Robin Blaser and Oppen, is especially useful for thinking about *Seascape*. DuPlessis defines segmentivity as "the ability to articulate and make meaning by selecting, deploying, and combining segments" (*Blue Studios* 199). Any given poem or body of work, however, may foreground its segmentivity to a greater or lesser degree, and Oppen does so increasingly via his use of page space: "Oppen's later poetry seems continuously to be stopping at virtually every line, at every porous white-space caesura, and then picking up the commitment again to go on" (188). Elsewhere, DuPlessis remarks that "in Oppen, especially later Oppen, the lines, line by line, are organized serially. I mean that literally: each line or small group is like a distilled poem, section, aphorism. Then these are placed 'end-for-end.' This gives the sense of space, depth and extent in Oppen—each line acts as if it is a section or stanza of a poem—even, each word does" ("Topos" 47). How this constructivist poetics plays into the post-Objectivist serial form of DuPlessis's own long poem *Drafts* is the (or one) subject of my next chapter.

# 7

# Macro, Micro, Material

## Rachel Blau DuPlessis's *Drafts* and the Post-Objectivist Serial Poem

Enough to look at here
For the rest of a lifetime
—Rachel Blau DuPlessis, "Draft 85: Hard Copy"[1]

"Objectivist": the best-known and earliest definitions of the term come from Louis Zukofsky's early essays, "Program: 'Objectivists' 1931" and "Sincerity and Objectification," which both appeared in the February 1931 special feature in *Poetry* that Zukofsky guest-edited. Zukofsky stresses Objectivist over Objectivism (a term he is careful to avoid) since "the interest of the issue was in the few recent lines of poetry which could be found, and in the craft of poetry, NOT in a movement" (*Prepositions* 214). In his definition, Objectivist refers to the "*desire for what is objectively perfect, inextricably the direction of historic and contemporary particulars*" (189; emphasis in original). Out of this desire, "writing occurs which is the detail, not mirage, of seeing, of thinking with the things as they exist, and of directing them along a line of melody" (194). What is commonly emphasized in this formulation is the first phrase, "the detail, not mirage, of seeing," accurate rendition of the image, but in the interests of my argument here, which requires a capacious definition of the term "things," I'd like to stress equally the second: "Thinking with the things as they exist."[2] These are the features of "sincerity," moving toward, in the best-realized poetic work, what Zukofsky calls the "rested totality" of "objectification—the apprehension satisfied completely as to the appearance of the art form as an object," "writing . . . which is an object or affects the mind as such" (194). Sincerity also involves the art of omission, of the cut or the gap that is central to serial form: "When sincerity in writing is present the insincere may be cut out at will and information, not ignorance, remains" (201). As a way of seeing and of embodying those perceptions in poetic form, then, Objectivist sincerity moves toward seriality.

In "'Recencies' in Poetry," the introduction to his 1932 *An "Objectivists" Anthology*, Zukofsky expands upon some of these principles in ways relevant to a major experiment in post-Objectivist serial form, Rachel Blau DuPlessis's *Drafts*. More than in his previous essays, Zukofsky emphasizes what he calls "context—The context necessarily dealing with a world outside" of the poem (207). The Objectivist poem-as-object is here "an inclusive object," "binding up and bound up with events and contingencies," socially embedded by definition (207–8). George Oppen writes similarly, many years later, that the "act of perception" is "a test of sincerity, a test of conviction" projecting "the sense of the poet's self among things" (*Selected Prose* 31–32). This location of the poem in a social world was always implicit in Zukofsky's "historic and contemporary particulars," but it becomes explicit in his later formulation in a way important for thinking about DuPlessis's socially saturated work.

In the introduction to their germinal essay collection, *The Objectivist Nexus*, DuPlessis and Peter Quartermain review the basic principles of the poetics in question: "The term 'Objectivist' has come to mean a non-symbolist, post-imagist poetics, characterized by a historical, realist, anti-mythological worldview, one in which 'the detail, not mirage' calls attention to the materiality of both the world and the word" (3). They go on to connect Objectivist poetics with serial form: "The Objectivists, with their decided sense of the line and their inventive serial organization, use the basic nature of poetry—its 'segmentivity'—to articulate social meanings" (4).[3] "Seriality is a central strategy of the Objectivist poetry of thought and of its constructivist debate with a poetics of presence and transcendence" in ways that directly impact the post-Objectivist: "All writers absorbing the Objectivist example consider the praxis of the poem to be a mode of thought, cognition, investigation—even epistemology" (7, 3).[4] Beyond the obvious example of her own poetic practice, discussions of seriality or serial form run throughout DuPlessis's critical work, from essays on Robin Blaser and Oppen to those on the long poem as a genre and on her own poetics. The following observation on Lorine Niedecker can stand for much of her theorizing specifically of Objectivist seriality:

> In its segmentivity and sequencing, its deliberate fragmentation, and intense economy, its building a poem by accumulating moments of sincerity, and its materialist claims, [Niedecker's] "Paean to Place" is written saturated with objectivist premises and practices. . . . It builds meaning by the cut of the fragments and the blaze of white space between the parts. ("Lorine Niedecker's 'Paean to Place'" 162)

"One of the mid-1960's inventors of seriality along with Oppen and (from another poetics) Jack Spicer," Niedecker generated "a version of seriality as a mode of reflective moments playing realist images and meditative pensiveness against one another" (163). At the same time, versions of serial form lie at the Objectivist movement's very roots: in Oppen's *Discrete Series* (1934), in Zukofsky's "Poem Beginning 'The,'" or in Charles Reznikoff's nineteen-section *Rhythms* (1918) and his twenty-two-section *Rhythms II* (1919).[5] Serial form is the Objectivist answer to the problem of the long poem: the problem of how it may be possible to write one in the twentieth century, and the question of whether a long Imagist (or Objectivist) poem is possible. In chapter 5 I quote Pound's observation that "I am often asked whether there can be a long imagiste or vorticist poem," and his answer, with some qualifications, is that "I see nothing against a long vorticist poem" (*Gaudier-Brzeska* 94). Objectivist seriality (in itself diverse and by no means monolithic) came to provide one means by which such a poem might get written.

As an analytical tool, what DuPlessis and Quartermain call the Objectivist nexus is a "three-dimensional model of participation, production, and reception over time" that "allows one . . . to attend to rupture as well as continuity, and to dispersion as well as origin" (22). But it is also a space of ongoing poetic practice, and as such is precisely post-Objectivist (or in DuPlessis's term, "neo-Objectivist") ("Objectivist Poetry and Poetics" 99). "The Objectivist nexus" thus provides a framework for thinking about poetry "after" (chronologically, and on the model of) the Objectivists, poetry that is part of the Objectivists' ongoing reception and legacy.[6] In *Drafts* DuPlessis continues the Poundian and Objectivist notion that technique is the test of a woman's sincerity, that an ethos and an ethics emerges from the writer's attitude toward materiality—that of the object world and of language. For DuPlessis, "this makes an ethic of writing emerge simultaneously with the making of language. The basic 'rule' of technique is that every single mark, especially the merest jot and tittle, the blankest gap and space, all have meaning" (*Blue Studios* 210).[7] We might note the materialist language here (mark, jot, tittle, gap, space), the connection of linguistic materiality to ethics, and the location of meaning in the small, even the microscopic. Every material textual detail has meaning in what DuPlessis calls the "through-composed" long poem—"for me a poetics is expressed philosophically via the detail"—and that constitutes one definition of what it means to associate technique with sincerity (*Surge* 11). In this chapter, I explore some of the ways in which these post-Objectivist concerns with the material detail and its mystery, and with scale—the relationships among micro, macro, and monumental—play out through her long serial poem *Drafts*.

In her preface to *Surge: Drafts 96–114,* the final volume of *Drafts,* DuPlessis returns us to some of the basic features of the project, "certainly a work saturated in an objectivist ethos" (13). This ethos is defined partly by an Oppenesque sense of "the mystery that has always generated the poem. Perhaps the words for this mystery are IT and IS. These poems have, at any rate, returned to those concepts as an insistent continuo—or obbligato" (3).[8] Oppen's "Psalm" offers the canonical Objectivist statement of this ethos: "The small nouns / Crying faith / In this in which the wild deer / Startle, and stare out," lines preceded by the exclamation "that they are there!" with its awe before the mystery and strangeness of being (Oppen's deer have "*alien* small teeth" [my emphasis]) (*New Collected Poems* 99). To return to DuPlessis: "The poem certainly wants to talk of the mysteries of 'it.' And 'she' [the title of Draft 2] is faced with that 'it' and with all of it" (*Surge* 12).[9] The preoccupation with "IT IS," then, is a fundamental part of *Drafts*'s objectivist ethos. In "Draft 33: Deixis," DuPlessis cites "a statement by Louis Zukofsky [that] offers the poetics of this kind of examination of the smallest words" (*Drafts 1–38* 225). The key part of Zukofsky's 1946 statement reads as follows: "'A case can be made out for the poet giving some of his life to the use of the words *the* and *a*: both of which are weighted with as much epos and historical destiny as one man can perhaps resolve. Those who do not believe this are too sure that the little words mean nothing among so many other words'" (10; *Drafts 1–38* 225–26). DuPlessis weaves references to the principle of the "little words" throughout *Drafts,* often in ways that call up Oppen or Zukofsky. As one example: "Little words, / worming into incipience. / 'The a.' / Then, half-contrary, / 'a the'" (*Drafts 1–38* 180).[10] "The" (the title of "Draft 8") and "a" are tied to DuPlessis's move away from the bounded lyric and to her earliest imaginings of *Drafts*: "(*No more poems, no more lyrics. Do I find I cannot sustain the lyric; it is no longer. Propose somehow a work, the work, a work, the work, a work otherhow of enormous dailiness and crossing*)" (*Pink Guitar* 147). This chant-like repetition invites a reading of *Drafts* as a kind of "the-work" and "a-work" immersed in the "enormous" (Zukofsky's "epos and historical destiny"). But again, DuPlessis's own "little words" are other: "it" and "is." I focus the next phase of my discussion on the operation of those two words in *Drafts,* following along the line of one that "Draft 1: It" inaugurates.[11] Tracing this particular line through *Drafts* will allow me to foreground not just the pervasive presence of the material object, as fact, value, and idea, throughout *Drafts* but also its foundational presence at the poem's beginning and at each rebeginning.

*Drafts* has two entirely appropriate epigraphs, raising as they do questions of attention to minute detail and of the appropriate form for "ungainliness," the latter term from Zukofsky's "'*Mantis,' An Interpretation*": "Feeling this, what should be the form / which the ungainliness already suggested / Should take?" The first epigraph, from Clark Coolidge, reads thus:

> The minutest details of
>    sunlight on a shoe . . .
> had to be scribbled down,
>    and with *extensions.*[12]

Consistent with these considerations of "minutest details" and of the form their scribbling down and multiple "extensions" might take, the project begins with nonhuman subject and object, "Draft 1: It"—both material and grammatical object, and the key Objectivist pronoun. Subsequently, every Draft on the line of one, the beginning of every fold, that is, every rebeginning *in medias res*, uses the phoneme "it" in its title: "Incip*it*," "Spl*it*," "In S*it*u," "P*it*ch Content," "Veloc*ity*." More generally, the use of "little" words as titles—"It," "She," "Of," "In," "Me," "The" in the first eight Drafts alone—establishes early on their importance for the poem. At the same time, *Drafts* begins with a questioning of Objectivist premises, or at least the desire to extend them: "To reinvent 'attention' is narrow tho tempting," though one "reinvention" that DuPlessis does embrace is that of the page as a visual and performative site for self-reflexive attention to language (*Drafts 1–38* 4). "Draft 1" features multiple iterations of the phrase "it is," the linguistic, philosophical, and ethical foundation of *Drafts*. One such iteration, "I / is it" (4), anticipates numerous later variations throughout the poem on Rimbaud's "je est un autre" but lays out early DuPlessis's preoccupation with the self's relationship to the object world, including the objects that are words. Reinvented attention will focus on the materiality both of language and the page, of "putt (pitting) the tiny word / litt / it / on stage in a 'theatrical' space / a / space white and open a flat / spot a lite on / it" (*Drafts 1–38* 5). Why "pitting," "litt," "lite?" One effect is to highlight, sonically and visually, the omnipresence of "it." If one persistent intertext is Robert Creeley's formulation from *Pieces*, "it—/—it," there is another reference to Creeley, and to his well-known "As soon as / I speak, I / speaks" (Creeley, *Collected Poems* 391, 294).[13] For DuPlessis's "Object (pronoun) / squeaks its little song its bright white / dear dead dark," but at the same time, "CANO"—"I sing"—so that "I" and "it" become equally the subjects or source of the long song that is *Drafts* (*Drafts 1–38* 5, 4).[14]

If "It"—as title and as pronoun—encodes Objectivist materiality, one aspect of that materiality in *Drafts* is its self-reflexiveness, a persistent "spoilage of / presence" (*Drafts 1–38* 3) in the work that differentiates it from much Objectivist writing. From the beginning, *Drafts* is occupied with the material conditions of language and of its own (and any print-based poetry's) production: "It's / framed marks that make / meaning is, isn't / it?  Black // coding inside  A / white fold open" (2).[15] In "Draft 20," another beginning—"Incipit"—focuses on "it is" in a way that connects "it" again to the poem's self-reflexiveness, its "aura of endlessly welling commentary // folding and looping over / **I**s" (131). The large, uppercase boldface "I" links visually with a similar **T** five lines later to form "**IT**." This passage gives us DuPlessis's commitment to "it is" as a kind of fate, reflected in the dominant iambic rhythms of the Anglophone tradition: "And that was it. / It sentenced me for life" (131). Thus writing from "it is" constitutes a baseline measure of the objectivist ethos of *Drafts*, while linking "it" to and opening "it" into moments of midrashic self-reflexiveness marks an extension of that ethos, as an ongoing theorizing of poetics enters into the poetry itself to a far greater degree than in the original Objectivists' work.

In "Draft 39: Split," the beginnings of the third fold, "'It' mark dots / down on the page" (*Drafts 39–57* 2). It does indeed, and those dots, again reminiscent of Creeley's *Pieces*, help construct the seriality of the form. "It," like Zukofsky's "the" and "a," has a historical destiny (not to mention density): "But speak of how that 'it' emerged // it's 'there' it's 'where' it's never what // you think  Might be" (2). "That 'it' emerged," among other sources, from a literary and philosophical history that is encoded in the iambic rhythms of these lines and that includes one especially relevant iambic pentameter couplet, Charles Reznikoff's canonical image of Objectivist it-ness to which DuPlessis refers multiple times in *Drafts*: "Among the heaps of brick and plaster lies / a girder, still itself among the rubbish" (*Poems of Charles Reznikoff* 107). Also hovering here is what DuPlessis calls the "always palpable / stripped intransigence" of George Oppen: "No way seeing is-ness / no way saying it-ness / except resistance," that point where the Objectivists' ethos meets their variously left politics (*Drafts 39–57* 197, 3). "It" moves as a kind of bass line through "Draft 39" via deliberately obtrusive rhyme: "it," "legit," "split," "bit" in one eight-line sequence. As always in *Drafts*, "it" is both material world and text, detail and plenitude, micro and macro, as we move from this comment on Beverly Dahlen's *A Reading*—"'Reading "it" / by the endless invention of "it"'"—into the quintessential encapsulation of what "it" means in and to *Drafts*: "Where 'it' // splits and doubles between the little (unspoken) and the looming // (unspeakable)"—the totality (11). "Draft 39" then concludes, in one of the many allusive summaries of the project, in a playful use of Williams's three-step line rendered iambically: "To cast a dot of matter forth // and, farther, farther, troll it out, // through cusps of darkling antecedent sea" (12) That darkling sea gestures simultaneously toward Arnold's "Dover Beach," toward Homer and the "darker, antecedent sea" (*Drafts 1–38* 10) that closes "Draft 1," and toward the possibility of the female-authored post-Homeric long poem, called up in "Draft 1"—as tongue-in-cheek imperative? As declarative?—via the use of Homer's famous adjective in "little girls little legs jump the wine dark line" (9).

The self-enfolded serial poem in multiple books has to keep concerning itself with (re)beginning, restarting every nineteen Drafts at its material base, "It." By "Draft 58: In Situ," her fourth beginning, DuPlessis acknowledges the challenge of any "simple beginning, in situ, / that is, in the middle," as the poem confronts the impossibility, for her, of certain Objectivist ideals and of practices historically associated with the epic: "I just wanted simplicity, or relief, / wanted to list items" (*Torques* 1, 3). However, "it lists [i.e., leans], it tilts—the it of all of this: / How account for it; how call it to account?" (5) Meditations on the traditional epic beginning, *in medias res*, break down in the face of political rage and human loss (a student suicide), as does the Objectivist impulse toward documentation or recording, the all-inclusive ambition to write a tale of the tribe, and the convention of the epic catalog: "This was to be a straight-line list, / itemizing what was at stake" (1). Like "Draft 58: In Situ," the next poem in the line of one, "Draft 77: Pitch Content" begins the volume *Pitch: Drafts 77–95* by considering how to begin and by personifying the "it" that drives all of DuPlessis's rebeginnings: "'*It wants to write. It wants me to write it*'" (*Pitch* 1), in an epigraph from Hélène Cixous. After the epigraph, the first line of text has the effect of a Zukofskyan beginning, invoking both his little words and his long poem: "A," that line reads, and it's awfully hard for a reader of the Objectivists not to complete it as "A / Round of fiddles playing Bach" (Zukofsky, *"A"* 1). In contrast to that social plenitude, we have "A / first page empty, blank and null" (*Pitch* 1)—the blank verso opposite this recto. For all that, however, sound and music do dominate this Draft that echoes *"A,"* "the It / of impercipient vibrato" (4)—here, "it" is all sound. In "Draft 96: Velocity," by contrast, "it" is all speed and motion—verbs like "pulse," "push," "surge," "plunge," and "sweep" dominate the first sentence (*Surge* 23). Zukofsky may well be present here also at the end of this last beginning, in a closing sentence that "*calls outright to A*" (26), Zukofsky's key little word and the first letter. The more visibly modernist presence, however, is Williams, not just in DuPlessis's use of his triadic line but in the reference to his great poem of (re)beginning, "By the road to the contagious hospital." In "Draft 96: Velocity" the figure for "it" is a swallowtail butterfly, "gripping down" like Williams's plants, babies, and new American poems: "Rooted they / grip down and begin to awaken" (Williams, *Spring* 13).

Just as each volume of *Drafts* begins by returning to the ground of "it is," so each one closes with a variation on the ongoingness of poetic labor, of the work with "it is" that will end only with death: hence the doubled invocation in the last two lines of *Drafts 1–38* to "work until it tolls / *And work until it tolls*" (267). *Drafts 39–57* moves toward these lines while linking "workplace" and "nekuia," mundane space of daily labor and necromantic poetic rite: "It is hard to know why / this site is so implacable / but it is, clearly it is" (*Drafts 39–57* 221–22). *Torques: Drafts 58–76* closes with endlessness, with rebeginning, and with the citationality that forms one core aspect of DuPlessis's poetics. The volume's last page brings the invocation to "Begin! / Here! And Here!" while its last words appropriate the mail artist Ray Johnson on (self-)appropriation: "'My works get made and then chopped up, and then reglued and remade, and then chopped up again, the whole thing is really endless'" (*Torques* 136)—reasserting, at a point of temporary closure (the end of the book), the open-ended constructivist nature of the work, something close to an infinite series.[16] Similarly, on the last page of *Pitch: Drafts 77–95*, "it" imposes itself yet again on the reflective poet: "Is this what I wanted to say? / It is said. Is it what I wanted? / It is what came out. / . . . / It chose me" (172). Thus chosen, one can only continue writing beyond the ending, and "Draft 95," via the image of restarting a faulty watch, "ends" by anticipating the work ahead: "I knock it hard to start it up again, / hitting the table where I do my work" (172).[17] The earliest parts of "Draft 1: It" date from May 1986, when "it?  that? // plunges into every object / a word and then some" (*Drafts 1–38* 1). One hundred fifteen Drafts later, in 2012, the poem is both concluding and ready to continue beginning with the Objectivist "it":

> There are so many tasks. To start.
>
> Up. Again.
>
> Like this. The is, the it.
>
> Id est:
>
> So vector the crossroads once again!
> Volta! Volta! (*Surge* 160)

Thus, on "it is" ("id est"), the two little words that have driven it, and on another turn (volta), DuPlessis's post-Objectivist *Drafts* concludes in a (its) beginning, "closes without ending" (1).

So, little words, big poem, a poem that persistently addresses and enacts ratios of scale. "It is" turns out to be crucially connected to issues of scale, and of interpretation, in this contemporary poetics of Mass Observation: "These are poems challenged by—moved by—the plethora. . . . Here is a typical situation: small to large, tiny to largest. It is about the plethora of stars, that vastness, and the dot or yod, the most minuscule mark. That *it is*. That we can read it" (*Blue Studios* 214). As a simultaneously formal and social question, that of scale is insistently, though complexly, gendered in *Drafts*. DuPlessis is drawn, as poet and critic, to the creation of "large and encompassing structures with a female signature," following on such female modernist models of "writing a gigantic oeuvre, a mound of oeuvre" as Dorothy Richardson and Gertrude Stein ("Interview" 404). Early in her critical career, she claims "in women's writing, . . . there is an encyclopedic impulse, in which the writer invents a new and total culture, symbolized by and announced in a long work, like the modern long poem"—a work motivated, that is, by "the thrilling ambition to write a great, encyclopedic, holistic work, the ambition to get everything in, inclusively, reflexively, monumentally" (*Pink Guitar* 17, 9). At the same time, however, as a poem in the Objectivist tradition *Drafts* is also committed to a constructivist poetics of close attention to the immediate concrete detail or fragment, refusing any kind of panoptical perspective, a constructivist poetics that is also a feminist poetics of writing against the long epistemological, cultural, and literary tradition of coding the detail female. Around the time that DuPlessis began *Drafts*, Naomi Schor offers a "feminist archaeology" of the detail in which she analyzes its "participation in a larger semantic network, bounded on the one side by the *ornamental*, with its traditional connotations of effeminacy and decadence, and on the other, by the *everyday*, whose 'prosiness' is rooted in the domestic sphere of social life presided over by women" (4). But Schor is equally interested in the redeeming of the detail as a site of value within materialist and realist modernism: "The ongoing valorization of the detail appears to be an essential aspect of that dismantling of Idealist metaphysics which looms so large on the agenda of modernity" (3–4).[18] Thus an Objectivist poetics, in this view, becomes a way to undo the feminization of the "detail"; *Drafts* engages ongoingly with this gendered history and modernist degendering of the detail.

A foundational essay on the question of "scale" in women's long poems remains Susan Stanford Friedman's 1990 "When a 'Long' Poem Is a 'Big' Poem," in which she ventures "some generalizations about women's status as outsiders in relation to the genre and the self-authorizing strategies in which they have engaged to penetrate and transform its boundaries" (721).[19] "In this horizontal-vertical discourse," Friedman argues, in which the long poem asks "big" or "deep" questions and does so at length, "vast space and cosmic time are the narrative coordinates within which lyric moments occur, the coordinates as well of reality, of history" (722). While I question whether Friedman's account of women's relationship to the genre of the long poem continues to pertain, it remains a compelling historical account: "Rooted in epic tradition, the twentieth-century 'long poem' is an overdetermined discourse whose size, scope, and authority to define history, metaphysics, religion and aesthetics still erects a wall to keep women outside" (723). Without using the term, Friedman refers here to the totalizing impulse; in response to that impulse, DuPlessis uses the serial form of *Drafts* to construct what she calls "an anti-totalizing text in a situation with totalizing temptations" (*Surge* 2). In the face of Friedman's accurate claim that the woman's long poem is no longer centered on a male hero's quest, *Drafts* maintains "the general aura of quest just as a baseline," though that baseline has its limits: "not hero, not polis, not story" (*Drafts 1-38* 9, 102).[20] But it does so in the interests of "a distinct demasculinization of the genre," of moving away from the long poem "as a masculine discourse of important quest-ions" while maintaining its scale and ambition (Friedman, "'Long' Poem" 724, 733).

What are the different kinds of scale or ratio about which one could talk in *Drafts*? There is scale at the level of language, where DuPlessis mainly focuses on the micro: the serif, the tiny visual mark, the point (iota, yod). Then language is persistently felt as inadequate to the articulation of the macro, of enormity or plethora (both recurring terms in the poem). There is scale at the level of perception: what can be seen at the tiniest level as against a cosmic or astronomical scale, the microcosmic or the "micro-moment" and the macrocosmic. By the time DuPlessis invokes Blake's grain of sand in *Pitch*, the reader has been waiting for it for quite some time, while the term "micro-moment" lets us know there are questions of temporality at work too.[21] Scale in the area of genre or poetic method would set the monumentality of *Drafts* against the method of constructing this massive nonwhole that "closes without ending" out of fragments, debris, "little stuff," bits and pieces, moments of what once was called "lyric."[22] Even the extensive notes to *Drafts* can be seen to participate in this ratio: "The note. The Note! a feminist task of the Scholiast!—the annotation, condensing enormous cultural pressures into a tiny meaningful margin, tracking around the monumental, following traces" (*Pink Guitar* 130).

I want to think about the possibilities of an antimonumental monumentality as one approach to what is, after all, at 992 pages one of the longest long poems of the twentieth and twenty-first centuries—large scale without monumentality as a way to claim, and as an analogy for, poetic authority without hierarchy.[23] Sheer mass in poetry, DuPlessis suggests, can itself constitute a cultural intervention, an obstacle that requires negotiation: "The modern/contemporary long poem often exists to put an unassimilable mound of writing between yourself and culture as usual; a large realignment of what you know and what you see takes shape in it" ("Lyric" 37).[24] At the same time, this "mound" is composed of the debris or rubble that forms one central motif in *Drafts*: "Perhaps the experimental long poem of our era smashes the epic into lyric shards as a social critique precisely of the social ethos of the epic," its totalizing tendencies (39). *Drafts* is both the practice of and "also a theory of debris," "*theory of the shard*" (*Torques* 133; *Drafts 1–38* 180). We can map macro, micro, and questions of gender onto DuPlessis's concerns with monumentality and its shattering into rubble, a recurring term that will actually end up returning us to DuPlessis's Objectivist roots. (In the next chapter, I discuss DuPlessis's relation specifically to Poundian monumentality, itself reduced to rubble by the end of the *Cantos*.) In particular, "Draft 15: Little" contemplates the project and method of this millennial and monumental nonepic: "Not hero, not polis, not story, but it. / It multiplied. / It engulfing. / It excessive," "the little / stuff agglutinating in time, debris" (*Drafts 1–38* 102). The seemingly throwaway term "little" is simultaneously here a poetic or formal and ideological commitment, with its own lineage running, as I've been arguing, through the Objectivists and—in the recurring image of "debris"—through Walter Benjamin. And here that "little" term "it" is linked simultaneously to the macrocosmic—"it" is what is multiplied, engulfing, excessive—and to the counterepical agglutination of *Drafts* (including the accumulating moments of sincerity that cumulatively establish the Objectivist ethos).

The dialectical relationship between macro and micro is fundamental to DuPlessis's project: "This conflict or incommensurability of little and large and its unstable resolution . . . might be what incites anyone to write a long poem in the first place" ("Lyric" 50). And the "conflict or incommensurability" finds its appropriate form in post-Objectivist seriality. "Draft 49: Turns & Turns, an Interpretation" is a poem formally and conceptually in dialogue with Louis Zukofsky's two-part "'Mantis'" and "*'Mantis,' An Interpretation*" (the source of DuPlessis's epigraph to *Drafts 1–38* on "ungainliness" seeking appropriate form, as it does throughout *Drafts*). The lineated essay "Turns, an Interpretation" poses this question and answer: "What is the form for motion, what is the form for dialectical shim, / for self-quarreling and readjustment—serious, humorous? / It's seriality: / its quick shifts and sectors, / its questions at each moment of articulation" (*Drafts 39–57* 121). Importantly for DuPlessis, the nature of seriality refuses resolution: "What single message from [Oppen's] 'Of Being Numerous'?" (121).[25]

Via the trope of debris, let me return to Charles Reznikoff's couplet from his 1934 volume *Jerusalem the Golden*:

> Among the heaps of brick and plaster lies
> a girder, still itself among the rubbish. (*Poems of Charles Reznikoff* 107)

In ways centrally relevant to *Drafts*, this is partly a poem about the interconnectivity of singleness and plurality, "*a* girder" and "*heaps* of brick and plaster." More precisely, it is also about distinctive singleness, what one might call "it-self-ness," and its relationship to a muddying plurality, the indistinct "heaps" and "rubbish." Oppen repeatedly invoked this poem as an iconic, almost foundational or originary, moment in Objectivist poetics and nearly always misquoted it, substituting "rubble" for "rubbish." In turn, DuPlessis consciously adopts this misquotation, returning to "rubble" as a persistent motif throughout *Drafts*: rubble as the shattered fragments of a broken whole but rather more poignant and even elegiac a term than the more judgmental "rubbish." In one formulation, amid "the faceted refraction / of choices and debris" we find "the girder amid, between, among, above, / the rubble under, on, from, next to, within"—little words making up what DuPlessis calls "prepositional debris" elsewhere in the poem (*Pitch* 82, 20).[26]

Monuments and their breakage recur throughout *Drafts* as a figure for the work's form, method, ethos, and cultural politics. Given "the monsters to whom / Monuments are built," it's no surprise to encounter the following faux cross-reference: "As for monuments—/ see ambivalence" (*Pitch* 56, 44). But these monuments do not survive intact; what survives is the trace, at least tentatively, somewhere, sometimes, even as it "makes no claims / that it will survive" (105). As well as the erosion of male power by time, the statue of Ozymandias to which DuPlessis alludes in "Draft 87" represents, as it did for Shelley, "monumentality / broken and scattered" into "trace elements," "which implies / not that trace / is outside of structure, but that it is / the shattered bits of former structure" (92). "Improbable Babel left in rubble, / This poem almost became its own erasure. / Almost blanked itself out" but was able to "let in fissure, fracture, broken shard" (129). Returning to the image of *Drafts*'s opening page, where handwritten capital Ns take the form of mountains, this is the way to "make the book an imitation mountain but with real hard strata. Data" (134): the poem made up of the shards of its own always already shattered monumentality, on the scale of a monument but with none of its features.[27]

# 8

# *Drafts* and Fragments

## Rachel Blau DuPlessis's (Counter-)Poundian Project

To say this project [*Drafts*] was involved with and against Pound from the start is almost tautological.
—Rachel Blau DuPlessis, *Blue Studios*

This chapter positions itself in relation to my epigraph on Rachel Blau DuPlessis's massive, multiyear serial poem *Drafts*, what she calls a "series of interdependent, related, canto-length poems" (*Blue Studios* 211). "*Drafts* and Fragments," of course, both is and is not Poundian, invoking the titles both of Pound's first book of cantos, *A Draft of XXX Cantos*, and his last, *Drafts and Fragments of Cantos CX–CXVII*. Typographically, however, the italics in my title mark DuPlessis's *Drafts* and its relation both to Pound and to fragments. DuPlessis has turned and returned to Pound throughout her career as poet and critic, from her 1970 Columbia dissertation "The Endless Poem" (Pound's own term, from a letter to Joyce, and what DuPlessis calls a "predictive rubric" for her own poetry [*Blue Studios* 189]), to a long 1981 essay on George Oppen and Pound, to energized discussions of Pound in *The Pink Guitar* (1990), *Blue Studios* (2006), and *Purple Passages* (2012) to—throughout—*Drafts*. Pound and Williams are two of the poets at the core of the "Objectivist continuum" (Davidson, *Ghostlier Demarcations* 23), with its multiple offshoots. I address Williams's reception by one generation of that continuum in chapter 12. Here, I want to offer a brief case study of one poet's responses to the far more politically problematic Pound. I do not mean to suggest an ongoing (and especially not filial) debt to Pound on DuPlessis's part. But I do mean to suggest a serious ongoing engagement and argument, with Pound as a figure, with his work, and with particular aspects of experimental modernism for which DuPlessis reads him as standing. "Reads him as standing": I should stress that I'm considering here a poet-critic's reading of Pound, and that, like many readings of poets by other poets, it is partial, motivated, self-interested, sometimes tendentious. With gritted-teeth neutrality, DuPlessis begins the endnote to "Draft 61: Pyx" thus: "Ezra Pound has been an essential modernist for Anglo-American poetry, and among the practitioners haunted by his work and his career, I would count myself" (*Torques* 138). That word "haunted" is carefully chosen. Pound is both foundational and to be moved away from, complexly enabling and an object of resistance, and DuPlessis describes *Drafts* as "a modulation from the Poundean mytho-informational model as the master genre of long poems to a Creeleyesque or, better, Oppenesque notational, social and secular proposal" ("Considering the Long Poem")—a "modulation" in the direction of serial form, with the term "secular" reminding us of the deliberate absence of anything like Pound's "Eleusis" in *Drafts*.[1]

Related to the shift from the "mytho-informational" to a "notational" model is the (gendered) question of scale. I discuss scale in, and the scale of, *Drafts* in chapter 7, and the sheer size of the *Cantos*, along with Zukofsky's *"A"* and Olson's *The Maximus Poems* the largest in a century of large poems, is everywhere present as a fact "behind" *Drafts*, which itself consciously engages from a female-authored perspective "the whole area of cultural ambition, to open up into the largest kind of space, the challenge of scope itself" ("Interview" 403). DuPlessis triangulates the importance for her of a male example like Pound with ongoing, large-scale production among female modernists: "Both Dorothy Richardson and Gertrude Stein were doing the same thing, writing a gigantic oeuvre, a mound of oeuvre, to separate themselves definitively from all of the tradition of the novel and . . . of thinking / writing that went before in order to start a new tradition" (404). In "Draft XXX: Fosse," which invokes Pound both in its use of Roman numerals, calling up *A Draft of XXX Cantos*, and its use of the Poundian word "fosse," the underworld site in "Canto I" of empowered (male) prophetic speech, DuPlessis associates herself with a Poundian tradition via citations from or allusions to Oppen, Zukofsky, and Armand Schwerner. But "cunningly" (Odysseus-like) she focuses on their more scaled-down moments: "Mimics little words / (flat pebbles), / brings them all to the *a* / or to the *the* of 'be'" (*Drafts 1–38* 188).[2] Importantly, in this nuanced negotiation, "little" gets disarticulated from its received association with the feminine by its association with male precursors and contemporaries.

I return later to the question of the "notational," but initially, I want to work with the idea of the fragment. It is connected to three central aspects of DuPlessis's and Pound's poetics, three sites at which or ways in which DuPlessis both declares her own poetics and argues with Pound: gender, authority, and reading. There is a long epistemological, cultural, and literary tradition of coding the fragment female (it is little, incomplete, etc.), and indeed DuPlessis herself has been a key figure in unpacking that tradition. Her most consistent critique of Pound is a gender critique that foregrounds his promoting "forms of modernist maleness and, more loosely, of poetic genius [that] depend, as subject positions, on proposing and maintaining a dehistoricized, despecified female figure" (*Blue Studios* 124). As a central example, DuPlessis analyzes the "work of interpretive erasure" (132) that Pound performs, in "Portrait d'une Femme," on the feminist writer and activist Florence Farr. Pound's production of a particular version of modernist maleness "is probably one of his most culturally influential acts within the reception of modernism, as well as its production" (135). DuPlessis already noted in an earlier essay who is absent from the memory poems of the *Pisan Cantos*: the female editors, poets, "and other women cultural workers whom Pound knew. He mentions none. The loss, the erasure, the missing" (*Pink Guitar* 42). Pound's poetics of particularity, that is, fails notably to attend to particular historical women as historical actors (43).

In DuPlessis's reading—a reading directly relevant to our thinking about the form of *Drafts*—Pound actually started the *Cantos* with analogies for the poem's projected form that were "both more 'female' and more popular/populist than the cantos later became" (*Pink Guitar* 46): the bag of tricks, the rag-bag, the quilt, the circus booth, the spilled catch of fish. As we know, he largely rejected or reworked the so-called Ur-Canto I from which these images derive, and early on he questions whether his "many fragments" are "less worth" poetically than the unifying central figure of Robert Browning's eponymous Sordello; addressing Browning, he writes, "You had one whole man? / And I have many fragments, less worth?" ("Three Cantos" 115). The goal became mastery, masculine formal authority, so that for Pound, "[major form] began as a 'rag bag,' a market mess of spilled fish, but became the form of *Analects*, of codes, a great man's laws. *The Cantos*" (*Pink Guitar* 9). Fragments and notes become, later in the *Cantos*, less the basis of form than a measure of failed totalization: "My errors and wrecks lie about me. / And I am not a demigod, / I cannot make it cohere" (796). "Notes" are inadequate to capture the invisible wholeness on which Pound continues to insist: "It coheres all right / even if my notes do not cohere" (797). In other words, for DuPlessis, "Pound is saying that the work failed because its strategies were too feminine" (*Pink Guitar* 46–47). To reframe the argument in its baldest form: *The Cantos* starts out as a female poem, becomes or aspires to become a male one, and finally collapses in its own originary femaleness, reconceived not as formal potential but as detritus.[3]

DuPlessis's contestation with Pound's example takes place, among other sites, on the grounds of the institutional and the pedagogical. Thus in "Draft 57: Workplace: Nekuia," the instructive epic descent into the underworld does not reach the "fosse" of Pound's "Canto I" and of DuPlessis's own "Draft XXX: Fosse." Rather, it is associated with that most mundane of sites, the poet-academic's office: "This is the place I work, / *This is the workspot, the office*" ( *Drafts 39–57* 188). If it is, punningly, *"a sacred office, scared and / or scarred"*—with the sometimes uneasy relationship between poet and scholar perhaps reflected in that between the italics and roman typeface—one still has to walk in every day and "turn on the work-processor" (188). This is a poetry openly engaged with Pound, that asks (tongue-in-cheek) for Tiresias or Virgil or a *Guide to Kulchur*—"Was there a guide"—and that clearly echoes "Canto 45":

> With profit, with profit,
> even the babies
> cannot crawl or suck
> unscathed. The suture occurs
> on the level of cell, in interiority, so that: (*Drafts 39–57* 189)

It is a poetry "that speaks in (and for) the convergence of quirks" (echoing the "quirks and tweaks" of the original "Canto 1") via Poundian "statement, counter-statement, and huge sections / that don't settle anywhere" (194).

If Pound helped invent modernism as the art of the fragment, nevertheless in DuPlessis's reading his "use of fragment and parataxis became a totalitarian and mystical way of carrying out objectivist poetics (*totalitarian*—meaning totalizing and authoritative)." As she continues, Pound "used the fragment to headline affirmative ideas he wished to promulgate," since he "held he had already investigated and was declaring (establishing) permanent results" (*Blue Studios* 189). This position is complicated by arguments such as Christine Froula's discussion of the enhanced authority paradoxically gained by Pound's occasional admission of error, and by Charles Bernstein's insights into how the fractured nature of Pound's formal choices at every point contradicts the aggressively self-confident rhetoric of his public statements on poetics (and everything else).[4] In raising a question about the authoritative/authoritarian in Pound, Bernstein unintentionally offers what can serve as a precise overview of the method of *Drafts*:

> Is cultural megalomania a symptom of being overwhelmed by the incommensurable and intractable autonomy of fragments, that will not submit to a unitary measure, hierarchically predetermined, but which insist on making their own time and space, their own poem: never yielding to the totalizing of the autocratic arbitration of their place but allowing their own whole to come into being, not Coherence on the Pound standard, but a coherence of the displaced—disseminated and desecrated—making a home where it is to be found, where it occurs? (*Poetics* 122)

But the Poundian fragment becomes "totalitarian and mystical," "authoritative," in DuPlessis's reading partly because it is inadequately investigative, used by Pound under the sign of the luminous detail radiating its self-evident truth. In contrast to the tendency, by the mid-late 1930s, for "Pound's poetry [to] settle into his own repeating codes," because "certain values or discoveries are treated as settled" ("Objectivist Poetics" 130), then, her own title, *Drafts*, signals "investigation without allegiance" (*Blue Studios* 250). In a phrase that echoes through *Drafts*, one "can choose to investigate" (*Drafts 1–38* 188) in ways that Pound too often did not. (As Oppen once observed, "if Pound had walked into a factory a few times the absurdity of Douglas' theory of value, which Pound truculently repeats in the Cantos, would have dawned on him—it sometimes pays to have a look And to keep still till one has seen" ["Adequate Vision" 17].) [5]

*The Cantos* begin in a tension between form and ambition, DuPlessis suggests: "If the cantos were to remain personal, quirky, situational, Pound would have had to resolve the issue of authority and of claim he made immediately in those 'pre-Cantos'" (*Pink Guitar* 47). That is, he would have to find a way to embrace mess and contingency more consistently, as a method, and locate poetic authority there. Increasingly, however, "Pound was perplexed by, and resistant to, historical fluidity and its demands on praxis. He wanted things settled once and for all" ("Objectivist Poetry and Poetics" 134). Via DuPlessis's own use of the fragment, *Drafts* counters the masculinist, anti-Semitic obsession with cleanliness, antisepsis, and historical fixity that marks Pound's darkest years: "*Drafts* is pleased to be an unclean, female-penned poem filled with jots and tittles and thoroughly contaminated by traces of the Hebraic. *Drafts* is a poem filled with debris, rot, fragment, corners in which collages of trash collect" (*Blue Stu-*

*dios* 250)—"the categories filth / refuse, shit, debris" (*Drafts 39–57* 153), Pound's vision of hell.

These issues of rhetorical authority that I have been circling around are inseparable, for DuPlessis, from the long-standing question of the reader's relationship to *The Cantos*' difficulty, a topic she has addressed at various points in her career. Faced with Poundian difficulty, DuPlessis argues, "The reader is slid to scholiast, to epigone, to apologist" (*Pink Guitar* 47)—to student, we might say. In this critique, even while Pound thought he was encouraging scholarship, his most influential and original poetic moves were some of his most disempowering: "By radically decontextualizing sources and erasing syntax, [Pound] created a reader who was perpetually evacuated of ways of knowing and, by being perpetually baffled, was made ignorant" (*Blue Studios* 249). Starting with its title, however, *Drafts* distances itself from the confident didacticism that marks Pound's approach to knowing. Both more self-reflexive and more intellectually exploratory than *The Cantos*, in "Draft 57" "the project finding itself out / is itself," asking itself (and ventriloquizing the often-baffled student-reader of the high modernist epic) "*why not simplify this / what will these intricate layers achieve*?" (*Drafts 39–57* 188). In "Draft XXX: Fosse," one of the poems that DuPlessis refers to as an explicit "not-*Canto*," she asks us to "imagine a reader, who would resist / and not resist," "resist / and still articulate" (*Drafts 1–38* 189) a far less forceful pedagogy than that offered by *il miglior fabbro*: "The instruction it offers / is delicate, maybe misplaced," the "it" here referring to a "little book" that is not the little book of Pound's "Envoi" but an Ann Hamilton artist's book "whose words are covered / one by one / with the smallest pebbles" (187), metonyms for the shards out of which DuPlessis, honoring Pound, constructs her demystifying text. If *The Cantos* try to answer their opening "trenchant call across the fosse / to activate / something / is it prophecy? / is it instruction? / is it mourning?" *Drafts*, itself responding to that trenchancy, will "step across" the fosse in far more contingent fashion, "not as demanded in foundational commandment // nor as refused in annihilating compleynt // but just in the course of things // casting oneself to the same winds" (*Drafts 1–38* 192).[6]

The more positive perspective here would see Pound as writing a poem against mastery, except that he exempts himself as author: that is, *The Cantos* are written against everyone's mastery but his own, though that eventually fails too. For DuPlessis, the relationship to the reader is embroiled in Pound's authoritarian rhetoric, involving "the ruthless fantasy that interpretation, discussion, partial understanding, patient unfolding are all contemptible" (250). I think Pound allows for the possibility of the earnestly bumbling lay reader more often than DuPlessis suggests, that his view of reading and readers is less monolithic than she suggests (though certainly miscalculated or misguided much of the time), and that it changes in the course of his career.[7] More to the point here, however, is this question: What is one way for the contemporary writer of the complex serial poem to address the issue of difficulty inherited from Pound? One answer: the use of endnotes, not as addendum but as an intrinsic rhetorical feature of the poem's overall architecture.

DuPlessis has acknowledged *Drafts* as a bricolage of citations from the beginning, and that citationality is reinforced by the poem's paratextual apparatus, its endnotes: a total of 42 single-spaced pages of notes to the 115-poem sequence. "Draft 61: Pyx," one of the most explicitly counter-Poundian drafts, contains this envoi:

> Go, little lines,
> singing in my sullen ear;
> go, half-baked work
> noting, and by the notes begin
> a process of greeting.
> Of gritting.
> Without illusion.
> Darkly, I listen. (*Torques* 22)

While the imagery of noting and notes here refers to the method and music of *Drafts*, and to DuPlessis's main technique for giving texture or "grit" to the work, it also has a third reference: that is, one function of the endnotes is to "begin / a process of greeting" the reader.

DuPlessis's endnotes make explicit what is implicit in the Poundian project. As Jerome McGann writes,

> A poem containing history, written in the twentieth century, means not simply "the tale of the tribe," but the self-conscious presentation of such a tale. It is therefore a poem which will have already theoretically imagined a critical edition of itself. A twentieth-century poem containing history will have to invent and display, somehow, at least the equivalent of footnotes, bibliography, and other scholarly paraphernalia. (*Textual Condition* 129)

This position accords with DuPlessis's account of the long poem's features in a 2008 paper: "Often such a text reorganizes the library; it is a poem that deliberately, nobly, even maliciously absorbs and transposes Great Works of the past while adding its own reading list, including itself." In a note, she adds "not only a text that needs a library, indeed, it is a text that *is* a library—a text itself indebted to, synthetic of, and burrowing through a pile of archival and literary materials, often ones self-declared as vital" ("Considering the Long Poem"). *Drafts* is acutely aware of, and ambivalent about, the institutional context of its own production and reception:

So then it was DAWN,
Dawn over the PMLA
bibliography

articles, books, festschriften
shrive me! father! (*Torques* 21)

We know what the "Poundean mytho-informational model" demands of its readers. The "notational" mode of *Drafts* will not only operate via brief, contingent observations—notations or notes—but will also provide notes to its notes. The porous textual boundary of *Drafts* bleeds into paratext; radically incomplete, there is always something "next" to it. Endnotes can have a range of rhetorics and purposes, but in *Drafts* they suggest that authority does not reside solely within the text, that some kind of supplement is both necessary and appropriate. Indeed, a number of these notes foreground their own nonauthoritativeness, or the writer's own learning process: "It is from this article that I first learned about Mass Observation" (*Drafts 1–38* 271). A combination of the precise and the casual, the notes resist consistent formatting: they include full citations, partial citations, relative noncitations or bare mentions. At one extreme of punctiliousness we find the following: "The last line is an almost-accurate citation from Bonnie Costello, 'Planets on Tables: Still Life and War in the Poetry of Wallace Stevens.' *Modernism/Modernity* 12.3 (Sept. 2005), 451" (*Torques* 137), scholarship as the language of poetry. At the other end of the spectrum: "John Berger, on Picasso" (*Drafts 1–38* 271), or "among other sources, some undergraduate students saying particular things," or "'little i' comes from somewhere I can't now remember" (276). We are invited not so much to investigate allusions or something "behind" the text, to pursue sources, as simply to note their existence. The trope of saying that a line has a source without knowing what it is points to citationality as a fact of the text rather than actually explaining or locating the citation. On the whole, further investigation will not yield further information or insight. What is at work, then, is not Poundian allusiveness, with DuPlessis playing Carroll Terrell to her own poem, but an ethics and aesthetics of acknowledgment and dependence on others.[8]

Appropriately, if one of the endnotes' functions is to construct a space of greeting between writer and reader, the notes occasionally offer directions on how to read. The note on "Draft 23: Findings" contains the following explanation of the poem's procedural construction: "The reader might already have surmised that each section of this poem both enacts an hour of the day and also refers or alludes to the prior Draft corresponding to its particular number" (274). The note to "Draft 36" gives us that poem as procedural self-citation: "Draft 36: Cento . . . is a 'patchwork'—a poem in which every line is cited, often from epics. This is a partial cento, built of 99 lines—and that, for its simple allusion to the wrong word, 'cent,' or one hundred. Here at least every third line is cited, 'borrowed' from my own long poem" (277).

I have reviewed quite extensively so far DuPlessis's own accounts of her project, not inappropriately in the case of this persistently self-descriptive, self-examining, self-questioning poem ("the poem is like a self-gloss mechanism," as she puts it ["Interview" 407]). But if, as DuPlessis writes, "I wanted to make an alternative *Cantos*, a counter-*Cantos*" (*Blue Studios* 250), what does a specific counter-canto look like? How does it engage with Pound? What I pursue here is less a detailed reading, more what I consider a demonstration of method. "Draft 61: Pyx" is one of three poems in the sequence (the others are "Draft XXX" and "Draft 57") in which "*Drafts* explicitly positions itself as not-Cantos" (278n9). At the same time, it includes numerous citations from the *Canti postumi*, Massimo Bacigalupo's edition of outtakes and uncollected drafts of *The Cantos*.[9] That is, *Drafts*—or at least this Draft—incorporates Pound's drafts. It is divided by boldface subheadings, often punning in their fracturing of language and bringing play into sites of Poundian authority and homosociality. The opening section, for instance, features a "lone" female speaker resisting an unspecified "tour [of] his office" led by an "old man" who "tapped his cane, surrounded / by other men / showing the faculty or facility / a faculty for what?" (*Torques* 21)—a scene that seems somehow to splice Pound at the Ezuversity or St. Elizabeths, with his famous cane and attended by neophytes, with the young DuPlessis's sense of marginalization in a male-dominated academy. (Regarding the poet's cane, DuPlessis surely knows Amy Lowell's poem "Astigmatism," in which, in an allegory of masculinist canonizing, "the Poet"—apparently Pound—whacks the heads off various flowers with his assiduously crafted "walking-stick / Of fine and polished ebony" because none of the flowers are roses) (12). And the title of this introductory section? "INTRO DUCE," split in half to read as an "intro [to Il] Duce" and to invoke Pound's hero Mussolini.

The next section, "BEG IN," returns to notes again, or more specifically to the idea of a "melodic germ," a very un-Poundian splicing of music and infection just as the self-descriptive "dirty rumbled tune" (*Torques* 25) runs counter to the cleanly precisions of Poundian melopoeia. But DuPlessis acknowledges that "smelling 'the stench of stale oranges'" (the phrase comes from "Canto 14") involves "a touching quotidian / a domestic sensitivity / amid influx of beetles, / broken cloacas, / and meeds of merde" (*Torques* 22), a counternote within the satiric violence and vulgarity of the hell cantos. DuPlessis uses an aural and typographical tweaking of a Poundian phrase to consider the curve of his career: "Was it hell rot or 'he'll rot'?" (22), suggesting the later rot of Pound's mind and values. And yet in 1945 Pound was still capable of something approaching the fierce incredulity of the hell cantos in a way that speaks to the present: as cited in "Draft 61," "**my mind stretched to the bursting point / with this enormity / with the continuity of the gun-sales**" (23).

While DuPlessis and Pound share that quintessential modernist method of making "evidence" and "findings" out of "clutter," "pilings," "clippings," the passage in which DuPlessis lays out this commonality moves in a more Poundian direction in its invocation of the "moon afloat, / silvery eclipses cool down / in luminous cloud-shadow" (23). The seductive rhetoric of Poundian pastoral here invites the question of how to disidentify from the more problematic aspects of his poetics: "How to resist a world-system?" (23). The counterchallenge is "How to get a handle on it / How to keep the rage complex" (25)—something that, one would have to say, Pound tended not to do in, for instance, the obsession with credit and conspiracy reflected in this outtake from the *Cantos* that DuPlessis quotes: "**ledt hoo vill rhun de harmies, / if I can gontroll th gredit**" (25). Again, however, it is a dialectical Pound we have here, the phonetic spelling of the anti-Semitic conspiracy theorist next to the vivid imagery of the World War I about which Pound continued to write for years: "**greasy flame of dead gas flare // a thick air / and a stifled silence**" (25).

DuPlessis talks back to Pound most explicitly as "the extra 'r'" in his misspelled "**Mt. Arrarat**" (27). This Jewish woman imagines herself othered as victims of the Holocaust were, through a process in which Pound actively participated. Thus, like all admirers of Pound's poetry, she has had to come to terms with his Fascist politics, and particularly his lack of political self-doubt. Her speaker asks incredulously, "and never halting? never faltering?" (28) This speaker imagines herself as she might be perceived from a hypothetical Poundian perspective, "you stupid nothing r," "the little tiny Jew / poking a nose somewhere / to find something" (28). The Jew as nosey plague-carrying rodent: "contaminated by traces of the Hebraic" indeed. During World War II Pound wrote, in another outtake cited in "Draft 61," "**How is it, I said: that the ghosts are so gathered?**" These ghosts are simultaneously the impetuous, impotent dead of "Canto I," cited a few lines later, the characters populating Pound's memory, and the dead of the Holocaust: Jerome Rothenberg's *dybukkim*, soundless voices, "these Shadows [who] make antiphonal claims // as words that fail" (29)—for in *Drafts* (as for George Oppen), to write, to enter language, is to fail.[10] "The page [is] a cavernous echo chamber / of that" (30), capturing the shadows and silence of the dead in an echo chamber antiphonal to that echo chamber of the self from which Pound delivered his Rome broadcasts.

What remains powerful in Pound for DuPlessis? What she calls the "grief and intransigence" (*Pink Guitar* 42) of the *Pisan Cantos*, for one thing. She observes that "over the course of writing a [multigeneric] long poem, one genre can grow in importance (. . . elegy for Pound in the *Pisan Cantos*)" ("Considering the Long Poem"), and indeed elegy—the poetics of memory and loss—is one crucial mode in *Drafts*. And she "acknowledge[s] . . . his political rage and despair, and his hyperstimulation, for he is literally overwhelmed, drowned in data, in the storm of history, in the floods of mud, water, in the dangerous pools in the early cantos" (*Blue Studios* 247), Malatesta up to his neck in the swamp of "Canto IX." For DuPlessis, this is one defining condition of her poetry: a response to "scale far beyond any humanist tempering . . . the universe, the earth, our history and politics, the sense of the past, and the more febrile sense of the future: in short, plethora, hyper-stimulation, an overwhelmedness to which one responds" ("Considering the Long Poem"), such that "the long poem is a work of mastery during which you submit to your own powerlessness" (*Blue Studio* 240). Another explicit not-canto, "Draft XXX: Fosse," refers, in one of its many moments of self-description, to "a book of the unraveling voice / incapable and swamped / in the same time as the self" (*Drafts 1–38* 188), and for DuPlessis it is *that* Pound who can still compel: the unraveling voice, incapable, swamped in time, "saturation / beyond catalogue" (20).

# 9

## "Drawings with Words"

### Susan Howe's Visual Feminist Poetics

> Letters are sounds we see. Sounds leap to the eye. Word lists, crosses, blanks, and ruptured stanzas are points of contact and displacement. Line breaks and visual contrapuntal stresses represent an athematic compositional intention. . . . Spaces between letters, dashes, apostrophes, commas, crosses, form networks of signs and discontinuities.
>
> —Susan Howe, *The Birth-mark*

> What if these penciled single double and triple scorings arrows short phrases angry outbursts crosses cryptic ciphers sudden enthusiasms mysterious erasures have come to find you too, here again, now.
>
> —Susan Howe, *The Nonconformist's Memorial*

The extensive critical commentary on Susan Howe now pays increasing attention to the material, visual dimension of her poetry—page layout, deployment of white space, her many forms of palimpsestic text or overwriting, reproduced visual images and diagrams.[1] If one could agree broadly at the time with Howe's 1993 complaint that critics "very rarely" "consider poetry as a physical act . . . [or] look at the print on the page, at the shapes of words, at the surface—the space of the paper itself" (*Birth-mark* 157), the generalization no longer applies to her own readers. In this chapter I examine the visual aspects of Howe's poetry via some questions that, while sometimes addressed in these readings, still warrant further treatment: How do page and typographical design connect to Howe's particular brand of feminist poetics? And relatedly, how do the multiple possibilities for reading created by Howe's visually exploded page and use of space relate to her examining and decentering of a frequently patriarchal authority? To see Howe's use of page space solely or too persistently in gender terms would be to narrow the range of its effects, to impose on her a version of her own (admittedly arguable) opinion that "women who take a theoretical position are allowed to take a theoretical position only as long as it's a feminist theoretical position, and to me that's an isolation" ("Interview" [by Keller] 21). At the same time, as Rachel Blau DuPlessis argues, gender questions in Howe (which are nearly always historiographical questions at the same time) do frequently take the form of "line breaks, page canvas, the use of space/silence/silencing/ the piercing of whiteness" (*Pink Guitar* 132). To this extent Howe's visual page—especially in the work from the first half of her career that helped establish her reputation and that I focus on here—invites a gendered reading.

Howe's beginnings as a painter are well known, and critics have proposed various terms that are applicable to discussing her use of the page as a kind of canvas.[2] In an essay on Anne-Marie Albiach that is directly relevant to Howe's work, DuPlessis writes of the "visual text or page poem"—"a concerted, intended, and forthright use of the white space of the page, not as neutral, unnoticed, and uncritically accepted, but as a deliberate ground for the text's typography and placement." And this "page poem has a transgressive aim" ("'White Fiction'" 168, 170).[3] Nathaniel Mackey's term for the foregrounding of the visual, material aspects of the poetic text is "graphicity." For Mackey, as for DuPlessis, the graphic impulse suggests "a principle of tolerance . . . for its disruptive, de-formalist thrust, often outright celebration of it" (123). While Johanna Drucker uses the terms "graphic poetics," "visual poetics" and "graphical aesthetics" ("Not Sound" 239–40; "Graphical Readings" 269) to theorize her attention to all the graphical elements of the written page, including the most conventional, these terms remain particularly useful for what Drucker calls "works [like Howe's] that conspicuously explore the potential of graphicality as their initial impulse" ("Not Sound" 240) in a post-Mallarméan tradition. Finally, Michael Davidson's notion of the "palimtext" captures usefully both the material forms of Howe's layered intertextuality and their ideological implications: "As its name implies, the palimtext retains vestiges of prior inscriptions out of which it emerges. Or, more accurately, it is the still-visible record of its responses to those earlier writings" (*Ghostlier Demarcations* 68). When this mode makes marginal(ized) and so-called authoritative texts collide, as it does in Howe's hands, "the poem as palimtext becomes a window onto forces of stabilization in the culture at large" (92).

These palimtextual or palimpsestic "prior inscriptions" are partly comprised of the (gendered) history of poetry, and considerations particularly of the "blank" page as palimpsest, with its roots in H.D., reach a critical mass in the experimental women poets of Howe's generation and after. As Susan Gevirtz puts it, in the context of thinking through a feminist avant-garde poetics, "neither [screen nor page] are blank—ever—they arrive already written upon" (655).[4] Rosmarie Waldrop writes similarly that "the blank page is not blank. . . . Whether we are conscious of it or not, we always write on top of a palimpsest" (207). For DuPlessis, the title of her 1987 book *Tabula Rosa* "implied that both mind and writing space are infused and inflected with gender in manifold ways; the page is never blank; it is already written with conventions, prior texts, and cultural ideas" ("Darkest Gush").When Kathleen Fraser says "as a contemporary writer, I have been called back to this blank page again and again," she refers to H.D.'s invoking "the blank pages / of the unwritten volume of the new" as "a literal invitation of breathtaking immensity and independence to contemporary woman poets" (55). For Fraser, not unlike Howe, "my page wanted to be inscribed as if it were a canvas" (57). Fraser summarizes the connections between gender and the visual page in a 1988 essay:

> The frame of the page . . . has provided for many contemporary women poets the difficult pleasure of reinventing the givens of poetry, imagining in visual, structural terms core states of female social and psychological experience not yet adequately tracked: hesitancy, silencing, or speechlessness, continuous disruption of time, "illogical" resistance, simultaneous perceptions and agendas, social marginality. (142)

Meanwhile, closer to the present, in the "Working Note" to her erasure project on Shakespeare's sonnets, *Nets* (2004), Jen Bervin writes, "When we write poems, the history of poetry is with us, pre-inscribed in the white of the page; when we read or write poems, we do it with or against this palimpsest" (np). In this conceptual project, Bervin "stripped Shakespeare's sonnets bare to the 'nets' to make the space of the poems open, porous, possible—a divergent elsewhere." Notably, the part of "sonnets" that fades into the background to produce her title is "son."

Before advancing to my main argument about graphicity in Howe, about her palimtextual/palimpsestic "page poems" or "visual pages," it is worth contextualizing further this aspect of her work. Craig Dworkin summarizes usefully what Howe's page poems are *not*. They are not Olsonian scores for performance; they are not sites for experimentation with the materials of printing—ink, type, font, and so forth; they are not shape, picture, or pattern poems; they are not concrete poetry (*Reading the Il-*

*legible* 32–34). While her pages are indeed not designed as keys to breath or performance, however, Howe's poetry remains much more in the line of Olson than in that of the international avant-garde traditions of visual poetry traced by Willard Bohn and Drucker.[5] More significantly, for Howe, page space is directly connected with the feminine in Olson: "The feminine is very much in his poems. . . . It has to do with the presence of absence. With articulation of sound forms. The fractured syntax, the gaps, the silences are equal to the sounds in *Maximus*. That's what [George] Butterick saw so clearly. He printed Olson's Space" (*Birth-mark* 180).[6] Along similar lines, Fraser proposes Olson's importance more generally—even given his unsympathetic gender politics—for contemporary female practitioners of a visual poetics. She argues that women writers investigating "the visual potential of the page" "would have lacked such a clear concept of PAGE as canvas or screen on which to project flux without the major invitation Olson provided . . . this, in spite of his inclusive/exclusive boy-talk" (176). These writers, then, have claimed Olson's experiments "for entirely different uses and meanings—notations mapped directly out of the very lives Olson tended to discredit by his act of non-address" (177).

Fraser's argument and the perhaps surprising juxtaposition of space and the feminine in Howe's reading of Olson help address the risk of essentializing "space" in approaching Howe's page poems. The issue is how space on the page is deployed and populated—not in what the space "is," then, but in how it is used. The differences between and within male and female uses of space (with Olson, Howe, and Albiach representing three points on that spectrum) make it clear that we cannot mark page space as intrinsically gendered; the question is what space means in Howe, not what it means, period. DuPlessis points out that in Albiach's *Mezza Voce* the blank page is gendered male: "*The donné of this work is that the male figure is the page on which the woman is attempting to write*," with whiteness as the possibility of male erasure of the female word ("'White Fiction'" 170). In Howe, however, as DuPlessis argues elsewhere, white space functions in an implicitly gender-based way "as a trope for an anti-authoritarian practice. The foregrounding of otherness. The critique of centers, hierarchies, authorities. The suspicion of dominant meaning. The apprehension of power" (*Pink Guitar* 133).[7]

Not surprisingly, Howe connects her design of page space to her painterly beginnings. She has remarked that if she could paint her writing, "it would be blank. It would be a white canvas. White" ("Speaking" 42), and as she moved from painting (in which she worked in collage forms) to mixing pictures, paintings, and lists of words in artist's books, she "always left a lot of white space on the page" ("Interview" [by Keller]

5). Howe suggests elsewhere in this interview that the word for her is also fallen, finite, a corruption or interruption of the "infinite purpose or purposelessness" of the page: "In poetry I am concerned with the space of the page apart from the words on it. I would say that the most beautiful thing of all is a page before the word interrupts it" (7). At the same time, the word on that page/canvas is itself always visual too: "Words, even single letters, are images. The look of a word is part of its meaning" (6). Such remarks echo observations from her essay "The End of Art" twenty years earlier on the letter as visual: in Ian Hamilton Finlay's environmental concrete poem "Fisherman's Cross," "there are no vertical letters, just as there are no sharp sounds to pull the ear or eye up or down," Howe writes, and she reads Finlay's "Homage to Malevich" in terms of the effects of "vertical letters" and "round short letters" (*Quarry* 219–20). (As she writes in a 1988 symposium on the poetic line, "First I was a painter, so for me, words shimmer. Each one has an aura. Lines are laid on the field of a page, so many washes of watercolor" [Untitled 209]).[8] She stresses that the visual design of her work is intended to register what she calls a "meaning connection" among its overlapping parts: "The getting it right has to do with how it's structured on the page as well as how it sounds—this is the meaning" ("Interview" [by Keller] 8). We should take as foundational for Howe Mallarmé's epochal statement that "the Page . . . is taken as the basic unit, in the way that elsewhere the Verse or the perfect line is" (*Collected Poems* 121–22).[9] Given that the structure of Howe's page is integral to its meaning, as readers we need to consider how that is so and to do so in a way that goes beyond, without necessarily neglecting, notions of imitative form.

Introducing her 1994 interview with Howe, Lynn Keller notes that "[Howe's] writing embodies absence . . . in its dramatic use of space on the page" (Howe, "Interview" 1). This is a useful formulation, not least in its paradoxical notion of embodying absence (or what Howe calls "the presence of absence" in Olson). The question then becomes, whose absence is thus embodied, and how? That question moves us toward the connection between Howe's use of the visual and her distinctive feminism, toward understanding how her page space and design reflects forms of and responses to the erasure and silencing of female historical presence(s). In one of the earliest (1982) essays on Howe, and against the backdrop of "endless discussion groups dealing with the topic of the 'poli[t]ically correct' woman writer," Tina Darragh reads Howe herself as "placing her work firmly in the matriarchal tradition," her method for doing so "experimentation with the patterns of words handed down to her" (547–49). Typically in Howe the female runs as a visible thread (one of her recurrent images, as it has been for many women writers) through the work, appearing and receding. No sooner does the figure of Mary Magdalene enter "The Nonconformist's Memorial," and theological history, via a quotation from St. John's Gospel, than "the act of Uniformity // ejected her" (*Nonconformist's Memorial* 5), in appropriately evenly spaced, left-justified, uniform lines. Over the next few pages, however, Mary returns as a subscript to disrupt this uniformity, as an echoing, marginal presence in upside-down lines. Use of reversed text (6; see fig. 9.1), Howe says, "conveys [Mary's] erasure" from canonical accounts of the resurrection but also her continuing repressed presence: "I was trying to illustrate the process of her interruption and erasure, and that she's continuing through these narratives" ("Interview" [by Keller] 11). Woman is the reversed underside of this sequence; or to put it another way, subversion (etymologically, "overturning from underneath") within the text is gendered female: "Pronoun *I* or her name // Or break its boundaries" appears upside down to complicate the "intractable ethical paradox // Vindicated by uprightness" (20; see fig. 9.2), including the uprightness of the page itself. "She" appears, that is, typed semilegibly under and within the "upright" male text, as "Undertype Shadow Sacrifice," "Waiting for a restoration / and righteousness" (26).

In Peter she is nameless
Actual world nothing ideal

headstrong anarchy thoughts
A single thread of narrative

She was coming to anoint him
As if all history were a progress

Figure 9.1. Susan Howe, *Nonconformist's Memorial*, p. 6

Intractable ethical paradox

Or break its boundaries
Vindicated by uprightness

Pronoun *I* or her name
utter immensities whisper

Figure 9.2. Susan Howe, *Nonconformist's Memorial*, p. 20

Rendering visible the female, textual, or historical (in Howe these three typically intertwine) "Undertype Shadow" requires Howe to reconstruct the page. In her preface to "A Bibliography of the King's Book or, Eikon Basilike," she reiterates, using Pierre Macherey, the familiar position that any discourse is "'coiled about an absent centre which it can neither conceal nor reveal'" (50)—an "absent centre" that suggests the instability of authorship, the untraceability of origins, the textuality of history. It seems that from the first Howe saw these issues taking visual form in the sequence:

> So I wanted to write something filled with gaps and words tossed, and words touching, words crowding each other, letters mixing and falling away from each other, commands and dreams, verticals and circles. If it was impossible to print, that didn't matter. Because it's about impossibility anyway. About the impossibility of putting in print what the mind really sees and the impossibility of finding the original in a bibliography. (*Birth-mark* 175)

Given these remarks on writing "Eikon Basilike," it is appropriate that, after Howe's customary prose preface, the sequence begins in instant breakdown. The first poem (see fig. 9.3) is a canvas of erasures ("nfortunate," "un ust"), erratic spacings, archaic-seeming nonce words achieved by the inversion of letters ("u" becomes "n" in "Futnre") and actual archaic spellings ("comand," "woule"), Latin and French ("OMne," "envions"), typographical slippage ("Mans"), jammed-together double meanings (the weaving term "beering" and the notion of royal "bearing"), a whole range of "obwructions transposed"—this latter phrase printed upside down, fittingly enough—into a poem (*Nonconformist's Memorial* 51). Unpacking a poem like this parallels the uncertain twists and turns of the historiographical and bibliographical process generally and more specifically Howe's own process of researching the *Eikon Basilike*. Like Howe herself, we find ourselves confronting a text with no center, offering multiple possible directions for reading. This is what it is like—for writer and reader—to try and catch the "Horrifying drift errancy" (*Nonconformist's Memorial* 66) of history.

At one level, the "absent center" of this sequence is the ghostly King Charles I—the absent center of patriarchal power—who may or may not have written the book, the *Eikon Basilike*, whose provenance and history Howe investigates.[10] But in "Eikon Basilike" as elsewhere Howe also renders the persistently sought absence in visual terms and genders it female: "She is the blank page / writing ghost writing" (*Nonconformist's Memo-*

Oh Lord
o Lord
different from
Laws
zeal
transposed
beering
OMne
envions
obwructions
comand

nfortunate Man
s

un ust
woule
Futnre
audPaged doe of Title-page

Figure 9.3. Susan Howe, *Nonconformist's Memorial*, p. 51

*rial* 68), that "she" phasing into tentative agency as a "ghost writing" (or, more declaratively, "she is . . . / writing"), as if to anticipate Anne Waldman's call in her "Feminafesto" "that the page not be empty female awaiting penetration by dark phallic ink-juice" (24). Along with its other subjects, Howe's poem concerns not just the "fanatical swift moving authority" (*Nonconformist's Memorial* 72) of the Puritan regicides but how the grammatical and judicial "Sentences" of "Judges and ghostly fathers" constitute the "Opening words of *Patriarcha*" (71), and how, in such a history, the female is only a trace—a term that, as both noun and verb, recurs throughout Howe's oeuvre. A thread or trace left by those ancient workers in thread, "Archaic Arachne Ariadne," a long-standing but tenuous mythic presence, "She is gone she sends her memory" (69). Yet that memory floats visibly through the text, for instance in the broken summary of the Ariadne myth. "Trace weft" (79), Howe instructs herself, and we realize that this female weft can be traced back to the "beering," a dividing of the warp, of the sequence's first poem (51). This "weft" or "Thread," this "Thought" of the "daughter" (and daughter of the king, Minos) winds through the "*Centuries*" tangled on Howe's page (79; see fig. 9.4).

Both in this sequence and in a larger patriarchal history, this female face has been gotten rid of, hidden, swaddled, clothed ("SWADLIER Centuries I No rhid Face CLOATHE" [79; see fig. 9.4]). But Howe's page makes "dominant ideologies drift" (80), and the thread of the female, of Ariadne, drifts through the history and texts that would obscure it. Rachel Tzvia

utmost

light

mote

Spir e

Therfrom
evry
edge
all

Ariadne — led Theseus — Illimited

let down — in every

perceptive

Minos' from
daughter Thread

Sphere

pierced
Light symbolism

Thought — Trace
weft

daughter

SWADLIER Centuries — I No
rhid

Fire — To her — Face

fate — CLOATHE

distant

the lay

Island place
deathless

Place they stood on
Stars

away who remember
Flood — Crown

she wore
and the sea

Eyes — up

to
Fire

Figure 9.4. Susan Howe, *Nonconformist's Memorial*, p. 79

Back refers to "the gendered antinomian" in the sequence, a figure familiar from *The Birth-mark*, "represented by the female subject appearing midway in the text and, in multiple guises, hovering over the poem for a number of pages, only to disappear and then reappear more forcefully at the poem's close" (150). This subject appears as the "fictive Pamela" (*Nonconformist's Memorial* 49) of Sir Philip Sidney's *Arcadia*, whose presence John Milton uses to argue the *Eikon Basilike*'s inauthenticity, and reappears later as the same "heathen woman / out of heathen legend" (67); she appears as an unnamed sister figure, and as the wife of Bishop John Gauden, the cleric who claimed authorship of the *Eikon Basilike*. In the last poem of the sequence (see fig. 9.5), her name may be unstable, "ARACHNE" or "Ariagne"; it may still be inverted and thus made harder to read, in the interstices of another text; but it enjoys a central place on the page, capitalized next to the male SUN as his equal, companion, and inversion. Like Arachne, Howe has been subtly "winding wool" through the "Eikon Basilike" sequence, "trace" and "weft" bending and stretching on this page but holding, her female "thread" on the righthand side running through the male military "shield"—a shield from the separated letters of which emerges female potential and purpose, the homophonic "she'll."[11] And so we conclude with "soft thread," but soft thread with "a twist," in a way that calls up Ariadne, an apocryphal Shelley poem cited in the *OED* entry for "weft," and the first poem of the sequence. "Weft" threads cross from side to side at right angles to the warp threads with which they are interlaced, the ends of which are divided into the beers referred to in the sequence's beginning. A weft-way thread is *twisted* to the right in spinning. But "weft" can also mean a streak of cloud, as in "To the Queen of my Heart," once thought to be written by Shelley: "And thy beauty more bright / Than the stars' soft light, / Shall seem as a weft from the sky."[12]

Like much of the French feminist theory, particularly that of Julia Kristeva, circulating at the time of Howe's writing these sequences and being read by her and many other experimental women poets, Howe's poetics associates the feminine with rupture, gaps, erasure, absence—visually, with various forms of fragmented text or "empty" space.[13] "She must be traced through many dark paths"—isolated at the bottom of the page after a lot of space, almost like a footnote, in the Kulchur Foundation version of "The Liberties," and on her own page in the Sun and Moon reprint, but either way "to be read by guesswork through obliteration" (*Europe* 162, 163).[14] Howe comments explicitly on her association of space with the suppressed feminine when she says: "If you are a woman, archives hold perpetual ironies. Because the gaps and silences are where you find yourself" (*Birth-mark* 158). Or rather, we might say, where you don't find yourself, the spaces where you would find yourself if you were there: as

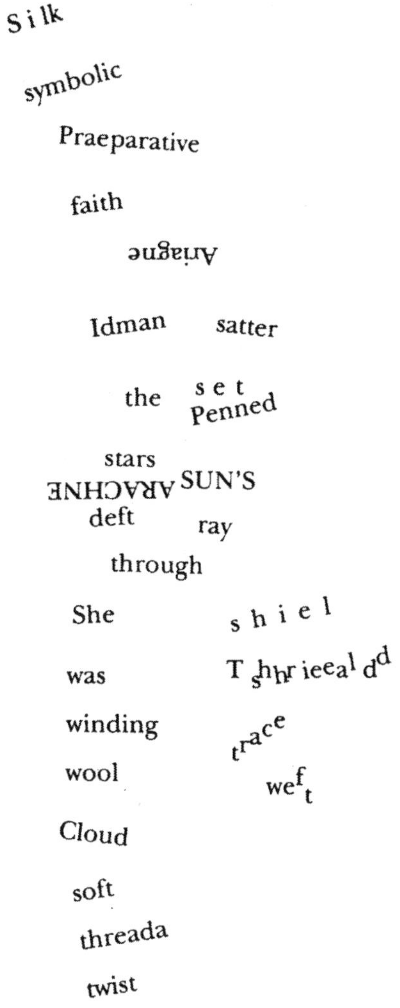

Silk

symbolic

Praeparative

faith

Ariagne

Idman satter

the set Penned

stars

ARACHNE SUN'S

deft ray

through

She shiel

was T shhr ieeal dd

winding trace

wool weft

Cloud

soft

threada

twist

Figure 9.5. Susan Howe, *Nonconformist's Memorial*, p. 82

Harryette Mullen writes, "of a girl, in white, between the lines, in the spaces where nothing is written" (22). If "the real plot [is] invisible," (*Europe* 169), as Howe puts it in "The Liberties," then we must look to invisibility for the real plot.

In the section of "The Liberties" called "Formation of a Separatist, I," both the formation of a female self and the lifting of Jonathan Swift's beloved Esther Johnson out of historical invisibility are accomplished visually. In contrast to the section's beginning in full predication with a male warrior who "swung his sword / said he would slash and slay" (204), the historical female self is reconstructed out of single words arranged in a porous block on the page. Amid that construction (set up on the previous page by a buried narrative of building in white stone like the white of the page) "Stella" (Swift's name for Johnson) is freed from the closed parentheses of history to become a part of the primary text:

stirring inlaid (      ) enclosure
                    stellar

—the parenthesis not quite wide enough to contain her (204). "The Liberties" had begun by connecting the materiality of print and female silence: "Page in her coffin. . . . / Do those dots mean that the speaker lapsed / into silence?" (158). Finally, however, visuality and materiality help produce an emergent self: "Print   pen   dot   i   still / hole   yew   skip   1" (206). Print and pen dot (or complete) the "i," which is emerging tentatively as widely spaced fragments of text, unsure if it is whole or "hole" and with its relationships guardedly encoded in pun ("yew" and "i"). "I" in these pages is simultaneously Stella, *King Lear*'s Cordelia, and Howe, who is "formed" in a complex combination of visual compression, erasure, and displacement. Her name enters as a riddle complete with an (unnecessary) key that resembles a key*board* and that contains elements of textual mystery ("enigma," "crypto,"), the male ("mastif"), and the female ("femiated"): "e n i g m a s t i f e m i a t e d c r y p t o a t h."[15] Place becomes writing ("graphy," with the "geo-" dropped), and Howe's "I" emerges out of Ireland only by being displaced to the next line and then needing to "re-land" ("reland / I") (209).

Countermanding the power represented in "The Liberties" by Swift, Lear, and the slashing warrior, Howe insistently uses visual design in her work—as I have already suggested with regard to *Eikon Basilike*—to render suspect notions of authority and centrality. She drafts poems and keeps notes in blank notebooks, on a page where "there is no up or down, backwards or forwards. You impose a direction by beginning" ("Interview" [by Keller] 6)—a description that could apply equally well to the reading of her own more visually hyperactive pages. Those pages radically destabilize our typical reading processes, collapsing the very categories of the vertical and the horizontal. Howe often constructs a page so that it is hard to know either where to begin or in what direction to proceed.[16] Indeed she resists the idea of an authoritative or "right" reading even of her own pages: "The way they look profoundly affects the reading, for me, anyway. I can't speak for anyone else" (13). Through their layout, the poems deny the possibility both of an authoritative point of view within the text or an authoritative movement through it. In Howe's page poems, what cannot be read from one point of view can be read from another. No one position is central; "singularities of space" create "possibilities of choice" (*Birth-mark* 181).

"He / said you know print settles it" (*Nonconformist's Memorial* 150). According to this unnamed male authority, print stabilizes a manuscript (such as Emily Dickinson's) and appears to resolve unanswered questions it might raise. "Print is sentinel," guarding against surprise, against irregularity (150); "print beats imagination back" (*Birth-mark* 66). This is the view that Howe takes of the editing of Dickinson's manuscripts, a view that has had significant influence in Dickinson studies. Especially relevant here is the relationship that Howe lays out, in commenting on Dickinson's editorial history, between visually normalizing print conventions and questions of patriarchal authority, tradition, custom, and propriety. Howe reads Thomas Johnson's editing of Dickinson's handwritten manuscripts as the exercise of male editorial control over an innovative female writer's visual disruptiveness, over the marks of her excess.[17] For Dickinson's editors and the institution (Harvard) that they represent, "the conventions of print require humilities of caution. Obedience to tradition. Dress up dissonance. Customary usage." In practice this means that, for instance, "lines will be brought into line," "subdivided in conformity with propriety" (*Birth-mark* 140). As a result of such editing, Howe argues, "provoking visual fragmentation will be banished from the body of the 'poem proper'" and "the production of meaning will be brought under the control of social authority" (140), even as the gender-coded "polyphonic visual complexity" (141) of Dickinson's manuscripts resists that control in the interest of a visual "scattering" of meaning, "indirection," "uncertainty," "indecipherable variation" (148)—meaning as excess, not access.

The element of self-description and self-justification in Howe's account of Dickinson's manuscripts should be clear. "Lines trail off interrupting sense. Margins perish into edges tipped by crosses and calligraphic slashes" ("Women" 79)—comments like this describe equally a Dickinson manuscript page and many Howe pages. In the case of Dickinson, editing such pages involved the exercise of a royal, almost divinely ordained, male power: Dickinson's editor, Johnson, who "has chosen a sovereign system for her line endings—his preappointed Plan" (79). Howe uses the space of her page actively to destabilize such relations between margin and center. She creates "a page space that is a canvas of margins" (DuPlessis, *Pink Guitar* 136), perhaps nowhere more bluntly than in two pages of "Melville's Marginalia" (*Nonconformist's Memorial* 96–97) (see figs.9.6 and 9.7). The first page quotes that canonical defense of centralizing literary institutions, Matthew Arnold's "The Literary Influence of Academies," while a vertical

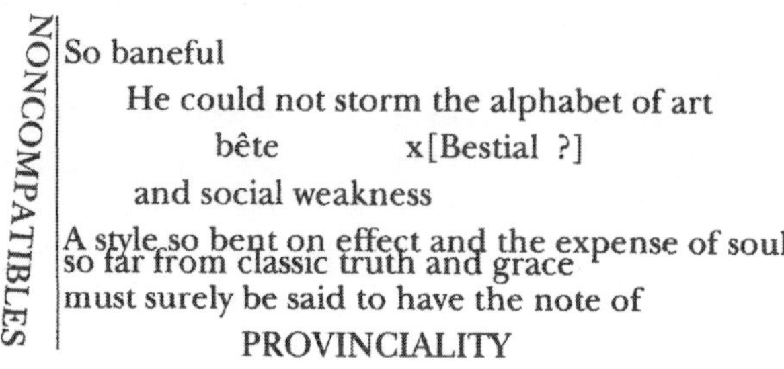

NONCOMPATIBLES
So baneful
He could not storm the alphabet of art
bête x[Bestial ?]
and social weakness
A style so bent on effect and the expense of soul
so far from classic truth and grace
must surely be said to have the note of
PROVINCIALITY


Figure 9.6. Susan Howe, *Nonconformist's Memorial*, p. 96

line firmly marginalizes from that text, at an opposing angle, the word "NONCOMPATIBLES," a class that the obscure and eccentric nineteenth-century poet James Clarence Mangan (and perhaps Howe herself) would surely fit. The opposite page has been emptied of its authoritative, evaluative discourse, however; "SIMPLETONS," visually connecting with "NONCOMPATIBLES," is similarly marginal, but the center has been emptied and the margins are shaky, uncertain—two nonparallel lines on the left, broken on the right, and on both sides no longer confidently vertical. And though not explicitly so in these two poems, these margin-center relations are typically gendered for Howe. In "Melville's Marginalia," Elizabeth Melville and Mary Shelley are writers in the margins of Promethean male texts, and, as elsewhere in Howe, the unpacking of margins that she announces as her project yields female presences, in a nice phonetic parody of canonical male bonding as three female Shakespearean musketeers replace Dumas's male trio: "I will dismember marginalia / 'l' for 'i' and 'i' for 'l' / Ophelia Juliet Cordelia" (*Nonconformist's Memorial* 146).

One could readily work through numerous other examples of the intersection of visual design and a gender-based social critique in Howe's early and midcareer work: the groping investigation of a father-daughter relationship and of the idea of the hero via the partial marks and sounds on an open page in *Secret History of the Dividing Line*; the visual regulation of the female-named Hope Atherton's discursive wanderings in controlled square forms and the mythic or prehistorical female presence searched for throughout "Articulation of Sound Forms in Time"; in "Thorow," the comparable search for "she, the Strange, excluded from formalism," whose "forms of wildness . . . become desire and multiply" (*Singularities* 41) in the shattered pages and floating word fragments that conclude that sequence. In these sequences, as well as in those I have touched on here, we can see some of the ways in which Howe visually, as well as thematically

Figure 9.7. Susan Howe, *Nonconformist's Memorial*, p. 97

and stylistically, answers her own question: "How do I, choosing messages from the code of others in order to participate in the universal theme of Language, pull SHE from all the myriad symbols and sightings of HE" (*My Emily Dickinson* 17–18).

This "pulling" calls for work with margins, space, thread, invisibility—visual figures of the feminine, from Emily Dickinson (at least that far back) to Howe. And to, among others, Rae Armantrout, alluding (it is possible to argue) to Dickinson but in a way equally applicable to Howe. This stanza from Armantrout's "Getting Warm" provides a fitting conclusion to a discussion of Howe's visual poetics:

> She is in the dark,
> sewing, stringing holes together
> with invisible thread.
> That's a feminine accomplishment:
> a feat of memory, a managed
> repletion or resplendence. (*Necromance* 43)

Armantrout's lines, which ironize her central image in the act of claiming it, may remind us of R. P. Blackmur's notorious description of Dickinson as "a private poet who wrote indefatigably as some women cook or knit. Her gift for words and the cultural predicament of her time drove her to poetry instead of antimacassars" (49). Years later, Dickinsonian imagery of hair, filament, cobweb, veil, and mesh is explicitly central to Armantrout's short essay on "I had not minded—Walls." Armantrout writes of Dickinson's poem that "the vehicles of the metaphor, the adamant cobweb, the battlement of straw, and the veil hiding dragons, might be seen as depictions of deceptive feminine weakness. I called my selected poems *Veil* in tribute to this poem of hers" ("Looking for Trouble" 5).

Howe herself responds to the overdetermined nature of such imagery when she objects with energetic skepticism to Sandra Gilbert and Susan Gubar's depiction of Dickinson as a "spider artist" engaged in "artful stitching": "Who is this Spider-Artist? Not *my* Emily Dickinson. This is poetry not life, and certainly not sewing" (*My Emily Dickinson* 14).[18] Certainly not; and like Armantrout's quixotic antiseamstress, Howe constructs her "feminine [and feminist] accomplishment" in and out of far-from-empty space. Howe's Dickinson is a visual poet, and when "words are in danger, dissolving" in Dickinson's work (23), that happens visually as well as semantically, just as Howe accomplishes what she praises in Dickinson, a "re-ordering of the forward process of reading" (51), "forward progress disrupted reversed" (24). Howe's, like Dickinson's, is a poetics of female and feminist self-exploration conducted visually, a poetics of "coding and erasing—deciphering the idea of herself" (76).

# 10

## Authority, Marginality, England, and Ireland in the Work of Susan Howe

> One of the problems I have always had has been the pull between countries. A civil war in the soul.
> —Susan Howe, "Speaking with Susan Howe"

Susan Howe's 2003 publication of *The Midnight* makes thematically explicit much of what is formally implicit in her earlier work regarding the variegated importance of Ireland to her writing. Among many other subjects, the sequence "Scare Quotes I" (*Midnight* 41–86) meditates on Howe's relationship to her Irish mother and to Ireland, to other Irish familial connections (her great-aunt Louie Bennett, suffragist and union organizer), and to Irish poetry (anthologies, Yeats). Through childhood memories of her mother's and her own involvement in the theater, and of her mother's love of Yeats, Howe explores in a far more openly autobiographical mode than in her previous work "the maternal Anglo-Irish disinheritance" (*Midnight* 66). Howe states as commentary what her previous poetry has enacted formally: "There were always three dimensions, visual, textual, and auditory. Waves of sound connected us by associational syllabic magic to an original but imaginary place existing somewhere across the ocean between the emphasis of sound and the emphasis of sense. I loved listening to her voice" reading Yeats aloud (75). Later in the memoir, Howe summarizes: "This is how it was to grow up with my mother as sanctuary and choir" (80).

Before *The Midnight*, Howe had often framed Ireland's biographical and creative meaning for her in terms of the gendered binary "mother/Ireland" and "father/U.S."—a somewhat unnuanced set of terms, perhaps, but a powerful psychological reality for Howe. (On having her credentials questioned by staff at Harvard's Houghton Library, "I feel the acne rosacea on the Irish half of my nose getting worse" [*Midnight* 122], she writes.)

She recalls the family library (and her father's study) of her childhood as divided between her mother's Irish books on one side and her father's American books (along with classics and dictionaries) on the other. More significantly, she says, "I remember that the Irish books represented freedom and magic. The others represented authority and reality" ("Speaking" 40). Commenting in the preface to *Frame Structures* on her father's biography of Justice Oliver Wendell Holmes, she writes:

> He called the first chapter "The Stars and the Plough" probably because that's the title of *The Plough and the Stars.* Sean O'Casey's play about the Easter Rising, named for the symbol on the flag of the Irish citizen army, is one of my mother's favorites. The stars are the ideal the plough reality. I guess my father meant to put reality first. (17)

Putting the "plough" of reality first, of course, is exactly what her father does not do with this chapter title. But more to the point is the view of her parents that Howe's minor misreading makes clear here, with her father the voice of mundane reality and American scholarship in contrast to her mother's association with idealism, with expressiveness, with Ireland, and with the arts—a complex array of connections for a poet who became an influential Americanist. Granted the risk Howe runs here of romanticizing or stereotyping the "freedom and magic" of Ireland, this set of associations still connects Ireland and mother in tension with a patriarchal authority represented by father and Harvard, and later, I will argue, by Matthew Arnold and England.

Possessed by that transitional passage of identity through which (New) English people became Americans, Howe has throughout her career used figures from American, English, and Irish literary and political history to address the issues of colonization, authority, and marginality that are among those central to her work. Put another way, what Ireland represents to Howe underlies her fascination with, and helps drive her writing about, the antinomian strain and settler colonialism in American history. While the Ireland-US dynamic is now understood to be fundamental to Howe's work, there remain few sustained critical treatments of how it plays out.[1] Critical emphasis on Howe's use of American history has tended to obscure or underplay a career-long concern with Ireland that begins with her use of the Irish landscape and her invocation of an ancient, mythic Ireland in such early work as *Hinge Picture* (1974), *The Western Borders* (1976), and *Secret History of the Dividing Line* (1978). The prose preface to *Frame Structures*, her 1996 gathering of four early books, places them in an autobiographical context that fills in Howe's Irish ancestry. *The West-*

*ern Borders* and *Secret History of the Dividing Line* also juxtapose, within themselves, the Irish and North American colonial contexts, while *Cabbage Gardens* (1979) addresses itself to Irish colonization. In *The Liberties* (1980), Howe treats gender formations past and present through her attention to an Anglo-Irish literary patriarch, Jonathan Swift; his historically and literarily marginalized muse Esther Johnson; and her own roots as an American poet of Irish descent looking on herself as a "semblance / of irish susans / dispersed" and "A PENDULUM SWUNG BETWEEN TWO COUNTRIES" (*Europe* 213, 163). (The earlier "irish susan" is her grandmother Susan Manning, to whom Howe dedicates the book.) *The Defenestration of Prague* (1983) calls up the Irish Protestant-Catholic conflict by reference to an earlier such conflict, the 1618 Protestant defenestration of two Catholic officials that sparked the Thirty Years' War. And in "Melville's Marginalia" (1993), Howe puts the noncanonical nineteenth-century Irish poet James Clarence Mangan at the center of an extended meditation on marginality, exclusion, and a colonial cultural authority embodied in the figure of Arnold.[2] Howe constructs a provocative critique of literary and social authority out of her own sense of Anglo-American relations and her preoccupation with North American and especially Irish colonial history. I consider how that critique develops by looking briefly at the place of Ireland in some of Howe's earlier poetry before lingering somewhat longer on "Melville's Marginalia."

In *Hinge Picture* (1974), Ireland is primarily present in the short final section, where it first appears in an Irish proverb—"All roads lead to rooms"—juxtaposed with a line from "Hansel and Gretel": a juxtaposition I mention only to point out again the often-noted association between Ireland and the world of fairytale, myth, and ancient story that runs throughout Howe's work. Yet, even in this early work, it is not too far-fetched to hear a veiled threat against the colonial center—the kind of threat that later becomes much more prominent in her work—couched in Howe's variation on a nursery rhyme: "Oarsman, oarsman, / Where have you been? / I've been to Leafy, / I've dismembered the Queen" (*Frame Structures* 52). In Howe's version, the original's visit to the colonial center (London) has been transformed into an act of violence against Queen Elizabeth I, the queen of Spenser's Ireland. One can hear "Irishman" behind "oarsman" and "Liffey" behind "Leafy," while the more explicit "I've dismembered the Queen" oddly anticipates the deconstruction of (gendered rather than colonial) cultural hierarchies proposed in a line written close to twenty years later: "I will dismember marginalia" (*Nonconformist's Memorial* 146).[3] Further, it is through sound—so crucial an element of composition for Howe—that she encodes her sense of her Irish ancestry in much of her work: "Eras and eras encircled by sea / the barrows of my ancestors have spilled their bones / across the singing ear in hear or shell" (*Frame Structures* 54). Such lines are saturated with aural echoes and variations of the name of Eire or Eireann: era, ear in, hear or. We might compare also the aural play on "air ha" / "-ear" / Eire in "The Liberties": "whistling would in air ha / nameless appear" (*Europe* 176). Howe returns to this phonemic cluster, which symbolizes for her the triple association of mother, Ireland/Irishness, and (poetic) sound, in *The Midnight.* At one point, she moves from a photograph of her eight-year-old mother watching an *aero*plane (my emphasis) to two juxtaposed entries in Mary Manning's last address book for "Aer Lingus" and "Audio-Ears" (*Midnight* 119). Later in the volume, questions of pronunciation and sound segue into a metonymic chain of near-homophones and anagrams, from "air when it is stirred up calls out Spirits of Place. Adjacent acoustic spirits" to "Eire" ("not a normal word") to Lake "Erie" and on to "aary," apparently a phonetic splicing of "airy," "Eire," and "aerie" (145, 166).

After a chiasmically riddling nursery-rhyme epigraph projecting nostalgia for a lost or missed place—"Oh would I were where I would be! / There would I be where I am not" (np)—Howe's third book, *The Western Borders,* begins with an uppercase "IRELAND" that connects visually with the next uppercase word in the sequence, "SONG," establishing the connection recurrent in Howe between Ireland and the poetic. Howe then invokes various colonial contexts by moving from Ireland to the colonization of New England and incorporating references to Egypt and to the conquering of Greece by Philip of Macedon (Demosthenes, the seashore speaker of Howe's poem, spoke against Philip [5]).[4] A mythic poem of Ireland, "Fallen Jerusalem Island," draws simultaneously on Gaelic legend (Lir, the "King who wears surge of the sea on his forehead" [13] and who reappears in "The Liberties")[5] and Christian legend (bringing "other small gifts for the baby"). Howe juxtaposes it strikingly with a poem apparently of the colonization of New England, "The Plains of Abraham":

> NEW PILGRIMS HAVE BEGUN THEIR TASK
> THE DENSE FOREST WILL BE CLEARED AWAY
> THEY ARE BUILDING AN ANCIENT COLONY. (14)[6]

These uppercase lines are followed by another uppercase phrase that visually recalls the opening IRELAND, "BOSTON HARBOR," with sailing ships eventually ending up at "the american strand" (19), another form of "western border" colonized by the English.

In this way *The Western Borders* exemplifies Howe's remark in the preface to *Frame Structures* that "my early poems project aggression" (29). The aggression of the 1979 *Cabbage Gardens* involves the colonization of Ireland. In the epigraph from Boswell, Samuel Johnson snorts at the possibility of writing something called "'The Cabbage-garden'" but then changes his mind to observe that

> one could say a great deal about cabbage. The poem might begin with the advantages of civilized society over a rude state, exemplified by the Scotch, who had no cabbages till Oliver Cromwell's soldiers introduced them; and one might thus shew how arts are propagated by conquest. (*Frame Structures* 74)

Following on this supposedly causal relationship between colonization and culture (crucial to Howe's poetics is Walter Benjamin's thesis that every document of culture is a document of barbarism), the poem begins in a history of invasions that seems to have lasted for "aeons"—"The enemy coming on roads / and clouds / aeons"—before alluding to the loss of one specific town: "Cashel has fallen" (75) to Cromwell's forces.[7] Subsequently one dominant strand in the poem concerns the efforts of the "people of the / Land / darkened / Perilous" (77) to construct defenses and resist the colonial power. On that land "I plough the earth / till ruts are ramparts" (78). Later we hear of the castle windows that "provided / light / and / served / as / watchtowers // overlooking / the / surrounding / countryside" (82) and the sea from which the invaders would come: "Stood on the ramparts of the fort / the open sea outside" (86).

In *Secret History of the Dividing Line* (1978)—published before *Cabbage Gardens* but written after it—Howe juxtaposes Irish and North American colonial experience as she does in *The Western Borders*. Howe has insisted that "*Secret History* is American" ("Speaking" 40); it constitutes an extended play around the meaning of Mark, the name of her father whom she always associates emphatically with her American side, and the source text is her father's edition of Justice Oliver Wendell Holmes's Civil War letters and diaries. While all this is so, however, this American history passes indirectly through Ireland, as the sequence moves early from Holmes's letters and historical information on New England ("THE FIRST ENGLISH CHILD BORN IN NEW ENGLAND WAS NAMED PEREGRINE OR THE WANDERER" [*Frame Structures* 91]) to an ancient Irish town that is a long-standing site both of invasion from the outside and of civil war: "We enter the ancient town of SWORDS. . . . According to ancient records, SWORDS was burnt by the Danes in 1012, 1016, 1030, 1138, 1150, and 1166 A.D.; and in 1185 it was taken and sacked by

O'Melaghlin, King of Meath" (92). Through fragments of echoing sound that call up Ireland's name as she does in *Hinge Picture*, Howe suggests an analogy between her groping for connection to this ancient history and her address to her father: "O / where ere / he He A // ere I were / wher // father" (93). (Here, in a complexly intertextual moment, "father father" echoes the dedicatory poem of Charles Olson's *Call Me Ishmael*, after Howe has used early in her sequence Olson's well-known formulation from that book, "THE LAST FIRST PEOPLE" [90].)

The history of American migration does dominate the sequence—partly under the sign of Olson, another radical half-Irish poet with Harvard connections, with the early allusion to *Call Me Ishmael* and the working with a central theme of that book, in Howe's words "the journey first / . . . / westward and still westward" (*Frame Structures* 95). Nevertheless, the Irish context still haunts the background, via, for example, "the old, wild, indomitable sea-kings / vikings" (105) who both invaded Ireland and reached North American shores. These are Howe's ancient fathers, and whether it is she, her literal father, or both who are now "stranger and sojourner" remains ambiguous: "Stranger and sojourner // as all my fathers were // horned sages sailing in ships // icy tremors of abstraction" (109). Conflating autobiography and national history, Howe concludes both "Secret History of the Dividing Line" and *Frame Structures* itself with a final grid poem that frames both a restlessly dispersed Irishness—"sh dispel iris sh"—and a truncated Americanness, "Americ" (122), with the hush ("sh") of her own initials.

The Ireland of Howe's early life and work is simultaneously an ancestral home and a place of myth, legend, fairytale. In this poet obsessed with colonial American beginnings, Irish legend often constitutes an imaginative Other to material history. As Peter Nicholls argues, "it was her mother's Irish background that first offered Howe clues to what she calls a 'wildness' somewhere outside history" ("Unsettling the Wilderness" 587–88)—the "SONG" of poetry that *The Western Borders* connects visually, via the use of capitals, with "IRELAND." In commenting on Edmund Spenser, one of the figures behind "The Defenestration of Prague," Howe observes that "in *The Fairie Queene* Ireland may be the uncodifiable spirit of Poetry" ("*Difficulties*" 25); I would set next to this her remark that "maybe margins shelter the inapprehensible Imaginary of poetry" (*Birth-mark* 29).[8] However, Howe's "'wildness' somewhere outside history" also never leaves behind material history, including the Irish history to which she feels so connected. In "The Defenestration of Prague" Howe calls Ireland her "myth sanctuary" (*Europe* 146), a place where—in an image that projects her recurrent concern with the untraceability of historical origins—"my Picts //

Ride unutterable // Oldest chronicle" (131). Yet it is also a place where this "Visionary soul / remembering Rebellion" can track the "Massacre pattern in history" (143, 134). In "The Liberties," which makes extensive use of Gaelic myth, that pattern takes the form of parallels between narratives of gender and colonization: Lynn Keller has shown effectively how for Howe the position of women in "The Liberties" is "partially analogous to that of Ireland and of colonized peoples more generally" due to "their common entanglement in systems of domination and oppression in which language plays a key role" (*Forms of Expansion* 198). Ireland as "the uncodifiable spirit of Poetry," then, never comes separate from the codes it seeks to violate.

In "The Liberties" the mythic and the autobiographical most obviously meet in Howe's use of Irish subject matter:

> The subject of Swift, Stella, and Vanessa was mythic for my mother and many other Irish writers. I grew up on it. It was another Grimm's fairy tale. But real. So when I began this time, I was really trying to paint that part of the landscape of Dublin in words. I was trying to get the place, a foreign place that was home to my mother, on paper. I thought I could understand my mother that way—I might go back to my grandmother. (*Birth-mark* 166)

All the while, however, pulling against her Irish roots is Howe's sense of her outsider status as a half-Irish poet who has, after all, lived nearly all her life in the United States: "I hope to return to Ireland someday but will always be a foreigner with the illusions of a tourist" (*Nonconformist's Memorial* 108). In a 1986 interview, Howe also describes herself in the terms she uses for Swift in *The Liberties*: "One of the problems I have always had has been the pull between countries. A civil war in the soul" ("Speaking" 37). A few years later, she speculates that Swift's being "constantly wrenched between England and Ireland when he was a small child . . . helps to explain the fracturing of language in his writing" (*Birth-mark* 166). It is not too hard here to substitute "Howe" for "Swift," given her other comments along these lines.

To note Howe's "civil war in the soul" enables us to register the complexity of an "Irish" identity on her part that can occasionally seem to oversimplify in the process of mythologizing itself. As Will Montgomery observes, "what is essential to any reflection on Howe's relationship to Ireland is a consideration that an Anglo-Irish—not an Irish—sensibility is at issue" and a realization of "the culturally displaced quality of Anglo-Irishness—doubly displaced in Howe's case by re-plantation in the United States" (1, 18).[9] Howe reflects this displacement in her persistent shifting among terms, a shifting that leaves identity unstable and its origins somewhat obscured: she writes as "Hiberno-English" (*Midnight* 154), "as a half-Irish or half-Anglo-Irish woman" (126), and her ancestors "the Bennetts and Mannings are Irish and not Irish so we haven't the secret of our first ancestral parents" (59). When Howe turns to the Irish poet James Clarence Mangan in "Melville's Marginalia," she turns to the subversive example of his shape-shifting identity, his counterfeiting and hoaxing, his embrace of inauthenticity.

Granted these complexities, for some years early in her career Howe did associate Ireland with the poetic, the marginal, the antiauthoritarian, the "uncodifiable," and all of those with the female. Though the under-discussed "Chanting from the Crystal Sea" and "Secret History of the Dividing Line," both legible as "American" texts, date from 1975 and 1978 respectively, it is around the early mid-1980s that Howe is commonly understood to have entered a more noticeably "American" phase with the work gathered in *Singularities,* with *My Emily Dickinson* and her essays on Dickinson, *The Birth-mark,* and "Melville's Marginalia." But even the latter sequence is an extended investigation of issues of "minority," cultural authority, and marginality, metaphorized through the colonial relationship between England and Ireland and through the figures of the elusive poet James Clarence Mangan and the English cultural law-giver Matthew Arnold. Although it is less central to "Melville's Marginalia," Howe—drawing on a centuries-long allegorical connection in Irish cultural and literary history—makes the same conflation of woman and Ireland there as in *The Liberties.* Catherine Nash demonstrates how the long-standing personification of Ireland as woman in both colonialist and nationalist discourses has served conflicting purposes, both subversive and oppressive. On the one hand, Nash notes "the allegorization of Ireland as woman in the 18th-century classical poetic genre, the *aisling,* following colonial censorship of the expression of direct political dissent." On the other hand, she points to "the colonial feminization of Ireland," part of "colonial efforts to control what was considered 'an essentially feminine race,'" and then how in the present "the continued use of the notion of Ireland as female . . . endorses and strengthens the signifying use of women in Ireland, their erosion from Irish history, and their contemporary silencing" (229, 234). In other words, as Ailbhe Smyth argues, in a contemporary postcolonial context that adapts this traditional personification to the purposes of redefining nation, "women powerless under patriarchy . . . are maintained as Other of the ex-Other, colonized of the post-colonized" (qtd. in Nash 241). Nash goes on to connect the nineteenth-century Ordnance Survey mapping of Ireland, on which Mangan worked, with control of the feminine, a connection both politically charged and made possible because the nation being mapped has also been feminized. "Melville's Marginalia" moves through layerings of unwitting complicity whereby Mangan, with his "'feminine softness'" (*Nonconformist's Memorial* 107), works on a project designed by the colonial master whom he resists to regulate his own feminized nation. (Directly relevant here for its own feminization of the Irish and of Irish literature is Arnold's 1867 *On the Study of Celtic Literature.*) As Howe knows, quoting Mangan's editor John Mitchel, "Roisin Dubh means Ireland" (*Nonconformist's Memorial* 125); and the identification (like the notion of the "virgin wilderness" that Howe deconstructs in *The Birth-mark*) is hardly a neutral or benign one.

The appeal of Mangan, whose work Melville annotated vigorously, is both biographical and poetic for Howe. "Why was I drawn to Mangan?" she asks herself; "only that I remembered the song called 'Roisin Dubh' from childhood and my great-aunt's garden one summer years ago beside Killiney Bay near Dublin" (*Nonconformist's Memorial* 105). The appeal is also typographical and aural, for this poet whose visually dramatic pages and ear are so crucial a component of her work: Mangan is "the man with the name so remarkably like *margin*" (105). Howe describes the impetus of the sequence as follows: "I thought one way to write about a loved author would be to follow what trails he follows through words of others" (92)—specifically, the marginal notes that Melville wrote in his books and that are preserved in the scholarly text that gives Howe her title, Wilson Walker Cowen's 1965 doctoral dissertation *Melville's Marginalia*. But the sequence is not "about" Melville in the sense that *My Emily Dickinson* is "about" its eponymous subject. Indeed, "Melville's Marginalia" is as much about Howe's reading of Mangan—and, in a concealed but very real way, of Arnold and cultural authority—as it is about her reading of Melville and Melville's reading. Much more than it concerns Melville, the sequence concerns marginalia and marginality, distinctions between major and minor, the central and the peripheral, and their interrelations; after all, "'the writing of Irish history is possible only because of the care with which the British Museum has preserved Irish materials'" (*Nonconformist's Memorial* 95).

Howe establishes these concerns succinctly by beginning with a headstone-like epitaph memorializing a minor playwright, Philip Massinger, as an alienated "stranger" (83). (Later we learn that "a quotation from Philip Massinger opens [Mangan's] 'Fragment of an Unfinished Autobiography': '. . . A heavy shadow lay / On that boy's spirit: he was not of his fathers'" [87].) There follows, under the title "Parenthesis," a "Brief Chronology of James Clarence Mangan" that furthers in various ways the notion of the marginal or the secondary. Proposing Mangan's life as a "parenthesis," Howe suggests how it has come to be seen as a dispensable part of a longer (historical) sentence. Furthermore, with the exception of some added details and the last entry, which speculatively connects Mangan to Melville's Confidence Man and Bartleby through brief quotations from those two texts, Howe bases her chronology almost directly on another peripheral or paratextual document, the appendix to David Lloyd's critical book, *Nationalism and Minor Literature: James Clarence Mangan and the Emergence of Irish Cultural Nationalism*. By the end of the chronology, however, we have the main preoccupations of the sequence in place: the political activism in Ireland of a canonical English poet, Shelley, and a noncanonical Irish one, Mangan; and the marginal or "isolato" characters of a canonical American novelist, Melville, with their capacity for cultural resistance and commentary and for a dispersed subjectivity that itself constitutes a form of such resistance and commentary. The common feature, as Michael Davidson puts it, among these "widely disparate anglophone authors" is that they "represent political resistance and mass appeal that stand in opposition to British cultural elitism, embodied by someone such as Matthew Arnold" (*Ghostlier Demarcations* 86).

Aside from her choosing to begin with a parenthesis, Howe's repetition of "What is a parenthesis?" makes it clear that that question is of more than passing (or marginal) grammatical interest to her. She devotes most of a page to a passage in which the schoolboy Mangan is the only one in his class who can answer the question. Mangan's answer: "'I should suppose a parenthesis to be something included in a sentence, but which might be omitted from the sentence without injury to the meaning of the sentence'" (*Nonconformist's Memorial* 93). Later, Howe repeats the question immediately after observing that Mangan "has been all but forgotten by serious literary criticism" (105). He has himself become a parenthesis, that "which might be omitted" from the canon "without injury to" it. Then the question arises a third time in a context that connects it to what Howe presents as Mangan's insistent undermining of authenticity, of origins—an undermining conducted from his parenthetical or marginal position in a way that Deleuze and Guattari theorize as characteristic of a minor literature. The line "What is a parenthesis" concludes the first half of a fourteen-line poem (a faux sonnet) apparently constructed of fragmented and often punning phrases from Mangan's prose. Through her selection of quoted materials in this poem, Howe suggests that Mangan writes "half-whimsically," in "derision half-seriously" (130); a punning reference to "what is Moore" alludes to the Orientalist-Celtic mix of Thomas

Moore's popular poem *Lalla Rookh*, the authenticating footnotes of which Mangan parodied in his own work (Lloyd 119) and to which Howe returns briefly in *The Midnight* (155). "If the reader please" turn "to his originals," then that reader may find only dubious or untraceable origins. Howe reinforces the question of dubious authenticity by intercutting these two phrases with "house" and "hovel" (*Nonconformist's Memorial* 130). The last "house" and "hovel" we saw in the sequence was a fictional one in which Mangan claimed to have lived, until the editor of his autobiography said, "'*This is purely imaginary; and when I told Mangan that I did not think it a faithful picture, he told me he dreamt it*'" (97). How appropriate, then, that the second half of this fourteen-liner, following the line "What is a parenthesis," should begin with the line "Long passage on fallacy" (130).

So what does all this have to do with England, Ireland, and cultural authority? In "Melville's Marginalia," Ireland is the parenthesis to England's sentence, the margin to England's page, just as Mangan is the margin or province to Matthew Arnold's center, and Melville's Bartleby is the margin to that center of capital, Wall Street, and its concern with a different margin, that of profit. Indeed, Howe moves between Melville's Arnold and Melville's Mangan. She describes how, having spent a day examining Melville's marginalia to Arnold's *Essays in Criticism*, she turned to a "heavily scored paragraph" from John Mitchel's introduction to Mangan's *Poems* that stands in "marked contradiction" (106)—in contradiction, I take it, of Arnold. Noting "how completely British criticism gives the law throughout" the English-speaking literary world, Mitchel describes Mangan's resistance to such claims to cultural authority, in a passage that Howe quotes at length:

> For this Mangan was not only an Irishman,—not only an Irish papist, —not only an Irish papist rebel;—but throughout his whole literary life of twenty years, he never deigned to attorn to English criticism, never published a line in any English periodical, or through any English bookseller, never seemed to be aware that there was a British Public to please. He was a rebel politically, and a rebel intellectually and spiritually,—a rebel with his whole heart and soul against the British spirit of the age. (106–7)

The Arnoldian authority that Mangan resists has appeared earlier in the sequence, via quotations from Arnold's essay "The Literary Influence of Academies." Specifically, Howe recasts into two poems, with some excisions, Arnold's comments on the historian A. W. Kinglake (fig. 9.6):

A style so bent on effect and the expense of soul
so far from classic truth and grace
must surely be said to have the note of
PROVINCIALITY. (96)

To describe such failures of taste Arnold uses two terms that Howe also quotes, "baneful" and (from the French) "bête." Transposed into the context of "Melville's Marginalia," these snippets work to describe not Kinglake but Mangan, to explain from the point of view of the cultural center why "he could not storm the alphabet of art." The phrase "and social weakness" picks up further on Arnold's critique of Kinglake, from a point where Arnold distinguishes the sustained or recurrent stylistic excesses that mark provinciality from a merely "momentary, good-tempered excess, in a man of the world, of an amiable and social weakness" (*Poetry and Criticism* 278). "Provinciality" is perhaps the key term here, for Arnoldian language like "province" and "center" is part of a colonial discourse. And outside the left margin of this short poem, separated from the text by a firm (morally upright?) vertical line, we find capitalized and slanted the word "NONCOMPATIBLES"—surely an appropriate term for Mangan and Arnold. Do we find any "noncompatibles" in Arnold? Well, it turns out that we do, or at least we find "incompatibles"—the title of an 1881 Arnold essay, referring to what he calls in another title "Irish Catholicism and British Liberalism."

A related recasting of Arnold occurs a couple of pages later. The phrases "Rapidity without ease / Effective without charm" (*Nonconformist's Memorial* 100) (fig. 10.1) are again clipped from Arnold's comments on Kinglake's style, which "has glitter without warmth, rapidity without ease, effectiveness without charm" (*Poetry and Criticism* 277). That style falls short of the Attic grace that in Arnold's essay embodies the classic, the style of the center characterized by the features of Homer's style with which Arnold concludes his essay "On Translating Homer" and which Howe playfully stands on their end like parodic Greek columns: "The pure lines of an Ionian horizon / The liquid clearness of an Ionian sky" (*Nonconformist's Memorial* 100). The flaws that Arnold criticizes in Kinglake extend "far beyond what the French mean by *fatuity*" (*Poetry and Criticism* 278) and into the realm of the "bête" that Howe cites four pages earlier. But as the phrases "rapidity without ease" and "effective without charm" are visually crossed with a citation of their source, Arnold's 1865 *Essays in Criticism*, they come to apply as much to Arnold as to his subject. Arnold becomes "effective without charm," and in a transposition from verb to adjective, "mean by fatuity."

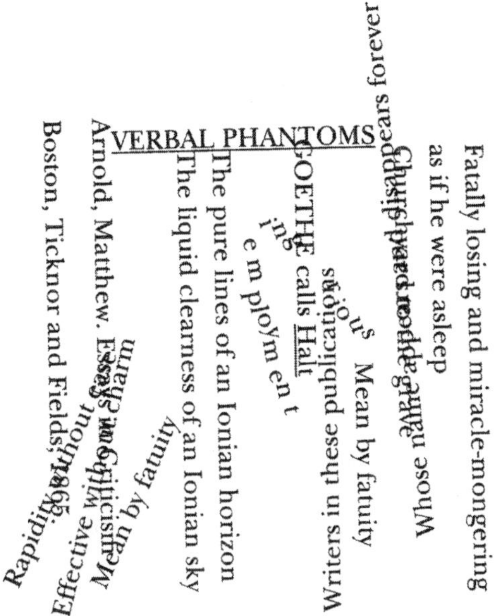


Figure 10.1. Susan Howe, *Nonconformist's Memorial*, p.100

Elsewhere in "Melville's Marginalia" Howe constructs poems, their sources openly acknowledged, from two other Arnold texts: "A SPEECH AT ETON" and "A FRENCH ETON or, Middle-class Education and the State" (*Nonconformist's Memorial* 98) (fig. 10.2). The first of these poems reinforces the implied argument with Arnoldian stylistic centrism that Howe has been conducting, by quoting this sentence from "A Speech at Eton": "And I might go yet further, and might show / you in the medieval world, *eutrapelia*, or / flexibility, quite banished, clear straight / forward Attic thinking quite lost; restraint / stoppage, and prejudice regnant!" (98; Arnold, *Complete Prose Works* 9:34). Between the second and third lines, however, is disruptively sandwiched the phrase "The Unrealities," Mangan's title for his translation of Schiller's "Die Ideale" in his *German Anthology*, in his copy of which Melville marked lines on the ephemerality of fame. Inserted between "restraint" and "stoppage, and prejudice," meanwhile, "The Field Imaginary in American Studies" may well be said to be characterized by those qualities with which it is associated through juxtaposition here. Certainly, this is one assumption of *The Birth-mark*, Howe's radically revisionist work of American literary history contemporaneous with *The Nonconformist's Memorial*.

The second poem, "A FRENCH ETON," is perhaps even more rele-

Must be fall or swerve

must be block or wedge

ADEQUATE EXPRESSION

Re-
venge is
honorable

A SPEECH AT ETON

And I might go yet further, and might show

you in the medieval world, *eutrapelia*, or

The Unrealities

flexibility, quite banished, clear straight

quietism stoicism

forward Attic thinking quite lost; restraint

The Field Imaginary in American Studies

stoppage, and prejudice regnant!

It is pleasant to think of the small blonde sprite of 1811 tripping in and out of the Derby Square school, who may have looked, more than once unawares, on Shelley's boyish self as he went crusading through the streets with Harriet.

Louise I. Guiney, "James Clarence Mangan, A Study," 1897.

A FRENCH ETON or, Middle-class Education and the State

Less can be immediately good taste Prose

critque radical radical visible subsurface

To cry with *Oberman*

we are all terrae filii

All my
estate
or property
all
quotations
from
books"

Between real authors
and the makers of dictionaries
blunders

Government says Burke
(to go back to Burke again)
"is a contrivance of human wisdom
to provide for human wants"

Subject of the idea (to quote from *The Excursion*)

Figure 10.2. Susan Howe, *Nonconformist's Memorial*, p. 98

vant to my argument here, in splicing material from Arnold's 1864 essay by that title with material from "The Function of Criticism at the Present Time."[10] The quotation from Edmund Burke on government as "a contrivance of human wisdom / to provide for human wants'" derives directly from "A French Eton" (Arnold, *Complete Prose Works* 2:302). Howe's citation seems intended both ironically—the English could hardly be said to have adopted this view of government with regard to Ireland—and as a reminder of the conflicts involved in culturally or state-mandated control of language, with "dictionaries" overwritten at right angles to "Government" as if ambiguously in collusion and contradiction with each other. The scrutiny of Arnoldian authority continues in Howe's use of "The Function of Criticism." In that essay Arnold sets the voice of the practical person embedded in his or her social interests against that of the disinterested critic. The former voice cries, in a phrase that Howe cites, "'We are all *terrae filii*,' . . . 'all Philistines together'" (Arnold, *Poetry and Criticism* 251). Mangan has already ironically co-opted the anti-Arnoldian "Philistine" position, however, in taking "Terrae Filis" (*Nonconformist's Memorial* 86) as a pseudonym—the phrase "terrae filii" in "The Function of Criticism" itself deriving from an attack on Arnold's perceived cultural elitism that Arnold has sought to turn against his attacker. Howe's goal here is to offer a "crit[i]que radical radical visible subsurface" (98) of the cultural authoritarianism buried in Arnold's promotion of "good taste Prose." This is Howe's version of laying bare the device: making the subsurface visible in a radical critique that exposes the roots of its object, with, perhaps, the "i" missing from "critque" as a parody of Arnold's "disinterestedness" (the antithesis of *My Emily Dickinson*). When Arnold reiterates his famous claim that "I am bound by my own definition of criticism: *a disinterested endeavour to learn and propagate the best that is known and thought in the world*" (*Poetry and Criticism* 257), he reiterates this buried authoritarianism. When Howe revises the first phrase to read "I am bound by a definition / of criticism" (*Nonconformist's Memorial* 125), the definition becomes explicitly not her "own" but "*a* definition," an institutional one with the spectral authority of Arnold behind it.

I mentioned Deleuze and Guattari earlier, and their influential theorizing of a minor literature—a paradigm that also underlies one of Howe's central resources for "Melville's Marginalia," Lloyd's *Nationalism and Minor Literature*—is useful for understanding Howe's treatment of Mangan and Arnold further. It is worth stressing how Deleuze and Guattari propose a specifically non- or anti-Arnoldian definition of the "minor" by making a political virtue out of a relative paucity of talent and by seeing the "minor" less in terms of individual quality, more in terms of its potential for collective social action. A minor literature defined in this way may have isolated major writers, but generally the lack of talent in a minor literature reduces the possibility for individual masterful "enunciations" separate from the collective, in positive ways: "Scarcity of talent is in fact beneficial and allows the conception of something other than a literature of masters" so that "literature finds itself positively charged with the role and function of collective, and even revolutionary, enunciation" (*Kafka* 17). The minor frames itself in an oppositional relationship to the major (and usually colonial) language in which it is written: Kafka's German, Joyce, Beckett, and Mangan's English. The pun in "a literature of masters" suggests what a minor literature like the nineteenth-century Irish of Mangan resists: "There is nothing that is major or revolutionary except the minor. To hate all languages of masters" (26).

One further feature of a minor literature is that, to cite Deleuze and Guattari again, "the message doesn't refer back to an enunciating subject who would be its cause" (*Kafka* 18). That is, the minor resists claims to essential identity, at all levels, from the individual to the national. On this point, Lloyd diverges from Deleuze and Guattari. He sees the literature of nineteenth-century Irish nationalism as "minor" in the more conventional sense of a fledgling literature aspiring to become major through "the production of an authentic Irish identity" (xi). But he sees Mangan as continuing a writing that remains programmatically minor in the Deleuzian sense. In ways that should help our reading of Howe, Lloyd points to Mangan's effort "to undermine the priority given to distinctive individual voice in canonical criticism" (23); to his "questioning the principles of originality and autonomy that underwrite [the bourgeois] conception of the subject" (25); and to his persistent "refusal of identity" (22)—or at least the identity assigned to him under a nationalism inseparable in its models of subjectivity from the imperialism it would resist. If, as Lloyd proposes, the ideological function of a major national literature lies in its claim to a representative status that reconciles differences within the nation, a reconciliation that requires "the alienation of [the reader's] autonomy in the aesthetic work," then a minor literature will critique this alienation, the claim to representativeness, and "the concept of the autonomous subject as the essence of the human" (19). It will often do so via a "perpetuation of non-identity" (22) that resists rising to "representative" status. This resistance, along with "an equivalent refusal to ground the possibility of identity on the recovery of origins," constitutes the minor's critique of one strategy (or effect) of major literature, "the reproduction of an original or essential identity at a higher and self-conscious level" (22).

All of which really does relate to "Melville's Marginalia," for as the penultimate line in the sequence has it, "Obedience we are subjects Susan" (*Nonconformist's Memorial* 150). Howe consistently highlights those aspects of Mangan's life and work that (disobediently) problematize ideas of authenticity, authorial and self-identity, and national identity: his bogus translations of nonexistent texts (86), the fictional moments in his autobiography (93, 97), his multiple pseudonyms, his biographical elusiveness, the attribution to Mangan of another's texts that were themselves published under an anagrammatic pen-name (Irys Herfner for Henry Ferris), even his addition of "Clarence" to his given name. In Mangan—to cite various points in the sequence—"originality dies out" (124); we get "an author-evacuated text," "the subjectless abject" (113); or we get an author who produces "a polyglot anthology / out of no materials" (129), out of nonexistent poems, who "was not the polyglot / he pretended to be" (128), who resignedly remarks, "I will 'do' the song / out of the Jacobite / Counterfeit" (133), and who openly admits to translating poems "of questionable authenticity" (94).

Howe quotes James Joyce's comments on "all the names and titles that [Mangan] gives himself," and then immediately turns to the *Encyclopedia Britannica* entry that describes Mangan's work "lying buried . . . under so many pseudonyms" (*Nonconformist's Memorial* 108–9). One of these pseudonyms was "The Man in the Cloak" (Mangan made up a German poet, Selber, or "self," notable for his cloak), and Howe foregrounds this motif of veiling as an aspect of Mangan's resistance to the identity that Irish literary nationalism would assign him. Like Hawthorne's Rev. Hooper, "he put a veil on his face," a "voiceless reclusion veil" (113, 149). If the veiled statue at Sais is an image of truth in Friedrich Schiller's poem of that title, Mangan treats it in terms of counterfeit and masking, compressed by Howe into the remark "Counterfeit when you / look artist of Sais" (133).[11] She cites Mangan making fun of contemporary myths of origin that claimed spurious etymological connections between Gaelic and various Semitic languages: "According to / Vallency every Irishman is / an Arab" (135). At the same time, all joking—or cloaking—aside, we find the unattributed assertion that "no cloak smothers my mirth" (143). It is from this position of elusive but mirthful self-marginalization that Howe finds an Irish poet mocking cultural identity as did her beloved Melville, to the point where the sequence might well be called "Melville's Manganalia."[12] Indeed, her use of the image from Schiller may well contain an oblique (veiled) reference to Melville, who alludes to Schiller's poem in chapter 76 of *Moby-Dick* "For unless you own the whale, you are but a provincial and sentimentalist in Truth. But clear Truth is a thing for salamander giants only to encounter; how small the chances for the provincials then?

What befell the weakling youth lifting the dread goddess's veil at Sais?" (257). In the context of "Melville's Marginalia," the Arnoldian overtones of "provincial" only add another intertextual layer, although Melville's use of the term predates Arnold's.

One risk here is of reducing the Irish strain in Howe's poetry to a predictable anticolonialist argument. The interest and strength of her work, however, lies in its textual uncovering of multiple interlinked forms of authority, most of which are themselves textually reinforced: the patriarchal authority of Harvard and the father, as well as the colonialist authority not just inscribed in such oppositions as "province" and "center" but generated by that center. As a citizen of a colonial power herself ("complicity battling redemption," as she puts it [*Singularities* 55]), Howe's position is complex; this is not simply a case of the empire writing back. Howe's concerns with margins, both social and typographical, is a long-standing one, and her investigation of the term is driven as much by a poet's associative imagination as it is by a thematized politics. When Mangan is "the man with the name so remarkably like *margin*" (*Nonconformist's Memorial* 105), sound play becomes a site for hearing the links among isolation, marginality, gender, and silence: "Strond strund stronde strand. The margin submerges phonic substance. A mother's thread or line is ringed about with silence so poems are" (*The Birth-mark* 37). Self-consciously an Irish American poet, Howe uses an Irish poet and Ireland itself as tropes to destabilize the power relations and forces of marginalization inscribed both in canonical colonial texts and in the "text" of colonialism itself.

# 11

## Bruce Andrews, Writing, and "Poetry"

A criticism consisting entirely of quotations should be developed.
—Walter Benjamin, "Program for Literary Criticism"

Genres are fucked; *disturb* the creature.
Bruce Andrews, *Ex Why Zee*

### Poetic Essays, Critical Prose Poems

Raising some fundamental questions, the program for the 2010 Penn/Columbia "Rethinking Poetics" conference read in part

> The category of Poetry has been enormously generous—taking in works that would otherwise find themselves generically orphaned, accepting experiments that other genres did not want, constantly expanding and adjusting its criteria for centuries. But that capacious kindness has also led to difficulties, and the usefulness of the category is inversely related to its breadth. Why do we still talk about "poetry" at this late stage–after deconstruction and intermedia and hybridity? What does the genre still do for us?

One speaker at this conference was Bruce Andrews, of whom Jed Rasula writes "within a nation's literature there are authors whose writing in its entirety constitutes the limit-work of a given genre. Andrews may be the paradigmatic instance of American poetry at its limit" (*Syncopations* 107). Rasula's claim provides a useful way into thinking about Andrews's poetry and its address to the very category of "poetry." As Rasula continues, "to liken Andrews, on the strength of the identifying trait 'poet,' to Dave Smith or Sharon Olds, is to be grotesquely disoriented," for his "poetry is emphatically antiliterary. It cannot be read in any customary sense, because it will not conform to the presentational apparatus of textual norms" (108,

113). Reading Andrews's 1992 book *I Don't Have Any Paper So Shut Up, (or, Social Romanticism)* in relation to the "ugly feeling" of disgust, Sianne Ngai writes that "the desire of this poetry is to become intolerable—in particular, intolerable to the extent that it cannot be absorbed by the pluralist economy of an aesthetic eclecticism" (349). Two aspects in particular of Andrews's work help constitute it within recent American poetry as "the limit of the limit" (Rasula, *Syncopations* 107): his restive, unstable splicing of poetry and critical essay, and the largely undiscussed visual aspect of his poetics. Both these features find Andrews, in his own words, emphatically "stripping away the foundations . . . of allegiance to genre" ("Reading Notes" 199).

Key to Andrews's countergeneric practice is his version of what Joan Retallack calls the poetic essay, with its potential "to violate or exceed generic expectations" and its limit-testing antiabsorptiveness: "Essays, like poems and philosophical meditations, should elude our grasp just because their business is to approach the liminal spectrum of near-unintelligibility" (*Poethical Wager* 48). "Oblique vectors ricocheting between authoritative generic poles, describing unforeseen patterns" (56): in the kind of essay that most interests Retallack, the specific genre boundary being tested is that between essay and poetry (and in ways different from the lineated verse essay). Thus, in Leslie Scalapino's *Objects in the Terrifying Tense Longing from Taking Place*, "there is no separation between essay and poetry" (67), while Scalapino's *New Time* "exemplifies an investigative poetics that conflates essay and poem" (Retallack, *Poethical Wager* 60)—a conflation equally characteristic, Retallack argues, of texts such as Tina Darragh's *a(gain)²st the odds* and Rosmarie Waldrop's "Alarms and Excursions."

Rachel Blau DuPlessis theorizes the essay by arguing that "essays tend to call the genre into question. . . . The nature of the essay asks one to resist categories, starting with itself" ("*f*-Words" 23). In ways directly relevant to what she calls Andrews's (and others') "critical prose poems" (22),[1] DuPlessis lays out the essay's heterogeneous, polyvocal nature as a form of writing that "ruptures the conventions—especially the scientistic ethos of objectivity—of critical writing" in "unabashed textual untransparency, conglomerated genre, ambidextrous, switch-hitting style" (25). "All margin, marginalia, and interstitial writing," "the essay is a way of representing struggle, crossings, and creolized exploration" (20, 28).

Historical commentary on the essay confirms DuPlessis's view. Lauren Mailhot describes the essay as "a polymorphous *genre*," "multiple, fragmented, shattered"; "its discourse is opaque" and characterized by a move toward "theory-practice" (74, 75, 88). Late in the twentieth century, however, at the time when Andrews was writing much of his work on poetics, its potential remained untapped by most critics and theorists. In 1989, at the tail end of poststructuralism's thorough assimilation into the American academy, James R. Bennett surveyed 8 anthologies of contemporary literary criticism and theory containing 280 "essays" or extracts, and found only 1 selection (DuPlessis's own "For the Etruscans") "significantly subversive" in its deviation from the norms of "the massive analytical tradition" (108). Bennett looked in vain for techniques such as collage, pastiche, word play, "the 'crot,' or fragmentary, autonomous passage; labyrinthine/fragmentary sentence juxtapositions (or wholly one or the other); the list or catalog; 'double-voice' or plural voices; 'repetitions/repetends/refrains'; and language variegation" (107)—all features, to varying degrees, of Andrews's essays but not of normative academic discourse.

The first issue of *This* magazine in 1971 carried Robert Grenier's untitled review of Robert Creeley's *A Quick Graph*. Meditating on the implications of this work for poets writing criticism, Grenier argues that

> a kind of critical writing which does not now much exist will have to be made dominant: one in which the intention to say something is accomplished in a form possessed, first, of all the self-sufficient factness of the actual poem/prose being discussed. . . . In the work that matters, comment is finished, *there will have to be no essential difference between criticism and poems.* ("Review," my emphasis)

One feature of what Ron Silliman calls the "collective critical project" of Language writing was to propose "the critical essay as an art act in and of itself" ("Dysfunction" 187). While Andrews does not propose this position directly himself, it provides a useful frame for reading his critical and theoretical prose in relation to his poetry, even while "prose" and "poetry" themselves are terms that his work destabilizes.

It is no accident that the terms "Language poetry" and "Language writing" have historically been used more or less interchangeably, for it is the line between poetry and prose, between practice and theory, that many of those writers, and Andrews particularly, have most insistently questioned and dissolved. In a 1989 *Minnesota Review* symposium, Andrews and Charles Bernstein note how Language writing "presses questions . . . about the distinctions between verse and prose or between poems and essays about poetics" (Andrews, *Paradise and Method* 109–10). To an unusual degree, Andrews's own prose foregrounds the value of critical writing as writing, as an enactment of a poetics; except by implication, it does not derive its value or interest from its service to an argument or text outside itself. "Equals What?," a projected section of *I Don't Have Any Paper*

*So Shut Up* first published in a manifesto issue of the *Washington Review of the Arts*, questions its own generic status: "This is not so-called language writing. . . . So it's what, art, just formalist social theory?" (202) One could say much about how Andrews blurs generic boundaries via his prose poems (*I Don't Have Any Paper, Strictly Confidential, Divestiture—A*) and the kind of work discussed later in this chapter: visual poetry, verbal/visual collaborations, journal fragments, word cards. I want to focus for now, however, on how he addresses genre in what is nominally "theory" or "criticism," on how his criticism contests the frame separating critical and cultural theory and poetic practice. Though not as exclusively as they once did, instrumentality and an unproblematized transparency of argumentative meaning still commonly define the procedures of critical prose (as they do here, admittedly, and even as they get questioned in theory), even more so than in the autobiographical free verse lyric once so often cited as the antithesis of Language writing—and they did so during the period that Andrews was writing the work eventually collected in *Paradise and Method*. It is worth examining, then, how Andrews disrupts those criteria in one of the subgenres where they are most often taken for granted. In Andrews's thinking, to explore/explode genre is to explore/explode instrumentalization: the more his texts resist categorization, the more they resist and question being turned to institutional "use." This does not mean that one cannot tell the difference between an Andrews poem and an Andrews essay. It does mean, however, that he uses similar strategies in both forms, and one result is that the nature of poetry and criticism becomes one implied subject of his work in both modes. For Andrews's work, more than for any of his peers, the term "writing" is precisely appropriate.

Central to Andrews's practice of the poetic essay are the anticlosural qualities of his prose. (DuPlessis: the essay "contests any notion that writing or thinking leads to unity, system, abstraction, mastery" [*Blue Studios* 40].) While institutional context (the academy) dictates far more pressure toward closure in the critical or theoretical essay than it does in poetry, Andrews's literary work has always operated outside this context. The academy may form one important context for the consumption of his work but has not shaped its production. Sentence fragments, ellipses, shifting typefaces, fragmentary paragraphs, abrupt and unannounced shifts in and out of quotation, dialogic or collage forms, a principled refusal of the conventions of argument—these are some of the features of Andrews's criticism, just as they are of his poetry. As a critic and theorist, a worker in poetics, Andrews is interested in texts that are, in the title of a short essay on Susan Howe, "Beyond Suture." Yet to refer to "a short essay on Susan Howe" is already to misrepresent Andrews's "critical prose" (another term that needs to be placed under erasure in discussing his work). For Andrews's writing "on" individual poets is his most fractured, least conventionally expository prose, the prose where the authorial self is most dispersed. "Beyond Suture" is "made up of phrases, separated by dashes, taken from [Howe's] published works" (*Paradise and Method* 227). It is punctuated, or punctured, by precisely thirty-eight of Andrews's own words, in the form of uppercase paragraph headings: "LET THE VERB BE 'REOPEN'—'REORDER'" (232)—an anticlosural echo, I take it, of "Let the circle be unbroken.". It is through the minimalist gestures of these headings that Andrews suggests where Howe's poetry echoes his own interests: "I LOST PERSPECTIVE"; "THE FIX IS OFF"; "LANGUAGE MAKES MORE GAPS"; the lack of "A SELF-SUFFICING LEXICON"; "THE SOCIAL" (232–33). From one point of view, a rather traditional notion of criticism is at work here: presenting the poetry in question and letting it speak for itself. But Andrews does not merely present; he rearranges so as to make a new text, the collage structure of which matches that of Howe's originals.

This method takes particularly vivid form in a 1990 essay on Michael Davidson. Andrews's title, "These Are Not My Words—Sorry about Ink on defective cover . . . ," reflects his dispersal of the writing subject, a dispersal unsurprising from someone who has read thoroughly and written favorably on Roland Barthes.[2] Except for bold capitalized subheadings that reflect Andrews's own preoccupations as both poet and theorist—"**REPRESENTATION**," "**MEDIATION**," "**SIGN SYSTEM**," "**SUBJECT**," "**ANTI-SUBJECT**" (220–23), and so on—the text consists entirely of quotations from Davidson's work. But if these are not Andrews's words, their arrangement is his. He de-lineates Davidson's poetry into prose (a gesture complicated by the fact that some of that "poetry" looks like prose in the first place), grafts Davidson's words (which turn out actually not to be his words either) into his own sentences, his own meaning and reading. "Out of a desire to stand over history, poetry lifts the veil from the hidden beauty of the world and makes familiar objects be as if they were not familiar" (220): here the material on either side of the comma derives from two separate sections of Davidson's *Analogy of the Ion* (the words following the comma derive in turn from Shelley's "A Defence of Poetry"). This strategy foregrounds Andrews's concern with syntax and with constructivist method (and, thematically, with defamiliarization). The words always precede the writer: the essay's deliberately overdetermined first sentence, "in the beginning was the word" (219), echoes Davidson's own beginning, "There would be a first word and it would permit the first one to speak it" (*Analogy* 7). The writer, then, becomes one who reconstructs the relationships among words. Andrews's goal is not exegesis (his second sentence reads, "There is no use in clarifying the text" [*Paradise and Method* 219]), not the creation of a secondary so much as a parallel text.

Relevant to any consideration of the "author" in Andrews's work is Barrett Watten's commentary: "There appears to be no psychology in the work, no structural other than the text; everything is on the surface. . . . The human subject is reduced [to] the status of an equivalent sign, including the subject of the writer, who is as dispersed as any element in the work" (*Total Syntax* 159–60). Are we seeing here the widely touted death of the authorial subject? Not exactly—rather, an investigation of and change in the author function. On the surface, Andrews's work can sometimes seem impenetrably private. Yet the notion of a "private" writing presumes an authorial subject lurking within or under or behind the text, a subject whose experience and imagination it becomes the reader's job to tease out, a producer of what students like to call "hidden meaning." Any efforts to tease such a stable subject position out of Andrews's work will be consistently frustrated. As much as any other Language writer, Andrews has rendered the author function irrelevant to a reading of his work—one reason why the blandly nondescript "creative nonfiction" or "lyric essay" are inadequate terms for his prose. Thus the text's very resistance to probing, its impenetrability, makes it paradoxically public, a material body residing in the public domain, unconcerned with "*private transaction*," a domain that the writer, through the public system of language, "*enter[s] as public figure*" (*Paradise and Method* 26). As Watten comments, "by taking himself apart [the poet] places his judgment in the world" (*Total Syntax* 57). Appropriately, then, he describes that work in technological and constructivist rather than in organicist or expressivist metaphors: in Andrews's "Funnels In," for instance, "the inner space of language is being altered by a mechanistic act," the verbal effects those "of a word machine that he has set up, like a wave generator or a conveyor belt"; similarly, "I Guess Work the Time Up" is "a kind of fantastic machine, each line a conveyor belt of semiotic rubble, funny poking things—to flip on the switch is to get action" (18, 160).

Andrews's engagement with other poets is often insistently dialogic, to a greater degree even than his other prose. Far from assuming the authorial self as a stable source of critical judgment, insight, and commentary on some writing "Other," the model for his critical essays is closer to that of conversation. Thus his essay on Ron Silliman, "Self/Ideology: Corpses That Devour Their Own Flesh" (*Paradise and Method* 208–14), takes the form of a strictly formatted alternation in end-stopped lines, without commentary, of selections from Andrews's own *I Don't Have*

*Any Paper So Shut Up (or, Social Romanticism)* and Silliman's *Tjanting*.[3] This proceduralist dialogue becomes a kind of antiessay that turns prose into poetry, that takes phrases and sentences from Silliman's and Andrews's prose and recasts them in poetic lines in a way that resonates with contemporaneous work like Charles Bernstein's "Artifice of Absorption" and "A Defence of Poetry" or Bob Perelman's "The Marginalization of Poetry"—work published both as poetry and as essay in different venues.[4] "Solicitation/Keyboards," a "hybrid essay collaboration . . . pushing at some genre constraints" (*Paradise and Method* 215), and Andrews's contribution to a special issue of *The Difficulties* on David Bromige, is a similar collage text. It includes a Bromige letter to Andrews, quotations from Bromige's *P-E-A-C-E*, a snippet defining "solicitation" (perhaps in response to having an essay "solicited"), floating sentence fragments ("A sighting of . . . . / A praxis of . . . ." [216]), all in the service of investigating the term and idea of "totality." Parodying the formulaic quality of much conventional criticism, Andrews intersperses rule-generated paragraphs in which the keyboard provides the sequence and first letter of the words: q, w, e, r, and so on. These paragraphs begin by offering a fair imitation of critical prose of the "Response to Bromige" type: "Question whether either reason tallies your unchallengeable intuition of prior aesthetic soundings demanded for general heuristic judgments" (216). But Andrews quickly leaves this flirtation with "sense" behind, so that a few paragraphs later we get to "quack, whack, eek, roar, thanks, yell, utter" (217). The essay turns into noise, or at least into words for noise, the representation of noise.

In 1986, Andrews published a—what? an essay? a prose poem?—titled "Social Topography." Here are the first two paragraphs, the "introduction":

> Geometry of the personal. Topology of . . . A stepwise advance, progression against . . . A permanent grid. (23, 17) Roles, models, forms—with which social strata are portrayed. (4, 11)
>
> Trapped with self meaning trapped with the whole of it all / 'tyranny of distance' / and closing knotty concentric patterns / with the presumption of pattern / confusion and otherwise. (21, 26, 8, 4, 9) (*Paradise and Method* 197)

This text may offer a topography of "social strata," but, constructed as it is out of quotations from Lyn Hejinian's Tuumba chapbook series, it is equally a social topography of Language writing itself, published in a magazine that is part of the landscape being defined, *Jimmy and Lucy's House of K*. It is also something like a bibliographical essay, concluding with its source texts numbered, listed alphabetically by title (not author), and dated: "1. *ABC*. Ron Silliman. 1983. / 2. *a.k.a.* Bob Perelman. 1979. / 3. *Alogon*. Michael Palmer. 1980" (199). Neither an orthodox essay nor "poetry," "Social Topography" is that oxymoron, a pure hybrid.

It is normative syntax and the sentence in Andrews's criticism that, as in much of his poetry, most consistently comes under attack. Here is the first paragraph of Andrews's review of Dorothy Trujillo Lusk's *Redactive*: "Trip hazard!" ("Redaction" 37)—a tongue-in-cheek warning as to what lies ahead for the reader of Lusk's book, and perhaps of the review. From this point the review moves through a series of short, characteristically staccato paragraphs, none more than five sentences or phrases long. Some are composed entirely of sentence fragments: "Implicit lines within. Unfigured, de-slurred, bigger as foresight. Using the desk as a ceiling." Andrews describes his subject and registers his responses not through discursive strategies but through short, sharp phrases: "A device purée," "extreme cuts fondly demolitional," "system caesura" (37–38). Similar in method is "Pulsed Scale," a review of Abigail Child's *Climate/Plus*: "Globed & shaped resistible—frontiers beside attention paratactic breeding, matrix wobbly intrinsic (noise) capacity's magnificence proliferates" (126). One might venture a "reading" here. That which seems self-enclosed and fully formed, "globed & shaped," is in fact "resistible." It is resistible through "attention" to what lies at or beyond the "frontiers" of a pervasively administered society ("managed, administered to be a job," Andrews writes earlier), however—an attention that operates not through the normative structures of hypotactic syntax but through "paratactic breeding," that locates itself "besides" (the root meaning of "para-"). Such disruptive "breeding," such "proliferation" of "(noise) capacity's magnificence," may be both cause and effect of the "matrix" becoming "wobbly." More to the point, however, is the way in which Andrews's writing itself breeds and proliferates meaning by its syntactic fragmentation and collision, following its own injunction from earlier in "Pulsed Scale" to "hybridize edge" (126).

Andrews frequently embraces a formulaic or self-consciously proceduralist structure in his essays. His use of rule-generated paragraphs in the Bromige essay is one form of this; another is the alternating structure of the Silliman essay. Yet a third is his use of section headings—on the surface, another academic convention. Along the lines of his Howe and Davidson essays, he organizes an essay on Barrett Watten (in which Watten is never named) under capitalized subheadings: ZERO DEGREE, POLITICS, EXPLAINING, and so on. (Of the twelve headings, seven also show up in the Davidson essay and in "Transatlantic," Andrews's introduction to the anthology of experimental London poets, *Floating Capital*, giving some clue to the consistency of his concerns.) Some sections, justified only to the left margin, could be read as poetry; most look like prose; all are less than a page long, with Andrews showing little interest, then, in sustaining an argument. And he uses for his title that of one of Watten's own most mathematically ordered books, *Under Erasure*, a serial poem that moves between italicized and roman-face tercets (as Andrews's essays often do), each tercet ending with three ellipses.

Andrews's introduction to *Floating Capital* is similarly formulaic—and I mean this term descriptively, not evaluatively. It begins as conventionally as any essay Andrews has written, with two paragraphs on the internationalization of music and the question of artistic "global transplants," followed by a third beginning with this thesis statement: "*Floating Capital*, published in the U.S., represents another such transatlantic communiqué, reflecting & anticipating a more attractive cross-fertilization" (*Paradise and Method* 246). But by the fourth paragraph, the essay has moved into the more recognizable Andrews mode of mostly short paragraphs made up of phrases and sentence fragments. Each paragraph begins with a one- or two-word question—"Radicalism?" "Politics?" "Social explanation?" and so on (247)—followed by a staccato sequence of comments, occasionally in grammatically complete sentences, mainly in the form of phrases or sentence fragments. (This procedure—one of "constructivist method & artifice" [247], to quote the essay itself—is anticipated at the end of the more orthodox third paragraph, which concludes "Questions—Responses" [247], the last phrase to resemble a conventional prose transition occurring in the essay.) Thus each paragraph begins not with a topic sentence but with a topic fragment, couched as a question. The point here is that the essay's structure, as much as its style, draws attention to its own artifice: a measure, in Charles Bernstein's terms, of the work's antiabsorptiveness in a mode conventionally designed for absorption.

As in his poetry, and again in direct transgression of the conventions of most critical discourse, Andrews foregrounds the graphic materiality of his prose—"a weightedness near-hieroglyphic in its matte" (248)—through a high incidence of uppercase letters, dashes, italics, parentheses: "Not futuristic jive—(Tract means Space Colony)—but *the world rewritten*. Edit Past" (247). Lack of transitions and fracturing of syntax further the disjunctive effect, and his comments on the writing that is his ostensible subject refer equally to his own method ("disjuncture=lack of adhesives, lingo sequenced staccato"; "note the resistant syntax incineration" [248–49]). His diction is equally resistant in its deliberately jaw-breaking neologisms:

"surrenderably," "readableable," "amphitheatricalized," "depreposterousize" (249–50). Though Andrews concludes with the conventional trope of a poetic quotation (unattributed, however) that sums up the issues of the essay, any actual effect of conventionality has by this point been erased by all that precedes it. In other words, Andrews invokes conventions of the critical essay—establish background to open the essay, quote to close it—to draw attention to the rhetorical frame and to highlight the gap between that frame and the energies at work within it and finally uncontained by it. One phrase from this essay could stand for the goal of Andrews's whole critical enterprise: "Not a self-allegorizing Ruin of discourse but Opportunity" (250).

This cut-up, constructivist prose—"cut-up-ish swoon experimentation Language" (247)—draws attention to its method as much as to its content. "Method," for Andrews, is where philosophy, politics, and poetry meet, the site of the "epistemopoetical" (247). (We might recall Charles Bernstein's aphorism that "all writing is a demonstration of method; it can assume a method or investigate it" [*Content's Dream* 226].) And in "Transatlantic" method is content, inviting the reader to make distinctions that the seamlessness of more orthodox prose might gloss over. "Methodics discriminate," Andrews writes, and they do so through acts of constructivist artifice: "edges, scarred lexicons," "Intuitive breaks & bumps & broadjumps to Parabolize Identity," "margins, cuts, hinges, stets & stops," a textual "surface worked-over, sawtoothed" (*Paradise and Method* 248–49). Refusing to accept "that constructivist method & artifice should be confined to well-mannered incremental moves within a regime of stylistic niceties" (247), Andrews cultivates an aggressive critical poetics characterized—to draw some further terms from "Transatlantic"—by "rips," "fracture," "amputations," "jam-up" (247–48). Paradoxically, Andrews's criticism exhibits some of the surface features of academic prose: a high incidence of the copula and of passive verbs, abstract nouns, lots of "-ists" and "-isms." Once subjected to his constructivist method, however, these features get abstracted from their usual status as conventional stylistic features of literary and social theory and become available for new uses.

Artifice and construction have been central to Andrews's poetics from the beginning:

> 1. Do you love the audience? Certainly we do. We show it by getting out of their way. 2. A sound, a rhythm, a name, an image, a dream, a gesture, a picture, an action, a silence: any or all of these can function as 'keys.' 3. Language is the house we live in. 4. The words are there to massage. (*Paradise and Method* 3)

These sentences kick off the self-quoting text "Index," one of the earliest of Andrews's collage or constructivist essays on poetics. (The numbered citations are, in order, from John Cage, Jerome Rothenberg, Jean-Luc Godard, and Andrews's then-wife Ellen.) And this is the beginning of another self-quoting "Index":

> ALL OF MY FRIENDS ARE DEAD
> AMERICA SHOPS
> AM I ALIVE
> ANIMAL DICKS IN BED. (*Ex Why Zee* 19)

This "Index," another constructivist text, rewrites (reprints? reconstructs?) as a poem the alphabetically ordered table of contents from Andrews's collection of prose poems, *I Don't Have Any Paper So Shut Up (or, Social Romanticism)*—poems that, in a gesture of aggressive artifice, take their first clause as their title in each case.

Even in the midst of all this genre blurring, as I have said, typically one can still tell the difference between an Andrews poem and an essay, in terms of purpose, publishing context, and often typographical layout. Nevertheless, there remain moments of genuine generic ambiguity. *Wobbling*, a collection of poems written in the mid-late-1970s, contains "Methodology," a critical prose poem that focuses on the implications for contemporary practice of "the tradition," "traditional poetry" (45)—admittedly a rather reified category in Andrews's treatment of it.[5] Reading in "the tradition" throughout this piece is associated with nostalgia for a lost stability, for some imagined historical moment "as if once ever still." The poem's rhetoric, then, is insistently one of returning: "It's part of the whole endeavor to get back," "finally to regain," "trying to be ever regaining," "we did want to go on with another reminiscence," "wanted to read traditional poetry so regain retain." Andrews's problem with this effort "finally to regain" the values associated in his view with traditional poetry, those of aesthetic "quality" and timelessness ("arrest rhythm of old time"), seems to be, at first, that whatever this poetry offers, "it's been *done* accomplished": "you read it but don't get the most acumen . . . so give it a rest." If the "rhythm of old time" also suggests traditional prosodies, this conflicts with the rushing kinetics of Andrews's own piece, a single unpunctuated three-quarter-page paragraph that moves like a "dance flood room giant Niagara speedster." Andrews mocks the vagueness of humanist appeals to tradition, the difficulty of defining its value: "Well it *had* done some other else however thing elusive." Yet he also seems to attribute substance to that "elusive thing," and to suggest that it might be worth retaining: "Whatever *aspects* of actual life were gift alarm continue *those*." The difference between this moment and Andrews's preceding critique of "getting back" resides in an approach to reading, in a shift away from a nostalgic and unreflective devotion to "quality" and timelessness, and toward a set of reading conditions in which "now audiences set junctures" (45)—a shift, to return to the poem's title, in the "methodology" both of reading and writing about reading, and a shift crucial to the development of Language writing at the time this piece was written.

"Methodology" is preceded by a poem whose title sounds like it was pulled straight from Foucault: "'At any rate this discipline is primarily contrary to any form of verbal apology of eroticism.'" Evoking poststructuralist theory as part of its intertextual field, the poem goes on to incorporate comments on its (Andrews's) own operations as a writing that "banishes the gestural," where "presence is *depreciated*" even though it "has left traces," and where "the unapproachability" can be read as "say a code / a social hieroglyphic" (43–44). These are the kind of poems that Ron Silliman may well have in mind when he writes of *Wobbling* that "Andrews's poems are far from theory-determined, engaging in such issues more as a boxer might an opponent" (["Review"] 155). The misplaced charge that Language writing is theory driven has haunted its reception from the beginning. But a thorough reading of Andrews's work makes clear that investigations of the poetry-criticism or praxis-theory boundary have actually characterized that writing from a point before the academic hegemony of poststructuralist theory that has often been misunderstood as having produced Language writing.

Commenting on what he takes as some representative excerpts of Andrews's work, Bob Perelman writes that "for readers who are not familiar with Andrews the politics of such writing would probably be difficult to fathom" (*Marginalization* 99). Like most poets' writings on poetics, however, Andrews's essays construct a social and political context for his poetry, a context necessary for a reading of his most disjunctive work. They constitute not only a frame of reference for new readers but also the familiarity itself that more seasoned readers (like Perelman) might claim for themselves. That is, "those who know Andrews's poetry . . . and what he stands for" (99) do so partly through his essays, which are an integral part of his writing practice, not an excrescence on the body of his "real" work in poetry.[6]

A critique comparable in subject and method to "Methodology" from Andrews's midcareer work appears in his 1995 volume *Ex Why Zee*. "Choose Your Weapons" began as a spoken text for a movement improvisation by the New York dancer and choreographer Sally Silvers. It energetically attacked conventional dance training, both balletic and modern, and more generally the idea of "training" in any art where, from Andrews's point of view, "there *is* no tradition, there is only illegitimate authority" (*Ex* 18). In a further moment of generic instability, the spoken text becomes something other when it is published: an essay-poem that treats training as constraint, regulation, petrification, paralysis, "the properly precocious easy safe and inoffensive, guide to excruciatingly correct behavior" (17). The text thus functions as interpretation or explanation of itself, theory as praxis. No wonder the book's jacket blurb asserts punningly "Here are primary texts," as if out of some anxiety that they might be taken as "secondary," mere commentary.

In most critical writing on poetry, one conventional marker of difference—though a marker that Language writing always problematized—between "primary" and "secondary" texts, poetry and poetics, practice and theory, is the poetic line. But the line no longer functions as such in much of Andrews's work, and a piece like the 1995 "Index" highlights the line's conventionality as a marker of generic difference. In a five-paragraph essay on prosody (a parody of the five-paragraph theme, and perhaps a tongue-in-cheek nod toward pentameter), "Lines Linear How to Mean," Andrews argues the homogenizing and closural effects of orthodox lineation: "a constructed continuity," "a static & isolating & securing closure of purpose" (*Paradise and Method* 119). Andrews's equally constructed alternative, embodied as well as stated in the disjunct phrases that make up his most characteristic unit of composition, is "constant crease & flux, a radical discontinuity as lack, jeopardizes before & after, stop & start, . . . troubling us to locate ourselves in formal terms" (119). Again, the effect and goal of this strategy applies equally to Andrews's critical/theoretical work, where, as in his poetry, he thinks of "lack of (regular, traditional) closure as generative": "It foregrounds an artificial, constructed process, a denatured measure of kinetic shifts, registers of differentiation," "refusing the normatively linear" (119–20). Consistently Andrews's accounts of his writing project apply equally well to all aspects of that project: poetry, essays, performance texts, reviews. Insisting that the argumentative and stylistic conventions of critical prose are also social conventions, Andrews is drawn both as reader and writer to "work inclined to contest, rather than bail out of, the context; the content. To send it up, short-circuit some of its particulars & maybe its shape, its agenda, its organizing principles" (206). Thus his essays seek to inquire into what has come to be called the social construction of reality by "withholding the usual allegiances of syntax, style, decorum, or subject (the idealisms of subjectivity *and* the partialities of subject matter)" (111).

Such examples suggest the range of possibilities for alternative critical practice that are thrown up by Andrews's attack on the theory-practice binary. His prose offers a constantly self-undermining point of view and language use that, because of its very self-undermining, does not and cannot claim authority (or even authorship, in the usual sense) for itself. Characterized by a manner, a set of tropes, more than by a critical voice, it profoundly questions the conventional features of normative criticism that serve to shore up the permeable boundary between poetry and poetics. Andrews's prose represents a stout resistance to such institutionalized modes of expository reading and writing. Because Andrews assumes that all writing has an ideological basis, the expository, too, must be subject to disruption from within: it cannot be seen as "taken-for-granted" (one of Andrews's favorite adjectives) neutral commentary. As he puts it in "Equals What?" when he sardonically notes the effect of pronouncing the labial plosive "p," "I spit every time I use the word 'expository'" (201); or less punningly and more bluntly, in "Be Careful Now, You Know Sugar Melts in Water," "the expository is hideous" (127). Or is it "less punningly," if the expository, in all its deceptive transparency, should turn out to "hide us?"

## Visual Materiality, Writing and "Poetry"

While I have hardly used the term "materiality" in the preceding discussion, it is an intrinsic formal feature of Andrews's poetic essays or critical prose poems that also reflects this creolized genre's ambitions toward social critique—"politicized poetic prose," as Rachel Blau DuPlessis calls it, "intransigent willful writing" ("*f*-Words" 17, 16). But another form of materiality is equally important to Andrews's counterpoetic project: the visual. Except for Lyn Hejinian's discussion of the relationships among acoustic, linguistic, and graphic line and her comments on Andrews's "'Field work,' where words and lines are distributed irregularly on the page" (*Language* 43), Peter Quartermain's analysis of the work's "topological features" (166), some early remarks by Ron Silliman on "Andrews's *page-as-field*" as an implicit critique of "the line [as] the predominant current signifier of The Poetic" (*New Sentence* 61–62), and William Howe's master's thesis, the visual components of Andrews's work have received relatively little attention.[7] Yet that work often exhibits great visual inventiveness, and Andrews himself wrote in his first book that "the way words fit into a sentence or a line (or a line of thought) doesn't grab me as much as how they relate to the space and silence around them. I like the edges, discreteness, fragments, collision" (*Edge* np). The vast visual range of Andrews's writing includes extensive manipulations of typography; minimalist gestural shapes, evoking (without forming) letters; block-like overwritten glyphs; drawings and diagrams; word circles, word and phoneme wedges, word grids, lists; drawings, pseudoscientific diagrams, and diagrams for performance; words in graphs, charts, spreadsheets, boxes; instructions for a gallery installation; pages variously perforated or divided by vertical and horizontal, solid and dotted lines; words linked by arrows or separated by hand-drawn landscape forms like coastlines; page designs that run from the scattered and dismembered to the strictly symmetrical to the blank (the 1976 *Vowels* alternates written and blank pages). I read the visual text in Andrews not as expressivist or as bearing a direct relation to thematic content (as in Susan Howe) but as part of his overall project to counter politically suspect modes of representation using the tools of a materialist poetics. From this point of view, reading Andrews's visual poetics does not aestheticize that aspect of his writing so much as it locates it within the overall social formalism of his poetic project. Further, consideration of the visual in Andrews (including such projects as *BothBoth*, his verbal/visual collaboration with the English poet and artist Bob Cobbing, and *Joint Words*, the collaboration on fourteen small cards with John Bennett) has the advantage of opening up numerous contexts for understanding his writing: concrete and other visual poetries, his intermedia work, his immersion in avant-garde cinema, as well as the more general preoccupation of the early Language school with material textuality. Equally importantly, these various contexts and the visual poetics that they partly shaped give us in turn a window onto Andrews's disidentification with the genre of "poetry" and his antipathy for the dominant poetries of his time.

As I've been suggesting, "poetry" is a rather problematic term for much of Andrews's project; considering the role of the visual or graphic in his work, his enterprise of "foregrounding in a pretty drastic way the materiality (& social materiality) of the reading surface, down to its tiniest markers" (Andrews, *Poetics Talks* 2) suggests just why that is so. Andrews did not come to poetry from a literary background, and indeed stresses as a positive the absence in his experience of "a schooled, institutionalized background concentrated on creative writing or so-called English, with predictable socialization into (the instigation of a commitment to) academic neo-Victorian verse or the timidly 'free' alternatives of '60s classrooms" (*Paradise and Method* 78). Rather, as he puts it, "my interests as a student were predominantly in avant-garde activity in a wide range of art fields—theatre, film, music, dance (a little bit)—and I had read some radical modernist literature," artistic practices that "seemed, with few exceptions, more radical and uncompromising than what I was familiar with in current literary work" (93, 78). Given the nature of his work, his earliest publishing possibilities came from "people in other types of experimental poetry, heavily influenced by concrete, visual works, sound work, performance kinds of things" (94), and he continued to publish work with presses and magazines oriented toward visual poetics such as John Byrum's Generator, mIEKAL aND's Xexoxial, and Crag Hill's *Score.*

Andrews describes his writing structurally (especially the process of producing his later work) by analogy with experimental cinema: "Writing is a constructing of previously generated materials, similar to what some of my filmmaker friends do—go out and shoot short chunks of footage, go into the flatbed, assemble films in the *editing* process . . . Again, more like people shooting film, single-framing or very short bursts of footage, ten feet, fifty feet, a hundred feet of film" (103–04). (Meanwhile, Brian McHale compares Andrews's process "to audio sampling and mixing in a recording studio" [181]). As a beginner, Andrews saw his work as "a kind of literary writing, or experimental writing, more than I thought of it as poetry." Subsequently, however, "it was clear that the only future for anything I did . . . was going to be under the category of poetry, as defined by other people" ("'How Poignant'" 193–94). Attention to the visual or graphic in Andrews, then, places his work in an expanded cultural field that includes avant-garde activity in all the arts and, more specifically, visual poetries from Italian Futurism to Lettrism to concrete poetry to conceptual art—identifications that Andrews maintains in his writing by continuing to publish work like *Ex Why Zee,* a book of performance scores that documents his involvement in the worlds of experimental music, theater, and dance.

Within this context of multiple intersecting arts, the conceptualism of the 1960s and 1970s is particularly important to any consideration of how Andrews's work, and especially its graphic components, emerged. In *Art Discourse/Discourse in Art,* Jessica Prinz focuses on "works by artists for whom language is an essential constituent part of art" (1), and we can read much of Andrews's writing in relation to the conceptual art of Kosuth, LeWitt, Smithson, Weiner, and others, with the influence of Duchamp behind them. Indeed, Prinz closes with comments on "the close tie between Language poetry and Conceptual art," claiming that "what the Language Poets share with the Conceptualists is an acute sense of the materiality of language" (166–67). Carla Harryman addresses conceptualism's significance for the San Francisco Language-writing scene, and especially for poets' theater, as follows: "Conceptualism's attention to materiality, frame, context, and space influenced all the arts . . . and many if not all of the writers associated with Language writing" (29). In particular, via reference to a range of conceptualist discourses, Harryman sketches a cultural moment marked by the "presentation of experimental works as critical lectures" and "co-presentations of poets and performance and conceptual artists' works in contexts that diminished the distinction between 'poet and artist'" (28).[8] Such forms of conceptualist materiality as performance directions, postcards, and instructions for installations (with their origins, perhaps, in Fluxus event scores or Duchamp's notes for his boxes) all show up in Andrews as "poems." If the attitude of the first conceptualist, Duchamp (whom Marjorie Perloff sees as producing a "series of proto-language poems . . . in the mid-teens" [*21st-Century Modernism* 90]), was antiretinal, that of the early Andrews can often seem antireading (at least in the conventional sense of "reading").[9] If Duchamp's question was "can one make works which are not works of 'art?'" (qtd. in Perloff, *21st-Century Modernism* 81), Andrews's seems to be "can one write poetry-like works which are not works of 'poetry?'"

Perhaps the most sustained discussion of the relationship between avant-garde poetics and the role of language in conceptual art, Liz Kotz's *Words to Be Looked At*, addresses precisely this issue. Commenting on the 1950s collage experiments of John Ashbery and Jackson Mac Low, Kotz argues that "ultimately their works tended to recontain these experiments back into something all-too-recognizable as poetic form" (139):

> By remaining within the orbit of poetry, . . . even radical poetic practices tend to reaffirm a set of conventions that were elsewhere thrown into question. Just as Cage's work, in the words of George Brecht, "remained music," so too did these radical experiments of Ashbery and Mac Low "remain poetry." It was up to artists such as Carl Andre, [Vito] Acconci, On Kawara, Lawrence Weiner, and Warhol to follow through on the implications of these experiments. (134)

Meanwhile, "poetry appeared, in the 1960s art world, as a potential field for investigating language as such and, in particular for exploring the behavior of words on the page" (138). One index of this crossover is Vito Acconci and Bernadette Mayer's editing between 1967 and 1969 of the six issues of *0 to 9*, a mimeo publication juxtaposing poetry and "texts by conceptually oriented art world figures" (118) that Andrews read eagerly.[10] It is against this background that Andrews's visual poetics most strikingly resists recuperation as poetry. In an art world context, conceptualism may represent the dematerialization of the art object, in Lucy Lippard's phrase;

in the overlapping contexts of the art and poetry worlds, it represents the rematerialization of the word under the sign of poetry, even as a writer like Andrews questions the appropriateness of that sign for his work.

Andrews's active engagement with the visual arts and with verbal-visual cross-fertilization is reflected in his coediting (with Charles Bernstein) of *L=A=N=G=U=A=G=E* magazine, which featured visual and conceptual artists (Susan Bee, Carl Andre, "language-based sculptor" Lawrence Weiner),[11] filmmakers (Abigail Child, Henry Hills), book artists, visual poets, and intermedia artists (Johanna Drucker, Karl Kempton, Karl Young, Dick Higgins), and a revived Futurist, Gino Severini. The magazine included numerous reviews of visual-verbal works, and graphic texts by David Bromige, Douglas Messerli, Laszlo Moholy-Nagy, Barrett Watten, Severini, and Brita Bergland. Consistent with *L=A=N=G=U=A=G=E*'s genre-blurring project, reviews and graphic texts were sometimes one (in the cases of Bromige and Messerli). Andrews's own contributions included his commentary on visual components and conceptualism in the work of Michael Frederick Tolson ("Layout"), Ernest Robson ("The Politics of Scoring"), and Loris Essary ("Line Sites"); his cut-up selection of phrases from poet/filmmaker Frank Kuenstler's already-cut-up *Lens* ("And for Anything That I Could Call My Own Thinking"); and his two-part bibliography of articles relevant to experimental poetics, with its heavy emphasis on art and film journals ("Articles").[12] Even more apposite and striking, though much less well known, is the Andrews-edited issue of *Toothpick, Lisbon, and the Orcas Islands* (5 [Fall 1973]), with its almost complete emphasis on the graphic text and its juxtaposition of early Language writing with work by conceptual artists such as Robert Ashley, Arakawa, LeWitt, Weiner, and Acconci.[13]

One project that shows Andrews's visual poetics moving beyond poetry and the book is *Joint Words*, his 1979 collaboration with John Bennett. The title suggests two of Andrews's central artistic values, collaboration and materiality: words produced jointly by the coauthors, and words that function as "joints" in the construction of meaning. In *Joint Words*, distributed in a small envelope that evokes mail art but is not actually mail-able, fourteen four-by-two-and-a-half white cards each feature two words, which one could read as a kind of rearrangeable parody sonnet (one card = one line) and a project somewhat analogous to Robert Grenier's contemporaneous, though much larger, *Sentences*. Except for two apparent neologisms, "kak" and "kaak," the twenty-eight words (or perhaps twenty-seven, since one card reads "boom boom") are all complete and semantically meaningful in English, though not all resolve into meaningful phrases when combined.[14] Meanwhile, the "apparent neologism" carries as much relevant weight as any word in the packet, evoking the materialist poetics of Khlebnikov and Kruchonykh: in Russian, "kak" is the middle term in "the letter as such" ("bukva kak takovaia") and "the word as such" ("slovo kak takovoe").[15] *Joint Words* is anticipated by texts like "Song No 154," "Song No 156," and "Song No 124" from *Love Songs*, written in the fall of 1973 and probably the least love-song-like work ever issued under that title. "Song No 124" prints twenty-nine cards, each one featuring a two-word noun phrase ("the" plus a noun); one corner is cut off the cards, like sales tags in a department store, a technique to which Andrews returns in the later "Lasting Kiss Removal" (*Designated Heartbeat* 41–48). Part poem, part conceptual art, "154" and "156" consist of two vertical lists of words designed for visual display outside the confines of the book: in Andrews's directions, "*separate index cards placed on a table or shelf or in a display cabinet*" (*Love Songs* np). Although "Song No 156" is similarly designed for "*separate index cards placed within sight of Song No 154*," they are in fact separated in the book, so that they cannot be viewed in relation to each other, and the book placement conflicts with the proposed gallery or art space placement. In another sense, however, the page becomes the gallery space, so that what Kotz writes of Vito Acconci can apply equally to Andrews: "An 'installation' of words on the physical space of the page analogous to an installation of objects in the physical space of a room, [Andrews's] poems use words as objects to be accumulated, arranged, stacked, dispersed, and moved" (156).

A key distinction for framing the visual aspects of Andrews's work as a critique of poetry-as-usual, a way of rethinking poetics, is the institutionally imposed and maintained one between poetry and writing. He comments as follows: "I remember . . . when the term 'language poetry' started getting thrown around, and my initial nervousness about the term stemmed mostly from the P word rather than from the L word—that I thought of it as language writing, a term I wasn't all that displeased with, because it suggested almost a new genre, or a new subgenre possibility that hadn't yet been defined" ("How Poignant" 194)—one outside the received (or perceived) boundaries of poetry. In this context, Johanna Drucker's definition of "writing" is a useful one: "the visible form of language from the level of the marks to the letters" (*Figuring* 232). That is, "writing exists . . . along a broad spectrum from the most elemental gestural trace to the standard sign" (59), incorporating "marks, strokes, signs, glyphs, letters, or characters" (57). This expanded view of "writing," far more than any notion of poetry, can help us understand the place in Andrews's oeuvre of publications like *StandPoint*, a "visual sequence" ("W O R K" 286) from 1977 published in 1991. *StandPoint* is a ten-page eleven-by-eight booklet;

each page features nine framed images within one large frame. This sequence consists of minimalist gestural shapes, sometimes just one stroke per frame. Some of the shapes evoke natural forms somewhat as many of Robert Grenier's hand-drawn letters do (fig. 11.1); some evoke visually key terms of Andrews's poetics like that of "suture" (fig. 11.2);[16] others evoke actual letters, so that one can detect variously a sequence of Is or sideways Hs, a V, a U, a large O, a twiggy Y, a K, a distorted H, a backward P (figs.11.1–3). Unreadable in any conventional sense as poetry (as Drucker puts it, "traces of somatic gesture remain unreadable because they stop short of participation in the symbolic system" [*Figuring* 66]), *StandPoint*'s nonlexical (though not nonsignifying) marks are readable as part of Andrews's career-long investigation into how visual materiality signifies and into what constitutes writing.[17] Late in writing's history, these traces nevertheless locate themselves at the very beginning of writing and signification. In Drucker's words, the trace is "that materialization of gesture which makes the first line of demarcation against which meaning can be produced. Such a trace produces the differentiating boundary which renders meaning possible" (66).[18] If Andrews is "interested in the basic foundational structure of meaning, in its material form in the sign" (*Paradise and Method* 106), *StandPoint* is one visual form that interest takes.

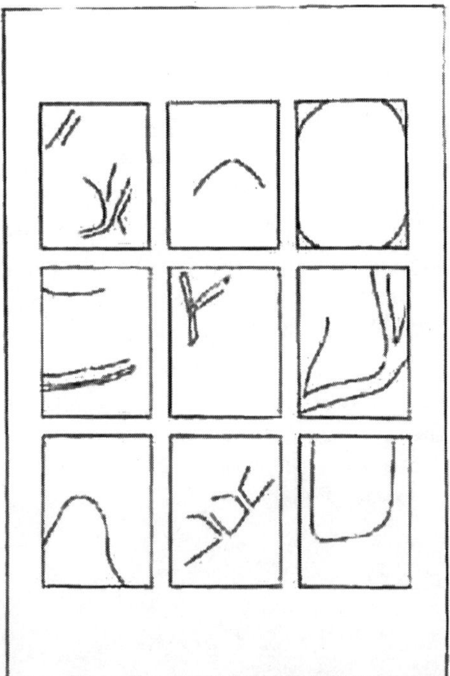

Figure 11.1. Bruce Andrews, *StandPoint*

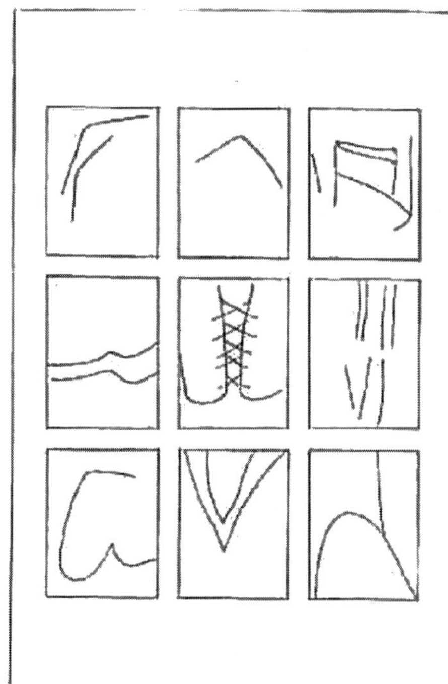

Figure 11.2. Bruce Andrews, *StandPoint*

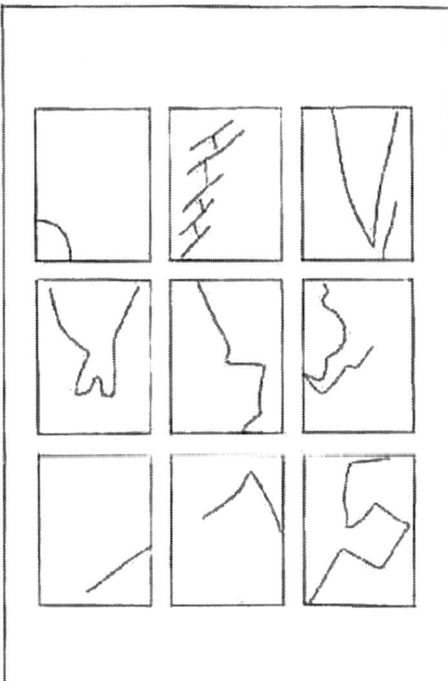

Figure 11.3. Bruce Andrews, *StandPoint*

Such "non-word" material ("W O R K" 288) has been part of Andrews's work ever since *Factura* (the earliest work in which dates from 1969), and on into the glyph-like figures in *Love Songs* (written in 1973) and the rough, unstably geometrical drawings of "Unit Costs" (published in the 1987 *Give Em Enough Rope* but written in 1980) (fig. 11.4). Given his investment in visual materiality, it is unsurprising that Andrews would publish a "non-word" collection like *Factura*, after the Russian Futurists' term for attention to the materiality of one's medium. (*Faktura* was originally a visual art term adapted for poetry. Russian Futurist attention to language "relied on the imposition of the notion of *faktura*, attention to the making of a work of art, especially to the resultant qualities of its surface, onto verbal material" [Drucker, *Visible Word* 175]). *Love Songs* contains hand-drawn landscape-like forms, surrounding the words and creating particular clusters of connection and separation (fig. 11.5); it contains composite glyphs, with the letters barely detectable and syllables or words

moss however house of cards

Dip prom

Sweetspot

Audio Awared-ness for the Consumer
positioning as box

Stars at night

Nameless erratically epistle
scissors reveal post office
vacant anus highlight interminable pegged wafer

Hen-mark on breast open breast drawers
's Self throat
dice throw

This *is* always going to be competing *with* others ('I heard you') in contexts where the others will invariably *be* presented ('let me wait to cocaine') as authoritative

Tail end—*it's all the substance*

Took hints
mangled matter

Respiration rate—turmoil ontology
tunnel re-entry as if dye spread over

Enter as public figure

May see backwards
low foreboding
literal & otherwise terrorist turnstile zoo flag

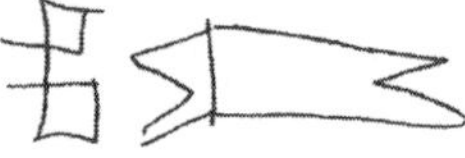

If cellophane wrapped around the body could be a spiritual awakening

Governance
I'm hostelry of facts

Lower as seismograph movements minus taxation

Sousa crypt

Obtrusive crotch house arrest

Anthemic power of

& I couldn't resist making my little point

Quick floorshine beat hairnet disembodiment

But it's not all that easy to

Not quite inaudible

General's deviant hot teenage assets

Figure 11.4. Bruce Andrews, *Give Em Enough Rope*, pp. 34–35

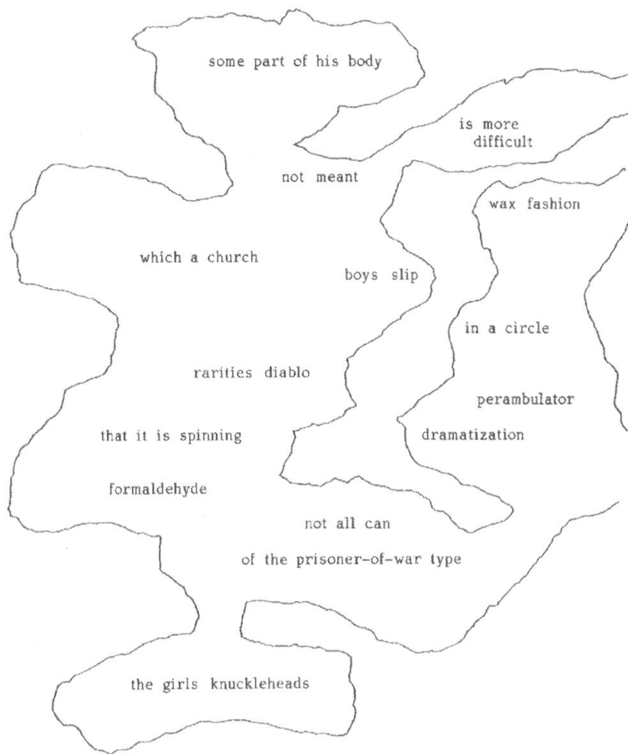

NO 116
some part of his body
is more difficult
not meant
wax fashion
which a church
boys slip
in a circle
rarities diablo
perambulator
that it is spinning
dramatization
formaldehyde
not all can
of the prisoner-of-war type
the girls knuckleheads


Figure 11.5. Bruce Andrews, *Love Songs*

barely formulable out of them.[19] Songs 144–46 are wordless "poems," occupying some point between the "post-semiotic" poems of Steve McCaffery's 1970 *Transitions to the Beast* and gallery maps (fig. 11.6).[20] But the use of drawings also seems to elicit what could be read as moments of self-critique. "No 11" repeats six simple hand-drawn shapes in an irregular sequence through a pageful of boxes or frames, over the handwritten statement "so now you've got the small ball of wax." Perhaps an emphasis on framing and visual design risks producing slight or repetitive results, curtailing the "total" social perspective that Andrews has increasingly aspired to in his work, so that the whole ball of wax is merely a small ball.[21] As Andrews asks in an early journal entry, in a parallel moment of self-questioning, "*who says* a poem which is based on the integrity of the word [or the mark] will instead allow the reader to be in charge?" (*Divestiture—E* np)[22]

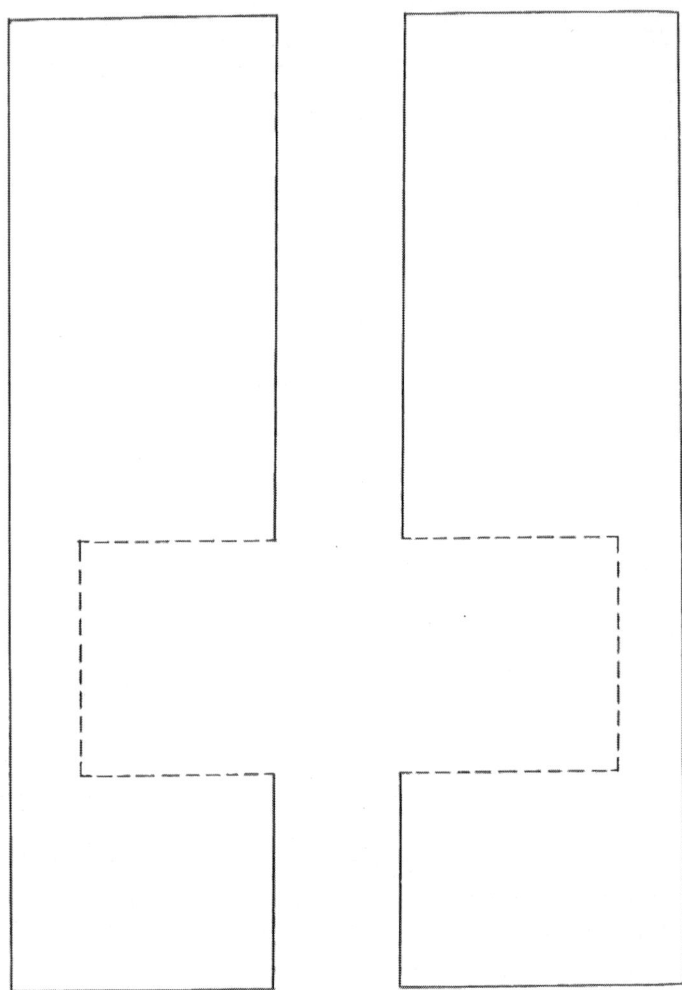


Figure 11.6. Bruce Andrews, *Love Songs*

A different kind of gestural trace shows up in Andrews's highly self-conscious use of handwriting, as that apparently most intimate and idiosyncratic form of physical production becomes another means to foreground the importance of materiality for his work. He comments on his handwriting in a couple of early journal entries:

> My handwriting—& casual proclivity for printing—the *style* of it, the angular precision—isn't completely a personal gesturing, or expressiveness, but is, really, an attempt from long ago to echo the *text*: to transform my writing into a reflection or personal figuration of "text"—a result, another one, of my whole love affair and obsession with print, with the qualities which differentiate or distinguish it as text: "textuality." (*Divestiture—E* np)

And again, "my handwriting—had to be 'printlike' so I could *read my writing* just like it were a book, text" (*Divestiture—E* np). Andrews's handwriting, that is, takes its form from his desire to defamiliarize it as a somatic production and have it take its place in his published work as a material form that will "echo the [printed] text," writing that aspires to the condition of typing. Thus, for example, on the cover of one of his earliest books, *Edge*, the title and author name are handwritten but barely detectable as such, and an important statement of poetics about halfway through the book comes in the form of a handwritten letter in which Andrews compares the words on his page to "the interrelated pieces of a nonrepresentational ceramic sculpture" (np)[23]

Handwriting offers a graphic example of poetry as an individual human production even as, in Andrews's case, it evokes the mediation of print technology in its appearance. In ways that have implications for the work of Robert Grenier that I discuss in chapter 13, Andrews's handwriting as reproduced proposes not some tension between the human or organic and the technological but a tension within any possible idealization of handwriting itself as primary or "natural." He renders the demarcation between handwriting and print fuzzy when his handwriting looks like a typeface. Print itself, of course, is not a neutral or transparent medium. Just as in early Language writing's materialist critique of rhetorical transparency, where one cannot simply look through the words to the truth behind them, one cannot look through the print to the words, since those words are print before they are anything else.

Is there, then, what William Howe calls a "politics of typography" (Brady et al. 200) in Andrews? Andrews's most visually splintered or porous work raises what is in part a political question: What holds these linguistic monads together? The unit of composition in his early work is frequently the single word, word fragment, or letter. In that work the social tensions around connection and disconnection are thematized visually. In the sequence "Film Noir," written in 1974, a high percentage of the phrases and sentences begin with a bold (noir) capital in a typeface different from the rest of the text. Beyond the title itself, "Film Noir" begins with an invitation to visual focus: "**I***ris in*" (*Getting Ready* 30), Andrews writes, combining an emphasis on the iris with a suggestion of the eye/I "risin[g]." The bold capitals make those letters seem separate from the words of which they are otherwise part. In the same sequence, different italicized typefaces on the same page serve to separate words from each other even as they are juxtaposed, along with the use of capitals and lowercase letters in multiple sizes, italicized capitals, lowercase roman—in this context, suddenly a choice among options rather than the default option or unconsidered norm—and bold-face horizontal lines. The idea of a politics of typography rests on defamiliarization, asking us to consider how unconventional typographical formats or shifts can bring a reader up short, can bring one to notice and denaturalize print's otherwise authoritative transparency. (Recall Susan Howe's formulation, "Print settles it.") The journal collection *Divestiture—E* contains a number of writing ideas focused on just such disruptions: "causal arrows in causal modeling," "tilted or enlarged letters in the middle of a sentence," "drawn larger, letters fill-in-able," "randomized typography," vowels rendered in italics, "pieces based on Gregg's shorthand" (np).[24] Drucker nicely summarizes the connection of all this to issues of authority and subversion:

> The threat to linguistic authority made by the manipulation of the words on the page was that it returned the written language to the specific place, instance, conditions of production—it became a highly marked text. The unmarked text, the even gray page of prose and poetic convention, appeared, as it were, to "speak itself." Its production codes lent the text a transcendent character. The text appeared, was there, and the unmarked author was indeed the Author of the Text as pure Word—with all the requisite theological resonance. (*Visible Word* 46)

The marked text, then, becomes by contrast antiauthoritarian and antitranscendent. Meanwhile, behind that "even gray page" of convention there lies an image from those ur-materialists and theorists of *faktura*, Khlebnikov and Kruchonykh, describing letters as political prisoners in "The Letter as Such": "You've seen the letters of their words—strung out in straight lines with shaved heads, resentful, each one just like all the others—gray, colorless—not letters at all, just stamped-out marks" (257).

Shaved heads and straight lines: one particular point where Andrews's experiments with visual layout and typography intersect with his privileging of writing over poetry is that once-defining feature of poetry, the line. Writing of Andrews's *Love Songs,* Lyn Hejinian distinguishes among the acoustic line (defined by the interweavings of sound in performance), the linguistic line (defined by syntax and vocabulary), and the graphic line, which offers multiple possibilities for ordering since it can be constructed in a number of different directions ("Hard Hearts" 64). Here, of course, the cliché of readerly production rears its head—"all the *words* to which this / gives rise" ("No 157," *Love Songs* np), as Andrews puts it—but to view Andrews's more visually oriented work through that framework both makes the concept concrete and suggests one impulse behind his page designs: active reader engagement. I do not think that idea needs yet one more reiteration, but I do want to look briefly at some other implications of his work with and play on the idea of the line. Hejinian's graphic line refers to an invisible mental line that the reader draws from one piece of language to another across the space of Andrews's open page. But *Love Songs* also contains all sorts of literal lines: a vertical perforation separates two halves of the page, but porously, as do his frequent ellipses; punningly, at the bottom of "No 166," "rulers draw lines," so the line becomes both the point of division and an exercise of power. In "Song No 113," performance "directions" are rendered graphically by arrows that thus become part of the text and visually collapse any line between the text and the directions that might be thought of as somehow outside it (fig. 11.7). Far from announcing the writing as poetry, Andrews's multifarious lines point away from literature toward performance and the art world. In Peter Quartermain's reading of Andrews, for instance, many of Andrews's "lines" constitute one more trope directed against "Poetry" as those drawn lines "[parody] the poetic line graphically: where traditionally poetry suppresses the multiplicity of connections between words, these lines enhance them, and by emphasizing the graphic qualities of writing emphasize the sheer physicality of words" (172). (While it is hard to agree with Quartermain that poetry suppresses multiplicity of meaning, I take him to mean that conventional syntax and lineation somewhat reduce or control such multiplicity in contrast to the open spaces of Andrews's pages.) Claiming Andrews for poetry requires a certain suppression or bypassing of the insistent visual component of his work; indeed, that intense visuality is one way in which the work resists such claims to assimilation. If such resistance is ultimately unsuccessful, given that Andrews's work continues to be read under the sign of poetry, it nevertheless demands of readers some serious reflection on the social construction of "poetry," that increasingly capacious sign, in the late twentieth and twenty-first centuries.

But for all the variousness and inventiveness with which Andrews

SONG NO 113

| Speed | Pitch | Volume | |
|---|---|---|---|
| | | | whenever thorough befoal hems |
| ↑ | | | able again<br>able cut |
| | | ↑ | so negligibly |
| | ↑ | | fretful |
| ↓ | | | snake fuelling |
| | | | pep guard<br>then than is |
| | | ↑ | oral |
| ↓<br>↓ | | | floor<br>saints |
| | | | should curves all my go up |
| | | | moonshining |
| | | | beauties |

Figure 11.7. Bruce Andrews, *Love Songs*

treats the idea of the line in his early work, one problem arises, acutely explored by P. Inman. While multiple productive connections are possible among the words and part-words laid out on Andrews's page, when each word occupies its own space or line in carved isolation it approaches the very iconicity that Andrews seeks to explode. Inman wonders if the lines in Andrews's earlier writing read "as tableaux," with the poem overall a "still-life stood on its head" and "the sculptural, edged quality" and "physical presence and tangibility of the lines" producing an effect of stasis: "the early work as paused. A constant push against momentum." In Inman's reading, "a visual writing, disavowing penetration. * * * Pure scan . . . visual surface" can even come to seem, against its own best intentions, "authoritarian." He notes Andrews's subsequent recognition of "the need for another mode of line, one that'd forestall objecthood," a move away from "a line which was always already there" toward the page as "the shape of a signal," with "all the impulse such a signal could take spread over the page, rather than manipulatively positioned" (88–89). Drucker writes of the visual line in general as "refusing to stay 'in line,'" however, "creating instead a visual field in which all lines are tangential to the whole, which is, in turn created as a figure from their efforts, their direction, their non-alignment" (*Figuring* 140). Consistent with this view, Andrews's essay on lineation, "Lines Linear How to Mean," confirms his characteristically disruptive intention for his lines as "suggesting an unmappable space, no co-ordinates, troubling us to locate ourselves in formal terms" (*Paradise and Method* 119).

If writing is recuperated into the institutional designations "poetry" and "literature" via interpretation, Andrews sets the graphic emphasis of much of his work against that process. The visually scattered pages characteristic of *Love Songs* and much of his other early work put the irreducibility of his language fragments in tension with the reader's impulse to order even the most recalcitrant microunits into larger units of meaning. Visual impact precedes and even pulls against the construction of a reading. Of Andrews's second book, *Acappella* (1973), Steve McCaffery writes, "the digital, gridlike quality of the syntax commands immediately a *visual* attention. One must pass beyond a seeing of the poem as an optical display to enter into the spatio-temporal activity of a reading" (*North of Intention* 23).[25] In this process, "the disposition to integrate units and the pressure to uphold their insular, non-semantic cipheralities equally call attention" (23). This tension parallels the one that Inman points to: fragment as mobile shard of language versus fragment as tiny icon. It is perhaps the tension itself within the text that deflects the charge of iconicity. In other words, the work's graphic nature actively exploits the tension between multiplicity of meaning and visual iconicity (while the pull between these different readings of Andrews's visual texts keeps those texts in play and resisting regularization).[26] Or as Andrews writes in his poem "Praxis," "the tissue of contradiction is pictured / as a criss-cross" (*Getting Ready* 42).

Andrews's collaboration with Bob Cobbing, *BothBoth*, concludes with the remark "watch the seriality drugs" (np)—regularized sequence (in one definition of "seriality") is a narcotic to be countered by careful visual attention.[27] This remark oddly echoes a poet very different from Andrews who also designed his pages to counter the soporific visual and cognitive effect of the conventional poetic line. In "The Book: A Spiritual Instrument" (an un-Andrewsian title if there ever was one), Mallarmé writes, "Let us have no more of those successive, incessant, back and forth motions of our eyes, tracking from one line to the next and beginning all over again" (qtd. in Drucker, *Visible Word* 56)—and whatever their differences, all later visually oriented poets are indebted to Mallarmé's redesign of the page. (Andrews's *Love Songs* shares certain structural and design features with Mallarmé's performance text *Le Livre* [*The Book*]).[28] Andrews is also quite as utopian as Mallarmé was, in a way that inclines me to conclude with an observation from Deleuze and Guattari that suggests the aspirations of Andrews's visual poetics: "Writing has nothing to do with signifying. It has to do with surveying, mapping, even realms that are yet to come" (*Thousand Plateaus* 4–5)—writing into the future.[29]

# 12

## "What About All This Writing?"

### Williams and Alternative Poetics

You Americans are obsessed with self-fashioned lineage, aren't you?
—Bob Perelman, *The Marginalization of Poetry*

To begin, a William Carlos Williams minianthology from what one might call the long 1920s:

—"Of course, it must be understood that writing deals with words and words only and that all discussions of it deal with single words and their association in groups"; "the only real in writing is writing itself" (*Imaginations* 145; *Embodiment* 13);

—"But can you not see, can you not taste, can you not smell, can you not hear, can you not touch—words? . . . Words, white goldenrod, it is words you are made out of"; "he objectifies the words as the material of poetry" (*Imaginations* 159; *Embodiment* 128);

—"Am I a word? Words, words, words—" (*Imaginations* 166);

—"So long as I can keep my mind free from the trammels of literature"; "[James Joyce] has in some measure liberated words, freed them for their proper uses. He has [to] a great measure destroyed what is known as 'literature'" (16, 169);

—"Liberate the words;" "FIRST let the words be free" (166, 172);

—"*The imagination of the listener and of the poet are left free to mingle in the dance*"; "the author and reader are liberated to pirouette with the words" (59, 149);

—"[*Kora in Hell*'s] excellence is, in major part, the shifting of category. It is the disjointing process" (285).[1]

Linguistic self-reflexiveness; attention to the materiality of written language; the self as constructed in and by language; a cultural politics of oppositionality, and especially opposition to literature; a Marinetti-like view of words in freedom, allied to the embrace of readerly freedom; the problematics of signification; generic hybridity enacted through various forms of disjunction and parataxis: in the decade of anthology chestnuts like "The Red Wheelbarrow," these were actually the central attributes of Williams's writing and thinking about writing. (Meanwhile, of course, subsequently canonical lyrics like "The Red Wheelbarrow" were themselves published, untitled, in the generically hybrid context of *Spring and All*.) They were also the attributes that drew a later generation of experimental writers to Williams, and it is that connection that I explore in this chapter.[2]

As Hank Lazer argues, recent literary history has given us two Dr. Williamses (2:19–28)—the Williams beloved of the first decades of creative writing programs, with his emphasis on quotidian detail and speech, and the Williams of the late 1910s and 1920s hybrid texts, the self-consciously avant-gardist Williams who proved a central figure for the most serious poetic avant-garde of the late twentieth century, the Language writers.[3] In particular Williams was crucial to the self-definition of Language poetics as it developed in opposition to the so-called workshop lyric, since under the sign of the plain-spoken, quotidian Williams this latter mode dominated much of American poetry through the 1970s and 1980s (including the anthologies I discuss in chapter 4). In contrast to this "attenuated version of Williams as poet of the quotidian," Bob Perelman recalls, it was "the romance of an oceanic, uncontrolled poetry as in Williams's 'The Yachts,' or *Spring and All* and *The Descent of Winter*" (*Marginalization* 12, 88) that constituted part of his appeal to a number of Language writers. Yet Williams's importance for Language writing and related experimental poetries, while widely acknowledged, is oddly underdiscussed in specific terms. Scholarship on Williams in the avant-garde contexts of his own times abounds, but work connecting him to later avant-garde poetics and to particular poets (Linda Kinnahan's *Poetics of the Feminine*, John Lowney's *The American Avant-Garde Tradition*) does not come up to the moment of his reemergence more generally in experimental poetries of the 1970s and beyond.[4] To begin addressing this critical and historical lacuna, I discuss briefly the second Williams's importance to certain crucial moments of self-definition early in the history of Language writing, examining how his name and work are used and invoked at those moments, and then look at his presence in the theoretical, critical, and poetic work of some of the movement's practitioners and certain fellow travelers. Reissued and renewed, the work of what is arguably Williams's most formally exploratory decade becomes crucial to a later moment of the poetic "new."

The first key moment and text in understanding the nature of Williams's importance to Language writing is the 1970 New Directions publication of *Imaginations* (issued in paperback in 1971), which brought *Spring and All* complete to a new audience for the first time after decades of unavailability. (The further importance of *Imaginations* was, and remains, its placement of *Spring and All* in coherent relation to Williams's other hybrid texts of the period, including *Kora in Hell*, *The Descent of Winter*, and *The Great American Novel*.) Equally crucial was Harvey Brown's Frontier Press edition of *Spring and All* from 1970, the edition in which a number of these poets first encountered that text. Ron Silliman recalls the importance of this edition for its inviting of "a renewed focus on the question of the relation of the poem to critical thinking"; it "gave young poets a new Williams, quite different from the one we thought we had known," "more radical," and "showed Williams to be a more accomplished theoretician than Ezra Pound" ("IX" 128).[5] Whereas *The Wedge* (1944) had been more important for the New American poets of the 1950s who constitute one precursor group for Language writing, Silliman asserts in 1981 that "many young poets today feel that [Williams's] finest work is to be found in *Spring & All* and the other books composed between 1920 and '32" (*New Sentence* 23)[6]—the work most readily found in *Imaginations*.

The year 1971 brought the first issue of Barrett Watten and Robert Grenier's *This* magazine, in which Grenier's widely cited essay "On Speech" marks a move away from Williams in Williams's own name.[7] He begins: "It isn't the spoken any more than the written, now, that's the progression from Williams" (496). In this now well-known formulation, the emergent Language writing move beyond the speech-based poetics of (in one version) the New Americans and (in another) the contemporary free verse lyric is couched as a "progression" from Williams. At the same time, however, Grenier invokes Williams to authorize this move, adapting his castigation of the sonnet and his trope of a tactically extremist rhetoric: "*To me, all speeches say the same thing,* or: why not exaggerate, as Williams did, for our time proclaim an abhorrence of 'speech' designed as was his castigation of 'the sonnet' to rid us, as creators of the world, from reiteration of the past dragged on in formal habit. I HATE SPEECH" (496).[8] In other words, as Perelman rightly points out, what is often taken as an inaugural manifesto statement of Language writing rests on a repetition of Williams: "This repetition of a prior originary act in the name of novelty is similar to Williams's destroying and recreating the world in the opening prose of *Spring and All*: Grenier wanted to join in the creation of an already created world. . . . His attack reenacted Williams's attack, with the workshop voice poem as the target rather than the genteel sonnet" (*Marginalization* 43).

The tendency among Language writers to use Williams in their developing arguments against a speech-based poetics is confirmed by remarks such as Silliman's that "[before Jack Spicer] one has to go back to William Carlos Williams' *Spring & All* to find a use of the line break as devoted to nuances of meaning" as distinct from the registration of or imitation of speech (*New Sentence* 157). Indeed, Silliman's early essays (from about 1977 to 1985) represent another site where Williams appears as central to the development of Language poetics, a trend culminating in Silliman's naming his germinal 1986 anthology of Language writing *In the American Tree* (after the Kit Robinson poem and KPFA radio show of that title but alluding also to Williams's *In the American Grain*).[9] Silliman begins his well-known 1980 essay, "The New Sentence," which theorizes a central concept of one branch of Language poetics, with the dramatic and perhaps exaggerated one-sentence paragraph: "The sole precedent I can find for the new sentence is *Kora in Hell: Improvisations* and that one farfetched" (*New Sentence* 63). This statement, of course, echoes directly Williams's own beginning of the Prologue to *Kora*: "The sole precedent I can find for the broken style of my prologue is *Longinus on the Sublime* and that one far-fetched" (*Imaginations* 6). For Silliman "the first American prose poet[s] of consequence" (*New Sentence* 83) are the Williams of *Kora* and the Stein of *Tender Buttons*. He goes on to specify what he finds important for his own practice in *Kora*: "The sentences allow only the most minimal syllogistic shift to the level of reference, and some . . . permit no such shift whatsoever" (84).[10]

For Silliman, then, Williams becomes a kind of ur-theorist of the sentence, in a way articulated by Stephen Fredman. Fredman in fact discusses *Kora* in terms that he frankly borrows from Silliman on the new sentence. For both Silliman and the Williams of *Kora*, a primary question is "what is a sentence?" and both address that question via a disjunctive, paratactically organized prose the central unit of which is Silliman's new sentence, or what Fredman calls the generative sentence. As an experiment in syntax-based prose prosody, *Kora* anticipates such work of Silliman's as *Ketjak* and *Tjanting*, work in which "the actual relationship between any of the clauses is always more potential than certain" (Fredman 50). Fredman argues, then, that "*Kora in Hell* asks for a reading that pays particular attention to its transitory surface, to the way words and things appear and are linked in the moment of its writing," a reading that "break[s] the normal reading pace [of prose]" (15–16)—just the kind of reading most appropriate for Silliman's own work, which Fredman addresses briefly later in his book.

In another essay, "Z-sited Path," Silliman engages in a more general discussion of Williams's influence on twentieth-century poetics—an influence so pervasive, he argues, that to describe someone's writing as Williamsesque is largely meaningless (*New Sentence* 130).[11] Out of this universalization of Williams's influence (130), Silliman wants to rescue one particular Williams.[12] One acknowledged site of that influence has been the creative writing workshop, and in a characteristically antagonistic early Language moment, Silliman inveighs against a neoacademic verse in which what remains are the mere surface features of Williams's poetry (135–36). More precisely, what remains are the surface features of one kind of Williams poetry—an image-centered concreteness and the simple vocabulary of everyday speech with those notorious Polish mothers lurking behind it. What has been lost or suppressed in many later poets' reading of Williams, Silliman argues, is "the identification of method with content"; the connection between "this [identification] and a broader social vision"; "the essential oppositionality of his work"; and "its challenge to the perceptual limits of the reader" (136), a challenge embodied for Silliman as for other Language writers in *Spring and All*. Part of what Silliman finds important is *Spring and All*'s emphasis on constructedness and defamiliarization, or in Williams's recurrent terms from that text, design, composition, and detachment. As Silliman puts it in a 1992 interview with Manuel Brito, "the onrush of capitalist technological development has permanently thrown over the organicist closure of 'natural' cycles. That understanding is what makes William Carlos Williams' *Spring & All* the defining poem of the first half of the 20th century, at least for me. I'm including the prose in that text in my definition of that work as a poem" ([Interview] 162).[13] The construction of *Spring and All* compels Silliman, then, rather than the more widely noted organicism of individual poems like "By the road to the contagious hospital."

Silliman acknowledges Williams's early inspirational force openly. At age sixteen, attracted by the book's color, he opened *The Desert Music* in the Albany, California, library, and although he had written nothing yet, the title poem convinced him that he would become a poet not least through its famous assertion "I *am* a poet! I / am. I am. I am a poet, I reaffirmed, ashamed" (*Collected Poems* 2:284).[14] *The Desert Music* helped him, he says, in "thinking through what a person in a text is" via Williams's "use of the word 'I'"; this and the older poet's "sense of nouns and facts and facticity" were what Silliman found central.[15] Later Silliman read the Frontier Press edition of *Spring and All* while writing his first book,

*Crow.* Again, he was struck by the use of the first person and the wonderful sense of detail ("Untitled") in a poem like "What about all this writing?" (*Imaginations* 113–15), which became a kind of talismanic text for Silliman (he cites it, for instance, in his 1987 book *Lit*). *Crow* begins with an epigraph from *Spring and All*—"the perfection of new forms as additions to nature" (*Imaginations* 140).[16] The "new forms" of *Crow* consist of thirty-two untitled short (often minimalist) poems in which idiosyncratic line breaks possibly modeled on Williams are used to heighten attention to easily overlooked details of language[17] and to create aural puns, homonyms, and multiple possibilities for meaning. Also as in Williams, the line is frequently visual in *Crow*, the poem typically constructed out of a registration of observed fact and a few sounds, themselves registered as facts. Lines like "on, o, blocks of wood. on / a lot" (*Crow* 12) combine the visual materiality of the repeated "o," the different sounds of "o," and literal detail (a truck up on blocks). Another poem moves by the smallest rearrangements of letters; from "rain" to "rain is" to "raisins" to "plows in the rain," as its "chokecherry" (2) recalls Williams's Elsie, "under some hedge of choke-cherry / or viburnum" (*Imaginations* 132). And in the same poem, in a context that echoes Williams, a line like "the rain is white" (*Crow* 2) surely plays on the rain and white chickens of "The Red Wheelbarrow."

After *Crow,* Silliman "wanted to explore the function of the 'I'" in a way that resulted in what he has called his "most Williamsesque work," the 1976 "Berkeley" ("Ron Silliman"). When one reads the opening lines, this comment seems surprising: "I thought you might be here / I was alone and it was almost two / I have enjoyed my lunch / I knew right away I made a mistake / I glanced back once / I mean it / I thought so" ("Berkeley" 63). How is this list poem Williamsesque? Well, again it depends on what Williams we are talking about. In "Berkeley," the "I" and other pronouns and deictics have no stable reference; the "I" changes line by line and is clearly not to be associated with the poet, especially when one learns that the text is constructed from a range of found sentences in unacknowledged literary sources. A procedural text like "Berkeley" programmatically reinforces the idea of "I" as a pronoun, a placeholder, and in its investigation of personhood as a language function it recalls the Williams of *Spring and All,* for whom the statement "nothing / I have done // is made up of / nothing / and the diphthong // ae // together with / the first person / singular / indicative // of the auxiliary / verb / to have" (*Imaginations* 104).

Granted the inevitable discrepancy between youthful enthusiasm for a precursor poet and mature revaluation, Silliman's valorization of *The Desert Music* still stands in apparent tension with his comment in "The Chinese Notebook" that "the failure of Williams to go beyond his work in *Spring and All* and the *Great American Novel* seems to verify Bergmann's assertion that nominalism inevitably tends toward (deteriorates into?) representationalism" (*Age* 58)—a statement that sounds just pompous enough, however, that it could be self-ironizing. However we weigh this remark tonally, it is also a particular kind of statement that is both constitutive of "The Chinese Notebook" (which takes the boundaries of poetry, poetics, philosophy and theory as a central subject) and made possible by Williams's example: a literary critical comment in a paratactic prose text written and circulated under the ambiguous sign of poetry. The surrounding context is revealing, furthermore, for its juxtaposition of Williams and Russian Futurism. What follows Silliman's praise of the 1920s Williams and critique of his later work is this polemical statement: "Futurism of the Russian school, especially the *zaum* works of the Group 41°, is the true existing body of experimental literature with which contemporary writers have to work" (58).

In other words, we can triangulate the relationship of Williams to Language writing partly through the historical Russian avant-garde, both literary (as in Silliman's invocation of Futurism) and theoretical—through Russian Formalism, that is, and more specifically through Viktor Shklovsky and the idea of *ostranenie.* Marjorie Perloff links *Kora in Hell* and *Spring and All* to Russian Formalism on this basis, that of an anti-Symbolist poetics in reaction respectively to Eliot and to such figures as Aleksandr Blok (*Poetics of Indeterminacy* 115–19). Margueritte Murphy shares Perloff's view of Shklovskyan defamiliarization as a paradigm for reading *Kora* (though she also invokes Bakhtin), pointing out that Shklovsky's "Art as Technique," in which he theorized *ostranenie,* appeared in 1917, the same year that Williams started publishing the improvisations of *Kora* in *The Little Review* (107–09).[18] The appeal of "Art as Technique" for early Language poetics is well known, but my point here is to note the common juxtaposition of Williams and Shklovsky: in Kit Robinson's talk "Song," for instance, or Barrett Watten's epigraphs to *Complete Thought.* Robinson reads Williams and Shklovsky as both writing "in opposition to Malevich's pure, spiritual sound poetry" (58). Williams's own terms derive from Marinetti: "Words occur in liberation" by virtue of the imagination's processes," and "to understand the words as so liberated is to understand poetry. That they move independently when set free is the mark of their value" (*Imaginations* 149). Robinson finds poetic evidence of this conviction in reading *Spring and All*'s poem VIII (sometimes reprinted as "At the Faucet of June") as a poem partly "*about* sound" (54), moving toward the image of "the son // leaving off the g / of sunlight and grass" (*Imaginations* 110). "The author and reader are liberated to pirouette with the words" (149), which include the homonyms sun/son and the bilingual pun on the French for sound, "son."

In the epigraphs to *Complete Thought,* Watten sets a phrase from Shklovsky's *A Sentimental Journey,* "Now I will write about things and thoughts" (where the apparent separability of things and thoughts has a resistant resonance for Williams's aphorism "No ideas / but in things" [*Collected Poems* 2:55]) next to a line from *Spring and All,* "In my life the furniture eats me" (*Imaginations* 113), where self becomes one with or consumed by objective context (*Frame* 85). He begins his 2003 critical book *The Constructivist Moment* with a similar juxtaposition, this time of Mayakovsky's "I feel my 'I' is much too small for me" (Mayakovsky 71) and Williams's "the contraction which is felt" (*Imaginations* 105) (xv): remarks of which Watten writes "I found both—as indices of larger aesthetic and cultural horizons—to be deeply generative when I first encountered them in the 1970s" (xvi). Watten reads Williams's phrase in terms of a recurring "gap or eruption in the discontinuous prose of . . . *Spring and All,*" a "gap or fissure in the texture of [Williams's] thinking" that in its "self-undoing negation" provides a space for fresh "construction," both formal and social. The discontinuities of *Spring and All* represent gaps in discourse that need to be acknowledged because "only then can we begin to construct" both the next art world and "a future world" (xvi–xviii). In Watten's poetry, such gaps will sometimes show up as ellipses associated with Williams: in "X," for instance, "clarity, outline of . . ." (*Frame* 81) simultaneously refuses the iconic organicism of Williams's original phrase ("clarity, outline of leaf") from the poem that became known as "Spring and All"; enacts the gaps that structure the sequence *Spring and All* and Watten's own poem, which itself juxtaposes moments of full predication and ellipses, sentence, and phrase fragments (including phrases ending with "of"); and suggests the (unfulfillable) desire for conceptual "clarity" and "outline." Early and late, Watten alludes to, responds to, or torques Williams in his work—in *Progress,* for example, or in the "To Elsie" section of *Bad History*—and his career-long working-through of the relationship among such categories as fact, thought, thing, and idea often seems to have Williams in the background.[19]

The "fissures" in *Spring and All* on which Watten focuses can be thought of as moments of breakage. In "A Sort of a Song," the first poem of *The Wedge* and the source for Williams's widely cited (out of context) aphorism "No ideas / but in things," set next to this apparent fetishizing of the image are the injunctions that "the writing / be of words," to "compose" and "invent" (*Collected Poems* 2:55). "Saxifrage is my flower that splits / the rocks"—superficially a concrete image but also a tautologically self-reflexive one for the reader who knows the etymology of "saxifrage" ("rock-breaking"). For many Language poets, Williams was instructive as a breaker as much as a maker, though in a way that does not deny his constructivist tendencies. In his 1979 talk "The First Person," Bob Perelman quotes *The Great American Novel*: "'Words. Words cannot progress. There cannot be a novel. Break the words. Words are indivisible crystals. One cannot break them—Awu tsst grang splth gra pragh og bm—Yes one can break them. One can make words. Progress?'" (148).[20] For a related perspective, we might consider Clark Coolidge's "Smithsonian Depositions," for which *Paterson* and Williams's *Selected Letters* are central source texts, and particularly its characteristic preoccupation with the geological and the crystalline: "Words and rocks contain a language that follows a syntax of splits and ruptures. Look at any *word* long enough and you will see it open up into a series of faults, into a terrain of particles each containing its own void" (26).[21]

The idea of the two different Williamses is also articulated explicitly in Charles Bernstein's defense of an oppositional, avant-gardist Williams in his influential 1983 MLA convention talk, "The Academy in Peril: William Carlos Williams Meets the MLA"—delivered, Hank Lazer writes, on the same day that Louis Simpson was celebrating the workshop Williams in another room at the convention (2:25). At issue for Bernstein, as for Silliman, is the canonization of a particular version of Williams: "As Williams passes through the narrow and well-guarded gates of official verse culture, it likely will be at the expense of so decontextualizing and neutralizing his work that it will be unrecognizable on his own terms" (*Content's Dream* 246), which were consistently oppositional. Thus, Bernstein argues, "his Williams may be a token inclusion in a canon that excludes what he stands for," "heard but not listened to" (246, 251). Two Williamses also feature in another 1983 Bernstein talk/essay, "Words and Pictures," but these two are opposed around what Bernstein calls a poetics of optics or of sight and a poetics of vision (137, 139). Bernstein critiques in Williams's Imagist/Objectivist work (his example is "The Lily") "the object-focussed, extratemporal, singled perspective that is, in actuality, a static idealization of the experience of looking" (137). Later Williams poems like "Tribute to the Painters" and "Shadows," however, represent in his view a movement "decisively away from the static, ahistorical 'thing seen'" towards a "poetics of vision": "an engagement of all the senses, and of thought, beyond the readily visible, the statically apparent" (159, 139). Meanwhile, like Silliman Bernstein stresses the significance of *Spring and All* "in the current [1982] flowering of paratactic (serially disjunct) prose-format poetry" (301): the New Sentence.

Just as there is no monolithic Williams, there is no monolithic Language version of Williams. Watten writes of the "'nonaesthetic' observed detail [as] the key to social insight" (*Total Syntax* 109) in Williams and compares the technique to Silliman's (although Watten also suggests that, unlike Silliman, Williams distances himself from the multiplicity of the social contexts that he invokes). Silliman frames the issue similarly when he praises Williams's sense of fact and detail and his ability to connect these formal choices "to a broader social vision." Bernstein, however, as I've said, finds the observed detail in Williams static and limited, contrasting it with the 1950s Williams who wrote of "the tyranny of the image / and how / men / in their designs / have learned / to shatter it" (*Pictures* 137).[22] The status of the image seems very much at issue in Grenier's "But," with its eponymous coordinating conjunction invoking opposition, difference, change: Williams's Imagism may have been viable once "but" not any longer. Here is the poem, dedicated to Williams:

> the young plum tree
> like a martini
> with new green
> leaves how metrical
>
> likely & con-
> versant it would
> have been *today*
> to write a true imagist poem. (*Phantom Anthems* np)

One reading might detect a certain wistfulness in that second stanza, a *desire* "to write a true imagist poem." That desire, if it is indeed present at all, is conditional and unfulfillable, however—"it *would* have been" (my emphasis). Williams has made the Imagist poem both possible and, ultimately, impossible for later poets. "The young plum tree / . . . / with new green / leaves" invokes any number of Williams lyrics, from "The Young Housewife" to "This Is Just to Say" to his many images of growing trees. But its apparent organicity is complicated, as it often is in Williams himself, by an improbable figure of speech: "like a martini" provides rhyme and assonance but otherwise functions as a faux simile (unless we want to jump from green leaves to green olives). If we read the title and dedication as part of a single (ungrammatical) sentence, "but for William Carlos Williams" we might still be attempting the "true imagist poem" today.

For writers such as Bernstein and Silliman—and perhaps unsurprisingly, given the shared commitment to breaking down genre boundaries in Williams's work of the 1920s and Language poetics—Williams's disjunct critical prose influences later prose poetry, even as Bernstein also writes that Williams "in his imagin[a]tive prose" (*Content's Dream* 450) was one model for the kind of writing encouraged in *L=A=N=G=U=A=G=E* magazine. In what can be taken as a statement representative of numerous Language writers' experience, Perelman says "For me, the complete version of Williams's *Spring and All,* with the fractured Dada-like prose, came out in 1970, not in 192[3]. And for most people it came out that way" ("Conversation" 534). One poetic-critical mixed-genre text that features Williams prominently is Perelman's *The Marginalization of Poetry: Language Writing and Literary History*—one of the most persuasive genealogies of Language writing, partly for being produced from within the movement itself. In the essay-poem "An Alphabet of Literary History," Williams appears first in section B:

> Meanwhile, back on the Nowheresville float,
>
> Williams was burning leaves of grass,
> trying to avoid the bitter smoke.
>
> He went inside and searched
> the refrigerator. The plums were gone. The
>
> cold of verbal construction was delicious
> in isolation but the question of
>
> social value remained in abeyance: there
> was really nothing to eat. (*Marginalization* 147)

This complexly intertextual moment finds Williams burning his bridges to Whitman (burning leaves of grass) in an allusion to his own "Burning the Christmas Greens" (one of Williams's many versions of the destruction/creation myth that Grenier repeats in "On Speech") while he is confronted with the "question of / social value" deferred, in Perelman's reading, in his own "This is just to say." Image (Christmas greens) becomes text (leaves of grass), and the cold of Williams's famous plums becomes the "cold of verbal construction," in a way that highlights the material textuality of his work. In this passage, then, the two Williamses meet and blur—the Williams of the fetishized concrete image, and the Williams of the material found poem, the refrigerator poem that becomes art. For Perelman, "This Is Just to Say" becomes a site at which to engage critically the political risks of an image-centered poetics, a poem "delicious / in isolation." Characteristically, Perelman manages here to combine a marijuana joke (after "burning" some "grass," Williams gets an attack of the munchies and "searche[s] / the refrigerator); invert Williams's original ("the plums were gone," eaten by someone else); and invoke the Depression-era poverty and hunger that forms the backdrop to Williams's 1934 poem ("there / was really nothing to eat").

Williams appears most centrally in section P of the poem, which is modeled structurally and in its diction on "The Descent" and begins thus: "Language writing beckons / as modernism beckoned. / Critical genealogy is a kind / of art **P**rose" (*Marginalization* 152–53). (**P** perhaps for *Paterson*, in book 2 of which the lines that became "The Descent" first appeared.) In Perelman's critical genealogy of this poem, Language writing is the descent to modernism's ascent. But to trace this narrative of only apparent decline is to produce "art **P**rose, / a sort of **P**oetics / even // a **P**oem" (153). It is to rewrite lines of genealogy and of poetry (Williams's own), and to produce the "new genres" remarked upon a few lines later in the poem. In taking us from prose to poetics to poem, this section of "Alphabet" (and the poem as a whole) models a sliding across and between genres that is exactly one of the lessons Perelman and other Language poets took from Williams, in this case paradoxically using one of Williams's more generically *un*ambiguous texts to do so.[23] Perelman's work has moved increasingly toward a hybrid mix of poetry, poetics, and commentary on his modernist inheritance, often in the mode of what would once have called the essay-poem, in the 2007 *Iflife* and in such poems as the January 2008 "Between Minsk to Pinsk," which has "WCW a source, along with Stein, of writing as a description of both the activity and the product the poems."[24] Here "WCW is both origin of language and plain-spoken thingness. It's as if canvases by the same painter were simultaneously seen as Pollocks and Hoppers" ("Between Minsk")—the two Dr. Williamses, one of whom would have been the first to note that the distance between Minsk and Pinsk is one letter.

Williams reappears crucially at the very end of *The Marginalization of Poetry* in the comic prose dream conversation, "A False Account of Talking with Frank O'Hara and Roland Barthes in Philadelphia." A fictionalized O'Hara sees the poet Perelman looking out of the window in the stereotypical gesture of the isolated poet, and writing, as if they were his own, Williams's words from "The Last Words of My English Grandmother," "What are those fuzzy things out there" (164). This moment initiates a brief exchange between "I" and O'Hara on the distinction between quoting and saying, which ends abruptly with Roland Barthes's interpolation that "You Americans are obsessed with self-fashioned lineage, aren't you?" (165) Williams here becomes the crux in a dizzying spiral of citation that raises serious questions about a speaker's ownership of their language. Both O'Hara and Perelman claim to be quoting Williams's grandmother, or, more precisely, quoting Williams quoting her.[25] In Perelman's genre-crossing critical history of Language writing, then, one that mixes straightforward literary history, close readings, an insider's narrative of a literary community, essay poems, and dream narrative, Williams occupies a privileged place, the final predecessor (outside of O'Hara and Barthes themselves) with whom the book leaves us.

Williams also figured centrally much earlier in Perelman's career, specifically in his first book *Braille* (1975). *Braille* was culled from a year-long series of improvisations, inspired by reading *Kora in Hell* (*Ten to One* 1)—a series written, Williams-fashion, at the rate of one improvisation a day and narrowed down to sixty-one lineated and prose poems for publication. In its interweaving of thirty-two prose and twenty-nine lineated poems, the structure loosely parallels the relationship between improvisation and commentary in *Kora*.[26] Incorporating the reflexive function of Williams's intervening commentaries into its own texts, and covering a wider formal range than *Kora*, *Braille*, written 1972–73, comprises a series of experiments in different sentence forms and lengths, in prose, and in usually stanzaic free verse. The last paragraph of "Youngstown," for instance, combines the sound play, methodological self-reflexiveness, speed of movement, and disrupted syntax or "brokenness of . . . composition" (Williams, *Imaginations* 16) characteristic of *Kora*:

> When to the sound of mind I bring these words scattering them ahead of me in exact statement bingo! then attitudes jar and what else do you have except an attitude to shine said the anthropocentric sun sing said the line of song say these things and see where they put me get me revealed the crooked cries of bingo the large task. (*Braille* 4)

Here an iambic opening clause and almost obsessive alliteration combine in statements of method ("I bring these words scattering them ahead of me," "say these things and see where they put me") and purpose ("attitudes jar") also marked by Williams-like exclamation ("bingo!"), phrasal and sentence fragments, and a speed of association created partly by these fragments and partly by the absence of punctuation.

Williams used the improvisational mode of *Kora in Hell* to counter the "rehash, repetition" of Eliot and Pound, "men content with the connotations of their masters" and producing "parodies of the middle ages" (*Imaginations* 24, 26)—poetry as reiteration of the canonical, of the words and tropes of others. Citation and the ownership of language form the basis of Perelman's discussion of Williams in his "First Person" talk. Perelman quotes passages from the beginning of *The Great American Novel* (where words are really the main character) on which he comments as follows: "Words are already created and so they've usurped Williams' function as a creator. Their meanings are already there ahead of his impulse to write them down. He can't get out of this impasse; he can't break the words and stay interested, and he can only identi[f]y with them mockingly" (148). Later in the talk he remarks, "I identify quite a lot with Williams, especially the early Williams and his growls and anger at the amount of prerecording in his head" (161). This sense of the poet's inevitably belated relationship to language underlies the citational quality central to Perelman's (and much other Language) writing, his habit of torquing relatively familiar moments from earlier texts into quirky, ironic versions of themselves. Williams is one of the writers whom he consistently tweaks in this way. In *Captive Audience* we encounter a version of the well-known formulation from "Asphodel, That Greeny Flower": locked into history and temporality, dulled by the trademarked voice of the news media, readers "sit staring / at the subtext of / their clock radios. People continue / to die miserably from the lack / of news to be found / *there*, too, doctor, / every day, as the display / changes a nine to a ten" (58–59).[27] In "To the Past," Perelman revisits the gendered voyeurism of "The Desert Music": "In some other poem / you wiggle your can / crazily, signifying America / for William Carlos Williams making music // in a gender / desert" (*Future of Memory* 63). That Perelman alludes to such canonical, easily recognizable passages of Williams is precisely the point: they are an unavoidable part of the overdetermined or prerecorded language that he is given to work with, and writing out of such a sense of language forms part of his kinship with Williams.

Williams's importance for Language and related innovative poetries has not manifested itself solely "in a gender desert"; that is, it has not been limited to the male practitioners whom I have discussed so far. However, women writers aligning themselves with Williams's more exploratory language practices have at the same time generally expressed a greater need to negotiate his gender politics. Without naming Williams, Lyn Hejinian remarks in *My Life* that "the work is probably a good deal wiser than the horny old doctor he was" (53), though her interest in and commitment to his work is clear from such texts as her review of Paul Mariani's 1981 biography, which I discuss later. Rachel Blau DuPlessis, whose resistant conversation with Pound I trace in chapter 8, confronts the issue most directly in her semiautobiographical essay "*Pater*-daughter," which she begins by noting the "conventional vocabulary of race and gender" even in the "radical literature" of *Spring and All* (*Pink Guitar* 41). By now this has become a widely assimilated observation about male modernists, precisely *because* of the work on gender narratives in modernism done by DuPlessis and many others. But it was significantly less so when DuPlessis originally wrote the essay in 1984 at a key transitional point in her own poetic career: the moment of *(HOW)ever* magazine (founded in 1983), a point following her 1970 Columbia University dissertation on Williams and Pound, "The Endless Poem," and between her revisionist feminist sequence "from The History of Poetry" (mostly written in the early 1980s) and "Writing," the 1984–85 ur-poem for her multivolume serial work *Drafts*.[28] After Williams's work of 1918–32 (from *Kora in Hell* to *A Novelette*), for DuPlessis "the great moments in *Paterson* occur when Williams releases his poem to pass beyond gendered limits into contradictory and swarming meanings," a poetics that she describes in Kristevan terms: "the writing in motion, a rhythm, a pulse, desire always and desire shifting" (59). The further terms in which DuPlessis describes *Paterson*'s importance for her read like a thumbnail description of her own *Drafts*: "the great confrontative entry into accumulation, discontinuity, fissure, rift" (61).

Acknowledging that Williams provides the basis for one kind of female-authored poetics, even as "the radicalness of the poetics is matched by the almost unquestioned conservatism of the gender ideas" (111), DuPlessis highlights from *Spring and All* two statements "that certainly invent modern American poetry"—"'to write down that which happens at that time' and 'to practice skill in recording the force moving'" (110).[29] She uses these statements as a paradigm for reading not just the work of Beverly Dahlen, her immediate subject, but a whole subsequent line of innovative women poets: "What does it mean when a woman writes down that which happens at that time [a historically devalued kind of women's writing] (thus, say, Bernadette Mayer's *Midwinter Day* [1982]). What, indeed, can it be to follow the force moving, recording it, for what moves, what writes, when the writer is a woman[?]" (111). Indeed, Mayer herself remarks to Alice Notley, in a January 27, 1980, letter quoted by Notley, that "I've always been very grateful to [Williams] for resuscitating the prose mixed with poetry form which is a form I like and seems like a good form to be in a hurry in" (Notley, *Doctor Williams' Heiresses* np).[30] Elsewhere Mayer makes explicit the linking of Williams's "force" and historical challenges for women writers: "Home deliveries, Dr. Williams and the force behind the rest. Women, this time, fierce love, what exists, hiding. Also is history and I can be like one. Not to have lost a place under everything above and a ground or pavement" (*Desire* 176). "Home deliveries" punningly juxtaposes the domestic sphere and Williams's obstetrics practice, while the next two sentences crisply compress "what moves . . . when the writer is a woman" "recording the force moving": the gendered politics of love and sexuality (though not only those subjects) both in the present and historically, the complex dynamics of suppression or invisibility ("what exists, hiding") and emergence ("not to have lost a place under everything").

DuPlessis writes of the woman poet's ambivalent imperative to "both follow [Williams] and leave him" (*Pink Guitar* 111) due to the combination of poetic radicalism and gender conservatism. Her own following occurs at various points in her serial work. Her notes on the 1984–85 "Writing," "a poem written very much under the regime of WCW,"[31] cite Williams's "January Morning," and while she does not make the connection explicit, the Williams poem probably offers her a model of serial composition and of a particular kind of dailiness. This suggestion is borne out by DuPlessis's quotation of "January Morning" in her "Draft 23." In the self-reflexive part 14 of this modular 24-part poem, one component of these "quirky manifestations. / Incidents of a time, spare and concise" is "the 'and' of Williams" (*Drafts 1–38* 152). Here are three sequential sections of "January Morning":

> V
> —and a young horse with a green bed-quilt
> on his withers shaking his head:
> bared teeth and nozzle high in the air!
>
> VI
> —and a semicircle of dirt-colored men
> about a fire bursting from an old
> ash can,
>
> VII
> —and the worn,
> blue car rails (like the sky!)
> gleaming among the cobbles! (Williams, *Collected Poems* 1:101)

This "and," preceded by a dash, begins 7 parts of the 15-part "January Morning" and gives that serial poem its paratactic structure of layered, brief incidents of a time—the structure, in those terms from *Spring and All* that DuPlessis cites, of writing down that which happens at that time. Meeting Williams's beginning in her poem's ending, and with another formal nod in his direction, DuPlessis quotes fragments of "January Morning"'s first stanza in her fragmentary final section: "'strange hours' / 'we keep' / That is, our lives" (*Drafts 1–38* 157). In the serial project of *Drafts,* the "isolate flecks" of Williams's "To Elsie" appear in a metapoetic moment as flecks of emergent language, "'isolate flakes' hybrid, subversive, inchoate. // The writing on the open page" (55).

Even as Notley celebrates Williams in her 1980 talk *Doctor Williams' Heiresses,* she records an ambivalence similar to DuPlessis's following and leaving: "There was always you. To love as a poet & to love & hate as a man." Though Notley's associations with Language writing are tangential, she first delivered *Doctor Williams' Heiresses* in the talk series now thought of as one key site of Language writing's West Coast development, the 80 Langton Street series, and it was published by Lyn Hejinian under her Tuumba imprint.[32] The talk begins with a playful genealogical narrative that leads up to the New American poetry and after, and to the more specific assertion that "the one named Alice Notley fell in love with her grandfather William Carlos Williams." The voice of Ted Berrigan expounds on the various possibilities that Williams opened up, but Notley is more interested in Williams's value for women writers: "You could use him to sound entirely new if you were a woman. . . . Williams makes you feel that you can say anything, including your own anything."[33] Notley suggests a view of gender as enablingly performative. In relation to Williams's self-construction as an American male, a woman poet can be both a female and a person: "'There's this way to be yourself, a woman, & person that has a lot to do with William Carlos Williams.'" (Though Notley also writes in this text "'I'm not all that interested in being a woman, it's just a practical problem that you deal with when you write poems.'") This performance, and Williams's value for his heiresses, involves for Notley a complex gender dynamics of closeness, identification, counteridentification, and reversal: "I like to reverse sexual identities whenever possible," she says in a 1988 interview, and

> *Doctor Williams' Heiresses* is about that. It's about my being able to relate to him and identify with him out of sexual reversal. I guess my theory was that . . . it was probably easier to be like Williams if you were a woman, because you couldn't be like him because you were a woman—and opposites can be same in spirit, and you could relate to a person like that in this whole opposite way—in a battle of the sexes way. ("Interview" 71)

DuPlessis's commentary in another context suggests how this sexual reversal in a female poet-reader (though Notley adds "I don't do that anymore" [71]), these moments of diffused, displaced, and often cross-gendered subjectivity, can have their roots in an aspect of Williams's work. "The shifts of gender positionality in the enounced are part of the labile attractions of early Williams" (*Genders* 32), as in a poem like "Transitional," she argues, and she reads Williams in terms of both the range and limits of gender mobility and split identification in his work (31–34). "Transitional" begins in just such a moment of a male speaker's split identification: "First he said: / It is the woman in us / That makes us write" (Williams, *Collected Poems* 1:40). In lines that save this split identification from being read as involving a conventionally internalized muse, the poem moves further into a gendered doubleness with the speaker's address to his (or "his") apparently male interlocutor: "We are not men / Therefore we can speak / And be conscious / (of the two sides)." Pushing such double identifications further, in the early poem "Dear Dark Continent," Notley breaks down gender integrity in a way that helps clarify her comments on Williams, by breaking down pronominal integrity: "I'm wife I'm mother I'm / myself and him and I'm myself and him and him // . . . // But I and this he (and he) makes ghosts of / I and all the *hes* there would be, won't be // because by now I am he, we are I, I am we" (*Grave* 8). This elasticity of gender identification—which in "Dear Dark Continent" could be read more conservatively as the wife and mother's merging with (male) family[34]—increases dramatically in range in, and becomes a central subject of, Notley's "September's Book." There "I" is variously "a man when I didn't / know it then" and "the famous crouching / Aphrodite of Rhodes" (76); later in the poem "I'm become this boyish-woman boy-woman little / girl butch" and have to "find my dead / brother self, sir, yes" (83). "Do you think we men want only to be babies & women want / to be perfect old men?" the speaker of one section asks; and later, "which of us is he & she?" (86, 89).

A different form of doubleness—her term—underlies Rae Armantrout's attraction to Williams's work. In a 1999 talk, Armantrout speaks of Williams and Dickinson as two of her early literary loves. In particular she cites what she sees as an erotic subtext running through "The Attic Which Is Desire," with its "narrow, vaginal column of text, transfixed by the ejaculatory soda" (*Collected Prose* 57). It is this doubleness in Williams (though he is hardly the only source of it) that appeals to a poet who describes her work as "a poetics of the double take, the crossroads" (59); her example of this tendency in her own writing is "The Creation."[35] As with Armantrout's own poetry, Williams's doubleness is achieved by compression. From her first undergraduate poetry workshop at San Diego State University in 1967, Armantrout remembers "reading 'The Attic Which Is Desire' and being awestruck at the concentration of meaning and feeling Williams had managed to contain in those few words" (*True* 57). She writes of Williams's "brevity" as part of her earliest positive response to him, and of "liking his early poem, 'Metric Figure,' especially" (36)—this encounter occurring through Louis Untermeyer's *Modern American Poetry*, which she was given by her high school English teacher (35).[36] As Armantrout says in formulating her reading of Williams (and of Dickinson): "I was drawn to poems that seemed as if they were either going to vanish or explode—to extremes, in other words, radical poetries" (*Collected Prose* 55).

The more specific linkage of the aesthetically exploratory and the erotic that Armantrout locates in her early reading of Williams likewise appears in her early poetry (and maintains itself through her career), for instance in an almost programmatic passage of the mixed prose-poetry text "Vice": "I understand the masochist. She wants to be jerked free of habit, thrown headlong into strange positions, unmanageable acts" (*Extremities* 27). Here the masochist is also the poet, desiring "strange" subject positions and a violent breaking up of linguistic norms or habits (though also ambivalently lacking in agency—the verbs describing her are passive, befitting the masochist). In a later piece, "Getting Warm" (*Necromance* 43), Perelman finds the poet achieving orgasm ("Exactly" 160), while I have read the same poem (in chapter 9) as moving toward a metaphorical description of Dickinson.[37] These two readings seem thoroughly incompatible. Combined, however, they would put encrypted sexuality together with a radically innovative female poetics in a way anticipated by Armantrout's earliest encounters with Williams.

In his reading of "Getting Warm," Perelman foregrounds the woman in the poem "concentrating on the spaces / between cries" (*Necromance* 43), and Armantrout's poetics of the double take does indeed also foreground between-ness—the moments or spaces between words, images, perceptions, stanzas, statements. She discusses Williams from this point of view in her talk "Poetic Silence." There she uses Williams as her first example of ways in which a writer "make[s] room in her work for silence, for the experience of cessation" (*Collected Prose* 24), citing in "January Morning" (to which we have also seen DuPlessis responding) Williams's use of ellipsis (his use of the initial "—and"), deliberate inconsequentiality, and "end[ing] on a note of irresolution" (25)—tropes characteristic of Armantrout's own poems. In this way, Williams "manage[s] to empty a moment into which questions then rise . . . , to make us feel the weight to silence, and of the world" (30).

The term that Perelman elsewhere associates with Williams's appeal, however, "oceanic," has a negative charge for Armantrout, who connects it with Cixous's *écriture feminine* in remarking that "[Cixous's] preferred text had a rather oceanic feel to it: seamless, boundless, transcending binary categories. I imagine this model could inspire some poets working today. I myself don't find it very useful." Her interviewer, Lyn Hejinian, responds "I would go even farther than you and express outright queasiness and even dislike of oceanic tendencies, whether they are expressed in poetry or in theoretical writings. They seem the result of very poor observation" ("Interview" 17).[38] Observation, meanwhile, is central to that aspect of Armantrout's poetics rooted in Williams: "Williams was the first poet I read seriously, and Ron Silliman was my first poet friend, so I guess I did start out in the Pound/Williams . . . Silliman school of poetics. By this I mean a notational observation of an 'outer' world combined with a keen attunement to the possibilities of form" (25).[39] We might recall here Silliman's own emphasis on the importance for him of fact and facticity in Williams.

Armantrout's emphasis on Williams's doubleness can return us, at least tropically, to the idea of the two Dr. Williamses, which also provides an organizing principle for "An American Opener," Hejinian's 1981 review of Paul Mariani's Williams biography. Hejinian critiques Mariani for his inattention to Williams's "sense of the weight and value of words" ("American Opener" 61) and for overemphasizing thematic interpretation: "It is not in terms of 'meaning' that Williams has exerted such a strong and beneficial influence on American letters" (64). Hejinian argues for the influence of a different Williams, a proponent of "a poetics in which the word is the concrete perceptible fact and the structure is tantamount to statement" (64), who begins *The Wedge* with the invocation, cited by Hejinian, that "the writing / be of words" (Williams, *Collected Poems* 2:55). If one function of the academy, as Silliman argues, is the social organization of writing into literature,[40] this Williams, the Williams of many late twentieth-century writers committed to formally exploratory work, stands outside literature, both as defined in high modernism and as defined in much of the premillennial poetry scene. This Williams is not the author of "The Red Wheelbarrow" or "Between Walls" but rather the linguistically self-reflexive Williams of lines like those I quoted earlier: "Nothing / I have done // is made up of / nothing / and the diphthong // ae // together / with / the first person / singular / indicative // of the auxiliary / verb / to have" (*Imaginations* 104). It is the Williams who pursued a cultural politics of oppositionality through a poetics of generic hybridity and a materialist attention to language as written. It is the Williams of the jumpily Dadaist "What about all this writing," invoked by Silliman in his book *Lit* via the quoted line "O Miss Margaret Jarvis" (53). That Silliman should allude to Williams's writing in the context of *Lit*, his term for institutionalized literature and his version of Bernstein's official verse culture, speaks exactly to the importance of the older poet for later experimental writing. Language and other exploratory poetics can be read as the apotheosis of that moment early in *Spring and All* when "the terms 'veracity,' 'actuality,' 'real,' 'natural,' 'sincere' are being discussed at length" (*Imaginations* 93). In engaging that discussion, Language writing especially was often accused by its detractors of opacity and incoherence. On these points, I conclude by citing the November 10, 1917, letter from Ezra Pound that Williams reprints in the prologue to *Kora*. Referring to some of the recently published improvisations, Pound writes, "I was very glad to see your wholly incoherent unAmerican poems in the *L*[*ittle*] *R*[*eview*]. . . . The thing that saves your work is *opacity*, and don't you forget it" (*Letters* 124). Rather than his much-vaunted clarity, it was this opacity, alleged incoherence, and disjoining of language from conventional forms of reference and subjectivity that proved foundational for at least one particular group of Williams's later poet-readers.

# 13

## Language Writing, Digital Poetics, and Transitional Materialities

One common critical trope in discussions of new media writing or digital poetics—as in most discussions of newness—involves the establishment of genealogies, and what Jay David Bolter calls "the connection between the hypertext movement and the avant-garde tradition" (*Writing Space* [2001] 160) is a widely proposed connection, even if a phrase like "hypertext movement" dates Bolter's version of the point. Bolter lays out what has increasingly become a standard line that includes Mallarmé, Apollinaire, Dada, Russian Constructivism, Lettrisme, concrete and visual poetry (most versions of the lineage also emphasize Marinetti).[1] Historically, these writers' and movements' productions, in Bolter's words, offer "expressions of a growing dissatisfaction with the conventional forms of print." But they do so "from *within* the technology of the printed page; they [stand] as a critique of the conventions of the medium" (153). This confinement to the page is finally what limits even such efforts as Marc Saporta's loose-leaf interactive fiction *Composition No. 1* "to resist the perfection of print" (151). It is also what often leads new media theorists back into a view of print as incorrigibly rigid. Thus Bolter writes of "the freeing of writing from the frozen structure of the printed page," of "liberating the text" from the page (*Writing Space* [1991] 21). Richard Lanham, considering "what happens when text moves from page to screen," argues that "the digital text becomes unfixed and interactive" and that as a result "the fixed, authoritative, canonical text . . . simply explodes into the ether" (31)—an imagined effect that is one social extension of George P. Landow's claim that "hypertext does not permit a tyrannical, univocal voice" (*Hypertext* 11) as print does. For Lanham as for Bolter, print is frozen, digital writing fluid: "Hot type was *set*. Digital typesetting programs *pour* or *flow* it" (44). For Landow, "unlike all previous forms of textuality, the digital word is virtual, not physical," and "the resulting textuality is virtual, fluid, adaptable, open" ("Twenty Minutes" 216, 218).

This view of print's confining fixity is closely connected to opposing views of "materiality," a source of considerable debate and persistent redefinition in the ongoing critical conversation about new media poetry.[2] Celebration of a liberatory immateriality pervades the early (mid-1990s) discourse surrounding new media. Throughout most of the 1996 special issue of *Visible Language* on new media poetry, for example, "the immateriality of new media poems" is held to be "truly transform[ing] the field of poetic communication" (Vos 222). When literary revolutions have not been claimed in the name of a return to "common" speech (see Wordsworth on), they have been claimed—at least in the twentieth century—in the name of an intensified materiality, the word and letter as such. From the perspective of at least some new media practitioners, however, we may be looking at our first immaterial avant-garde, with the twist that it is celebrated in a rhetoric derived from that materialist Marinetti. Within this particular line of discourse, poetry is constrained by taking on material or physical form. In an E. M. de Melo e Castro videopoem, however, "the page is no longer there, not even as a metaphor," so "the words and letters [can] at last be free" (141); in Eduardo Kac's holopoetry, the word is "freed from the page and freed from other palpable materials" (189). To anyone who has even a nodding acquaintance with Italian Futurism, this rhetoric of freeing the word will sound familiar.

In the immaterialist position, a version of the early theorizing about new media that I have cited in Bolter and Lanham, print is associated with such terms as stiffness, immutability, stability, solidity; it is given, static, fixed. The electronic text is associated with such terms as instability, variability, fluctuation, and change; it is oscillatory, malleable, a matter of fluid signs, of signifiers in motion. For Mark Poster, "the computer dematerializes the trace. . . . The writer encounters his or her words in a form that is evanescent, instantly transformable, in short, immaterial" (111). To sum up by quoting Eric Vos, "in terms of the labels often attached to new media, we are dealing with a virtual, dynamic, interactive, immaterial poetry" (216)—and who does not want to be dynamic and interactive? Other new media theorists, however, take a different view, captured in Matthew Kirschenbaum's position that "the tendency to elicit what is 'new' about new media by contrasting its radical mutability with the supposed material solidity of older textual forms is a misplaced gesture" when, among other things, we consider the historical evidence of ephemerality, unreliability, and fragility that textual studies provide. Loss Pequeño Glazier rests the argument of his *Digital Poetics* on "a recognition of the materiality of digital poetry texts" (3) and spends much of his book explaining the nature of that materiality. Johanna Drucker and N. Katherine Hayles both offer helpfully nuanced middle positions. Drucker draws on Kirschenbaum's distinction between the "phenomenological materiality" and "ontological immateriality" of the electronic text: "We perceive the visual form of the letter on the screen as fully material—replete with characteristics, font specifications, scale, and even color—even though the 'letter' exists as a stored sequence of binary digits with no tactile, material apparency to it in that fundamental condition" ("Intimations" 171–72). While Hayles grants the perceived immateriality of the digital text, of the "flickering signifier" or "screenic image" that is a product of code, "a light image produced by a scanning electron beam," she also defines materiality as "a selective focus on certain physical aspects of an instantiated text that are foregrounded by a work's construction, operation, and content" ("'Materiality Has Always Been'" 9–10), and as such it can be a feature of new and old media poetry alike.

It is within the context of this debate about the material features of the print and digital environments, and more generally within the practice of media archaeology as it impacts our thinking about radical poetics, that I position my argument. One well-known feature of the work produced by poets associated with Language writing is the redirection of readerly attention to the materiality of the word. (In this way, many Language texts can be seen as what Hayles calls technotexts, her term for work that foregrounds its own materiality or "inscription technology" [*Writing Machines* 25].) This interest expressed itself in multiple forms, but one underdiscussed form involves the visual component of Language texts—a visuality that I stress in my readings of Susan Howe and Bruce Andrews. Visual and concrete poetries are widely cited as historical precursors to new media poetries, but the visual and (re)combinatorial component of Language writing forms a significant bridge or transition between these two projects, especially in the work of the writers I discuss here: Steve McCaffery, Robert Grenier, and Charles Bernstein. Lori Emerson writes, "When transparency not only transforms into that which is valued above all else but also becomes an overriding, unquestioned necessity, it turns all computing devices into appliances for the consumption of content instead of multifunctional, generative devices for reading as well as writing or producing content" (xi–xii). Substitute "poems" for "computing devices" in this sentence and we have a remarkable parallel between the ideal of "invisible" or "user-friendly" interfaces and the fetishizing of transparency in the mainstream poem of the late twentieth century that Language writing so energetically critiqued. In the digital environment, Emerson seeks to counter the ideal of the transparent interface via attention to "digital literature that embraces *visibility* by courting difficulty, defamiliarization, and glitch and that stands as an antidote to ubicomp [ubiquitous computing]" (xviii)—the kind of work that I discuss here. She is interested, that is, in what Bernstein would call the antiabsorptive.[3]

In their different ways, McCaffery, Grenier, and Bernstein point us toward considering new media poetries as part of the ongoing project of, in the title of McCaffery and Jed Rasula's coedited anthology, "Imagining Language" in all its textural and material variety. Like practitioners in the realm of the "asemic," they have worked on the edge of what is usually called "writing," proposing that work ranging from nonalphabetic glyph-like designs to hand-produced letter-like drawings to barely legible palimpsests to simple pen strokes can be seen/read under the sign of poetry. In their visual works, and in the online representation of those works, they raise questions about seeing and reading, the mark and the sign, circulation and distribution, and the meaning of "materiality" that seem crucial to thinking about new media poetries. Meanwhile, new media technologies fulfill certain impulses toward different forms of materiality in Language writing that were perhaps only nascent or at least partly unfulfilled in the earlier stages of that movement. McCaffery's, Grenier's and Bernstein's work introduces into the critical conversation around new media poetries the idea of what I call here "transitional materialities": forms of visual text that interrogate the material limitations of the page-based, word-centered poem, that as acts of "protocybernetic anticipation," in Brian Lennon's phrase (85), look forward to the possibilities and achievements of digital poetics, and that often position themselves self-consciously as points of reciprocity between the print and digital environments.[4]

In such works as the very early *Transitions to the Beast* and *Broken Mandala* (1970), parts of *Evoba* (1976–78), the *Carnival* panels (1967–75), *Modern Reading* (1967–90) , and his video poems, McCaffery is insistently concerned with "allowing a type of reading to develop that was much closer to the classic category of 'seeing'" and with "a base sense of the materiality of the letter" (*Seven Pages Missing* 435, 434). He describes this aspect of his work in terms most appropriate to new media poetry, talking in terms of "animated letter shapes," "3 dimensional syntax," "*a network of non-linear signifiers*" (434, 437, 436). In particular, the transposition of *Carnival* onto the web was a key moment in McCaffery's effort to make concrete these claims to materiality as the work "deliberately problematizes the simple distinction between seeing and reading and offers itself for both distant viewing and close reading" ("*Carnival* Panel 2" 70). This web publication also reminds us that works like *Carnival* can now be circulated on a scale and in a form impossible before. Furthermore, they become readable in ways very different from, and sometimes in contradiction of, their writers' original intentions, and in the process of movement from page to screen, their nature as texts changes. With these texts, that process involves something more than or different from remediation, the importing of "earlier media into a digital space in order to critique and refashion them" (Bolter and Grusin 53) or "the cycling of different *MEDIA* through one another" (Hayles, *Writing Machines* 5). Their digital appearance helps actualize kinds of reading already immanent in the original. The process could more accurately be termed *rematerialization,* a shift in material medium or environment that raises a new set of aesthetic and theoretical questions about the texts.

In its original published form, *Carnival: The First Panel, 1967–70* is a packet of sixteen eight-and-a-half-by-eleven panels, stapled along the top edge but perforated along that edge to allow for tearing. One obvious way in which web publication changes *Carnival* is that it removes the whole component of manual de- and reconstruction, radically altering the material nature of the text. In that sense, it violates McCaffery's original directions for the book, which are only fulfillable once in any case—the book can only be torn up once. (Insofar as my library still has an intact copy, it has to be said that no library user has ever read the "book" properly. If I had charged it out and used it as intended, no doubt I would have incurred significant fines.) As McCaffery and bpNichol describe it, "*Carnival* is an anti-book: perforated pages must be physically released, torn from sequence and viewed simultaneously in the larger composite whole" (65). Peter Jaeger calls *Carnival: The First Panel* "a mechanical device that comes complete with its own instruction manual" (a book-machine, as McCaffery would call it), and those instructions, on a postcard that comes with the publication, read as follows: "In order to destroy this book please tear each page carefully along the perforation. The panel is assembled by laying out pages in a square of four." There is as much sly humor in that juxtaposition of "destroy" and "carefully" and in the politeness of "please" as there is in the inclusion of an errata sheet substituting three nonsemantic blocks of text for three others. (The dissident reader, of course, might lay out pages in various arrangements, much as Robert Grenier does in the reading of his drawing poems, which I discuss below.) As various readers have pointed out, then, echoing McCaffery's own description, it is necessary to destroy the book in order to read it; the book comes into being at the point of its own dissolution as a whole object. Examining closely how this antibook fares online by comparing the print and electronic version reveals what can be lost and gained in the move from one material environment to another.

Close to fifty years after its original publication, my library's print

*Carnival* is somewhat yellowed and rubbed out along the edges. Its slightly faint gray type and staples announce both its own small press origins and an affiliation more generally with alternative publishing institutions of the period. In other words, as a material object it embodies a particular phase of literary history in ways that its online presentation cannot possibly replicate. Nonhorizontal and nonrotating sections of text are, not surprisingly, much harder to read online; craning one's neck to view a monitor at ninety degrees is a tougher proposition than turning a sheet of paper. I have already pointed out how the book's original purpose cannot be fulfilled since it cannot be torn up online; it can be reintegrated but not disintegrated. From this point of view, digital presentation is more static, less susceptible to transformation and manipulation, than the original, and introduces into the digital *Carnival* an unintended level of semipermanence: a significant complication of the much-vaunted fluidity and productive instability of new media technologies (fig. 13.1).[5] And if these are metaphorical losses, there is also a small literal loss in the text's original digital appearance: because of the online version's slightly reduced scale, about a quarter-inch of the original's right margin is lost on each panel. Now, if the material environment of the web loses some semantically significant features of the original, what does it add? Mostly, the visual "noise" against which we measure information. At the top left of each panel, we read instructions for navigating the text: "CARNIVAL [in red] panel 1 map assembled previous next." At the bottom right, we get the necessary concession of the small press to market concerns that the original (though both are published by Coach House Books) could avoid: "order/tip online books mail chbooks CARNIVAL [in red]." If we agree with Jerome McGann that "the way poems are printed and distributed is part of their meaning" (*Black Riders* 168)—a principle so fundamental to my argument that I could well have used it as an epigraph—then surely the social meaning of *Carnival* changes with its entry into an online context that has attributes both of a gift and a market economy.

I hope it is clear that I mean this account as description and analysis, not complaint, especially when the original Coach House Books web publication made available not just both panels of the otherwise rare *Carnival*, in their individual segments and assembled, but also thirty five unpublished outtakes from Panel 2—a significant loss now that they are no longer accessible. McCaffery published the print version of "*Carnival* Panel 2," created between 1970 and 1975, in 1977. "At the time of its composition," he writes, "I conceived *Carnival* as a calculated intervention into the material stakes of poetics" ("*Carnival* Panel 2" 70). And what were

Figure 13.1. Steve McCaffery, *Carnival* Panel 1 (https://www.writing.upenn.edu.)

those stakes? An extension of Charles Olson's ideas about the typewriter as a writerly tool and "the repudiation of a breath-based poetics" (70), the principles so influentially articulated in Olson's classic essay "Projective Verse." *Carnival* seeks to offer both immersion in and distance on language, both reading and seeing: "The panel when 'seen' is 'all language at a distance'; the panel when read is entered, and offers the reader the ex-

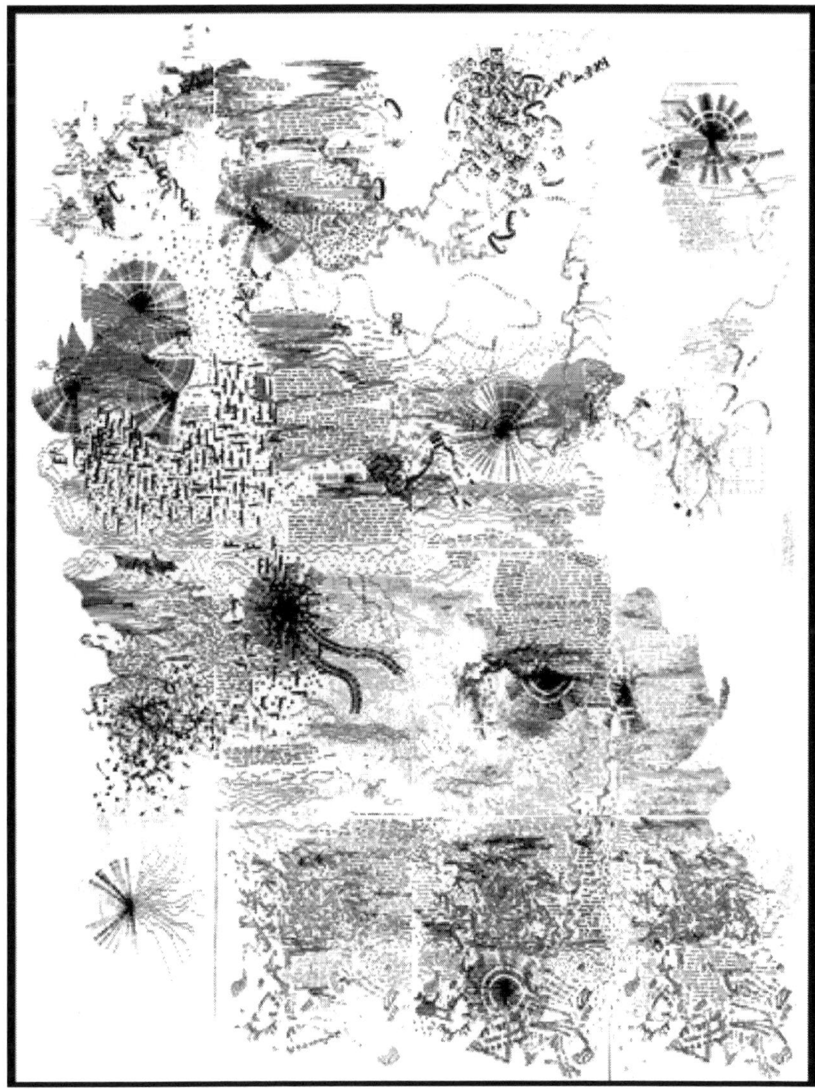

Figure 13.2. Steve McCaffery, *Carnival* Panel 2 (https://www.writing.upenn.edu.)

perience of non-narrative language" (*Seven Pages Missing* 446).[6] McCaffery says that "the roots of *Carnival* go beyond concretism . . . to labyrinth and mandala" (444), and even if we have a different experience of their scale, those shapes can clearly be discerned on screen when we view the panel assembled (fig. 13.2). However, since Panel 2 in its physical form is even more materially dense than Panel 1, that dimension of the work is inevitably lost. "*The Second Panel* places the typed mode in agonistic relation with other forms of scription: xerography, xerography within xerography (i.e., metaxerography and disintegrative seriality), electrostasis, rubber stamp, tissue texts, hand-lettering and stencil" (445), McCaffery writes. How to get all *that* online? Rather improbably, McCaffery asserts that "my own personal line of continuity goes back from *Carnival* to Pope's *Dunciad*," but the explanation is revealing. The typewriter was invented (or at least a typewriter-like machine was patented) in 1714, the year of Pope's enlarged *The Rape of the Lock* and one year before the first volume of his *Iliad*, allowing McCaffery to suggest by association that "the roots of the typewriter are Augustan; its repetitive principle is the principle of the couplet enhanced by speed. The typewriter oracled a neoclassical futurism that emerged in the mid-twentieth century as *poesie concrète*" ("*Carnival*" np). This enabling of a future avant-garde by neoclassicism may seem less odd later in this chapter when we get to the aesthetic and material importance of the typewriter's regularity and repetitiveness in a certain stage of the work of Robert Grenier.

The other McCaffery text that I want to discuss is actually a reading of a McCaffery text: Brian Kim Stefans's shockwave interactive animated reading of two pages (80–81) from *Rational Geomancy*, "Rational Geomancy: Ten Fables of the Reconstruction," a work that allows us to think of digital poetics not just as a way of writing but also as a way of reading and of writing reading. In the original pages of *Rational Geomancy*, McCaffery and bpNichol discuss Madeline Gins's *Word Rain* as "a book *about* the reading experience that necessarily *includes* the reading experience," and with photographed thumb-tips in the bottom left and right corners they replicate one feature of Gins's book: "An ambiguity exists between the page & its photographic reproduction. some pages are 'held' by thumbs. these thumbs are photographs which your own thumb holds" (80). Materiality self-reflexively trumps transparency in McCaffery and Nichol's Gins; meanwhile Stefans uses digital (the pun is appropriate in this case) technology to push this reading and the theorizing of the material book-as-machine a number of steps further, complicating the thematics of absence, presence, embodiment, and representation that recur in McCaffery's work. For Stefans's digital image of the thumbs gives us a multiply deferred or refracted presence: by the time of the online presentation, the thumbs are simultaneously Gins's, her reader's, McCaffery and Nichol's (as readers of Gins), their reader's, and Stefans's—who ends the chain by placing the thumb image on screen, beyond the reach of further thumbs (fig. 13.3).[7]

This process shows the capacity of a new media reading to highlight concerns already immanent in a previous text. On screen, traces of the body—like Robert Grenier's hands holding his little book *Pond I* in its online presentation (fig. 13.4)—stand as visible signs of its absence, a self-consciously rematerialized evocation of a previously material book, and in this way Stefans honors the Language writers' investigation of ideas of "presence" and extends them into another medium. As if to acknowledge that any reproduction of McCaffery's original will be somehow incomplete, in Stefans's presentation the top couple of lines are cut off and a shadow or stain across the book's gutter obscures a certain amount of text, which remains otherwise largely legible. Following the instructions—"click on the book to get a close-up"—produces a close-up of around fifteen lines of text featuring mobile details oscillating against a static ground to foreground certain themes. Letters dripping down the page from the phrase "word rain" explicitly call up Apollinaire's "Il Pleut," in a gesture of

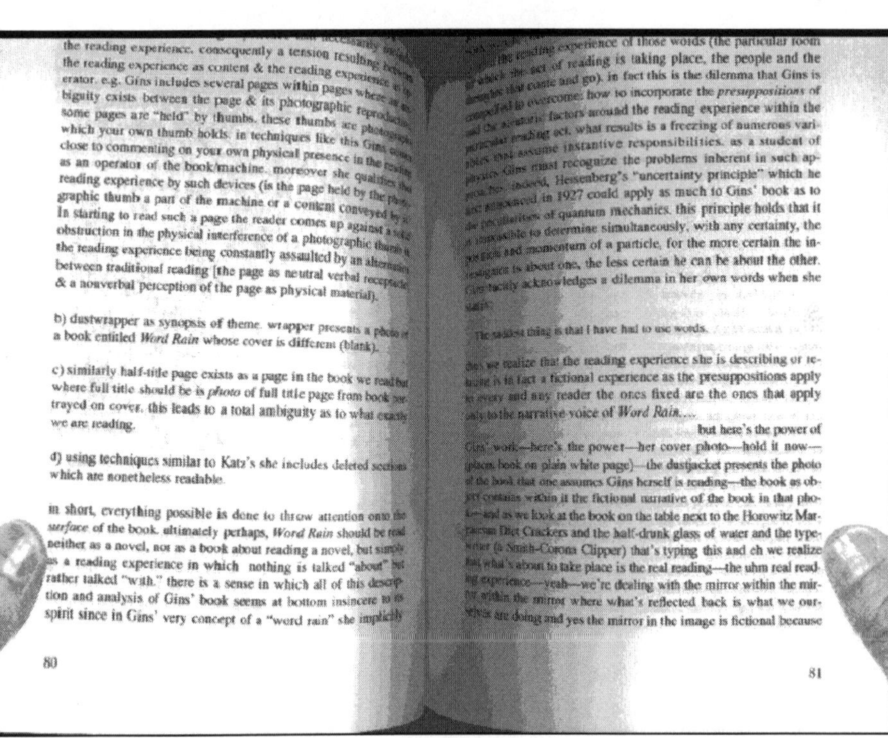

the reading experience. consequently a tension resulting [illegible] the reading experience as content & the reading experience [illegible] erator. e.g. Gins includes several pages within pages where [illegible] biguity exists between the page & its photographic reproduction [illegible] some pages are "held" by thumbs. these thumbs are photograph[illegible] which your own thumb holds. in techniques like this Gins comes close to commenting on your own physical presence in the reading as an operator of the book/machine. moreover she qualifies the reading experience by such devices (is the page held by the photo-graphic thumb a part of the machine or a content conveyed by [illegible] In starting to read such a page the reader comes up against a [illegible] obstruction in the physical interference of a photographic thumb [illegible] the reading experience being constantly assaulted by an alternation between traditional reading (the page as neutral verbal receptacle & a nonverbal perception of the page as physical material).

b) dustwrapper as synopsis of theme. wrapper presents a photo of a book entitled *Word Rain* whose cover is different (blank).

c) similarly half-title page exists as a page in the book we read but where full title should be is *photo* of full title page from book portrayed on cover. this leads to a total ambiguity as to what exactly we are reading.

d) using techniques similar to Katz's she includes deleted sections which are nonetheless readable.

in short, everything possible is done to throw attention onto the *surface* of the book. ultimately perhaps, *Word Rain* should be read neither as a novel, nor as a book about reading a novel, but simply as a reading experience in which nothing is talked "about" but rather talked "with." there is a sense in which all of this description and analysis of Gins' book seems at bottom insincere to its spirit since in Gins' very concept of a "word rain" she implicitly

80

[illegible] experience of those words (the particular room [illegible] of reading is taking place, the people and the [illegible] go). in fact this is the dilemma that Gins is [illegible] to overcome: how to incorporate the *presuppositions* of [illegible] factors around the reading experience within the [illegible] act. what results is a freezing of numerous vari[illegible] instantive responsibilities. as a student of [illegible] Gins must recognize the problems inherent in such ap[illegible] Heisenberg's "uncertainty principle" which he [illegible] in 1927 could apply as much to Gins' book as to [illegible] of quantum mechanics. this principle holds that it [illegible] to determine simultaneously, with any certainty, the [illegible] and momentum of a particle. for the more certain the in[illegible] is about one, the less certain he can be about the other. [illegible] acknowledges a dilemma in her own words when she [illegible]

[illegible] thing is that I have had to use words.

[illegible] we realize that the reading experience she is describing or re[illegible] is in fact a fictional experience as the presuppositions apply [illegible] every and any reader the ones fixed are the ones that apply [illegible] to the narrative voice of *Word Rain*. . . .

but here's the power of Gins' work—here's the power—her cover photo—hold it now—[illegible] book on plain white page)—the dustjacket presents the photo of the book that one assumes Gins herself is reading—the book as ob[illegible] contains within it the fictional narrative of the book in that pho[illegible]—and as we look at the book on the table next to the Horowitz Mar[illegible] Diet Crackers and the half-drunk glass of water and the type[illegible] (a Smith-Corona Clipper) that's typing this and oh we realize that what's about to take place is the real reading—the uhm real reading experience—yeah—we're dealing with the mirror within the mirror within the mirror where what's reflected back is what we our[illegible] are doing and yes the mirror in the image is fictional because

81

Figure 13.3. Brian Kim Stefans, "Rational Geomancy. Ten Fables of the Reconstruction," (http://www.arras.net)

Figure 13.4. Robert Grenier, from *Pond I* (https://www.writing.upenn.edu)

homage to one who is often cited as a modernist precursor to new media poetry (fig. 13.5). In another close-up, the words "problems" and "uncertainty" form a frantic dancing palimpsest over their originals in the base text; in yet another the first three letters of the alphabet buzz like annoyed bees over a stable background, as if to reference the debate over digital mobility and print stasis (figs. 13.6 and 13.7).

McCaffery, then, troubles the seeing-reading distinction in ways relevant for our thinking about new media poetry while his materially intensive texts variously point up the limitations of the electronic environment (in the case of *Carnival*) and its potential to extend the implications of a print text (in the case of *Rational Geomancy*). The publication online of Grenier's series "rhymms," "for Larry Eigner," "Greeting," and "Pond I," barely legible one-of-a-kind handwritten or hand-drawn poems rendered mostly in four different pen colors, raises a different set of issues: the electronic circulation of unique texts into instant availability and the consequent tension between reproducibility and aura, between current and ear-

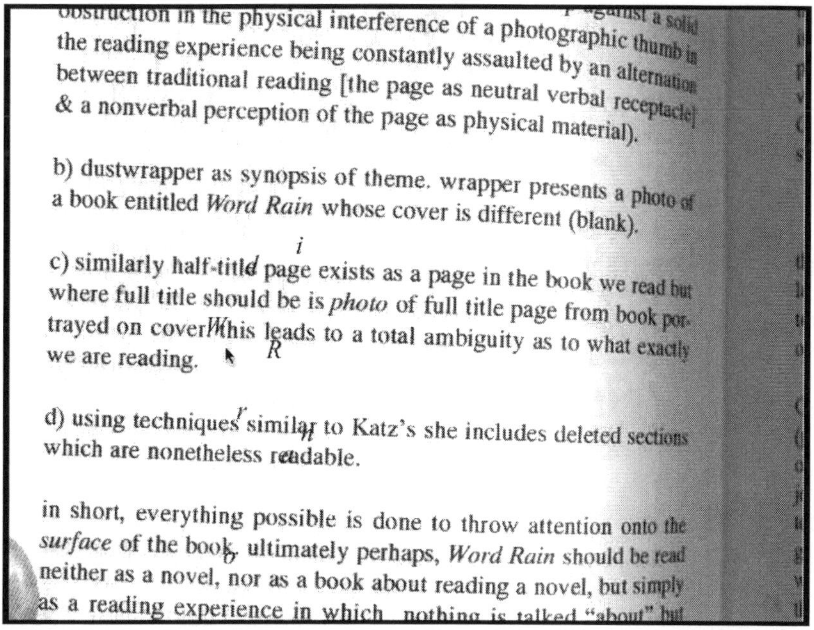

obstruction in the physical interference of a photographic thumb is ... against a solid
the reading experience being constantly assaulted by an alternation
between traditional reading [the page as neutral verbal receptacle]
& a nonverbal perception of the page as physical material).

b) dustwrapper as synopsis of theme. wrapper presents a photo of a book entitled *Word Rain* whose cover is different (blank).

c) similarly half-titld page exists as a page in the book we read but where full title should be is *photo* of full title page from book portrayed on coverWhis leads to a total ambiguity as to what exactly we are reading.

d) using techniques simila to Katz's she includes deleted sections which are nonetheless readable.

in short, everything possible is done to throw attention onto the *surface* of the book. ultimately perhaps, *Word Rain* should be read neither as a novel, nor as a book about reading a novel, but simply as a reading experience in which nothing is talked "about" but

Figure 13.5. Brian Kim Stefans, "Rational Geomancy. Ten Fables of the Reconstruction," (http://www.arras.net)

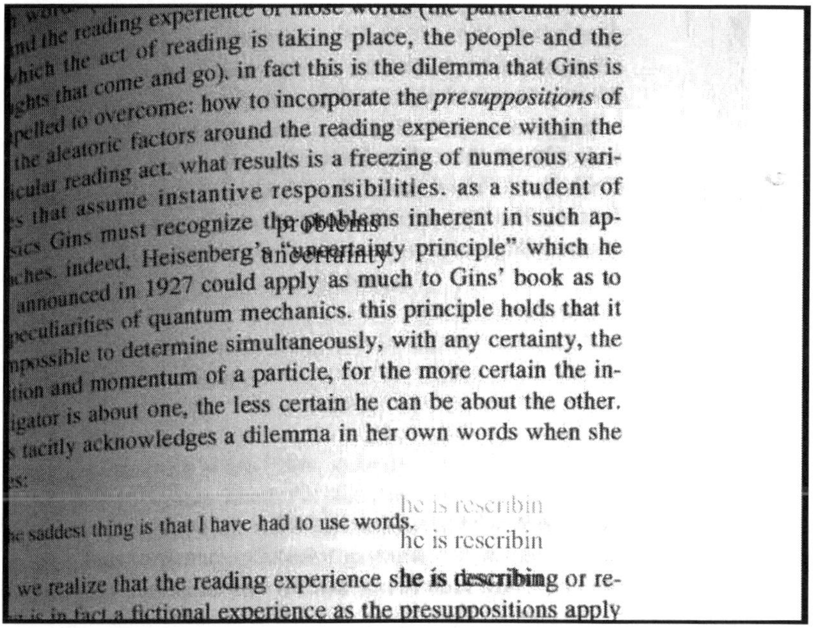

reading experience of those words (the particular room
nd the act of reading is taking place, the people and the
hich the act ... come and go). in fact this is the dilemma that Gins is
pelled to overcome: how to incorporate the *presuppositions* of
the aleatoric factors around the reading experience within the
icular reading act. what results is a freezing of numerous vari-
s that assume instantive responsibilities. as a student of
sics Gins must recognize the problems inherent in such ap-
ches. indeed, Heisenberg's "uncertainty principle" which he
announced in 1927 could apply as much to Gins' book as to
peculiarities of quantum mechanics. this principle holds that it
npossible to determine simultaneously, with any certainty, the
tion and momentum of a particle, for the more certain the in-
igator is about one, the less certain he can be about the other.
s tacitly acknowledges a dilemma in her own words when she
es:

he is rescribin

e saddest thing is that I have had to use words. he is rescribin

we realize that the reading experience she is describing or re-
is in fact a fictional experience as the presuppositions apply

Figure 13.6. Brian Kim Stefans, "Rational Geomancy. Ten Fables of the Reconstruction," (http://www.arras.net)

the reading experience. consequently aatension resulting between the reading experience as content & the reading experience as operator. e.g. Gins includes several pages within pages where an ambiguity exists between the page & its photographic reproduction, some pages are "held" by thumbs. these thumbs are photographs which your own thumb holds. in techniques like this Gins comes close to commenting on your own physical presence in the reading as an operator of the book/machine. moreover she qualifies the reading experience by such devices (is the page held by the photographic thumb a part of the machine or a content conveyed by it? In starting to read such a page the reader comes up against a solid obstruction in the physical interference of a photographic thumb is the reading experience being constantly assaulted by an alternation between traditional reading [the page as neutral verbal receptacle] & a nonverbal perception of the page as physical material).

b) dustwrapper as synopsis of theme. wrapper presents a photo of a book entitled *Word Rain* whose cover is different (blank).

c) similarly half-title page exists ...

Figure 13.7. Brian Kim Stefans, "Rational Geomancy. Ten Fables of the Reconstruction," (http://www.arras.net)

lier, even ancient, technologies of writing, between what Tim Shaner and Michael Rozendal have called, in discussing Grenier, emergent and residual technologies (48n.2).[8] Some words about Grenier's process and poetics are in order before moving on to these issues. It is worth remembering that Grenier has worked with loose-leaf forms of publication, outside of codexspace, throughout his career, ever since the now almost mythic *Sentences*: five hundred minimalist poems on five-by-eight index cards, written 1972–1977 and published in a foldup box in 1978. In the urgent search for or construction of historical precedents that marks moments of significant literary and technological change, even Grenier's closest readers disagree as to whether *Sentences* is an early form of hypertext. Bob Perelman argues that "while the lack of binding allows for any sequence, Grenier's allegiance is not toward any early version of hypertext" (*Marginalization* 46) but toward an emphasis on his materials. (I'd suggest it's not an either-or choice.) Charles Bernstein, however, includes *Sentences* in his list of "hypertext avant le PC" ("Mosaic") and even finds it pointing up, by contrast, one limitation of new media technologies: "You can't flip through a data base the way you can flip through pages or index cards. (I'm thinking, for example, of Robert Grenier's great poem of the 1970s,

*Sentences*)" (*My Way* 78). Complicating matters further, the original publisher of *Sentences*, Michael Waltuch, has made it available in a web-based version using a JavaScript code to randomize the cards but has also proposed that "the 'boxed version' allows for a 'freer' mode of interacting with the work than the online version." Grenier has produced more such publications than he has bound books. The drawing poems that he has been producing since the late 1980s, then, are consistent with this pattern.

Grenier describes the process by which he came to write these poems in a 1998 talk with the characteristically punning title, "Realizing Things." Language writing's emphasis on linguistic materiality always seems to have taken very literal form for Grenier. (Or, in a not indefensible reversal of that proposition, Grenier's literalist materiality became important for Language writing.) In a 1986 interview with Alastair Johnston, he says "as a writer what you do, whatever instrument you use, you make this mark, then that mark and that mark" ("Typewriter" 5), echoing his claim from a 1982 talk that "you start writing in relation to . . . writing materials" ("Language/Site/World" 230). In his account, at a certain point in his career typing came to defamiliarize the letter and immerse him further in the minute attention to language to which he was always inclined: "In the Selectric typewriter methodology, each letter is given an equivalent width—the i's are the same width as the m's, the l's are the same width as the w's—& I was able to count each letter as 'one' . . . & so that would be a further 'removal,' I suppose, & reengagement with the language process only" ("Realizing Things"). Partially handwritten poems started to come out of textual annotations on typescript that Grenier wished to preserve as part of the writing process, as in the 1984 poem "May Dawn Horizon Many Graces Pollen" from *Phantom Anthems*, at the same time as he also sought intensified materiality through type: "I got off the Selectric & went back to my highschool typewriter which made a darker image, with a dark ribbon—this was a manual—& that image somehow . . . I thought that was more, somehow, 'that of which it spoke' than the Selectric image . . . it was darker, denser" ("Realizing Things"). Apparently dissatisfied with his "delusion" that the manual typewriter would provide the sense of "a greater, hands-on tenacity or 'facticity,'" however, Grenier moved to handwriting or drawing poems with various combinations of the four color pens that he used in his proofreader's job.[9]

If "Grenier is interested in the phoneme as a thing in itself" (Watten, *Total Syntax* 9), he became equally interested in the grapheme as a thing in itself. Grenier himself offers a revealing pun when he speaks of "beginning to write letters by hand, to draw them into existence" ("Realizing Things"). He does literally draw his letters, creating shapes that sometimes seem to bear only a distant relationship to their alphabetic originals. But he also "draws them into [discrete] existence" out of a kind of Platonic ur-letter from which they emerge as much as they are constructed: "Letters draw themselves out of corresponding letter shapes . . . AS IF ALL WERE MADE FROM THE SAME LETTER" ([Untitled essay] 72). This is Emerson as postmodern materialist, the transparent eyeball now a transparent Uniball pen. Through this hands-on engagement with the materials of language, Grenier engages the material of the world: "The 'idea' is, if you focus sufficiently on the materials of language itself, possibly you'll be able to bring back to the participation in & with things a means of actualizing what's happening. . . . The farther you get into the structure of language itself, I've found, the more are you enabled at times to be able to go into the metamorphosis, the flow through things that Emerson speaks of" ("Realizing Things").

Grenier's narrative of his process directly reverses N. Katherine Hayles's account of the increased lightness of touch and the reduced "material resistance of the text to manipulation" involved in the move from manual to electric typewriter to keyboard ("Materiality of Informatics" 164). One could argue that part of Grenier's project is to reintroduce the resistance of touch (or the memory of it) in the face of this apparently dematerializing technology, proposing the body as a site of cultural resistance in much the way that Charles Olson—a crucial figure for Grenier, and another often cited as a print precursor for certain aspects of new media poetics—does in his 1953 essay "The Resistance."[10] If new "technologies modify the body's proprioceptive sense," as Hayles has argued (167), online presentation of Grenier's handcrafted work puts opposing materialities and opposing experiences of the body in productive tension. The question then arises (and it's one I want to keep open): Does web distribution dematerialize Grenier's emphatically embodied work, or does it paradoxically fulfill that work's project by foregrounding precisely these oppositions?

A related contradiction involves the electronic circulation of unique texts into more-or-less instant availability and the consequent tension between reproducibility and aura, between current and earlier writing technologies. Behind this tension lies the economics of production and distribution. Stephen Ratcliffe lays out the cost of codex production quite precisely, arriving by detailed argument at a figure of $22,000 in 1998 dollars for producing a print run of 400 of Grenier's then-current poems (*Listening* 119). Given the economic unfeasibility of such a book, Grenier's drawing poems have had their distribution through limited color xerox editions (David Baratier's Pavement Saw Press sold *12 from Rhymms* for

$20 a set in 1996, for instance); through gallery presentations (five hundred-plus slides of the work had been made public via a dozen showings and readings as of the time of Ratcliffe's writing in the late 1990s); and on the web.[11] As Karl Young, editor of the Light and Dust website where much of Grenier's work appears, writes,

> Robert Grenier's illuminated poems . . . present a number of problems in reproduction, distribution, and, for some, in reading. These poems are written in colored ink, and require color reproduction. Fourcolor process printing makes them too expensive to produce. . . . I hope that the web will help bring Grenier's illuminated poems out of the small and restricted circle of distribution in which they have moved, and make them available to a larger audience.

Especially in the handling of Grenier's work, however, this reaching out for an audience is not an unproblematic move. Far too pricey to produce in book form, these works derive considerable aura from the uniqueness, individual manual production, and unavailability of the original "hard" copies. As Bob Perelman proposes, Grenier's emphasis on his materials leads to "the special poetic or ontological value or magical potency that [he] seems to be trying to create" (*Marginalization* 53), a potency usually comprehended under the term "aura." Walter Benjamin, then, is not far in the background, and gives us one set of terms for thinking about the relationship between such aura and the "mechanical reproduction" of web publication in Grenier. At the same time, his famous claim that "the whole sphere of authenticity is outside technical . . . reproducibility" (220) has been rendered untenable not just by decades of poststructuralist theory and art practice but most recently by digital media.

In this interface between the most ancient and the most contemporary of text-producing technologies, as much as Grenier wants to return his work to the body, it cannot—if it is to be distributed—escape the machine. In reading Grenier's drawing poems electronically, we are confronted with the extremes of handcraftedness and technological mediation: extremes not immanent in the work but in the disjunction between its modes of production and distribution. From one point of view, Grenier's work of the last thirty years seems the absolute antithesis of new media poetry. From another, its digital presentation highlights the (in this case literal) inaccessibility of any original: online, we experience the web presentation of slides of photographs of one-of-a-kind handwritten poems the originals of which most people will never see. Paradoxically, their online reproduction can be seen both as a fulfillment and a contradiction of the originals' impulses toward personalized signature and fiercely specific attention to material texture.

Grenier's particular form of materiality is a retrospective (not to be confused with retrogressive) gesture driven by an almost Emersonian concern for natural origins. As Ratcliffe puts it, "the thingness of his writing . . . moves it backward, closer somehow to where it is that writing must first have come from" (*Listening* 125). Yet "naturalness" in Grenier is complicated. The artifice of his own reading style distances his voice from speech, and of course he is well known for his contentious but influential manifesto statement "I HATE SPEECH." At the same time, Ratcliffe finds the "shape of letters analogous to shape of landscape" in Grenier, "making the page itself a landscape" (121). Certainly, at the level of content, some of Grenier's graphic work is almost elemental in its minimalist focus on (to cite the "Pond I" sequence) "pond," "sky," "ground," "wind," "water," "sunshine," "minnows," "coyote." In one nicely ambiguous conjunction of natural imagery and textual materiality, it is hard to know whether to read #28 as "spelling" or [appropriately, misspelled] "saplling" (fig. 13.8). This evocation of and immersion in the organic seems to sit uneasily with the poems'

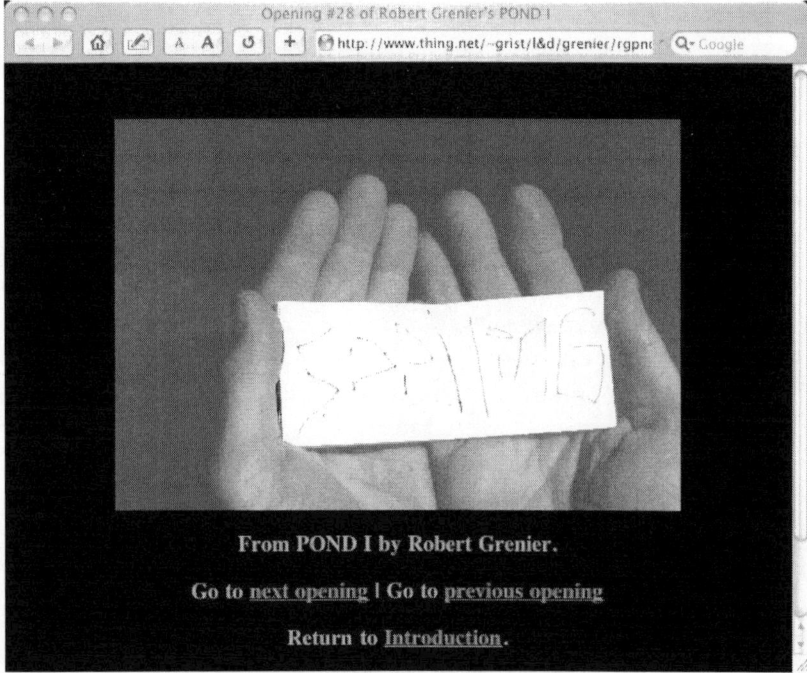


Figure 13.8. Robert Grenier, from *Pond I* (https://www.writing.upenn.edu)

digital presentation. As Michael Basinski points out, however, "Grenier has been able to invent a form of poetry that is suitable for the computer era but also moves beyond the stagnancy of text based poetry, visual poetry and performance poetry. His poems best utilize the capacity of the computer. He does this not by using a computer as a tool to manipulate text but as a medium to present" the work (33). Grenier's poetics exhibits a kind of materiality of organic form, as if language (as it was for Emerson) were at the heart of nature, and he adopts an organicist metaphor for his highly graphic aesthetic: "I wish more strange young poets wd dedicate life to making briers and blackberries out of words, letters etc. . . . for the fun of it" ([Untitled essay] 73). He wants poems that will embody—including visually—the prickly entanglements of those plants. The allusion to Whitman (the phrase "briers and blackberries" derives from "Out of the Cradle Endlessly Rocking," three lines of which begin the essay) is appropriate, since Grenier's materiality of organic forms sounds like nothing as much as Whitman's 1855 preface to *Leaves of Grass*, that title, of course, itself enacting a pun between nature and book. But for all its organicism, the fact that Grenier's work is so hard to reproduce in print pushes it toward the web as its "natural" home, and it fits at least one current if controversial definition of what Loss Glazier calls "e-poetry": "Works that cannot be adequately delivered via traditional paper publishing or cannot be displayed on paper. This would include innovative works circulated in electronic form" (163). Brian Reed observes that "as presented in [Grenier's] slide-lectures, such works as *rhymms* and *POND I* can seem, well, wholesome, caught up in an optimistic Emersonian affirmation of the essential goodness of nature, art, and humanity" (78). Other presentational contexts, however, including the digital, foreground Grenier's "opting for an amateurishness of execution by settling for at-hand materials," "a wavering, scrawny, hard-to-follow line" that "obstructs or counters the transcendentalist urges present in his verse . . . to stage a radical, insuperable split between spirit and matter" (79, 82). Grenier's hand-drawn poetry, then, demonstrates "the deconstructive potential of an improper (or perverse, untimely, inexplicable, inconvenient, deviant, etc.) emphasis on writing's materiality" (82).

As far from an evocation of the organic as one can get is the work of Charles Bernstein, who started out producing typographically manipulated palimpsests in the 1970s with his chapbook *Veil*. The visual explorations in his career since then have ranged from the many verbal/visual collaborations with his wife, the artist Susan Bee, to his cocuratorship of the 2001 *Poetry Plastique* exhibit, to colorful cyberpoems, to self-performing cyberessays that focus on the implications of new media for pedagogy and for what we teach about the "nature" of poetry. More than the other poets I discuss, Bernstein has theorized digital poetics, produced writing in that mode, and exploited the web's potential for circulation and as a site for discourses about poetry that share the genre-mixing techniques of page-based discourses. The sheer range and probing inventiveness of Bernstein's visually oriented poetic activities make him the ideal case study for examining how an engaged poet, critic, and teacher uses his own developing work in digital media to test the adequacy of current pedagogical paradigms for poetry and the relationship of new media to print-based poetries and to institutions of education, circulation, and reception.

These concerns form the core of Bernstein's electronic essay on poetics, "An Mosaic for Convergence," the clunkily ungrammatical title a synecdoche for the fault lines that the piece addresses. The essay is "based on a presentation at a 1995 conference at the State University of New York, Buffalo on 'The Convergence of Science and the Humanities.'" So much for the convergence. The mosaic is a matter of structure, of serial form: the essay consists of around twenty-four separate screens (or tiles), including the title screen, that are randomly reordered on each viewing so that no two visits to the essay will provide the reader with the same reading sequence.[12] The structure represents a digital version of the method Bernstein often uses in giving public talks, randomly shuffling through and reading index cards containing entries on his nominal topic—as Bernstein has it in one screen that anticipates a distinction from his book *My Way* (11), "not unstructured essays / *differently structured* // not structurally challenged / *structurally challenging*."[13] The screens contain a mixture of poems, aphorisms, jokes, and passages of critical commentary on digital poetics, its relation to the book and to the history of experimental writing, and its impact on the social and pedagogical institutions surrounding poetry. They cover a lively, diverse, and playful range of format, color, font, and background, confirming the kid-in-a-candy-shop pleasure that Bernstein expresses in a 1996 interview: "It's wild after a writing lifetime of assuming black ink on white paper to start to pick your background image—and not just your font and point size, but the color of the font" ("Interview" 20–21).

More specifically, one recurrent feature of the essay involves its visual and often tonal contrasts between figure and ground, and Bernstein has commented on the figure-ground tensions that came with working in HTML ("Every Which Way" 178–79). One screen, originally titled "Punic," addresses the discrepancy between the impact of new technologies on poetry and on academic institutions, historically slow to make structural adjustments to change. It begins: "As a poet, essayist, and university teacher,

I am particularly interested in the ways that the new computer technology affects the disciplines with which I am most involved" (fig. 13.9).[14] In conflict with the portentous, job-application seriousness of this beginning, however, stands the opening image, a book jacket photo of Bernstein comically altered by his daughter Emma and a bright blue, Kid-Pix-style background with black exclamation points descending like bombs, red-lipped mouths and flashing cameras, and the name of the perpetrator, Felix (Bernstein's son), inscribed here and there. Digital technology, then, enables Bernstein to create a tonal tension between straightforward, even earnest, exposition, and its visual context.

The mosaic organization of the essay also allows Bernstein to juxtapose, without resolving, competing views of new technologies' effect on academic discourse. On one screen, he finds it likely that "the ideological fixation on linear and expository discourse will be imported into this new medium"; on another, "hypertextual organization may finally help to break teaching, textbooks, and critical writing from their deadly boring fetishization of narrative and expository ordering of information" (a statement repeated in *My Way* 72). If institutional and pedagogical struc-

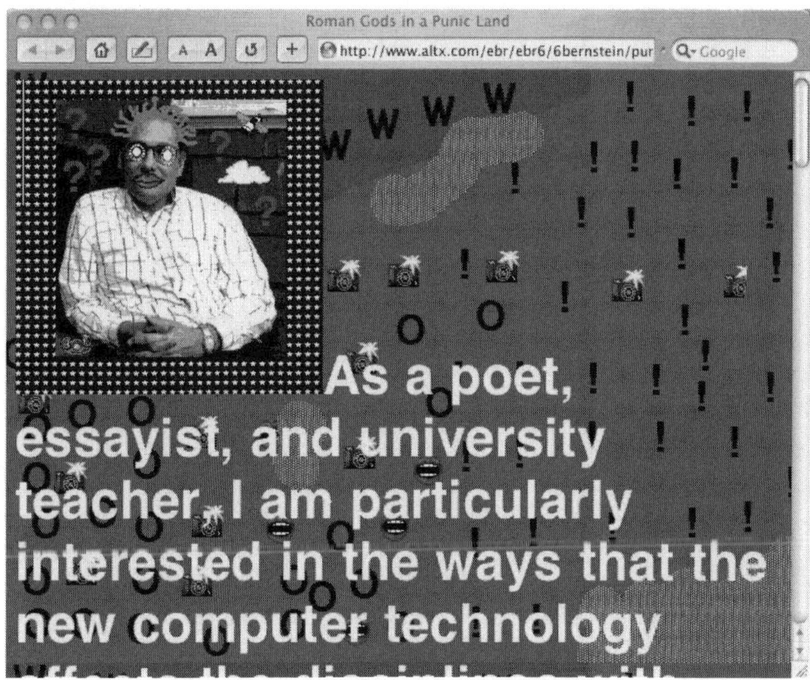


Figure 13.9. Charles Bernstein, from "An Mosaic for Convergence" (https://electronicbookreview.com)

tures rest on the normalization of book technology, as Alan Filreis argues, then Bernstein has suggested some sprightly alternatives.[15] Other sections, as Bernstein's page poetry often does, play off contemporary educational clichés that exploit electronic connectivity for profit (there's a poem called "Distance Learning"), or off the language of the web site: if "frequently asked questions" are FAQs (but not facts), "Frequently Unasked Questions," the title of one poem, are FUQs.

The digital medium provides Bernstein with a much wider palette with which to counter "the deadly boring fetishization . . . of expository ordering." Play with color and layout allow further possibilities for interrupting the tonal seriousness and structural predictability of normative academic writing (what he calls elsewhere "frame lock, and its cousin tone jam" [*My Way* 90]). The individual screens of "An Mosaic for Convergence," as I have suggested, insistently enact a tension between transparent expository content and obtrusive material presentation, the kind of clash of discourses that Bernstein pursues throughout his work and that the electronic environment further enables. That environment permits moments of defamiliarization like those produced by a screen such as "Textuaì," the legibility of which is obstructed by its presentation in partly nonalphabetic fonts (fig. 13.10). After reading such a screen, we no longer

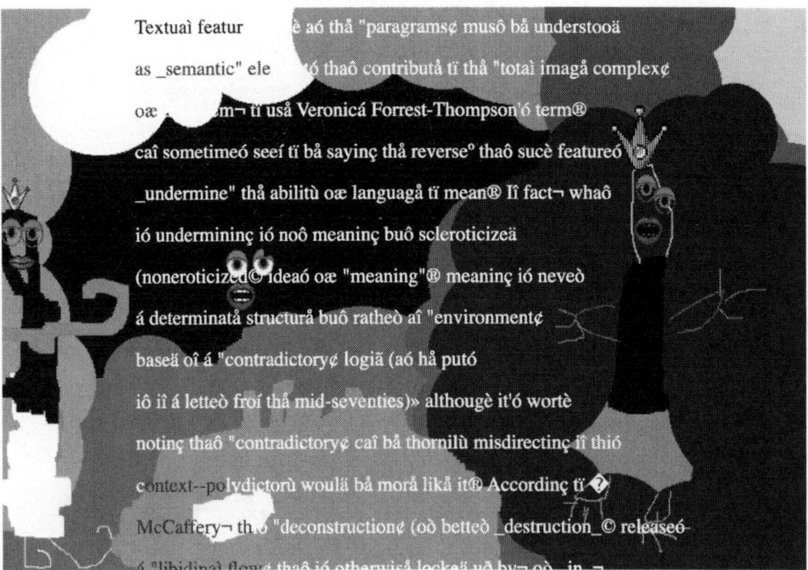


Figure 13.10. Charles Bernstein, "Textuaì," (http://writing.upenn.edu/)

take the alphabet quite so much for granted, and one result is that the normative presentation of a screen like "realpolitick"—two left-justified prose paragraphs on the commercial foreclosure of hypertext's radical open-endedness, in that most commonplace of fonts, twelve-point Times New Roman—suddenly becomes defamiliarized and seems highly designed, not inevitable but simply one set of choices among many (fig. 13.11).

"Realpolitick" itself also exemplifies the degree of rematerialization and textual migration within "Mosaic." Not only does the essay's overall context highlight or defamiliarize, by contrast, this screen's transparency, but Bernstein reformats a variant version of its first paragraph to make up another "Mosaic" screen. There it appears as a poem, centered on the screen and with a left-justified margin, on a ground of variously colored swatches that recalls Bernstein's "HTML Series" of poems; after twelve lines, a block of black space creates a distancing moment of discontinuity. In the original online version of "Mosaic," Bernstein's recycling of "Realpolitick" used the first paragraph of the text in a similar but even more colorful and visually playful form than that which appears in the ar-

As a structure, the paratactic links of a hypertextual environment short circuit narrative closure and foreground open-endedness - there is always another link. I take it as an axiom that commercial culture will shrink and privatize this radical, possibly unbearable, open-endedness by creating contained environments. Indeed, the privatization and commercialization of e-space is synonymous with containement - limiting links by imposing defaults that consumers will "choose" in the sense of choosing one commodity over the another. While the defenders of popular culture like to attack new art for being inaccessible, the fact is that it is hyper-commercialization of the communications media that most actively restricts access to "speech" by making inaccessible all that is not maximally profitable. Nor am I saying that limits are aesthetically or morally bad; on the contrary, they are the basis of aesthetics and ethics. But the aesthetic and political issue is what limits are chosen, who will do the choosing, how informed the choices will be, and who profits.

If you think I am being paranoid, consider the implications of a cartel composed of the major commercial producers of moves, music, computer operating systems, cable TV, networked computer operating protocols and systems, and games and entertainments for PC and networked computers. Call it Dreamworks Inateractive, Inc.; their dreams, your quarters. Netscape and Eudora may be free as shareware. You're dreaming if you think Microsoft Dreamworks will be.

Figure 13.11. Charles Bernstein, "Realpolitick" (http://www.altx.com)

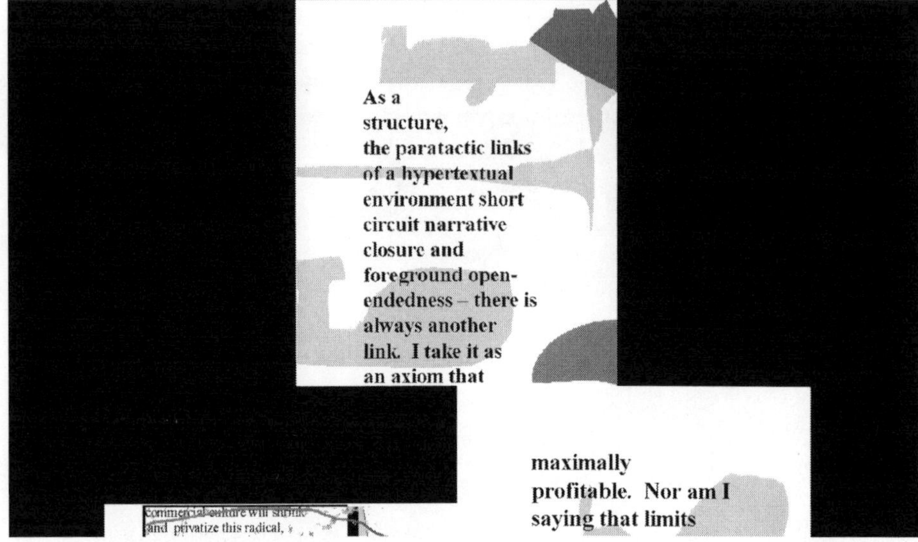


Figure 13.12. Charles Bernstein, "Access" (http://writing.upenn.edu)

chival version of "Mosaic" that I describe here; this iteration is available as a still under the title "Access" (fig. 13.12). At the level of content, Bernstein makes clear in "Realpolitick" and "Access" the appeal of the digital to an avant-garde poet: "As a structure, the paratactic links of a hypertextual environment short circuit narrative closure and foreground open-endedness." At the formal level, the visual conventionality of "realpolitick" makes a point about "frame lock," associating normatively presented prose with a politics of compromise; "Access," with the "same" text, uses the resources of HTML to embody the potential of parataxis and heightened materiality for reshaping the conventions of expository prose (and to pun on the fact of access to digital media and ideals of textual "accessibility").

Similar in form to "An Mosaic," "Electronic Pies in the Poetry Skies" originated in January 2001 as one of Bernstein's characteristically structured talks, in which he first shuffles and then reads from note cards pertaining to his topic. In its *Electronic Book Review* publication, as part of Marc Bousquet and Katharine Wills's online book *The Politics of Information,* the essay's arguments maintain their trenchancy while formally the piece becomes more static and linear than in its live performance. This version of the essay, imposing an order on the argument that other presentations disrupt, reflects Bernstein's previously cited observation that "you can't flip through a data base the way you can flip through pages or index cards"—distribution and readability for content trump formal exploration and surprising juxtaposition. The *EBR* version privileges a somewhat dystopian conclusion that remains the same with each reading, a conclusion in line with the title's (and essay's) ironizing of electronic democratic utopias: "There'll be pie in the sky when you die. / But not likely." The currently unavailable Coach House Press online presentation, engineered by damian lopes, randomized the essay by "shuffling" three slightly overlapping small screens that imitated browsers (Netscape, Internet Explorer, and Mozilla), with the content of each miniscreen changing about every ten seconds. Like Stefans's treatment of McCaffery and Nichol's *Rational Geomancy*, this presentation—part palimpsest, part juxtaposition—constitutes a reading of Bernstein's essay, as it foregrounds the material frames (the browsers) by which web access is both enabled and shaped. (Meanwhile, in a characteristic act of inverse remediation, Bernstein reprinted "Electronic Pies" in his 2011 print collection *Attack of the Difficult Poems*.)

Since Bernstein returns so frequently to ideas of layering or the palimpsest, it is unsurprising that the veil as both artwork and metaphor is crucial to his visual practice. He discusses the figure of the veil extensively in an interview with Manuel Brito, where he notes that the palimpsests of his chapbook *Veil* (written in 1976, published in 1987) were "produced by several layers of overtyping" (*My Way* 31), with Morris Louis's "Veil" paintings as one model. (Since Louis was born Morris Louis Bernstein, a biographical joke is also at work here: behind the veil of Louis's name change lies another Bernstein.) The veil suggests to Bernstein the materiality of language: "Our language is our veil, but one that too often is made invisible. Yet, hiding the veil of language, its wordness, its textures, its obstinate physicality, only makes matters worse" (32). The *Veil* chapbook is available as a pdf online, where, as Johanna Drucker points out, its circulation raises an issue similar to that raised by the rematerialization of McCaffery's *Carnival*: "The immaterial substrate, a mere display of code, has eliminated the production history and process, thus configuring a loss of information as its imaged form" ("Intimations" 166). However, individual pages of *Veil* tend to fade in their rematerialized HTML version. Even when enhanced, resolution is poorer in the HTML *Veil*, and especially the smaller pieces are much harder to read than in the print version, with the marks in parts barely detectable as letters.[16] In this format—as distinct from the original hard copy *Veil* and its pdf reproduction—the texts have become more available but less readable, even though Bernstein, stressing the graphic rather less than McCaffery, wants them to be read: "The writing was composed to be read, not only looked at: it is possible to read not just view these works" ("Mosaic"), which "are a form of writing, not design" ("My Veils"). At the same time, the materially intensive nature of texts like *Carnival* and *Veil* prompts useful speculation about the ambiguously material/immaterial digital environment. When a print text like *Veil* already foregrounds the materiality of its own letters, its electronic transformation intensifies any questions about the nature of electronic (im)materiality.

In their very rematerialization, the visually intensive works that I discuss throughout this chapter come to instantiate a minihistory of writing technologies. That is, as examples of transitional materiality, they mark the historical transitions or relations between media. This process emerges clearly through Bernstein's various visual series, each one "a visualization [of] the specific writing tools that I most used: the IBM Selectric typewriter, the fountain pen, and Microsoft Word for Windows" ("Mosaic"). Bernstein explains the process further: "'Veil,' the Selectric series from the late 70s, was made by typing new compositions over ones that I had just written. 'The Language of Bo[u]quets' from the early 1990s used pages of my writing notebook, overprinted with a xerox machine. The '*HTML Series*' was made using Word together with its built in HTML converter" ("Mosaic"). He lays out this history in a way that self-reflexively embodies it. The discussion begins with a paragraph of migratory text first used in "Every Which Way but Loose" (179) that proposes, uncontroversially enough, that "the new computer technology—both desktop publishing and electronic publishing—has radically altered the material, specifically visual, presentation of text." The screen appears in a Courier font that dates the text as page-based and alludes to *Veil*'s origins even as Bernstein argues that "it begins to seem . . . natural to think of composing screen by screen rather than page by page." Little seems natural, however, about this spiral of self-reflexive artifice as it proposes not a history of "supersession" of one medium by another, in Paul Duguid's term,[17] but one of a playful reciprocity between new and old media: "Reciprocity rather than hierarchy is a better way to understand the relation among the media" ("Mosaic").

This particular screen of "Mosaic" offers just one example among many of how Bernstein uses textual migration as a way to test both the capacities of different media and different realizations within a medium (since he moves text among different print sites and among different digital sites, as well as from print to the digital medium). The preface of Bernstein's 2001 book of poems, *With Strings*, reprints part of his discussion of materiality from his essay "Every Which Way but Loose." Similarly, much of "Mosaic" uses material that has appeared elsewhere: in *My Way*, *With Strings*, and "Every Which Way but Loose." The essay recycles a number of poems from *With Strings*: the first stanza of "mr. matisse in san diego" (79), "windows 95" (90), "Frequently Unasked Questions" (116), "this poem intentionally left blank" (121). In its electronic form, this last poem becomes (in white text on a black ground) "this link intentionally left blank"—the link left blank being no link at all, so that digital connection is jokily refused.[18] Bernstein's 1997 "Alphabeta" rematerializes a passage from the 1994 essay "I Don't Take Voice Mail" in *My Way* that he also uses in "Mosaic," on the relationship between hypertext and earlier writing technologies, and between hypertext and avant-garde antilinearity.[19] This migration of text from print essay to digital essay to prose poem is characteristic of how Bernstein uses multiple media as part of a practical strategy for de-essentializing poetry. Thus "Alphabeta" offers a statement visually or formally enabled by digital technology that simultaneously questions a central claim often made for that technology (the claim that, in the words of "Alphabeta," "hypertext" is "a particular innovation of computer processing" rather than a set of "technologies made available by the invention of alphabetic writing and greatly facilitated by the development of printing and bookmaking"). Another digital text, "Politics," consists in its original form of nine repetitions of the sentence "for all the utopian promise of technological optimists, the answer is not in our machines but in our politics"—a kind of digital proceduralist adaptation of the line from *Julius Caesar*, "The fault, dear Brutus, lies not in our stars but in ourselves."[20] In a self-reflexive critique of normativity, in this early version all nine iterations of the sentence are all perfectly aligned—by the machine. If the machine's "answer" is lockstep alignment (or justification), then we do indeed need a different politics. In three later versions—the screen that features in the archival "Mosaic" and the stand-alone works or stills titled "Politics" and "Politics2"—the text is far more scrambled, with its once-machinic presentation disrupted almost entirely by static or snow in "Politics2."[21]

Pre-Web 2.0, Bernstein produced a number of visually rich online poems in his "HTML Veil Series" (1996)—"Absolves," "Cannot Cross," "Littoral," "Illuminosities," "Alphabetica," "This Us" (which reappears as text in *With Strings*).[22] The central trope of all these pieces involves the layering of a brief English text over a visually denser, cross-hatched textual ground (somewhat like the overprinting of *Veil*). Granted, they are essentially static, immobile, or nonmorphing, even as they use the resources of html, digital art programs, and nonalphabetic font, and to this extent they remain outside some definitions of "digital poetry." In these examples of transitional materiality, however, the relationship between the textual and the visual, a long-standing preoccupation of Bernstein's, becomes itself one of the poems' subjects, with digital technology providing him with

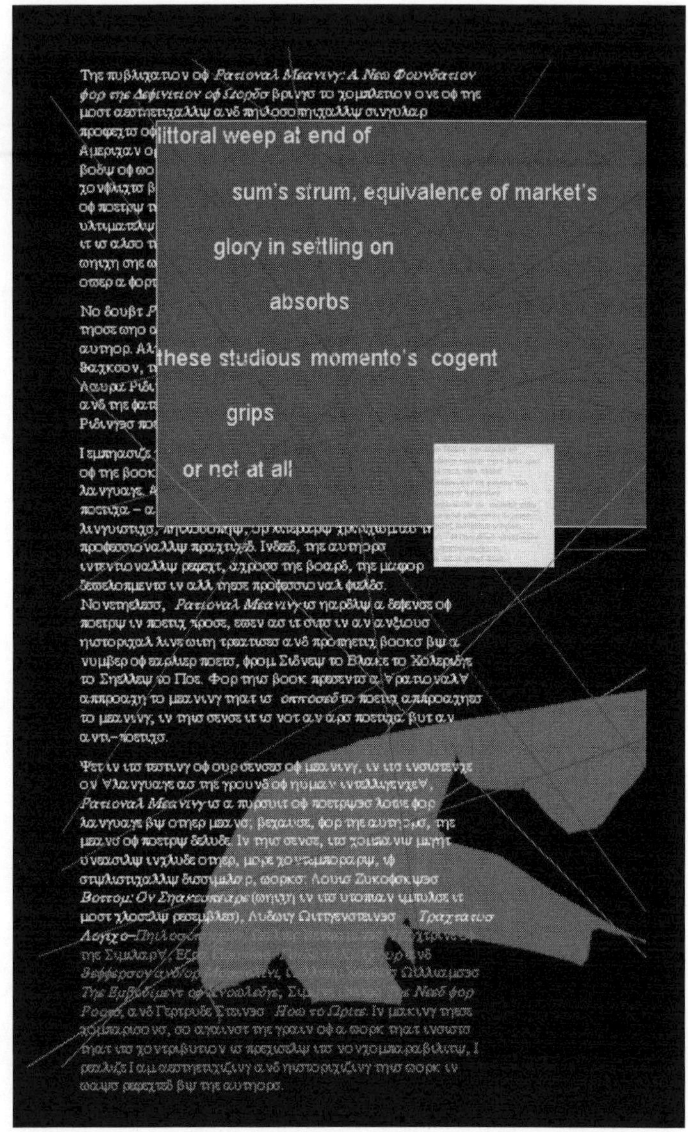


Figure 13.13. Charles Bernstein, "Littoral" (http://writing.upenn.edu)

the means to move a concern of his page-based work into a new medium. The poems consistently use digital technology to make self-reflexive points about the evolving history of print and digital media. In the obtrusively nonliteral "Littoral," for example, the background consists of the first four paragraphs of Bernstein's introduction to Laura Riding's *Rational Meaning*, "Riding's Reason" (*My Way* 255–56)—but again this is a background with a twist, going beyond remediation. The use of a nonalphabetic font, Symbol, renders the original script opaque, at the borders (or littoral) of the legible: the digitization of the text foregrounds its materiality, and even grants it a materiality that it previously lacked (or, more precisely, that was not previously prominent) (fig. 13.13). Looked at whole, Bernstein's online and print work forms a highly self-reflexive intertextual web, with reciprocity at every point created by the constant migration of text across media and its resulting transformation.

If we neglect the category of "materiality," N. Katherine Hayles argues, "we have little hope of forging a robust and nuanced account of how literature is changing under the impact of information technologies" (*Writing Machines* 19)—nor, I suggest here, an account of how some literature has anticipated or complicates that impact. Hayles assumes that when the materiality of the artifact changes, meaning is also transformed: "*The physical form of the literary artifact always affects what the words (and other semiotic components) mean*" (25). Her work makes clear how internally conflicted the category of "materiality," and its relationship to print, remains in theoretical analysis. Hayles argues that the emergence of the electronic text helped "bring into view by contrast the specificities of print, which could again be seen for what it was, a medium and not a transparent interface" (43). In other words, we are reminded that "literature was never only words, never merely immaterial verbal constructions" (107). Yet the acknowledgment of print's materiality, a positive for Hayles, is a negative for those theorists and writers who see the problem with print as being that it is entirely too material a medium. The concept of "transitional materialities," however, places different materialities on a spectrum rather than in opposition to each other. In what is, to be fair, a list of heuristic oppositions to which she herself does not necessarily adhere, Marie-Laure Ryan associates print texts with terms such as "unity," "order," "monologism," "sequentiality," "solidity." Readers of Language writing will recognize easily enough the inapplicability of these terms to that writing. Far more applicable to the poets discussed here are Ryan's opposing terms for electronic texts: "diversity," "chaos," "dialogism," "parallelism," "fluidity" (102). Looking at both the online work and the work online of these poets may help move the discussion and historicizing of new media poetries beyond such binary oppositions between the material attributes of print and electronic texts.

# Notes

## Introduction

1. The remark is reported by Horace Traubel in his foreword to Whitman's *An American Primer* (vii). In the full Whitman quotation from which I have selected, he uses the term "new" six times in the space of two sentences.

## Chapter 1

1. In order, these opening quotations come from the title of Ezra Pound's 1934 book, *Make It New* (London: Faber and Faber); Pound's 1917 essay, "A Retrospect" (*Literary Essays* 11); William Carlos Williams's prologue to *Kora in Hell* (*Imaginations* 23); and Loy (151). Loy anticipates Gertrude Stein's oft-cited 1926 observation that when an art work "is still a thing irritating annoying stimulating then all quality of beauty is denied to it" until the work is "accepted," to which Stein famously counters that "if every one were not so indolent they would realize that beauty is beauty even when it is irritating and stimulating not only when it is accepted and classic" (408).

2. See Roger L. Conover's editorial note in Loy (215–16) for further brief commentary.

3. Unattributed quotations in this paragraph derive from Loy's "Aphorisms on Futurism" (*Lost Lunar Baedeker* 149–52). Again, since I am quoting archival revisions, the words "Modern" and "Modernist" appear as "Future" and "Futurist" in Loy's published text.

4. *The Dial* had carried the cantos in its July 1920, August 1921, and May 1922 issues, along with sections of "Hugh Selwyn Mauberly" in September 1920. Thayer writes on March 27, 1923, that "I personally abhor Pound's cantos as I abhor his Paris Letters," however, and rejects the Malatesta Cantos: see Sutton (264). James Sibley Watson, in contrast, writing as "W. C. Blum," promoted the modernist poetics of Williams, Cummings, and Moore (and Pound in passing) in his May 1921 "American Letter." On Cummings's relationship to *The Dial*, see Cohen (9–27). Regarding Wharton: in *The Little Review* around the time of Thayer's comment, Jane Heap describes Wharton as being "as trivial and fluffy-brained as the society in which she plays" ("Notes" 36).

5. The dates 1920–29 reflect the incarnation of *The Dial* edited by Thayer and Watson, the most relevant one for my purposes. *The Dial* had started out as a Transcendentalist outlet from 1840 to 1844 and then enjoyed continuous publication under various editors starting again in 1880 and running until its 1929 demise. For historical overviews of the various magazines mentioned in my subsequent discussion, see the pertinent chapters in Brooker and Thacker.

6. These estimates derive respectively from F. Hoffman, Allen, and Ulrich (57) and Mott (171). Compared to that of some of *The Little Review*'s peers, with circulations in the hundreds, however, even a circulation of one thousand would have been significant. Without specifying numbers, Margaret Anderson observes that "as the *Little Review* became more articulate, more interesting, its subscription list became less impressive" (146).

7. Despite her publishing of, for instance, Emma Goldman and Arturo Giovannitti, however, Margaret Anderson's anarchism can sometimes seem less a political principle and more a generalized rebelliousness. Granted the possibility of irony in the following remark, she can sound like a parodic combination of Eliot and Pound when she writes, "I like monarchies, tyrants, prima donnas, the insane. I even like Mussolini" (41). Compare Adam McKible's observation that "Anderson made little to no distinction among political positions; her endorsements of activists relied entirely upon the perceived strengths and weaknesses of their individual personalities" (82).

8. *The Dial*'s success in spreading a particular version of modernism to a wider audience can be measured partly in circulation figures. By 1921, William Wasserstrom records, circulation had reached 10,000 (1). Although reliable circulation figures are surprisingly hard to come by for such a widely discussed journal, clearly circulation peaked in 1922–23, with the publication of *The Waste Land*. Eliot and the magazine were apparently good for each other. G. A. M. Janssens estimates a peak circulation figure of 18,000 in January 1923 (37), Wasserstrom a peak of 30,000 for November 1923 (80); Michael True puts the circulation still at just under 25,000 in 1925 (7), at a point where Janssens puts it at 10,000 (37). Watson recalled 22,000 as the peak (Janssens 38). Nicholas Joost offers a more reserved estimate of 18,500 copies being printed (not necessarily sold) at the end of 1922 (*Scofield Thayer* 254). Despite the discrepancy among these figures, even the lowest represents a substantial circulation for a magazine publishing at least some experimental material in all the arts. (The contrast is also dramatic with such modernist little magazines as *The Glebe* and *The Egoist*, with their circulations in the low hundreds.) The other consensus among these commentators is that the magazine's circulation declined rapidly in the years before it expired in 1929. Joost, for example, estimates a circulation of only 2,000–4,000 for 1927–29, and Watson estimates 4,000 annually for the years 1926–29––a figure that he considers the magazine's "natural" level (Joost 254).

9. Corroborating Joost's figures (*Scofield Thayer* 40), Lawrence Rainey cites deficits of $100,000 in 1920, $54,000 in 1921, and $65,000 in 1922 (93–94). G. A. M. Janssens finds *The Dial* losing $30,000–50,000 in its later years (37). Patricia Willis reports Watson telling her that *The Dial* expired because "Thayer's mother had been footing Scofield's half of the bills. She no longer wanted to support an effort in which Thayer was unable to participate" (58–59).

10. Wasserstrom attributes the authorship of the announcement to Watson (24). The terms of praise explaining Pound's award are more than a little surprising: Pound receives the award for, among other things, making *The Little Review* a more interesting magazine than *The Dial*.

11. Eighteen out of the thirty-seven poets who appeared in Kreymborg's first two *Others* anthologies (1916 and 1917) later appeared in *The Dial* (see Newcomb, "*Others*," 264–65).

12. [Marianne Moore], "Announcement," 90. One suspects Moore's hand at work in the language of this unattributed announcement, which like much of Moore's own work is constructed largely out of citations. The first phrase quoted appeared initially in praise of Moore herself, in the announcement of her 1924 *Dial* award. Nicholas Joost and Alvin Sullivan attribute the anonymous "Announcement" to Moore (25).

13. Mark Morrisson shows a precedent for some of these features, however, in still other publications, such as the *Continent* and the *Chicago Evening Post* (Morrisson 135).

14. *The Little Review* had criticized the "old" *Dial* as early as June/July 1915, as had

Pound in a 1917 letter to Margaret Anderson: "And *The Dial*, OH *gosh*, slosh, tosh, the dial, d,i,a,l, dial, Dial—the stationary part of a clock or other chronometer" (*Letters* 114).

15. Joost and Sullivan (36) attribute the anonymous "Comment" to Watson.

16. Joost and Sullivan (36) attribute the anonymous comment to Watson.

17. Both Wasserstrom (113) and Elizabeth Gregory, ed., *The Critical Response to Marianne Moore* (Westport, CT: Praeger, 2003), 53, attribute the announcement to Thayer. To be fair, Thayer's language also shows an earnest desire to remedy neglect of Moore's poetry, poetry that "has hitherto remained, among the unfortunate American public, so meagrely relished and so signally unacclaimed" (Thayer, "Announcement" 89).

18. Peter Ackroyd, *T. S. Eliot: A Life* (New York: Simon and Schuster, 1984), 126.

19. See Jaffe, *Modernism and the Culture of Celebrity* (73). Jaffe offers a compelling analysis, in marketing terms, of Eliot's place in and perpetuation of that literary economy of "originality, mastery, and scarcity" (71) that also goes by the label of high modernism. He describes "the closed system of interdependent, inter-signified names which enables the name of an individual author to circulate as elite currency. In the twenties and thirties, responding to modernism often meant trafficking in various authorial names like so many emergent currencies" (63).

20. On the relationship of *Vanity Fair* to high modernism, see Michael Murphy's "'One Hundred Per Cent Bohemia.'" Murphy notes the avant-gardist sympathies of editor Frank Crowninshield (62–63), analyzes how the magazine mediated between its "status as a piece of market-driven mass culture and the self-consciously 'high' modernism it would reproduce for its consumers" (68), and discusses more generally the slick magazines' "cultural function—the mass popularization of defiantly elite art" (76).

21. On Heap and the machine aesthetic, see Platt, "Mysticism in the Machine Age," 18–44.

22. For extended discussion of these dynamics in a later little magazine, see the chapter on *Origin* in my *From Outlaw to Classic* (114–43).

23. It was in the interests of this internationalism that Anderson had moved *The Little Review* from Chicago to New York. As she explains it, "the only way to make the L.R. the international organ I had planned was to publish it from New York where our position would be more commanding" (136). At the time of this move, the magazine also took Pound on board as foreign editor because of a shared belief in "the interest and value of an intellectual communication between Europe and America." *The Dial*'s internationalism stems largely from Thayer, who was heavily influenced even before he took over the magazine by Randolph Bourne's transnationalist thinking. Indeed, before Bourne died, Thayer had hoped to make *The Dial* a vehicle for his ideas and carry on the eclectic spirit of the short-lived *The Seven Arts*, to which Bourne had been a significant contributor. In changing his plans, he retained little patience with literary nationalism.

24. For more on these connections, see Platt, "*The Little Review*" (139–54).

25. For one well-known nationalist response to Jepson's commentary, see William Carlos Williams's prologue to *Kora in Hell*, where he counters Jepson's praise of Eliot with a critique of Eliot and Pound as "men content with the connotations of their masters," producing "rehash, repetition" even as Williams was writing out of the conviction that "nothing is good save the new" (*Imaginations* 23–24).

26. Regarding Pound's invocation of "the Wild Young American gaze," see Morrisson, *Public Face of Modernism* (133–66), on *The Little Review*'s marketing of and to

"youth": "Margaret Anderson explicitly and repeatedly made the connection between modernist art and literature and youth, and she tapped into the cult of youth to advertise the magazine" (143).

27. On the matter of "fun," Jayne Marek comments on the combination of ironic play and seriousness in Anderson and Heap's editorial self-presentation (64).

28. Williams recalls that "our poems constantly, continuously and stupidly were rejected by all the pay magazines except *Poetry* and *The Dial*," adding ruefully that "*The Little Review* didn't pay" (*Autobiography* 175).

29. It is hard not to hear in Crane's criticisms the tones of the wounded, rejected author. At various times, *The Dial* turned down his "Black Tambourine," "The Bridge of Estador," part of "The Marriage of Faustus and Helen," "Chaplinesque" (also rejected by *The Little Review*), "Stark Major," "Passage," and "At Melville's Tomb" (lost to *Poetry* after Crane refused Moore's request that he cut the fourth stanza). When Crane submitted "The Wine Menagerie," Moore cut it in half and changed the title to "Again." Conrad Aiken panned Crane's first book, *White Buildings*, in a one-paragraph *Dial* review after Moore had returned to Yvor Winters his positive review of the book "with a note chiding him for his enthusiasm" (Crane, *Letters* 32). Despite this pattern of rejection, Crane still placed ten poems with *The Dial*, twice as many as with *The Little Review*, and seven of these ten appeared between 1926 and 1929, under Moore's editorship. At the same time, Crane's relationship with *The Little Review* seems to have been equally ambivalent. Margaret Anderson rejected many of Crane's poems before accepting "In Shadow," and *The Little Review* published only four more Crane poems after this.

30. Joost and Sullivan (32) attribute the anonymous comment to Seldes. Although in its early years *The Little Review* emphasized American work, for much of its life—and especially during Pound's years as foreign editor, from 1917–19 and 1921–24—it was no more American in its orientation than *The Dial*. Perhaps due to its lesser visibility, however, it escaped the kind of criticism that *The Dial* suffered. It published a considerable amount of French Dada and surrealism and British and French work generally, along with special issues on W. H. Hudson, Picabia, and Brancusi. Anderson may have felt sufficiently self-conscious about the magazine's apparent Eurocentrism to designate two numbers, for June and December 1918, "American" numbers, but as Adam McKible has shown (59–107), *The Little Review* and *The Dial*, which each in its different way had a complex relationship to ideas of "place" and "space," were equally skeptical of the American "local" as a value in itself.

31. Joost and Sullivan (31) attribute the anonymous comment to Seldes. It is no small irony that Williams had read John Dewey's essay "Americanism and Localism," a powerful influence on his own thinking, in the June 1920 *Dial*.

32. About *Ulysses*, Pound was right. As a defense witness in *The Little Review*'s obscenity trial for publishing sections of the novel, Thayer supposedly admitted that he himself would not have risked publishing the work in *The Dial* (Anderson 220).

## Chapter 2

1. Charles Altieri, "From Symbolist Thought to Immanence: The Ground of Postmodern American Poetics," *boundary 2* 1.3 (Spring 1973): 605–42.

2. I discuss *The New American Poetry*'s influence on certain later anthologies in *From Outlaw to Classic* (30–32, 180) and here in chapter 4; see also Perloff, "Whose New American Poetry?" *The New American Poetry* was large for its time: it expanded during editing and outweighed its contemporary competition, and one early commen-

tator calls it "a huge book" (Garrett 229) at 454 total pages. Perloff is right, however, to point out its modest scale in relation to some of its later offshoots: Ron Silliman's *In the American Tree* at 628 pages, Paul Hoover's *Postmodern American Poetry* at 701 pages, or Douglas Messerli's *From the Other Side of the Century* at 1,135 pages ("Whose New American Poetry" 104). As regards the ongoing reassessment of *The New American Poetry*, I have in mind the conference marking the anthology's fiftieth anniversary at the University of Warwick on October 23, 2010; the question-and-answer session and a number of the papers presented at the University of Pennsylvania "Poetry in 1960" symposium on December 6, 2010; John R. Woznicki's edited collection of scholarly essays, *The New American Poetry: Fifty Years Later* (Bethlehem, PA: Lehigh University Press, 2013); and Stephan Delbos's 2017 Charles University dissertation, "Behind Enemy Lines: *The New American Poetry* and the Cold War Anthology Wars." For the reprinting of two other classic anthologies from the period, see the 2007 reissue of Larry Neal and Amiri Baraka, eds., *Black Fire: An Anthology of Afro-American Writing* (Baltimore: Black Classic), originally published in 1968, and the 2017 fiftieth anniversary reissue, in an expanded third edition, of Jerome Rothenberg's *Technicians of the Sacred: A Range of Poetries from Africa, America, Asia, Europe, and Oceania* (Berkeley: University of California Press).

3. For exceptions, see Cary Nelson's detailed and highly materialist narrative of editing his *Anthology of Modern American Poetry*, "Murder in the Cathedral: Editing a Comprehensive Anthology of Modern American Poetry," *American Literary History* 14, no. 2 (Summer 2002): 311–27, and Delbos, "Behind Enemy Lines," chapter 1. More briefly, see Rita Dove's comments on the permissions process and the enforced absence of Ginsberg, Plath, Brown, and others "that also fell victim to their owners' stranglehold" (li), in her introduction to *The Penguin Anthology of Twentieth-Century American Poetry*, ed. Dove (New York: Penguin, 2011).

4. Unpublished correspondence between Donald Allen and poets other than Charles Olson, Allen's reader reports for Grove Press, and a draft of his preface to *The New American Poetry* are cited with the permission of the authors and of the Mandeville Special Collections Library, University of California at San Diego. Both sides of the Allen-Olson correspondence are cited from the Charles Olson Papers, Archives and Special Collections, Thomas J. Dodd Research Center, University of Connecticut Libraries, and are used with permission. Allen's letter to me is cited with his permission.

Corman had envisioned a similar, though rather smaller (124 pages), anthology for a number of years himself. In May 1957, he asks Charles Olson to contribute to "'a careful selection of the most moving poetry that has been written since the end of the last war, in English . . . by poets who are not yet 50. . . . I feel for myself that such a dose is needed as a clear and potent corrective to all the crap that has been flung about and instead of all the diseased polemics'"; "'I've been suggesting this book around for several years, but no one picked it up'" (qtd. in G. Evans 150). Interestingly, Corman planned to pass on the traditional editorial prerogative and exclude himself. As regards his relationship to *The New American Poetry*: after signing a contract, he withdrew from the anthology because he did not think Allen was genuinely interested in his work.

5. On this point, *The New American Poetry* anticipates, in structure, purpose, and effect, Ron Silliman's *In the American Tree* (1986), the anthology that first helped define Language writing for many readers. Jed Rasula has rightly observed how the new theory, poetics, and criticism came largely from the New American side of the evolving poetry wars (*American Poetry Wax Museum* 224); and the 1950s mainstream aversion to statements of poetics also marked a generational difference from such New

Critical poet-critic precursors as R. P. Blackmur, Allen Tate, Robert Penn Warren, and Randall Jarrell.

6. The full text of Allen's form letter, contract, and project description is available in Maud (46–48). The eventual change from the safely neutral "modern" to the more polemical "new," though descriptively accurate, proved somewhat controversial. Although "newness" was as much an aesthetic and ideological as a temporal category for Allen, some reviewers took issue with the term "new," combined with the definite article, as implying claims to an inclusiveness that the anthology failed to attain—an inclusiveness, however, to which Allen explicitly did not aspire.

7. This paradox seems less strange when one considers the reification of the individual poet embodied in collections like, for instance, *The Morrow Anthology of Younger American Poets* (New York: Quill, 1985), can be traced to one strain implicit in *New American Poetry.*

8. Specifically, Allen considered the inclusion of Williams, Pound, Moore, H.D., Cummings, and—more surprisingly—Stevens.

9. The late addition of "Hotel Transylvanie" is particularly significant because it places O'Hara in explicit, and antithetical, conversation with Olson: "But I hold on / I am lyrical to a fault / I do not despair being too foolish / where will you find me, projective verse, since I will be gone?" (O'Hara 351). O'Hara is almost as substantially represented as Olson, with fifteen poems over thirty-one pages. His importance to the anthology's development, and the dialogic relationship between his and Olson's poetics that marks the final product (O'Hara describes himself as "the opposite of visionary" [Allen, ed., *New American Poetry* 249] in one Allen selection, "In Memory of My Feelings"): these are the subject for another essay.

10. "[T]he 'Harrison'" is "A Newly Discovered 'Homeric' Hymn"; "the Satyrs" is "The Lordly and Isolate Satyrs" (Olson 363, 384).

11. As early as July 17, 1958, Allen tells Duncan that he hoped to be "going to Gloucester to kick it around with Olson *again*" (emphasis added).

12. In this same letter, Allen writes that "the New American Painting show has come back from Europe and is installed in the Modern Museum—yesterday I studied it with care and came away with clearer conceptions of how to handle the anthology." The show's catalog juxtaposed brief artist statements with the reproductions of the artist's work and concluded with equally brief biographies and lists of one-person shows. Brad Gooch proposes that Allen based his anthology's eventual title on the title of this show, organized in part by Frank O'Hara and exhibited in eight European countries between April 1958 and March 1959 before returning to the Museum of Modern Art: Gooch, *City Poet: The Life and Times of Frank O'Hara* (New York: HarperCollins, 1994), 354.

13. The following fifteen writers from *The New American Poetry* were excluded from *The Postmoderns*: Helen Adam, Ebbe Borregaard, Bruce Boyd, Ray Bremser, James Broughton, Paul Carroll, Kirby Doyle, Richard Duerden, Edward Field, Madeline Gleason, Philip Lamantia, Edward Marshall, Peter Orlovsky, Stuart Perkoff, Gilbert Sorrentino.

14. While the complexities of Olson's sex/gender identification(s) are manifold, the feminized "aunties" may reflect not just a resistance to the possibility of including Moore and H.D. but his antipathy specifically to the gay Paul Goodman (admittedly, a contemporary, not a predecessor). Davidson (*Guys Like Us* 39–40) and Horowitz (2–30) discuss the troubled relationship between Goodman and the aggressively heterosexist (though not thoroughly hetero*sexual*) Black Mountain community.

15. Allen's correspondence with Jack Spicer contains exchanges over Allen's own poetry, which complicates Duncan's complaint about the anthology not being edited by a poet. Allen also observes that "Duncan was miffed because I had turned down several of his 'Structure of Rime' sections for EVERGREEN REVIEW" and "there was also some resentment re my greater interest in Olson" (letter to the author, October 9, 1996).

16. For further evidence of Duncan's insistence on keeping the right anthological company, see his short essay "A Partisan View." This piece is essentially a public letter regretting his participation in Thomas Shapcott's *Contemporary American and Australian Poetry* once he fully realized its failure of "measure and context," its exclusion or ignorance of some of the poets closest to Duncan (Olson, Creeley, Zukofsky) and of younger New American poets in the same tradition (Dorn, Williams, Wieners, McClure), and the "homogenised level" of the "maundering private susceptibilities" that he saw represented there (368). Duncan also withdrew from Paris Leary and Robert Kelly's *A Controversy of Poets* when, as Kelly puts it, "he saw that the other half was to include boring academicians and that the better boring academicians were not included" ("Nothing but Doors" 113).

17. Surprisingly, Duncan shared this view, even down to the specific examples cited, with Cecil Hemley, the reviewer of *The New American Poetry* whom Duncan excoriates in his essay "Ideas of the Meaning of Form." In "Within a Budding Grove," Hemley writes, "I defy anyone to tell me what this particular renaissance signified. A rebirth which includes Brother Antoninus and Lawrence Ferlinghetti is truly protean" (627).

18. Reviewers who discuss *The New American Poetry* in terms of "gangs" include: Wright (268–78); Bell, "a pretty exclusive fan club" (123); Zahn, "a cosy little club founded upon the impregnable mathematics of mutual admiration" (42); and Thwaite, "incestuous heel-treading" (298). In an omnibus review that begins with high praise of Howard Nemerov and ends by slamming Olson, Thom Gunn argues for the value of standing, as he puts it in his title, "outside faction." George Garrett argues that "schools and groups and clubs of poets are utterly foreign to our native scene" (236), though he applies this skepticism to both sides in the anthology wars. While some early reviewers accused Allen's poets (and by extension Allen himself) of using their alleged clubbishness as a form of aggressive self-marketing, the evidence suggests that marketing concerns were far from Allen's mind in editing the anthology. In his form letter to contributors, Allen hoped for sales of 5,000 copies in the first year. In fact, the text went through two impressions and 14,000 paperback copies that year, and in its first 10 years went through 16 impressions and 112,500 copies.

19. Like Duncan, Olson thought of himself as a coterie poet: he seems drawn to the motorcyclists of "The Lordly and Isolate Satyrs," published first in Allen's *Evergreen Review* and then in *The New American Poetry*, partly because they form a marginalized (male) clique, "the unadmitted, the club of Themselves" (Olson 385). Speaking in his role as anthologist and little magazine editor, Robert Kelly offers some useful comments on the idea of the "clique" in a 1976 interview. Kelly distinguished between publishing (and anthologizing) based on a sense of polemic and a sense of clique. "Polemic"—Duncan's "coterie"—involved a sense of shared purpose that cut across social boundaries and friendship; one could share a polemical goal with someone whom one disliked, as Kelly did with Robert Bly. The clique involved friendships that do not necessarily include shared intellectual principles; Kelly's friend Paul Blackburn "thought Deep Imagism was a lot of nonsense" (Kelly, "Nothing but Doors" 115–17).

From this point of view, *The New American Poetry* was compiled out of a sense both of polemic and clique. For relevant and valuable discussion of the concept of poetic coterie, see Lytle Shaw, *Frank O'Hara.*

20. On the matter of magazines, one widely acknowledged important precedent for *The New American Poetry* was the "San Francisco" issue of *Evergreen Review* that Allen edited in 1957. He thought of *Evergreen* as something "that would have a longer shelf life than the ordinary magazine. It would be a kind of little anthology of interesting reading" (Allen, "Don Allen" 133). The twelve issues of *Evergreen Review* that preceded the publication of Allen's anthology featured twenty-seven of his poets, twenty-three of them in the issues (1–8) that Allen edited; twenty poems from *Evergreen* issues 1–12 were reprinted in *The New American Poetry.*

21. For a more detailed discussion of this conflict, see Golding, *From Outlaw to Classic* (11–40).

22. Blaser writes in this letter that "the S.F. view of Wentley, lead [*sic*] by Duncan, is something less than mine or N.Y.'s." Compare Frank O'Hara's poem, "Les Luths," from October 6, 1959: "Everybody here is running around after dull pleasantries and / wondering if *The Hotel Wentley Poems* is as great as I say it is" (*Collected Poems* 343).

23. For one example of the resonance of *The New American Poetry*'s racial homogeneity for contemporary debates about race and the poetic avant-garde, see Cathy Park Hong's remark, in a widely discussed essay, that Jones's presence in the anthology (and in its 1982 revision, *The Postmoderns*) exemplifies both "tokenism at its most elegant" (249) and a whitening of avant-garde poetics that continues into the present.

24. In a September 24, 1958, letter to Allen, Jones writes, "Sorry, I haven't sent Tom Postell's poetry to you . . . but he was in Bellevue and I just managed to get him out yesterday."

25. Both Kyger (with whom Allen went on to share a sustained correspondence and friendship) and di Prima do appear in Allen and George Butterick's revision of *The New American Poetry, The Postmoderns.* Di Prima notes Allen writing to her that her exclusion from the original anthology "had been a severe oversight on his part" ("In Conversation").

26. Linda Russo comments on the gender context of Kyger's exclusion in "Introduction."

27. Through a case study of Kathleen Fraser, Megan Swihart Jewell offers a "reconsideration of the ways in which the gender imbalance of Allen's anthology—and the accompanying assumptions about women's relationship to poetic innovation—might continue to be reproduced by poets, anthologists, and critics alike" (135). See Jewell, "Becoming Articulate: Kathleen Fraser and *The New American Poetry,*" in *The New American Poetry Fifty Years Later*, ed. John R. Woznicki (Bethlehem, PA: Lehigh University Press, 2014), 133–54.

28. For a range of commentary on this aspect of Olson's poetics, and his embrace of a male-centered literary history, see Davidson, *Guys Like Us* (33–40); DuPlessis, *Blue Studios* (84–93) and *Purple Passages* (109–68); Hokanson; Howe, "Since"; Mossin (25–64); Perloff, "[Letter to Ralph Maud]"; and Ross (138–41, 147–55).

29. For more on the "compulsory homosociality" of the Spicer circle specifically, see also Ellingham.

30. Compare Davidson's argument that both the Spicer and Black Mountain circles embraced a postmodern sociopoetics that "often replicates phallic ideals of power, energy, and virtuosity that it would seem to contest" (*Guys Like Us* 29).

31. At moments, the "structural necessity" that Davidson notes can devolve into

a poetics of extremity that takes overt misogyny as a basic, unexamined premise and rhetoric. Thus, Ray Bremser presents mass killer Charles Starkweather as the man needed to clean away the impure products of America's "vast vagina":

> he would know how to handle the infinite
> putrid scumbags somebody's mother manufactures—
> he would annul your vast vagina
> into a finer
> better business bureau box of the mange! (353)

32. Five years after this report, in 1963 Cook became chair of, and transformed, the SUNY Buffalo Department of English, hiring Olson and Creeley to the faculty and bringing in, among many other distinguished and emergent writers, Duncan and O'Hara as visitors. In the poem "Some More Ostentation," set at the 1980 Houston MLA, Edward Dorn writes with sardonic affection of how Cook "burned down / a Techniques Panel with his IQ" (*Collected Poems* 676). Cook's importance in building something like a New American poetry program at Buffalo is a recurring topic in *At Buffalo: The Invention of a New American Poetry*, ed. Sean Pears (Lake Forest, IL: Lake Forest College Press, 2020).

33. Duncan, for one, did not especially want to be associated with Rexroth, however. On September 29, 1957, he writes to Olson that "Rexroth's loud mouthings and obscuring clouds of 'avant-garde' and 'disaffiliated' are a miserable association. He should have been shot a year ago, and saved us all from the big noise" (Bertholf and Smith 126). Duncan was responding to Rexroth's "San Francisco Letter," in which "disaffiliated" is a central term (as it is elsewhere in Rexroth's commentary from the period) and in which Rexroth writes "of all the San Francisco group Robert Duncan is the most easily recognizable as a member of the international *avant garde*" (10).

34. One factor that complicated the cultural binaries structuring the war of the anthologies was the money to be made from "academic" writing by a press generally identified with avant-gardism. *New Campus Writing No. 3* was published in 1959 by Grove, the press that published *The New American Poetry* only one year later and that constituted, as S. E. Gontarski argues, many 1950s readers' introduction to avant-garde writing (7). Equally relevant was the money to be made from avant-gardism itself. The common, though inaccurate, perception of *The New American Poetry* as a Beat anthology, combined with the marketability of Beat ideology, the concurrent publication of actual Beat anthologies, the increased visibility that Grove Press earned by winning its highly publicized censorship battle over *Lady Chatterley's Lover*: none of these factors can have hurt initial sales of *The New American Poetry*. As Daniel Kane remarks, Grove had developed for itself "a profitable naughty reputation," such that "*any* book featuring the Grove imprint during the 1960s essentially guaranteed a reader response characterized in part by expectations of aesthetic daring, shocking content, unique or 'avant-garde' textual practices, or at the very least titillating good times" (13–14).

35. I say "*claimed* that he wished to preserve" because, according to Allen, Spicer gave him a long list of work from which to choose ("Editor's Note" xxxi–xxxiii). Allen's first letter to Spicer about the anthology is dated April 11, 1958, and he already says that "I do hope to include Elegy 4 ['Imaginary Elegies IV'] in the antho." In later correspondence, Allen praised *After Lorca* but continued to like Spicer's early work best. On August 26, 1959, Allen wrote to Spicer that "the elegies are after all your finest achievement, ranking ahead of *After Lorca*, I believe." Although Spicer wrote in No-

vember 1958 suggesting the recently completed "Billy the Kid" as his contribution, he apparently did not disagree vehemently with Allen's choice, and in fact, he had previously written Allen that "what I would really dream of is having the whole Elegies in" (qtd. in Allen, "Editor's Note" xxxii).

36. Marvin Bell complains of Allen "surrounding" his poets "with all the academic nonsense some scholars use to ensure significance—a pigeonholing introduction, notes by the authors, and a bibliography" (122). George Garrett describes Allen's divisions into groups as "truly academic" (229) and conflates the terms "academic" and "educated" to collapse the differences among the New American poets and those in Hall, Pack, and Simpson's *New Poets*: "The claim that the conservatives were too academic is vitiated by the fact that almost all of the radicals are highly educated men" (228). Thus, the New American poets became "like their professed enemy," their poetry "conservative" (231–32). A generation later, Vernon Shetley argues that "the New American Poets . . . depended on their audience's identification and sympathy with modernism, and so, no less than the academic formalists, addressed themselves to a readership that had been created by the triumph of modernism in the university" (*After the Death* 15–16). While Shetley argues persuasively that the defining difference in the anthology wars was a difference between two readings of modernism, his further argument tends to posit a single entity called modernism that "triumphed in the university"—treating one form of modernism, that is, as if it were Modernism. Part of Allen's point, however, was precisely that the poetic "modernism" of the 1950s academy (Eliot, Frost, Auden) was not the modernism of the New American poets (Pound, Williams, Zukofsky, H.D., Stein).

Early resistance to Allen's construction of a self-consciously "antiacademic" anthology also appeared as an almost willful denial of the anthology's purpose, a denial manifested in part by complaints about the exclusion of poets whose *presence* would have been wildly inappropriate. Thus X. J. Kennedy disingenuously wonders how any book of new American poetry could exclude James Wright, Snodgrass, Merwin, and Lowell (all featured by Hall, Pack, and Simpson) (242). Anthony Thwaite notes that "this anthology chooses to ignore Wilbur, Lowell, Roethke, Louise Bogan, Hecht, Snodgrass," but at least he seems to get the point—" any American poet, in fact, who could by any stretch of the imagination be called 'academic'" (298). (Kennedy and Thwaite both featured in the second edition of *New Poets of England and America*.) After seeming to understand Allen's definition by exclusion of the "antiacademic," Cecil Hemley then goes on to read the anthology as aspiring to a wider representativeness than it really does, and so wonders about the absence of Wilbur, May Swenson, Jean Garrigue, Hoffman, Simpson, Snodgrass, Roethke, and Stanley Kunitz. Perhaps the most entertaining example of this trend among reviewers was Marianne Moore's commentary on the absence of Hoffman, Robert Bagg, George Starbuck, Garrigue, and, most remarkably, I. A. Richards.

37. Recall also Duncan's comment, quoted earlier, on "Ginsberg supplying what most English professors believe would happen if you kicked over the traces." Some reviewers demurred from this trend. Katherine Garrison Chapin argued explicitly that "the new poets are not merely negative in their approach" (25), while James Dickey admitted what he called the "aggressive gabble" of *The New American Poetry* as a possibly necessary response both to "the sober constipation of the Yvor Winters school and the chatty, knowledgeable aesthetic elegance" of *New Poets of England and America* (6).

38. To be fair, Kalaidjian's comment is part of an effort to locate points of overlap in the anthology wars and thus complicate the binary. He observes usefully that

"like their academic counterparts, the 'new' poets largely eschewed any overtly political commitments or affiliations in the wider social field" (7). Despite such exceptions to this generalization as Olson, Ginsberg, and Snyder, it is worth remembering that Rexroth announced the San Francisco Renaissance under the banner of "disengagement," though Lawrence Ferlinghetti objected strenuously to the term, and Rexroth's claims, in his poetics statement for *The New American Poetry*: "[Sartre] would give the horse laugh to the idea of Disengagement and the Art of the Beat Generation. Me too. And that Abominable Snowman of modern poetry, Allen Ginsberg, would probably say the same. Only the dead are disengaged" (412–13). Compare to Rexroth's position Robert von Hallberg's argument that "the Black Mountain poets were provocatively asocial" and that "the white avant-gardes of the 1950s remained beyond practical politics" (95); or Donald Hall's view that both sides in the anthology wars were equally complicit in a generational failure to engage any world beyond the domestic ("Ah, Love"). (Hall's equation of the domestic and the asocial deserves a critical scrutiny that would be digressive here.)

39. John Ashbery is an appropriate figure to embody the contingencies behind *The New American Poetry*. James Longenbach points out Ashbery's praise for O'Hara (the second most heavily represented poet in *The New American Poetry* after Olson) for his "independence from both the mainstream and the avant-garde" (103) and argues with some justice that Ashbery himself increasingly sought to find a place, in his own words, "between an avant-garde which has become a tradition and a tradition which is no longer one" (*Reported Sightings* 393). (Ashbery's phrasing echoes his characterization of O'Hara as "'too hip for the squares and too square for the hips'" [*Selected Prose* 81].) Meanwhile, along with claiming inaccurately that Ashbery did not appear in *The New American Poetry*, Shetley argues that "Ashbery and his work played no role in the 'war of the anthologies'" (*After the Death* 107). Far from it. For it was Ashbery's fate to preserve the temporary purity of absolute non-overlap in the anthology wars by being the last poet *cut* from *The New Poets of England and America*.

40. Along with doubling the number of interviews, the expanded edition adds to each interview an epigraph quotation from that interview, a biographical headnote detailing the poet's career (and sometimes Ossman's own relationship to it), and an endnote summarizing the postinterview career. It also adds a five-part organization somewhat reminiscent of *The New American Poetry*, an index, a preface, introduction, afterword, and audio CD, and more than triples the length of the Ginsberg interview. As a snapshot of the original moment, it is perhaps worth listing the interviewees from the 1963 edition: in order, Kenneth Rexroth, Paul Carroll, Paul Blackburn, Jerome Rothenberg, Robert Kelly, Robert Bly, John Logan, Gilbert Sorrentino, Robert Creeley, W. S. Merwin, Denise Levertov, LeRoi Jones, Edward Dorn, Allen Ginsberg.

41. Anderson's full comment on *The New American Poetry* as "the 'club book'" reads as follows: "All of those people have gone to school together or lived together or taught each other or corresponded for many years. Those are all close friends with only a few exceptions and those few exceptions are brought in by the close friends. That's the 'club book.' . . . There are names immediately I can think of who were left out. Bob Kaufman, for one, who is fairly well known." I address what Anderson calls—not knowing the story behind it—the "notorious and probably vicious omission" (*Sullen Art* [2016] 189) of Cid Corman earlier in this chapter.

42. Of the relationship of the New York school poets, "somehow too 'uptown' for *The Sullen Art*," to "the poets of the Lower East Side," Ossman observes that (at least from his perspective) "the two communities of writers seemed further apart than

the distance from Canal Street to the Museum of Modern Art [where Frank O'Hara worked]" (*Sullen Art* [2016] 13).

## Chapter 3

1. I chose these anthologies because they claim to represent a range of experimental practice (and it is worth noting how claims to cover the field of experimental writing in the 1990s continued to come from the editorial position of the white male). These ambitions stand in contrast to the more specific concerns of gatherings, contemporary with them, such as Walter Lew's *Premonitions: The Kaya Anthology of New Asian North American Poetry* (1995), Maggie O'Sullivan's *Out of Everywhere: Linguistically Innovative Poetry by Women in North America and the UK* (1996), and Mary Margaret Sloan's *Moving Borders: Three Decades of Innovative Writing by Women* (1998), with their emphasis on linguistically innovative work by Asian North Americans and by North American and UK women respectively. Historically situated "out of everywhere," in Maggie O'Sullivan's title, minoritized subjects have had a different relation to the "mainstream vs. margin" rhetoric of experimentalist anthologies from that of white male writers with whom they may have much in common aesthetically.

2. Meanwhile, neither the Weinberger nor the McClatchy anthology represents exactly what it seems to. *American Poetry since 1950*, self-consciously an anthology of historically marginalized work, programmatically excluded one major grouping within its own tradition of "innovators and outsiders," the Language poets, whom Weinberger saw as antihistorical: "The most vocal avant-garde of the moment, the Languages, were still in a militant phase of denying nearly everyone, except Stein and Zukofsky, who had come before them" (Weinberger, "Conversation"). Conversely, McClatchy's *Vintage Book*, still in print in its 2003 second edition and in many ways the quintessential mainstream anthology of the late twentieth and early twenty-first centuries in its choice of Bishop and Lowell as founding figures, excluded almost all examples of the scenic lyric that for most readers constituted the contemporary US mainstream at the time of its original publication.

3. For further discussion of Weinberger's and Hoover's anthologies specifically, and for further detail on how other later editors variously modeled their anthologies on *The New American Poetry*, see Golding, *From Outlaw to Classic* (30–35 and 179–81).

4. The poets that the Norton *Modern* dropped from the 1988 2nd edition and whom Hoover included in his own anthology are Ted Berrigan, Edward Dorn, Paul Blackburn, James Schuyler, and Gregory Corso; among others, Laura Riding and Louis Zukofsky also disappeared from the 1988 edition. The 2003 3rd edition of what is now called *The Norton Anthology of Modern and Contemporary Poetry*, with the input of third coeditor Jahan Ramazani, looks significantly different from the 2nd edition to which Hoover was responding, though not especially in the areas of Hoover's greatest interest. The 1988 and 2003 *Norton* included the same eleven poets from *The New American Poetry*; to that lineage, the 2003 edition added Howe, Hejinian, Palmer, and Bernstein but actually dropped three other poets whom one would associate with the New American line, William Everson, Irving Layton, and Diane Wakoski. Weinberger, meanwhile, apparently felt some distance from what he calls Hoover's and Messerli's "mammoth anthologies": "I found them reference books and not anthologies. Something to refer to, not to read" ("Conversation").

5. For a differing view, see Rasula, who acknowledges taking a "particularly skeptical line" in locating the more retrospective of the mid-1990s anthologies within that "site

of canonical debasement," the institutionalized "Wax Museum" of post–World War II American poetry (*American Poetry Wax Museum* 465).

6. Rasula observes that although Language poetry "has been repeatedly and favorably singled out in prestigious scholarly journals" and "routinely discussed in monographs," "there are *no* language poets to be found in over five thousand pages" of nine of the most visible and widely used poetry anthologies published between 1984 and 1996 (*American Poetry Wax Museum* 458–59).

7. The self-conscious oppositionality on which Weinberger's anthology rests also seems directed at Helen Vendler's *Harvard Book of Contemporary American Poetry* (1985), if we read as a polemical gesture his starting with Pound and Williams and ignoring Stevens just as Vendler did the reverse. This contrast serves as yet another reminder of how larger debates within literary culture—in this case, the thoroughly fruitless and now dated argument over modernism as the Pound or Stevens "era"—get played out in anthologies, often in unacknowledged ways.

8. In a further canonizing move, the anthology's jacket blurb—not necessarily authored by Hoover himself, I realize—makes "postmodern" and "avant-garde" synonymous with the category of "major poetry." The blurb describes the text as "the first anthology since Donald Allen's groundbreaking collection to fully represent the movements of American avant-garde poetry." This claim is followed by the far more generalizing and less tenable one that the anthology "offers a deep and wide selection . . . *of the major poets and movements of the late twentieth century*" (my emphasis). Despite his invocation of the anthology wars, it is only in the 2013 2nd edition that Hoover explicitly acknowledges *The New American Poetry* within the text as his most significant precedent: "This anthology began when, in 1991, I spoke to Barry Wade of W. W. Norton about the need for an anthology of poetry of the 'other tradition,' as none had been published since Donald Allen's *The New American Poetry: 1945–1960*" ("Preface" xxviii).

9. The frame had narrowed to the literary by the 2nd (2013) edition, where "avant-garde endures in its resistance to dominant and received modes of poetry" (xxxiii).

10. The alleged characteristics of these opposed "model poets" are familiar enough that they do not need reiteration here. (In the 2nd edition of 2013, Hoover seems to double down on "The Battle of the Anthologies" by giving it its own subheading in his introduction.) On a related issue, however, the "battle of the anthologies" (as discussed in chapter 2) usually refers to the differences between Allen's *New American Poetry* (1960) and Hall, Pack, and Simpson's *New Poets of England and America* (1957), with Hall and Pack's 1962 2nd edition a kind of follow-up entry in the debates. In framing the "battle" as one over Allen's collection and the 1962 edition of *New Poets*, Hoover grants *The New American Poetry* a chronological primacy that it did not in fact enjoy.

11. As I have noted, in 2003 the one-volume *Norton Anthology of Modern Poetry* became, in its 3rd edition, the two-volume *Norton Anthology of Modern and Contemporary Poetry*. Primary editor Jahan Ramazani observes of this new edition that one "priority has been to welcome into the anthology what John Ashbery has called an 'other tradition'—experimental poetry by modern avant-garde writers . . . extending to the contemporary avant-garde of Language poetry by Susan Howe, Lyn Hejinian, Michael Palmer, and Charles Bernstein" (xxxv). As of December 2020, the 2003 3rd edition—containing one author born after the publication of *The New American Poetry*—remains in print, just as its extension of the "other tradition" has remained the same for those fifteen years.

12. See Perloff, "Whose New American Poetry?" (104–23).

13. It is also the case, however, as some commentators have pointed out, that none of the collections radically reconceived the genre of the anthology itself. See, for instance, Lazer, *Opposing Poetries* (1:379n8). Richard Kostelanetz criticizes Hoover's *Postmodern American Poetry* for excluding what he considers a whole range of avant-garde work that might also have forced rethinking of the anthology's nature: "It completely omits sound poetry, visual poetry, neologistic poems, minimal poems, site-specific poems, video poetry, poetry holograms, computer poetry, and comparable experimental forms" (17).

14. While the term "post-Language" does not appear in *The Art of Practice* itself, publicity materials for the volume describe it as containing "over 400 pages of poetry generally considered 'avant-garde' or 'post-Language.'" In a review of the anthology much occupied with issues of lineage and with what is to follow Language writing, Daniel Barbiero writes, "The 45 poets included in this collection can all be seen as extending an open-form tradition that runs, roughly, from Pound and Williams through 'language' poetry via Surrealism, Objectivist & Projectivist verse, and points between and beyond." Thus, "although much of the work can legitimately be thought of as post-'language' poetry," it is also "very much part of a tradition" ("States of the Art" 7, 13). For more generationally specific and forward-looking collections from the period that also articulate various early forms of a post-Language poetics, see the double issue of *o-blek*, # 12 (Spring/Fall 1993), "Writing from the New Coast," edited by Peter Gizzi; Juliana Spahr, Mark Wallace, Kristin Prevallet, and Pam Rehm, eds., *A Poetics of Criticism* (Buffalo, NY: Leave, 1994); and Mark Wallace and Steven Marks, eds., *Telling It Slant: Avant-garde Poetics of the 1990s* (Tuscaloosa: University of Alabama Press, 2002). For critical commentary, see Steve Evans, "The American Avant-garde after 1989: Notes toward a History," in *The World in Time and Space: Towards a History of Innovative American Poetry in Our Time*, ed. Edward Foster and Joseph Donahue, 646–73 (Jersey City, NJ: Talisman House, 2002).

15. Compare Ron Silliman's historicizing of Language writing as involving a "complex call for a projective verse that could, in the same moment, 'proclaim an abhorrence of "speech"'—*a break within a tradition in the name of its own higher values*" ("Language" xv; my emphasis).

16. Barone and Ganick describe their editorial procedure as follows: "We asked each poet to choose his or her work for the anthology, but we asked for more pages than we planned to use. We then made a selection from each author's work. We hope that our anthology has some collaborative trace to its presence" (xv). One appeal of this approach is that it allows the poets significant input into the anthology's contents, in a way that recalls Donald Allen's correspondence with his contributors. But it remains unclear how one would locate the "collaborative trace," how a reader could tell in what ways, or even if, a selection was shaped by dialogue between editors and contributor. It would require archival research of the kind represented in chapter 2 to uncover many of those traces.

17. Without disputing Silliman's overall point, it is worth noting that eighteen of the forty-five poets in *Art of Practice*—40 percent of the total—are poets whom Silliman names as possible inclusions in an imaginary alternative version of *In the American Tree* ("Language" xx–xxi).

18. Key sites of such debates would include Cathy Park Hong's widely discussed essay "Delusions of Whiteness in the Avant-garde," *Lana Turner Journal* 7 (2014): 248–

53; the *Boston Review* forum "Race and the Poetic Avant-garde," March–April 2015, featuring eight contributors; Dorothy Wang's influential *Thinking Its Presence: Form, Race, and Subjectivity in Contemporary Asian American Poetry* (Palo Alto: Stanford University Press, 2013); the sequence of "Thinking Its Presence" conferences beginning in 2014 and named after Wang's book; Kenneth Goldsmith's March 2015 reading of "The Body of Michael Brown" and the more-or-less contemporaneous critical response to Vanessa Place's multiyear project of tweeting *Gone with the Wind*. In a contribution to the *Boston Review* forum, John Yau reiterates his critique (from a 1994 review) of the racial makeup of Weinberger's anthology: see Yau, "'Purity' and the 'Avant-garde,'" *Boston Review*, April 2015, accessed October 23, 2020, http://bostonreview.net.

19. Reframing the historical language-lyric tension as one between conceptual poetry and a pervasive lyric practice that sounds remarkably like its 1970s precursor, Marjorie Perloff registers some skepticism about the "precarious rapprochement" of *American Hybrid* as Swensen and coeditor David St. John "try their best to fuse mainstream and experimental tendencies." She acknowledges, however, that they "at least make the effort to forge an aesthetic consonant with the moment" ("Poetry").

20. In the context of my discussion here, 1999 represents a remarkably Janus-faced moment of retrospection and prospection: on the cusp of the millennium, *The New American Poetry*'s reissue coincided with the April 1999 conference "Where Lyric Tradition Meets Language Poetry: Innovation in Contemporary American Poetry by Women," in which Rankine and Spahr's book has its roots.

## Chapter 4

1. As I pointed out in chapter 3, Juliana Spahr wrote of her and Claudia Rankine's coedited anthology *American Women Poets in the 21st Century: Where Lyric Meets Language* (2002) that "this collection begins a dialogue between the two often falsely separated poetries of language and lyric" (11), and she repositions lyric (often associated with mainstream retrenchment in the late twentieth century) as a privileged site of—indeed, synonymous with—innovation: "Lyric is by definition innovative. When it stops being innovative it is no longer lyric" (13). Reginald Shepherd's *Lyric Postmodernisms* gathered twenty-three poets "whose work combines lyricism and avant-garde experimentation in a new synthesis I call, after Wittgenstein, lyrical investigations" (xi). For Shepherd as for Spahr, a millennial re-linking of the lyric with the exploratory has replaced the late twentieth-century association of lyric (or at least particular versions of it) with mainstream retrenchment: "No anthology has brought these contemporary poets together as writers experimenting and exploring within the lyric tradition to expand that tradition's boundaries" in "a new poetic synthesis" (xvii). I discuss Cole Swensen and David St. John's use of the term "hybrid" in chapter 3; in Swensen's introduction to the anthology *American Hybrid*, another figure that she proposes for American poetry's movement beyond "the two-camp model" is that of the rhizome, "a more laterally ordered network composed of nodes that branch outward toward smaller nodes, which themselves branch outward in an intricate and ever-changing structure of exchange and influence" (xxv).

2. Beach and Rasula differ in their approaches, however. Writing in the late 1990s, Beach finds that the long-standing mainstream-outsider split "has become even more visible" and "we have witnessed a new divergence of poetry into two opposing camps, each with an array of anthologies that seek to ensure a form of canonical status for the poets included" (82). But while Beach finds the face-off between "two opposing

camps" a live contemporary issue, Rasula, writing a few years earlier, finds it already old news. For their full discussions, see Beach (82–98) and Rasula, *American Poetry Wax Museum* (415–69).

3. For a similar approach to British anthologies of the same period, see Andrew Michael Roberts, "The Rhetoric of Value in Recent British Poetry Anthologies."

4. The fact that these anthologies also are all male edited deserves a separate essay in itself. Many female editors of the period tended to occupy themselves with the project of uncovering, documenting, and presenting historical and contemporary work by women. See, for instance, Florence Howe and Ellen Bass, eds., *No More Masks: An Anthology of Poems by Women* (Garden City, NY: Anchor, 1973), revised and expanded in 1993; Laura Chester and Sharon Barba, eds., *Rising Tides: Twentieth Century American Women Poets* (New York: Simon and Schuster, 1973); Erlene Stetson, ed., *Black Sister: Poetry by Black American Women, 1746–1980* (Bloomington: Indiana University Press, 1981); Marge Piercy, ed., *Early Ripening: American Women's Poetry Now* (London: Pandora, 1987); Maureen Honey, ed., *Shadowed Dreams: Women's Poetry of the Harlem Renaissance* (New Brunswick, NJ: Rutgers University Press, 1989); and, relatedly, Louise Bernikow, ed., *The World Split Open: Four Centuries of Women Poets in England and America, 1552–1950* (New York: Vintage, 1974). To the extent that, in their representation of contemporary writing, these anthologies tended to foreground work in realist lyric and narrative modes, "work readily fit for absorption into a mainstream canonical model of the poem" (Sloan, "Of Experience" 501), they received a response in such gatherings as Maggie O'Sullivan, ed., *Out of Everywhere: Linguistically Innovative Poetry by Women in North America and the UK* (London: Reality Street, 1996), with a sequel edited by Emily Critchley published in 2015; and Mary Margaret Sloan, ed., *Moving Borders: Three Decades of Innovative Writing by Women* (Jersey City, NJ: Talisman House, 1998). For summary and provocative analysis of the linkages among the categories "woman," "lyric," "innovation," and "mainstream" in this history, see the series of essays by Jennifer Ashton, "Our Bodies, Our Poems," *American Literary History* 19, no. 1 (Spring 2007): 211–31; "Sincerity and the Second Person: Lyric after Language Poetry," *Interval(le)s* 2.2–3.1 (Fall 2008/Winter 2009): 94–108; and "Lyric, Gender, and Subjectivity in Modern and Contemporary Poetry," in *The Cambridge History of American Women's Literature*, ed. Dale M. Bauer (New York: Cambridge University Press, 2012), 515–38.

5. Despite McClatchy's pretense in the *Vintage* anthology to a kind of Whitmanian connectiveness, his collection of critical essays, *White Paper: On Contemporary American Poetry* (New York: Columbia University Press, 1989), shows both the mutually reinforcing relationship of criticism and anthologies and his fundamental commitment to a New York and Ivy League–centered canon. *White Paper* devotes three essays to Lowell and one to Bishop, with whom McClatchy begins his *Vintage Book* and whom he calls there "the strongest poets of their generation," "towering models" ("Introduction" xxviii). *White Paper* also contains essays on Penn Warren, Berryman, Plath, Snodgrass, Merrill, Howard, Hollander, Clampitt, and Hecht.

On the matter of "inclusiveness," one of the most egregious *exclusions* in the *Vintage Book* is that of the three most explicitly homoerotic pages of Allen Ginsberg's "Howl," suggesting that the genteel tradition, paradoxically instantiated in a gay editor and perhaps in alliance with a publisher's reluctance to risk maximum marketability, is far from dead. The *Vintage Book* is one of the collections that remains in print, in a 2003 revised and expanded edition that adds twelve new poets and "A Note on the Second

Edition" while preserving the original introduction and cutting two poets (Alfred Corn and Marvin Bell). The collection remains aggressively asocial, at least in McClatchy's conception of it, an ideological vacuum ("preconceived and thumpingly defended ideologies of the right or left have less glamour and weight nowadays") happily sealed off from extrapoetic discourse: "Beyond the bounds of this book, the hollow wars continue," in a fallen world where other anthologies are tainted by "too many pages" of "loopy Language poets, dry-as-dust New Formalists, or New York School clones" ("Note" xxxiii). The book's asocial lyric space (how does it accommodate such poets as Charles Olson, Robert Duncan, and Adrienne Rich, one wonders?) is contradicted by McClatchy's canonizing impulse, which becomes even more explicit in his second edition, with the collection's debatable "variety" having "acquired a new solidity, and a genuine authority" associated with the original canonical text, the Bible: "This is a book you could swear on in a courtroom" (xxxiv). If we take McClatchy's claims at face value—though they can also be overlooked as an editor's standard hyperbolic privileging of their own moment—his contemporary canon has matched and surpassed the products even of the modernist period: "American poetry has never been more brilliant than it is today" (xxxiv).

6. In an examination of British poetry anthologies, Andrew Michael Roberts usefully analyzes the limits of claims to pluralism on both sides of the "mainstream"–"avant-garde" binary: "Although pluralism figures as a value in anthologies of both the 'mainstream' and the 'alternative' or avant-garde, in neither case does this pluralism extend to any significant inclusion of the work of the other, nor to any full recognition of its possible values." Roberts goes on to ask, "Are we faced with the paradox of anthologies which include only that poetry which accords with the editors' particular conception of pluralism and actually excludes other poetry, on the grounds that it is not plural enough, or plural in the wrong sort of way, not 'the best poetry'?" (119).

7. The terms of this debate over "schools" are directly reflected and anticipated in Paris Leary and Robert Kelly's *A Controversy of Poets*, still a fascinating exercise in juxtapositions and bipartisanship. This collection brings together two opposing tendencies in American poetry of the time: the cooked and the raw, to use the terms current then. Reconciliation or face-off? The editors themselves disagree. Anticipating the characteristic rhetorical strategies of later mainstream editors, Leary denies that there is really anything to argue about, that contemporary debates are a surface and ephemeral matter of "fashionable classifications" ("Postscript I" 559). Nominally coauthored, the anthology's preface urges (in a statement reprinted on the back cover) attention to poems rather than to schools:

> This anthology is designed to turn the attention of the reader to the contemporary *poem*, away from movements, schools or regional considerations. Hitherto some of these poets have been referred to . . . as belonging to this or that rival—and hostile—school. Such poetasting has served only to distract the reader from the *poem* and to divert his attention to supposed movements or schools, whereas the only affiliation finally relevant is that apparent from the work itself (xi).

Each editor wrote a postscript, however, and in his Kelly argues for exactly the opposition that Leary seeks to dissolve in his own postscript, between what Kelly calls "social decorative verse" and a poetics of "radical newness," between "the two classes of poets today" ("Postscript II" 564–65) that the anthology's division into halves, its title, and its framing by the two "sides" of the debate all reinforce. Neither Kelly's maintenance of this opposition nor Leary's dissolution of it is entirely tenable; what is revealing, and what resurfaces in later anthologies, is the structure of the debate itself, the centrist denial and the avant-gardist reassertion of conflicting interests.

8. Regarding one definition of "diversity" apposite to the construction of a mainstream poetics: in the introduction to the most visible and debated mass-market anthology of recent years, Rita Dove comments strongly (in an otherwise quite tonally neutral essay) on her experience in the highly competitive Iowa MFA program of the mid-1970s, where "poets were being raised like broods of chicks." She writes, "As the only African American and one of only three minority students in my two years there, I was spared the most bruising battles simply because the other members of the workshop didn't consider us as competition; we sat by, an invisible trio, as our white classmates slugged it out in the Iowa sandbox of American poetry" (*Penguin Anthology* xlix).

9. The closer one approaches the present, the more necessary it becomes to acknowledge exceptions to this generalization about university press poetry. Starting in the 1990s, books of poetry, poetics, and theory by writers working in various "alternative" modes appeared with numerous university presses: California, Wesleyan, Chicago, Harvard, Princeton, Alabama, Northwestern. As the publisher of major collections by, for instance, Charles Olson, Robert Creeley, Robert Duncan, and Louis Zukofsky, California also significantly supported poets in the Objectivist–Black Mountain line. At the same time, among these presses only Wesleyan maintains a genuinely eclectic contemporary poetry list open to nonmainstream work—a tendency whose beginning, interestingly, more or less coincides with the moment of Collier's retrospective *The Wesleyan Tradition* in 1993.

10. One might expect a canon as all-inclusive as that claimed by mainstream editors to be somewhat flexible, mobile, open to change. As evidence of the mainstream canon's inertia, however, consider that forty of the first forty-six poets in McClatchy's 1990 edition overlap with those in Strand's 1969 anthology.

11. On the issue of the "individual" poet, Rasula observes how, in paradoxical violation of its editors' intentions, the *Morrow*'s "tight juxtaposition of 104 poets . . . renders the poetic voice anonymous and collective as perhaps no previous anthology has done" (*American Poetry Wax Museum* 432), and Geoffrey O'Brien comments on how the *Morrow* reduces the range of its poets' work in other contexts to an "overwhelming unity of tone," so that "you start to feel that you're reading the work of a single author, that composite younger poet whom the editors define in their preface" (35). Compare also Walter Kalaidjian's critique of this aspect of the anthologies as marking "the period's political limit: one that actively led readers to invest in ideologies of bourgeois individualism" (14).

In *The Future of Memory*, Bob Perelman both pointedly parodies the Smith/Bottoms position and destabilizes his own "avant-garde" status in observing that his recent

> . . . writing seems pretty normal:
>
> complete sentences; semicolons; yada yada. I
> seem to have lost my avant-garde
>
> card in the laundry. (11)

12. Rasula argues that anthologists of alternative poetries like Eliot Weinberger, Paul Hoover, and Douglas Messerli share McClatchy's position "that letting [poems] 'speak for themselves' is the editor's primary obligation." While these editors do little to question the basic structural format of the anthology as a form, however, so that admittedly they too "showcase isolate poems" (*American Poetry Wax Museum* 466), they do not propose as explicitly as their mainstream counterparts this position about the poem's self-articulating value.

13. From this point of view, it may well be that the very phenomenon of the anthology conflicts with the aura of individual and asocial creativity that the mainstream collection projects. As Ann Lauterbach suggests, "there still attaches to the *idea* of the poet a belief that poetry should be, is, exempt from market forces, from brute commerce and commodification. And yet, into this abstract, distilled sanctity, the protected solitude of Rilke's Beloved, comes the Angel of History with his Anthology under his Wing" (100).

14. For an effective exposition of this aspect of Language writing's coalescence as a movement, see Perelman (*Marginalization of Poetry* 12–13) and Silliman et al.

15. See Perelman, "The First Person" (156, 160–62) and his further comments in *The Marginalization of Poetry* (113–14), where he writes "such an insistence on individuality, which is often translated into the aesthetic necessity of 'finding your voice,' masks the institutional circuits, the network of presses, reviews, jobs, readings, and awards that are the actual sounding board of 'voice'" (114); and Armantrout's parody "Traveling in the Yard" (*Precedence* 18).

16. Compare Allen's assertion in the preface to *The New American Poetry* that his poets "are our avant-garde, the true continuers of the modern movement in American poetry" (xi).

17. More recently, but along similar lines in claiming the disruptive and the carnivalesque as mainstream qualities, see K. Silem Mohammad's comments on Michael Magee's 2006 *Mainstream* (with its almost-eponymous poem "Mainstream Poetry," a parodic rewriting of Baraka's "Black Art"), that Magee quotes in his afterword to the book:

> Want to take seriously [Pixar-esque weasel/clown-faces behind me fleer and moue] for a bit here Mike Magee's reconfiguration of the poetic Mainstream. Others have pointed this out before, of course, but "mainstream poetry" as usually construed by its opponents is anything but. . . . A mainstream is a forceful, central current that carries in its path all the debris and livestock and entire vacationing families that get vortexed into it. It is not a carefully constructed iron walkway that escorts the effete peripatetic poet safely above a scenic view of the countryside and its filthy horizon. In the mainstream, you have to shout to be heard above the roar of the already-tired water metaphor I'm spinning out here. In the mainstream, the weasels with clown faces have uzis. The mainstream is the scary global video game we live in, everyday, and it has nothing to do with some absurd publishing scam within which a few bloodless surrealists and failed classicists and Tools of the Homespun False Consciousness get to define what is normative. (95)

18. For example, the Academy of American Poets' Walt Whitman Award, the Associated Writing Programs award series, and the National Book Critics Circle Award all started in 1975; 1976 brought the Princeton University Press and Houghton Mifflin

poetry series (now both dead); the Elliston Award was founded in 1977, and the National Poetry Series (far more diverse than most such series) and the Poetry Society of America's William Carlos Williams Award (now one of eleven PSA awards) in 1979. The L. A. Times Book Award was first granted in 1980, and in 1981 the first MacArthur Fellowships were given; see Rasula (*American Poetry Wax Museum* 519–47) and Holden ("American Poetry" 261). Only the years 1945–46 have seen a comparable eruption of award series. Details from the Devins Award's history provide concrete examples of how institutional networks in poetry sustain themselves. Gerald Constanzo used his 1974 prize money to publish the first Carnegie Mellon University Press poetry books in 1975; Jonathan Holden's award earned him his first academic job (Constanzo 5–6). The point here is not to demean Constanzo's labor and generosity or to begrudge Holden his employment. It is to make concrete the claim that mainstream publishing series and rewards tended to generate more series and rewards along similar lines in the period under discussion.

19. I cite this version of an analysis that appears also as part of Holden's *The Fate of American Poetry* because the book version drops any mention of the Myers and Weingarten anthology (in which Holden does not appear).

20. For a more general analytic history of the (British and American) poetry reading, see Peter Middleton, *Distant Reading: Performance, Readership, and Consumption in Contemporary Poetry* (Tuscaloosa: University of Alabama Press, 2005), 61–103.

21. Holden's praise of the *Morrow Anthology* echoes the terms, cited earlier in this chapter, in which Smith and Bottoms describe their representative younger American poet: "The mainstream of American poetry . . . has continued to be, whether narrative or meditative, in a realist mode that is essentially egalitarian, university-based, and middle-class, and to be written in a free verse that has, by and large, vastly improved since the sixties" (*Fate of American Poetry* 47–48).

22. My point here is not to argue the merits or demerits of the Longfellow revival that Dana Gioia's quite compelling chapter proposes; rather, it is to note the price of that revival in this publishing context, the exclusions with which it is associated in an academically sanctioned construction of American literary history that cannot imagine a parallel tradition of formal investigation running alongside the bland centrism that it unspokenly promotes.

23. A list of counterexamples from the period, of anthologies based on alternative publications and awards, would include Clayton Eshleman, ed., *A Caterpillar Anthology: A Selection of Poetry and Prose from "Caterpillar Magazine"* (Garden City, NY: Doubleday, 1971); Cid Corman, ed., *The Gist of Origin 1951–1971* (New York: Grossman, 1975); J. J. Phillips, Ishmael Reed, Gundars Strads, and Shawn Wong, eds. *The Before Columbus Foundation Poetry Anthology. Selections from the American Book Awards 1980–1990* (New York: W. W. Norton, 1992); and the two volumes of Douglas Messerli, ed., *The Gertrude Stein Awards in Innovative American Poetry* (Los Angeles: Sun and Moon, 1995–96).

24. For discussion of the category of the "academic" in Allen's influential anthology, see chapter 2.

25. Characterizations and critiques of the mainstream anthology, however, by no means all stem from its self-designated experimental Others. From a formally traditional perspective, R. S. Gwynn finds that *The Pittsburgh Book of Contemporary American Poetry* symbolizes "what the center holds"—"a marked uniformity of style and subject" (741). Vernon Shetley, who has written on poets as lionized in mainstream

circles as Bishop and Merrill, argues, as I have here, the false pluralism of mainstream poetics: "Though a rhetoric of pluralism obscures the underlying conformity, the range of stylistic options and models employed in the mainstream is in fact quite narrow; differences in outlook and approach are rarely so dramatic as to involve fundamental disagreements of principle that would be worth arguing publicly" (*After the Death of Poetry* 137).

26. In a January 29, 2008, blog post, Paul Hoover comments on how changes in the AWP's annual conference program complicate received (and once-accurate) views of it as an institutional bastion of mainstream poetics:

> At the Palm Springs AWP, 2001, Maxine Chernoff and I walked around looking for someone to talk to and found only Aaron Shurin, who was equally alienated by the Carolyn Kizer/Yusef Komunyakaa program dominant. Now all of that has changed. If you want to locate the avant-garde, you can find it [in] the Nassau Suite at the Hilton, second floor. I don't exclude myself. I'm on two panels at the forthcoming meeting in NYC, one of which I proposed on contemporary Vietnamese poetry. The other is Newlipo: Proceduralism and Chance Poetics in the 21st Century. ("Cahiers de Corey/2")

27. Compare Geoffrey O'Brien's characterization of the *Morrow Anthology* as a textbook of "academically respectable verse," "a display of officially sanctioned art, a veritable *poésie de salon*" (34).

## Chapter 5

1. "Clarity" turns out to be a complex and unstable category in Oppen, however, a term that involves phenomenological immediacy more than language and around which some of his more opaque statements cluster. In "Of Being Numerous," Oppen writes these oft-quoted lines that make up a complete section (# 22) of the poem: "Clarity // In the sense of *transparence*, / I don't mean that much can be explained. // Clarity in the sense of silence" (*New Collected Poems* 175). In his working papers, he notes to himself "Clarity I said, meaning—the clarity of Being I had no other concern" ("Anthropologist of Myself" 158). "Clarity" is not necessarily a *linguistic* property for Oppen: "I don't mean that much can be explained," and in any case (in a paradoxically clear and seemingly transparent claim), "words cannot be wholly transparent. And that is the 'heartlessness' of words" (*New Collected Poems* 194). Meanwhile, "clarity in the sense of silence" would render poetry unnecessary. On the category of "silence" in Oppen, see Izenberg (78–106); for useful comments on clarity and opacity in Oppen, see Weinfield, "Oppen on Clarity."

2. Oppen's absence from critical commentary on the long poem extends to Margaret Dickie's *On the Modernist Long Poem* and Joe Moffett's *The Search for Origins in the Twentieth-Century Long Poem: Sumerian Homeric Anglo-Saxon* (West Virginia University Press, 2007), though it would be fair to note that Oppen is hardly the ideal fit for the thematic focus suggested by Moffett's title. Moffett offers a few scattered remarks on parts of *"A"*; Peter Baker, who discusses Zukofsky more substantively, mentions Oppen in one footnote, though not as a writer of serial poems. In *Writing in Real Time: Emergent Poetics from Whitman to the Digital* (Cambridge University Press, 2017), Paul Jaussen focuses on how certain ongoing lifelong or multivolume long or serial poems change as they respond to historical events in the course of their being written; *scale*

is crucial to his argument in a way that would make Oppen's inclusion inappropriate. While acknowledging Oppen as "a poet who is most commonly perceived as an expert of the minute and particular," Matthew Carbery describes "Of Being Numerous" as "an excellent example of a long poem in which poetic extension comes about through the complex interrelation of its parts rather than through sheer volume," arguing for the poem's "mode of poetic extension" as "phenomenologically informed" (37).

3. For a contrary opinion on Oppen's tone and rhetorical stance, see Jonathan Galassi, who often finds Oppen "openly, even severely didactic" (167), a poet-teacher who sees it as his role to speak for others, not just for himself, or Oren Izenberg's characterization of Oppen's work as "larded with sententious and didactic passages" (82). Oppen himself claims that he tries to avoid didacticism, even at those points where it might be expected: "Very few of those poems that touch on the social-political ethic exhort" (Oppen and Oppen 46). In "Of Being Numerous," we might recall, he writes, "I don't mean that much can be explained"—hardly the stance of a didact. To place Oppen's tone, which he calls "impoverished" (*New Collected Poems* 220), accurately, one might contrast it with that of those two arch-didacts Pound and Olson. Carbery also briefly discusses Oppen's "resistance to didacticism" (40).

Noting that to "include history" for Oppen is more than a matter of breadth and scale, Henry Weinfield summarizes the ambiguous relationship that "Of Being Numerous" has to the modernist long poem tradition: "'Of Being Numerous' . . . is a poem that 'includes history' with greater depth than any we have had in recent years. Thus, although it makes no such claim for itself but even questions the validity of such a claim for poetry in the present, it carries the burden of the modernist version of epic, serving as both a continuation and a corrective to that tradition" ("'Of Being Numerous'" 379). The distinction represented by the phrase "modernist version" is key, for as Weinfield argues elsewhere, "Oppen is fundamentally opposed to the epic, because of its connection to empire and to warfare" (*Music* 69–70).

4. In questioning the applicability of Miller's and Gardner's paradigms for reading Oppen, I do not mean to deny Whitman's presence in Oppen's poetry. One could speculate that Whitman, one candidate for inventor of the American serial poem if we wish to look back beyond Mina Loy and Charles Reznikoff, and the first poet to write a language of New York, provided Oppen with one powerful precedent (among others) in American poetry for exploring the relationship between individual and society. On this point, "Myself I Sing" is an important transitional poem between Oppen's early work (especially "Party on Shipboard," which Oppen quotes in "Myself I Sing") and "Of Being Numerous." The title's allusion suggests that Oppen's concerns in the poem will recapitulate Whitman's in the lines that begin the final edition of *Leaves of Grass*—"One's-Self I sing, a simple separate person, / Yet utter the word Democratic, the word En-Masse" (3)—or that begin "Song of Myself": "I celebrate myself, and sing myself" (26). Oppen begins, however, by using his characteristic literalism to ironize the Whitmanesque stance: "Me! he says, hand on his chest. / Actually, his shirt" (*New Collected Poems* 56). Despite Oppen's interest in Whitman, then, he does not model the style, voice, setting, scope, or vision of his own serial poems on *Leaves of Grass*. In fact Bernard Waldrop, reviewing *The Materials*, contrasts the two poets, noting how in Oppen one finds "no rambling catalogs of things, no ranting that he is part of the whole universe" (51). George Monteiro reads "Night Scene" (*New Collected Poems* 137), which depicts a drunk about to attempt suicide by jumping into the Hudson River, as offering "wry commentary on romantic notions such as that of Walt Whitman's 'man in the open air'" (227).

5. For the modernist period especially, this canon remained for decades largely predictable and, for some critics, actually constitutive of modernism; referring to *The Waste Land, The Bridge, Paterson,* and *The Cantos,* Margaret Dickie argues that "together, the compositions of these poems compose the history of Modernism" (17). The discussions that I have cited so far also remain overwhelmingly centered on male writers, with only minor exceptions: Conte's half-chapter on Niedecker, Rosenthal and Gall's chapters on Dickinson, on Plath and Sexton, and their brief mentions of Riding, Rukeyser, Rich, and H.D. (though not of *Trilogy* or *Helen in Egypt*). In *Obdurate Brilliance,* Peter Baker devotes a half-chapter to Stein and a few pages to Bernadette Mayer. Despite extensive critical work on individual modernist women writers, commentary on the long poem and the serial poem *as genres* has historically overlooked women's writing in these forms.

While focusing on poems written by women since 1970, Lynn Keller's *Forms of Expansion: Recent Women's Long Poems* provides a valuable corrective to the largely phallocentric history of criticism and theorizing on the long poem. Keller discusses work by Sharon Doubiago, Judy Grahn, Brenda Marie Osbey, Rita Dove, Marilyn Hacker, Susan Howe, Beverly Dahlen, and Rachel Blau DuPlessis. For other discussions of the long poem that address the relationship between gender and genre, see Susan Stanford Friedman's essays "Craving Stories," "Gender and Genre Anxiety," and "When a 'Long' Poem Is a 'Big' Poem"; and Keller, "The Twentieth-Century Long Poem."

6. Ron Silliman's distinction between what he calls the serial poem as "formally contained" and the series as "potentially infinite" parallels Conte's between the finite and infinite series. For Silliman, the difference is partly one of imagined scale (either potential or actual), a difference between the poem conceived "as a book or tale" and the poem "taken as a lifework" ("I Wanted to Write Sentences" 15). Conte reiterates the argument of *Unending Design* in compressed form in his essay "Seriality and the Contemporary Long Poem," *Sagetrieb* 11, nos. 1–2 (Spring–Fall 1992): 35–45.

7. While I have concentrated in the opening pages of this chapter on book-length treatments of the American long poem or serial poem, it is crucial to mention the work of Rachel Blau DuPlessis on seriality, across a range of essays and book chapters: see especially "Blazes of Poetry," "Lorine Niedecker's 'Paean to Place,'" and *Blue Studios* (209–51). Writing about Oppen, DuPlessis offers one of the most succinct definitions available of the serial poem:

> Serial poems are sectional or modular works whose argument is built by the order of the parts, by the nature and montage cut of the parts (image, phrase, line, word), by the shape of blankness or space in relation to the parts, and by the varied intellectual and emotional relations of suture and leap among these parts. Seriality proceeds by vectors, adjusting to pressures on all sides and coming out with a situational path. (*Blue Studios* 273n5).

8. One contemporary model or source of inspiration for Oppen seems to have been Yves Bonnefoy's *Du mouvement et de l'immobilité de Douve*: see Nicholls, *George Oppen* (88–93).

9. Unlike Olson's and Williams's, Oppen's sense of place is rarely celebratory. He investigates "the meaning / Of being numerous" in the face of what he describes to Charles Amirkhanian and David Gitin as "the increasing meaninglessness or uselessness of New York City" and its loss of "even the historical meaning that it had" ("Conversation" 21). In this same interview Oppen describes San Francisco, his home in his

later years and the setting for another serial poem, "Some San Francisco Poems," as "much too clever a city and a very strange city," generating "a sense of isolation" from its location on "the bare edge of the continent and simply space beyond" (22). Oppen's use of place in his poetry, then, is generally willed. As Constance Hunting puts it, "Oppen's eye adjusts itself to geography not automatically but through willed effort. He makes the geography; it does not make him" (54). For more extended discussion of the effect of San Francisco on Oppen's work, see chapter 6 of this volume.

10. The comments on Olson are consistent with Oppen's evaluation of his work in his review "Three Poets," where Oppen admires the shorter poems of Olson's *The Distances* but finds "Maximus from Dogtown" labored and wordy, "the verse . . . creating unnecessary difficulties for itself" (*Selected Prose* 24). On this latter point, compare Oppen's critique of Olson and Duncan in a 1971 letter for their "copiousness and digressions—and . . . the proliferation of theories" (*Selected Letters* 405n10).

11. The relationship between poetry and thinking has received increased emphasis from Oppen's critics in recent years. It constitutes the organizing trope of Steve Shoemaker's edited essay collection, *Thinking Poetics: Essays on George Oppen* (University of Alabama Press, 2009); see also Peter Nicholls's discussion of Oppen's "poetic thinking" (*George Oppen* 76–82). Henry Weinfield rests perhaps the most detailed reading of "Of Being Numerous" that we have on the premise that "epistemological concerns are primary to Oppen from the outset of his career, . . . and one could argue that bringing them to light was precisely what his objective as a poet was" (*Music* 26). On the relationship between thought and action in Oppen, see Davidson, *Outskirts* (270–78). When Oppen himself describes his starting to write poetry again after his long hiatus, his terms are revealing: "I sat down with a piece of paper for the first time in twenty years and thought my way into a poem" (*Selected Letters* 127).

12. Oppen distances himself tonally and philosophically from Williams in "Of Being Numerous," section 29, however. If Williams's new world children, plants, and poems are associated with "quicken[ing]," a "stark dignity," and "profound change" as "rooted, they / grip down and begin to awaken" (*Collected Poems* 1:183), Oppen asks "is it not / In fear the roots grip // Downward / And beget // The baffling hierarchies / Of father and child" (*New Collected Poems* 182). In section 25, Oppen's "'pure products of America'" are not the population of Williams's "To Elsie" but "the children of the middle class" (177).

13. While various critics note Oppen's ethical concerns, see especially Woods (215–33) and (from a Levinasian perspective and with specific reference to *Of Being Numerous*) Jenkins (33–60).

14. Ezra Pound considered the feasibility of the Imagist long poem as early as 1914, in this note from his essay "Vorticism" reprinted in *Gaudier-Brzeska*: "I am often asked whether there can be a long imagiste or vorticist poem[.] The Japanese, who evolved the hokku, evolved also the Noh plays. In the best 'Noh' the whole play may consist of one image. I mean it is gathered about one image. Its unity consists in one image, enforced by movement and music. *I see nothing against a long vorticist poem*" (94; my emphasis).

15. As he says in his working papers, Oppen sees syntax as a means to separate as much as to connect words. It involves, for him, "a careful packing of a poem . . . to avoid destroying a word by its relationships" ("Adequate Vision" 29); "each WORD MUST BECOME SOLITARY" (27). One virtue of "little" words, Oppen says to Kevin Power, is that "they remain attached to the object" and "can be separated from each

other, that the word can place itself within the poem" (Oppen and Oppen 47). Similarly, in conversation with L. S. Dembo he sees one function of the poetic line "as separating the connections of the progression of thought" ("George Oppen" 180). Many critics note in passing the disjunctions that result from this view of syntax and the line; Perloff ("Shape"), Berry, and Oderman offer useful and sustained discussions of the issue. See chapter 6 for my own discussion of syntax in late Oppen.

16. The degree to which it is appropriate to say Oppen "returned" to poetry—a site of some debate among his readers—is usefully questioned by David Herd:

> It is difficult . . . to argue in any uncomplicated way that Oppen "returned" to poetry in 1958, as if he were going back or was picking up where he left off. Rather, as Heller reads the situation . . . what is at issue is a complex break in which one social practice, namely poetry, starts to seem viable again when the social practice which made it seem insufficient, namely politics, itself appears to have failed. And not poetry as Oppen had previously reckoned it, but poetry made of a new set of what, in the title of his second book, he called *Materials*, and composed in response to a new set of imperatives. Oppen, then, did not return to writing. Rather, in Peter Nicholls' full and demanding sense, he began again. ("'In the Open of the Common Rubble'" 147)

Herd refers here to Michael Heller's argument in *Speaking the Estranged* that Oppen "did not 'return' but in fact came anew to poetry, and in a greatly changed state of mind" (6) and to Nicholls's focus on "the completeness of Oppen's rejection of his own work" during his twenty-four years away from poetry, on his "beginning again," on Oppen's reacceptance of that earlier work "only after he had actually begun to write again" (*George Oppen* 28), and Oppen's statement that "I am starting now as if from scratch to write of things I knew nothing about when I was twenty" (*Selected Letters* 26). Oren Izenberg argues for a notable degree of *formal* continuity in Oppen's work "despite the profound changes internal to the poet": "His next poems, written after a quarter century's accumulation of worldly knowledge, are . . . not profoundly different in *kind* than his first ones" and "are not a true stylistic departure" from the earlier work (81). I return briefly to the question of Oppen's "return" in chapter 6.

17. Oppen's previously unpublished poem "Narrative" (not to be confused with the 1965 "A Narrative") begins in skepticism toward a canonical Western narrative the outcome of which is always already known: "How could those artists paint / The Virgin playing with her baby / In pure happiness? // The artist knows / How that story ended." Narrative in the arts offers less substantive knowledge than biology: "We have our knowledge: // Structure of the gene, the evolution / Of the ground // Deeper in our lives, in our minds / Than any song, than any pictures" (*New Collected Poems* 319–20). This particular version of narrative as involving the repression (in some cases) or adumbration (in others) of an already known conclusion would be thoroughly alien to the poet who insists that "we do not write what we already knew before we wrote the poem" (*Selected Prose* 44). In Oppen's thinking, narrative seems to have involved a kind of suspect explanatory distance from one's materials: "I think I have written what I / set out to say—I need / not now turn to narrative" (232).

18. This is Oppen's explication of the image in a letter to June Oppen Degnan, September 27, 1963: "Ouroboros of course is . . . the closed universe, the closed self" ("Letters to June" 223).

19. On producing "a decisive expression of a period," compare Oppen's remark that "perhaps an 'important' poem contains what could only have been said at that moment. As Eliot's Wasteland" (*Selected Prose* 186).

20. Compare Pound's description of *The Waste Land*, in a December 24, 1921, letter to Eliot, as "the longest poem in the English langwidge" (*Letters* 169).

21. Two particularly helpful articles discuss this feature of Oppen's work in more detail: see DuPlessis, "George Oppen," and Hatlen, "Opening Up the Text." Of the "five linguistic processes"—"interrogation, negation, repetition, interruption, and dialogue" (265)—that Hatlen uses to describe the movement of "Of Being Numerous," negation resembles most closely what I have called reversal and contradiction.

22. Heller (75–81) is one of the few critics to draw connections between Oppen and Stevens.

23. One intertext: a scene in Todd Haynes's *I'm Not There* involves a press conference after the film's version of Bob Dylan going electric at the Newport Folk Festival. A journalist says to the Dylan figure, "Jude Quinn" (played by Cate Blanchett), "I think we all know what the definition of 'people' is," and Quinn responds, "Yeah. Do we?"

24. See Oppen's own comments on the relationship between form and thinking in "Of Being Numerous," both in its beginnings and as he worked on the poem: "Of Being Numerous" was "conceived as a process of thought, section by succeeding section: but very drastic revision, rearrangement, re-writing (therefore) involved: changes in the thinking, too—something over a two-year process" (*Selected Letters* 209).

25. In "Two Romance Poems," the last-but-one entry in his 1975 *Collected Poems*, Oppen seems to see the simultaneous proximity and distance between people in the world as an organizational model for his poetry: "The people standing at a little distance / from each other, or in small groups // would be the poem." That he had "Of Being Numerous" specifically in mind is suggested by the fact that he quotes a prominent phrase from the earlier poem, "bright light of shipwreck" (*New Collected Poems* 261).

26. Wyatt Prunty, "Emaciated Poetry," *The Sewanee Review* 93, no. 1 (Winter 1985): 78–94.

27. Any claim for a connection specifically between *Of Being Numerous* and *Pieces* would be untenable because Creeley wrote most of *Pieces* between November 1967 and August 1968. At the same time, he would have had access to *This in Which*, containing "A Narrative" and "A Language of New York," and possibly to *Discrete Series*. And after the publication of *Of Being Numerous*, he continued his own work in serial form beyond *Pieces* into *A Daybook* and, more ambiguously since they are printed as separate poems, *Thirty Things*. For a more extended discussion of Creeley's work in serial forms, see my "Revisiting Seriality in Creeley's Poetry," in *Form, Power, and Person in Robert Creeley's Life and Work*, ed. Stephen Fredman and Steve McCaffery (Iowa: University of Iowa Press, 2010), 50–65.

28. Oppen seems, however, to have felt less commitment to this common processual poetics than Creeley, remarking in a 1975 interview that he had confidence "neither in the language nor in the accident of my own voice like Creeley" ("Interview" 15).

29. Commentary on the relationship between prosody and presence in Objectivist writing is characterized mainly by its multiple contradictions. Eleanor Berry and Marjorie Perloff agree on associating certain prosodic features with a prosody of presence. They disagree on where these features appear, which explains why Berry's Oppen sounds like Perloff's Williams. (Berry also makes more distinctions than Perloff between Oppen's 1960s writing and his early and late work.) Berry associates the frequent syntactic regularity and coincidence of line with syntactic unit in Oppen's 1960s work

before *Seascape: Needle's Eye* with his celebration of "a world of solidities and edges," a poetics of "naming and praising things of the world" (310, 315); for Perloff, "the presence of the moment is made manifest" in Williams through similar prosodic means ("'Shape of the Lines'" 229). Perloff explicitly *distinguishes* Oppen's prosody, with its "curious disruptiveness" by which "the text itself is . . . called into question" (227, 229), from Williams's. Bernstein echoes Perloff in arguing that Oppen's prosody leans away from effects of presence; yet their Oppen sounds like Hatlen's Williams, in whom we are asked to associate "syntactic dislocations" with attention to "sensory particulars."

Bernstein's metaphor of the hinge for Oppen's line break recalls Creeley's sense of his own line break as a "pivot" ("Interview with Robert Creeley" 58), and he suggests this prosodic "hinge" as one possible aspect of Oppen's influence. Before the publication of *Pieces*, Oppen expressed reservations about Creeley's line: "A lot of the worst of modern poetry, and it would be true of some quite good poetry, such as Creeley's, uses the line-ending simply as the ending of a line, a kind of syncopation or punctuation" ("George Oppen" 180). This statement echoes Oppen's observation in a daybook entry from the 1962–65 period: "Creeley finally largely mannerist one remembers the manner, not the poem" (*Selected Prose* 116).

30. In a January 1966 letter, Oppen writes that "Of Being Numerous" has "been a harrowing work for me, partly for the difficulty, a difficulty I suppose of courage or of honesty in permitting the imperfect to appear imperfect, and the difficulty of distinguishing that decency from the indecency of permitting mere sloppy work, a different kind of faking—. Imperfect, but I think it has to be" (*Selected Letters* 128–29). Willing to describe a Shirley Kaufman poem as "perfect" in a July 1970 letter to her, Oppen also praises the work for not being "'too perfect'" ("[Letter to Shirley Kaufman]").

## Chapter 6

1. See, however, David Herd's review of Oppen's *New Collected Poems*, which he values because "it gives a version of the poet not so well known"—"what really comes through here . . . are the poems of place, the poems of Oppen's largely itinerant lifestyle: not the poems in which he refines and argues, but the poems of Brooklyn, San Francisco, Mexico, France, Guadeloupe, Deer Island Maine" ("By Catboat to New York").

2. For brief biographical background on Oppen's early San Francisco years, see Oppen, "'Meaning Is to Be Here': A Selection from the Daybook," edited by Cynthia Anderson, *Conjunctions* 10 (1987): 193–94; Mary Oppen, "Conversation," 42–43 (which also contain comments on why the Oppens left New York); and Eric Hoffman, *Oppen* (21–33).

3. Heller remarks vividly that "the later poems, looking as though they have been shredded or blown apart, lie scattered across the page, gathered into seemingly dismembered clusters of text. The wide irregular areas of white space suggest the dictation of someone speaking into a wind, a favourite image in Oppen's work" (88). Heller reads Oppen's use of page space variously as "show[ing] where the pressure of articulation causes the poet to pause, to jump across linguistic and visual space, to bend or break the usual syntax of poetic language" (111) and as a means "almost to isolate and dissociate one word from another in order to bring into focus the burdens, linguistic, historical and poetic, that they bear" (2).

4. In particular, see Berry. For a strongly differing position, however, note Heller's claims that "the over-emphasis on *Discrete Series* tends to distort the picture of Oppen's career" (4) and that "the poetry Oppen wrote after his Communist period does not 'return' to anything that he had done previously. Instead, he is writing a radically

different poetry" (6). It seems to me that one can accept Heller's view that after his notorious twenty-five-year hiatus "Oppen did not 'return' but in fact came anew to poetry, and in a greatly changed state of mind" (6) without positing an absolute discontinuity between *Discrete Series* and his other work at the level of visual/page design. For more on the nature of Oppen's "return" to poetry, see chapter 5, note 16.

5. For a close reading of this poem that pays particular attention to syntax, see Jack Marshall, "On Late Oppen," *Big Bridge* 14 (2009), http://www.bigbridge.org.

6. See Berry, especially 310–12 and 315, for a useful discussion of this aspect of Oppen's work.

7. In possible response (and in another citing of first words), Simic uses as epigraph for his *Austerities* (New York: Braziller, 1982) the last lines of the first poem in Oppen's first book: "Of the world, weather-swept, with which // one shares the century" (*New Collected Poems* 5).

8. The increased self-reflexiveness of *Seascape* may partly embody Oppen's skepticism about poetry's ability to respond meaningfully to pressing political problems, a skepticism that in the 1930s had caused him to give up writing. Letters from the *Seascape* period return persistently to this concern: "Difficult again to believe in the importance of poetry. The army tightens up, some kids surely will be shot soon"; "[I] doubt any poem's adequacy" in the face of the Vietnam War; "one doubts poetry" (*Selected Letters* 187, 189, 230). In an unpublished poem from the early 1960s, "Maudit," Oppen imagines his sense of poetry's inadequacy to the social "stopping" him again as it had in the 1930s:

> I can be stopped
> Again anytime
> By, shame.
>
> The man sitting on his stoop, in a world of stoops, defeated;
> What can anything I have written mean to him? (*New Collected Poems* 326)

9. In reduced form, this passage becomes part of "The Book of Job and a Draft of a Poem to Praise the Paths of the Living" (*New Collected Poems* 244). It may not be too far-fetched to hear a punning observation about class hierarchies in these lines, raised as Oppen was in a class accustomed to being served by "the bellboy."

10. Compare Oppen's comment in a [1969?] letter to Diane Meyer, as he was contemplating "a next book, which possibly I can't write," that "maybe we—all of us—people—have come about as far as humans were ever fitted to go" (*Selected Letters* 185).

11. For more detail on this allusion, in the lines "All that was to be thought / Yes / Comes down the road" (*New Collected Poems* 213), see *Selected Letters* 408n16.

12. Oppen had first written to Schwerner responding to this work on August 5, 1964 (*Selected Letters* 101–2). Part I of Schwerner's poem "Prologue in Six Parts," in *Seaweed*, cites Oppen's "A Narrative." A further observation in the same review seems to confirm the element of self-description at work: "One begins to fear that poets of worth may be lost in the impenetrable welter of publication as once they were lost in general neglect" (*Selected Prose* 40). Oppen wrote the Schwerner review in the same year that he canceled a post–Pulitzer Prize reading tour.

13. Indicative of Oppen's tendency to move back and forth among poems, notebooks, and letters in his writing, one daybook entry (a comment on Reznikoff's well-

known "girder" couplet) reads "the syntax is arranged to control the order of disclosure upon which the poem depends" ("Adequate Vision" 29). Syntax and lineation were inseparable in Oppen's thinking: "My lines and the division of lines is not meant merely as a cadence of sound. It is an essential element of the syntax" (*Selected Prose* 120).

14. Oppen differentiates Olson's poetics from his own in "Three Poets" (*Selected Prose* 23–28). For some suggestive connections between Oppen and Olson, however, see Stephen Fredman, "'And All Now Is War': George Oppen, Charles Olson, and the Problem of Literary Generations," in DuPlessis and Quartermain (286–93).

15. On distance and otherness, see the unpublished poems from the San Francisco years "The Powers" (which repeats some form of the word "strange" twelve times) and "All This Strangeness" (*New Collected Poems* 343–46). In "The Powers" Oppen associates "strangeness" with, among other things, his aging, his Jewishness, language ("the words // themselves"), and—with the spacing characteristic of *Seascape*—his own poetics ("the turn   the cadence   the verse and the music   the essential // clarity,   plain glass,   strangest of all places" [*New Collected Poems* 344]). Compare his 1975 comment that "the word in one's own mouth becomes as strange as infinity—even as strange as the finite, strange as things" (*Selected Prose* 48).

16. Patrick Pritchett reads the use of white space in late Oppen as a figure for the poet's ongoing preoccupation with the idea of "clarity": "It's as if the only way for Oppen to write clarity is through these sharp incisions of white space." In the late work, Pritchett argues, "clarity becomes a kind of . . . para-notational blank space, a scission cutting into the material body of the poem"; it "can appear . . . only as and from the pauses within the overall shape of the poem, the white caesuras of its metrical breaks" ("Clarity or, Late Modernism).

17. For the most thorough physical description of Oppen's archive, his constructivist method, and its implications for questions of genre, see Davidson, *Ghostlier Demarcations* (64–78); see also Stephen Cope's introduction and textual apparatus (1–20) for his edition of Oppen's *Selected Prose.*

18. Despite writing in this November 1970 letter of "the final version of the SF poems" that he expected to appear "in the Fulcrum Collected" (*Selected Letters* 216), Oppen undertook considerably more revision for the poems' publication in *Seascape.* "The Fulcrum Collected"—the English edition of Oppen's *Collected Poems* published by Fulcrum Press in London in December 1972 (though contracted for May 1970)—features a thirteen-page section titled "Of the Needle's Eye 1968–1969." In that section, what became the untitled first poem of "Some San Francisco Poems" is printed as a separate poem titled "Rock Festival, Altamont, California"; the eventual seventh poem, "o withering seas," is not yet present; the sequence ends with "The Song," a short draft of what became "Song, The Winds of Downhill"; and Oppen subsequently revised other poems in the sequence, sometimes significantly.

19. Compare Rachel Blau DuPlessis's remark that "in Oppen, especially later Oppen, the lines, line by line, are organized serially. I mean that literally: each line or small group is like a distilled poem, section, aphorism. Then these are placed 'end for end.' This gives the sense of space, depth and extent in Oppen—each line acts as if it is a section or stanza of a poem—even, each word does" ("The Topos of the 'Thing'" 47).

20. Given that Oppen's revisions took his poems in an opposite direction from voice-centered narrative, it is ironically appropriate for Stanley Plumly, one practitioner of such a poetics, to describe *Seascape* in a generally laudatory review as "a poetry so committed to the object as to deny the possibility of its own voice" ("[Review of *Seascape: Needle's Eye*]" 104).

21. Though it is not immediately apposite to my argument, I should also note the likely personal component to Oppen's use of space, as he imagines the blankness of his own death. "Needle's eye . . . comes to the personal: the man individually facing the temporal" ("Anthropologist" 158), he writes, an observation that he repeats in a December 1972 letter to Michael Heller—"so imminently confronted by one's temporality" (*Selected Letters* 249). Daybook entries and letters from the period return repeatedly and bleakly to "the question whether any life can come out well alone. Whether a life can end well I try to face it" (184). Acutely aware as he seems to have been of time running out (though he was not yet sixty when he moved to San Francisco), the ending of "Anniversary Poem" poses the human challenge of Oppen's late poetry: "To find now depth, not time, since we cannot, but depth // To come out safe, to end well" (*New Collected Poems* 227). The space acknowledges the emptiness of the hope "to end well." Compare Peter Nicholls's treatment of this issue in *George Oppen* (140–41) and Heller's observation that the voice of Oppen's later poetry "is tonally so closely connected with aging and death that it is almost an overhearing similar to those extreme moments of near death during the war when scraps of remembered poetry would come to him" (62).

22. The early version of "Anniversary Poem" contained in the English edition of Oppen's *Collected Poems* preserves a variation of the phrase—"We said / —consenting— / *Objectivist*"—that is cut from the later American version. See Oppen, *Collected Poems* (London: Fulcrum, 1972), 151.

## Chapter 7

1. "Hard Copy" (*Pitch* 42–71) is a crucial document in DuPlessis's career-long conversation with the work of George Oppen. Specifically, this serial poem within the larger serial project of *Drafts* is in dialogue with Oppen's "Of Being Numerous," including (to note only surface features) the forty-section structure that mirrors Oppen's own and the direct echo of Oppen's conclusion (itself cited from Whitman), the phrase "quite curious." For sustained commentary, see Libbie Rifkin, "'That We Can Somehow Add Each to Each Other?': George Oppen between Denise Levertov and Rachel Blau DuPlessis," *Contemporary Literature* 51, no. 4 (Winter 2010): 703–35, and especially 723–31.

2. For DuPlessis on the "thing," see her essay "The Topos of the 'Thing.'"

3. See also DuPlessis, "The Blazes of Poetry."

4. Compare DuPlessis's recent and even stronger claim that "perhaps the most distinctive contribution of objectivist poetics is the mid-length to very long serial poem" ("Objectivist Poetry and Poetics" 95). On the connection of Objectivist seriality to "thought, cognition, investigation," see chapter 5's discussion of Oppen.

5. Charles Bernstein writes of Reznikoff that "with his first book, he introduced cubo-seriality into American poetry: serial poems that have a modular, rather than a sequential, relation to one another" ("Brooklyn Boy Makes Good"). I would also note DuPlessis's offhand but historically persuasive reference to "the invention of the serial poem in early modernism (possibly by Loy)" in her *Genders, Races, and Religious Cultures* (55). Mina Loy's "Songs to Joannes" was first published as "Love Songs I–IV" in the experimental little magazine *Others* 1, no. 1 (July 1915): 6–8, and the revised "Songs to Joannes," now in thirty-four sections, was published in *Others* 3, no. 6 (April 1917): 3–20, taking up the whole issue.

6. For more recent comments on the idea of writing "after," see DuPlessis's "After the Long Poem," *Dibur Literary Journal* 4 (Spring 2017): 5–13.

7. DuPlessis's frequent use of the phrase "jot and tittle" has encoded into it her awareness of Pound's anti-Semitism. See chapter 8 for her response to his assertion that "'not a jot or tittle of the Hebraic alphabet can pass into the text without danger of contaminating it'" (*Blue Studios* 250).

8. For recent observations on "IT IS," see DuPlessis's 2017 essay "Autobiography of a Practice": *Drafts* "manifests its commitment to seriality on a very large scale—you might say that the sections all point outward and inward as a series of explorations into the world and thus into IT. Into the two oddities of all oddities: IT and IS. These words indicate *being* itself (thus *Drafts* is an ontological poem). They also address being *itself*, within this cosmological and ecological poem, at times meditating on actual scientific findings as told by journalism, at times speculating on the universe."

9. DuPlessis seems to be invoking two relevant intertexts here, from Whitman's "Song of Myself" (another candidate for the first serial poem)—"I and this mystery here we stand" (Whitman 28); and from Oppen—"The self is no mystery, the mystery is / That there is something for us to stand on" (*New Collected Poems* 159).

10. The letter "a" recurs in *Drafts* as beginning, invitation, or "incipience": "Ask the letter A / and it may tell you // to continue," for instance (DuPlessis, *Collage Poems* 6).

11. For a valuable prior analysis of the "little words," including "it," in *Drafts 1–38*, see Libbie Rifkin, "Little Words and Redemptive Criticism: Some Points on *Drafts*," *HOW2* 1, no. 8 (2002), https://www.asu.edu. Regarding "the line of one," and the related terms "fold" and "grid," for readers unfamiliar with the structure of *Drafts*: between the writing of "Draft 19" and "Draft 20," DuPlessis writes, "I decided to repeat some version of these themes or materials in the same general order every nineteen poems, folding one group over another, making new works but works evoking motifs and themes in the former one—and also . . . generating new images, materials and themes as I went" in "a recurrent but free structure," a procedure but not a plan (*Surge* 7). Thus, with a "fold" every nineteen poems, the "line of one" would include Drafts 1, 20, 39, 58, 77, and 96, all in some degree of conversation with each other; the "line of two" would include Drafts 2, 21, 40, 59, 78, and 97; and so on. Starting with *Drafts 39–57, Pledge, with Draft, Unnumbered: Précis*, DuPlessis includes a diagrammatic "grid" laying out the structure of the lines and folds as it expanded with every volume.

12. The epigraphs appear in *Drafts* (Elmwood, CT: Potes and Poets Press, 1991), which includes Drafts 3–14 in the first book-length gathering of the project. When DuPlessis reprints these poems as part of *Drafts 1–38*, she replaces the Coolidge epigraph with one from Keats.

13. A variation entirely apposite for *Drafts* would be "as soon as / I speak, it / speaks," and indeed we find something close to that in "Draft 76: Work Table with Scale Models": "It / (still / speaking) / is still, speaking" (*Torques* 132).

14. DuPlessis's use of "cano"/ "I sing" invokes a canonical epic beginning, that of Virgil's *Aeneid*, as she notes in *Blue Studios* (234).

15. A different discussion from this one would examine how the material page in *Drafts* is not just thematized but insistently foregrounded through drawings, hand writing, double columns, typographic marks, bold face and italics, shifts in font size, capitals, obtrusive typos, blacked-out text, mail art, visual collage, and generous use of interlineal and intralineal white space, both an acknowledgment and an extension of the materiality of prior Objectivist texts. In these ways, *Drafts* has a deep kinship with the visually exploratory work of Susan Howe discussed in chapter 9. DuPlessis wrote some of the earliest commentary on this aspect of Howe's work (even connecting it to Oppen) in the chapter "'Whowe': On Susan Howe," *The Pink Guitar* 123–39. For

an important treatment of Objectivist and post-Objectivist materiality, see Davidson, *Ghostlier Demarcations* (64–93). On visual materiality specifically in DuPlessis, see Ron Silliman, "Un-scene, ur-new: The history of the longpoem and 'The Collage Poems of Drafts,'" *Jacket2*, December 14, 2011, http://jacket2.org.

16. In his discussion of the "infinite series" in *Unending Design*, Joseph Conte places the Objectivist work that he treats (Oppen's "Discrete Series," Zukofsky's *Anew*, Niedecker's "Lake Superior") in the category of the "finite series"—though one source for the phrase "infinite series" is the first section of Oppen's "Of Being Numerous."

17. It is notable that DuPlessis turns to a perfectly regular iambic pentameter to "start it up again," as if the continuing work depends both on a repeated return to the history of Anglophone poetry (encoded in the iambic meter) and on doing that history just enough violence to jog it into renewed life but not destroy it ("I knock it hard").

18. In the Preface to *Surge*, DuPlessis writes, "I don't want to say too much about scale and gender, because any stereotypical observation—however situationally true—risks restating (re-instantiating) patterns we want to reject" (9). One can assent without finding the comment disabling for considerations of scale and gender, especially when she moves immediately into a long paragraph on the history of female authorship.

19. The definitive book-length study of the female-authored long poem remains Lynn Keller, *Forms of Expansion*, which contains one of the earliest sustained discussions of *Drafts* as a "feminist serial long poem" (276).

20. We can take "not hero" here as "not Ezra Pound" (not Pound's sequence of heroic males in *The Cantos*) and, even more explicitly, "not polis" as "not Charles Olson" (in whose *Maximus Poems* "polis" features as a central term).

21. "Not so much the world in a grain of sand / but the grain of sand in the world / defines trace": *Pitch* (91); "micro-moment": *Drafts 1–38* (115).

22. Daniel Bouchard captures the macro-micro dynamic of *Drafts* nicely in his essay "A Little Yod and a Rocking Enormity: Reading 'Drafts,'" *Jacket2*, December 14, 2011, http://jacket2.org, where he lists images of smallness and uses of the word "enormous" (and its variants) side by side.

23. Compare Patrick Pritchett's comment that "the scale of *Drafts* is monumental; its focus anti-monumental," in his review, "*Drafts 1–38, Toll*," and DuPlessis's own description of *Drafts* as "a monumental task suspicious of the monumental" (*Blue Studios* 241).

24. DuPlessis's early comment on "how to indicate one's volume without squatting hibernations of mass" (*Pink Guitar* 133) may seem contradictory until we recall that—despite the implications of the "mound" metaphor—"mass" for her must also be mobile, labile, porous, and hardly a matter of "squatting hibernations."

25. For Zukofsky, the form for "thoughts' torsion," for "the actual twisting / of many and diverse thoughts" "is really a sestina," that strange combination of elegance and baroque ungainliness—but the sestina considered and used "as a force," not merely "as an experiment" in seeing if one can write a sestina (*ALL* 75–77).

26. Elsewhere in *Pitch*, in a self-lacerating definition of poetry and a theoretical reflection on Objectivist poetics, words are "a fetish substitute for the directness / of rubble" (49). As a recurring point of reference, Reznikoff's girder becomes almost a fetish object in later Objectivist-influenced writing. See, for example, the use by Zukofsky biographer and poet-critic Mark Scroggins of Reznikoff for the conclusion of his poem "Whiplash" (which also alludes to Oppen): "girder still itself." Scroggins, *Torture Garden: Naked City Pastorelles* (Brooklyn: Cultural Society, 2011).

27. With these opening Ns, I suspect an allusion not just to Wallace Stevens's "Poem

in the Shape of a Mountain" but to Basil Bunting's observation on Pound's *Cantos*: "There are the Alps. What is there to say about them?" (110). The first Draft and page of *Pitch* returns to this image in citing a phrase from Gershom Scholem, "'Letters took on / . . . the shape of great mountains'" (*Pitch* 1).

## Chapter 8

1. See also DuPlessis's remark that "*Drafts* was involved with Pound from its inception, but as a critical resistance to the impact of the work" (*Blue Studios* 250). On one aspect of this resistance, "opposition to the dominance of the Pound-styled editor" (60) and his investment in (historical) cleansing and efficiency, see Joshua Schuster, "Jewish Counterfactualism in Recent American Poetry." *Shofar: An Interdisciplinary Journal of Jewish Studies* 27, no. 3 (2009): 52–71, especially 58–60. For more on DuPlessis and Poundian epic, see Perelman, *Modernism* (53–68). For a discussion of non-Poundian models of serial writing important to DuPlessis—those of Robert Duncan, George Oppen, Beverley Dahlen, and H.D., along with Kurt Schwitters's collage practice—see Keller, *Forms* (242–51).

2. Readers of Oppen and Zukofsky will recognize the allusions to Oppen's celebration of "the small nouns" in "Praise" (*New Collected Poems* 99) and "the little words that I like so much" ("George Oppen" 175), to his sense that "that's where the mysteries are, in the little words. 'The' and 'and' are the greatest mysteries of all" ("Poetry and Politics" 38). Both Oppen and DuPlessis allude to or cite Zukofsky's statement that "a case can be made out for the poet giving some of his life to the use of the words *the* and *a*: both of which are weighted with as much epos and historical destiny as one man can perhaps resolve" (*Prepositions* 10). See chapter 7 for a more extended discussion of DuPlessis's citation of Zukofsky's statement, and her work with "the little words" and with "*the* and *a*" post-Oppen and -Zukofsky.

3. Again, without arguing for direct filiation, it seems fair to claim that *Drafts* is immanent in one aspect of the work of male modernist writers, including Pound, who were "drawn to the burble, the midden, sheer rhythm, a dance and not a mirror, an electricity" (*Pink Guitar* 62)—to *écriture féminine*, a revolutionary poetics that, as DuPlessis points out, did not extend to a rethinking of gender roles.

4. See Christine Froula, *To Write Paradise: Style and Error in Pound's Cantos* (New Haven, CT: Yale University Press, 1985); and Bernstein, *Poetics* (121–27).

5. As Lynn Keller rightly points out, one key aspect of seriality as a compositional method for DuPlessis is that "its aspirations are more modest, more investigative, than the grandly didactic cultural projects of modernist epic" (*Forms* 242). Late in life, Oppen wrote this fragment: "Only one mistake, Ezra! / You should have talked / to women" (*Selected Prose* 235).

6. It is appropriate for a long poem that always begins again that this echo of epic's inaugurating gesture appears on page 192 of the work's first volume.

7. I offer a more developed discussion of Pound's relationship to questions of knowledge, difficulty, readership, and reading in "From Pound to Olson: The Avant Gardist as Pedagogue," *Journal of Modern Literature* 34, no. 1 (Fall 2010): 86–106.

8. I am referring to Carroll F. Terrell, *A Companion to the Cantos of Ezra Pound*, 2 vols. (Berkeley: University of California Press, 1980, 1984), still the definitive reference text for Pound's sources in the *Cantos*.

9. Ezra Pound, *Canti postumi*, ed. Massimo Bacigalupo (Milan: Mondadori, 2002).

10. For the reference to *dybukkim*, see Rothenberg's poem "Dibbukim (Dibbiks)," *Khurbn and Other Poems* (New York: New Directions, 1989), 13–14.

## Chapter 9

1. See, for instance, Dworkin, *Reading the Illegible* (31–49). It was still possible for Dworkin to argue accurately in 2003—after at least fifteen years of Howe's experiments in visual prosody—for her use of page design as "one aspect of her work which critics have consistently noted but failed to seriously address" (32). While Johanna Drucker would take the position in her 2009 essay "Not Sound" that "the language of descriptive analysis for visual features [of poetry] barely exists" (238), Howe's critics have started increasingly to construct that language. Michael Rinaldo extends Dworkin's use of the term "illegibility" in "Breaking the Letter: Illegibility as Intersign in Cy Twombly, Steve McCaffery, and Susan Howe," PhD diss., University of Michigan, 2013. For sample close readings of some of Howe's more visually turbulent pages, see Back (158–62); Ming-Qian Ma, "Poetry as History Revised: Susan Howe's 'Scattering as Behavior Toward Risk,'" *American Literary History* 6, no. 4 (Winter 1994), especially 730–35; Bloomfield, "'Aftershock of Iconoclasm,'" who usefully notes the differences in Howe's visual page at different points in her career while connecting "Howe's disrupted pages and her enquiries into traumatic histories" (419); and Antoine Cazé, "Susan Howe: TransParencies: Leafing Through," *Jacket* 40 (2010), https://jacket2.org. Brian Reed, "'Eden or Ebb of the Sea': Susan Howe's Word Squares and Postlinear Poetics," *Postmodern Culture* 14, no. 2 (January 2004), http://www.pomoculture.org, focuses mainly on Howe's use of grids; Tony Lopez, "Susan Howe's Visual Poetics," *Études Anglaises* 61, no. 2 (2008): 202–14, pays particular attention to a page from "Eikon Basilike" and connects Howe's visual poetics to Pound and Olson. Elisabeth W. Joyce offers an overview of Howe's various visual techniques in *"The Small Space of a Pause": Susan Howe's Poetry and the Spaces Between* (Lewisburg, PA: Bucknell University Press, 2010), 101–27. Chelsea Jennings usefully notes a late-career shift in Howe's visual techniques as she moves toward a "facsimile aesthetic" of type-collages and reproductions of objects; see Jennings, "Susan Howe's Facsimile Aesthetic," *Contemporary Literature* 56, no. 4 (Winter 2015): 660–94.

2. For sustained discussion of Howe's beginnings in the visual arts, see Reed, "'Eden or Ebb of the Sea'"; and Kaplan Page Harris, "Susan Howe's Art and Poetry, 1968–1974," *Contemporary Literature* 47, no. 3 (Fall 2006): 440–71. Both acknowledge the importance of Howe's essay "The End of Art" for understanding the curve of her career.

3. For a companion essay to DuPlessis's, on "the space of the page as an active stage" and connecting Albiach and Howe, see Swensen, "Against the Limits of Language" (630). For white space as active and constitutive matter in Albiach (and Claude Royet-Journaud), with "the page as a stage on which the word-actors execute carefully choregraphed movements" (107), also see Rosmarie Waldrop, *Dissonance* (105–18). In a related essay, Waldrop connects the use of white space by Albiach and Royet-Journaud's generation—Howe's French contemporaries—to the violence and threat of World War II and a postwar sense of "the total crisis of society in our century" (125). Howe herself writes that she "saw signs of culture exploding into murder" in the news photographs through which she experienced World War II. She recalls that first experience with violence in terms that themselves recall her use of the page: thus "the blank skies over Europe" have an analog in Howe's white spaces, and her observation, from the wartime photographs, that "things overlap in space and are hidden" has its analog in her more criss-crossed palimpsestic pages (*Europe* 11, 12).

4. The gendered history of the "blank page" trope is a long one, but one critical *locus classicus* of second-wave feminism is Susan Gubar, "'The Blank Page' and the Issues of Female Creativity," *Writing and Sexual Difference*, ed. Elizabeth Abel (Chicago:

University of Chicago Press, 1982), 73–93. See also Jeremy Gilbert-Rolfe, "Blankness as a Signifier," *Critical Inquiry* 24 (Autumn 1997): 159–75. Book artist Keith Smith reminds us that a blank page may be composed as such (*Text in the Book Format* [Fairport, NY: Sigma Foundation, 1989], 44), and in the first chapter of *No Medium* (Cambridge: Massachusetts Institute of Technology Press, 2013), Craig Dworkin discusses various manifestations of the blank page constructed as such across the literary, visual, and plastic arts. It is worth noting, however, that Howe's work contains very few literally "blank" pages, and even fewer once her serial poems are transferred from small press to trade or university press formats. For a cluster of significant and influential essays on the related questions of the blank page and the female-authored visual page, see Fraser, "The Blank Page: H. D.'s invitation to trust and mistrust language" (53–62); "Line. On the Line. Lining up. Lined with. Between the lines. Bottom Line" (141–60); and "Translating the Unspeakable: Visual Poetics, as Projected through Olson's 'Field' into Current Female Writing Practice" (174–200).

5. Willard Bohn, *The Aesthetics of Visual Poetry 1914–1928* (New York: Cambridge University Press, 1986); Johanna Drucker, *The Visible Word: Experimental Typography and Modern Art, 1909–1923* (Chicago: University of Chicago Press, 1994).

6. George Butterick was the editor of numerous Olson texts, most relevantly *The Maximus Poems* and *The Collected Poems of Charles Olson* (Berkeley: University of California Press, 1983 and 1987, respectively).

7. It may be, as Marjorie Perloff has argued of a visually oriented "poetics of nonlinearity or postlinearity," that "the [visual] transformation that has taken place in verse may well be more generational than it is gendered" (*Poetry* 166), and one could hardly dispute that the page poem is a widespread practice among male and female poets. At the same time, women have often enacted that transformation in gendered directions, as ample examples in anthologies such as Mary Margaret Sloan's *Moving Borders* and Maggie O'Sullivan's *Out of Everywhere* suggest. As if to make a polemical point, O'Sullivan begins *Out of Everywhere* with five female practitioners of the page poem: in order, Howe, Joan Retallack, Tina Darragh, Paula Claire, and Diane Ward. For an overview of "specifically feminist possibilities of a visually-oriented poetics" (Frost 339) in the twentieth century, moving through the categories of modernist predecessors, "Compositions by Field," "Concretism," "The Prismatic Page," the "Performance Page," and "Photo-Text and 'Cinepoetry,'" see Frost 339–58.

8. For an extended meditation on the incandescent materiality of words and letters, relevant to Howe's comment that words "shimmer," see Michel Leiris's 1948 "Alphabet," in *Scratches*, trans. Lydia Davis (Baltimore: Johns Hopkins University Press, 1991), 31–63.

9. Peter Quartermain notes Howe's "deeply ingrained necessity to compose in units of one page," in *Disjunctive Poetics: From Gertrude Stein and Louis Zukofsky to Susan Howe* (New York: Cambridge University Press, 1992), 192—a "necessity" that reprint editions of Howe's sequences unfortunately sometimes undercut in compressing two or more poems onto a page. In contrast, Craig Dworkin argues that "the *line* . . . forms Howe's basic unit of both prosodic and spatial composition." This view rests, however, on the premise that Howe's page poems "arise primarily from the manipulation of lines rather than of individual words or letters" (*Reading* 33–34)—which is often but by no means generally accurate.

On Mallarmé: in a 2005 interview with Jon Thompson, Howe says that by the time she moved from using text in installations to page-based work, but had not yet read Olson (whom she first read in 1968–69), "I already knew Mallarmé's *Un Coup de dés*,

Artaud's writing and drawings, Duchamp's *Notes and Studies for the Large Glass*, writings by John Cage; I was familiar with the work of Concrete Poets, their use of page space and typography" (np)—a body of knowledge evident in "The End of Art" (*Quarry* 203–21). In particular, the typographic version of Duchamp's manuscript notes for *The Bride Stripped Bare by Her Bachelors, Even*, which provides the epigraph for Howe's first book, *Hinge Picture*, exhibits some of the visual features that later became characteristic of her work: deleted but legible words, underlinings, word lists, text at multiple angles, generous use of white space.

10. For another "absent center" that resonates with that of the *Eikon Basilike*, consider the blank pages at the heart of the Puritan pastor Thomas Shepard's notebook, discussed by Howe in her essay "Incloser." Shepard's book contains an abbreviated autobiography in one-half and "more improvisational commentary" (*Birth-mark* 59) in the other, with the two bodies of writing "positioned so that to read one you must turn the other upside down" (60), like a number of Howe's poems. Meanwhile the middle of the notebook is blank: "Eighty-six blank manuscript pages emphasize this rupture in the pious vocabulary of order. The reader reads empty paper" (58). Twice within a few lines Howe repeats "then there is the empty center" (59). Some of Howe's notebooks bear remarkable resemblance to the Shepard manuscript notebook: "There is no title on the binding of the notebook that contains the manuscript. The paper is unlined. There are no margins. There is no front or back. You can open or shut it either way" (*Birth-Mark* 59).

11. For a sustained discussion of the figures of textiles and thread in Howe, see Stephen Collis, *Through Words of Others: Susan Howe and Anarcho-Scholasticism* (Victoria, BC: ELS Editions, 2006), 39–43.

12. All unattributed quotations in this paragraph are from *The Nonconformist's Memorial* (82). "To the Queen of my Heart" can be found in Shelley, *Complete Poetical Works* (674), with the following editorial note: "Printed as Shelley's by Medwin; reprinted by Mrs. Shelley, first edition of 1839, but subsequently withdrawn as of doubtful genuineness." Thus Howe ends the "Eikon Basilike" with an allusion to yet another obscure inauthentic text. My thanks to Jerome McGann for his help in tracking down the "Shelley" poem. For a strong reading of the closing "Eikon Basilike" poems that also emphasizes the image of the thread, see Back (153–62).

13. For one apposite example of this widely proposed applicability of Kristevan theory to late twentieth-century avant-garde poetics, see Fraser, who connects visual experimentation in contemporary women poets with "the very female subjectivity proposed by Julia Kristeva as linking cyclical and monumental time"—"visual apparatus on which to construct formerly inarticulate states of being" (175). See also Kornelia Freitag's reading of Howe through the Kristevan concept of "women's time" (292–97) and, more ambivalently, DuPlessis, *Pink Guitar* (84–88). Contrast, however, Peter Middleton's argument that Kristeva offers "a theory whose definitions of language and rationality are far too narrow" to account for Howe's work: "On Ice: Julia Kristeva, Susan Howe and Avant Garde Poetics," in *Contemporary Poetry Meets Modern Theory*, ed. Antony Easthope and John O. Thompson (Toronto: University of Toronto Press, 1991), 81–95. In the various versions of her extensively reprinted talk "The Rejection of Closure," Lyn Hejinian cites then-contemporary French feminist theory throughout but connects its premises to avant-garde writing generally rather than specifically to women writers and their experiments in visual poetics. "Dear Unconscious scatter syntax," Howe asks in a Lacanian/Kristevan apostrophe in "Articulation of Sound Forms in Time," but the "Visible surface of Discourse" (*Singularities* 36), of "barbarous jargon /

fluent language of fanaticism" (31), in this case maintains itself against the feminized "muffled discourse from distance / mummy thread undertow" (32).

14. The first of these quotations appears in the poem's printing in *Defenestration of Prague* (New York: Kulchur Foundation, 1983), 75, at the bottom right corner of a large (ten-by seven-inch) page, disconnected from all other text on the page. "The Liberties" had first appeared as a 1980 pamphlet from Loon Books in London.

15. While the mastiff is a breed, I would suggest that Howe's "mastif" is culturally coded male. Compare Howe's use of the phrase "mastiff-father" in *My Emily Dickinson* (16).

16. Compare McGann, *Black Riders* (102), for whom Howe specifically breaks down "the law of the margin (left to right reading) and the law of headers and footers (top to bottom reading)."

17. For a book-length extrapolation of Howe's arguments about visual materiality in Dickinson's manuscripts, see Marta L. Werner, *Emily Dickinson's Open Folios: Scenes of Reading, Surfaces of Writing* (Ann Arbor: University of Michigan Press, 1995); and Werner and Jen Bervin, eds., *The Gorgeous Nothings: Emily Dickinson's Envelope Poems* (New York: New Directions, 2013).

18. In a 2003 interview, Howe acknowledges that "I've come full circle on the subject of sewing. Or sewing has come home to me. Dickinson *does* tap into the culture of women where lace making and embroidery were valued skills" and "it is true that many of her best poems concern sewing or thread or detail work—metaphorically." Looking back on her earlier observation in *My Emily Dickinson*, she says "Gilbert and Gubar rightly made the comparison to sewing in their *Madwoman [in the Attic]* chapter on Dickinson but in such a way that they made me want to throw it out." See her interview with Thomas Gardner in his *A Door Ajar: Contemporary Writers and Emily Dickinson* (New York: Oxford UP, 2006), 147–49. Howe has returned to various forms of fabric as synecdoche for the female and feminized in later sequences such as "Fragment of the Wedding Dress of Sarah Pierpont Edwards," "Bed Hangings," and "*Kidnapped*."

## Chapter 10

1. Exceptions include the chapters on Howe in Keller, *Forms of Expansion*; McHale; much of Back (61–106) on *The Liberties*; and Montgomery, especially 1–26.

2. The term "noncanonical" as applied to Mangan admittedly marks my, and Howe's, writing as located within an Anglo-American sense of canonicity or national tradition. In the Irish tradition, Mangan stands larger, taken seriously by writers from Yeats and Joyce to Thomas Kinsella and deemed worthy of a 1996 biography (Ellen Shannon-Mangan, *James Clarence Mangan: A Biography* [Dublin: Irish Academic Press]), a multivolume collection of writings from the Irish Academic Press, and a 2004 *Selected Writings*, ed. Sean Ryder (Dublin: University College Dublin Press) and *Selected Prose*, ed. Jacques Chuto, Peter van de Kamp, and Ellen Shannon-Mangan (Dublin: Irish Academic Press). The young Yeats published two short essays on Mangan in 1887 and 1891 (Thomas Kinsella and W. B. Yeats, *Davis, Mangan, Ferguson?: Tradition and the Irish Writer*, ed. Roger McHugh [Dublin: Dolmen, 1970], 21–27); Kinsella includes a poem in Mangan's voice, "Clarence Mangan," in his 1962 volume *Another September* (Dublin: Dolmen) and devotes a section to him in his historical overview of Irish poetry, *The Dual Tradition: An Essay on Poetry and Politics in Ireland* (Manchester: Carcanet, 1995), where he describes Mangan as having produced, amid much that is "miscellaneous, and often trivial in impulse," "the most important poetry written in Ireland in the nineteenth century until Yeats's *The Rose*" (49). Digital technology has enabled a

number of scanned reprints of Mangan's original texts. In 2009, Cornell University Library issued a digitally scanned reprint of Mangan's 1863 *Poems*, and 2010 brought a reprint of the John Mitchel edition of Mangan's poems (Charleston, SC: Nabu).

3. If Howe associates "dismemberment" with breaking apart authorities, and with an interpretive taking apart of "marginalia," she also associates it with the early traumatic break in her experience of her Irish family caused by the buildup to World War II "in the summer of 1938 . . . when Czechoslovakia was *dismembered* by Hitler, Ribbentrop, Mussolini, Chamberlain, and Daladier, during the Conference and Agreement at Munich. That October we sailed home [from Ireland] on a ship crowded with refugees fleeing various countries in Europe" (*Europe* 9, my emphasis). Howe would have been about sixteen months old at the time of this voyage, so it is hard to tell whether she is writing from memory or a learned narrative. The latter seems much more likely.

Howe presumably also knows Marianne Moore's "Spenser's Ireland," in *New Collected Poems of Marianne Moore*, ed. Heather Cass White (New York: Farrar, Straus and Giroux, 2017), 154–55.

4. For ease of reference, I have supplied pagination for the unpaginated original publication, using the first page of text as page 1.

5. The phrasing echoes the early lines of "Canto II," where Ezra Pound mythologizes the seal as "daughter of Lir" and invokes Homer's poetic "ear, ear for the sea-surge" (*Cantos* 6).

6. The imagery anticipates the "European grid on the forest" that is such a central figure of speech in "Thorow" (*Singularities* 45).

7. Some subsequent references in the sequence to ramparts, castle windows, and battlements may refer to Cashel; the town's defenses on the 358-foot Rock of Cashel date to the fourth century CE. The phrase "the open sea outside" (*Frame Structures* 86), however, suggests that Howe also has other fortifications in mind, since Cashel is an inland town.

8. Howe's working papers for "The Defenestration of Prague" contain numerous passages from *The Faerie Queene* and from Spenser criticism, and early versions of the poem contain more sections featuring Spenser's Florimell and Una than the final version. For exemplary scholarship on and analysis of Howe's use both of *The Faerie Queene* and Spenser's *View of the Present State of Ireland*, see McHale, especially 229–33. Spenser's *View* could be said to anticipate Arnold's relationship to the "provinces" discussed later in this chapter. As McHale puts it, Spenser "exposed what he regarded as the failures of the Elizabethan colonial regime in Ireland, and advocated a more aggressive policy aimed at reducing the country to order" (229). But as she does with Arnold's texts, Howe splinters the *View* via citations from the variorum edition, revealing that "the very text in which Spenser advocates the imposition of order is itself subject to the textual vagaries of manuscript transmission" (McHale 231).

9. Complications within the categories "Anglo-Irish" and "Anglo-Irish literature" are well discussed by Julian Moynahan, *Anglo-Irish: The Literary Imagination in a Hyphenated Culture* (Princeton, NJ: Princeton University Press, 1995).

10. Howe also uses a phrase from Arnold's "On Translating Homer: Last Words": "Subject of the idea (to quote from *The Excursion*)." The vertical placement of this phrase anticipates that of Arnold's other commentary on Homer and his classic style (*Nonconformist's Memorial* 98); it puts the pastoral monologues of Wordsworth's *Excursion* at cross-purposes with "Middle-class Education"; and it prefigures the pun on "subjects" (as subjectivities and as regulated citizens) with which Howe ends the sequence.

11. Friedrich Schiller's poem "The Veiled Statue at Sais" (also translated as "The Veiled Image at Sais") is most easily available in the German original ("Das verschleierte Bild zu Sais") at https://de.wikisource.org. For an English translation by Edward Bulwer-Lytton, a contemporary of Mangan's, see https://archive.org.

12. Compare Howe's observation that Cotton Mather's *Magnalia Christi Americana* "could be called 'Marginalia' *Christi Americana*" (*Birth-mark* 30).

## Chapter 11

1. The alternative term "essay-poem" seems inadequate because Andrews's work in a hybrid critical prose poem mode lacks the surface features of poetry—most notably, lineation—that have characterized that subgenre, even in manifestations of it that treat the line self-consciously as a visual and mathematical convention. Andrews's prose remains generally undiscussed in its own right, though see Brian Kim Stefans's substantial review of *Paradise and Method*. While Stefans argues that "genre issues . . . are not [Andrews's] concern," his qualifier is key: "apart from the question of the border between polemic and poem" ("Review").

2. See "Code Words" (*Paradise and Method* 190–92), Andrews's essay on Barthes's *Image-Music-Text*. It is relevant to recall that Davidson's *Analogy of the Ion*, in its mix of short poetic lines, Socratic dialogue, continuous prose, and single sentences rendered as long, Whitmanesque, end-stopped lines, itself meditates on genre boundaries. On the relationship between poetry and other discourse, at one point, Davidson's Socrates remarks (in character), "To propose that poetry involves knowledge is rank folly and is why poets should leave theory to those with academic positions or at least a federal grant" (18).

3. Two exceptions to this pattern occur. Sections 3 and 7 (from a total of 12) each consists of a single Andrews sentence: "Meaning means the elimination of identity" and "Language institutionalized theft" (*Paradise and Method* 209, 211).

4. Bernstein's "Artifice of Absorption" was first published as an issue of *Paper Air* magazine (4, no.1 [1987]) and then reprinted as a chapter of his essay collection *A Poetics* (Cambridge: Harvard University Press, 1992). In the final issue of *Paper Air*, (4, no. 3 [1990]), it is indexed both under "Poetry and Prose" and "Essays, Reviews and Commentary." Perelman's "The Marginalization of Poetry," first delivered as a talk at an academic conference, appears as the second poem in his *Virtual Reality* (New York: Roof, 1993) and as the title/lead essay in his critical book *The Marginalization of Poetry: Language Writing and Literary History* (Princeton: Princeton University Press, 1996). I discuss the different iterations and sites of Perelman's essay-poem "Guide to Homage to Sextus Propertius" (including its changing title) in "'Time to Translate Modernism into a Contemporary Idiom': Pedagogy, Poetics, and Bob Perelman's Pound," *Shofar: An Interdisciplinary Journal of Jewish Studies* 27, no. 3 (2009): 16–29. Most recently, the poem, now titled "Homage to Pound's 'Propertius,'" appears in Perelman, *Modernism* (47–52).

5. Bob Perelman observes "there is a real question as to how reified Andrews's own dismissal of conventional literature is" (*Marginalization* 97).

6. Brian McHale comments on Andrews "contextualizing and renarrativizing material from his own poetry, either by collaging it with other poetic material (his own or other poets'), or by weaving it into the fabric of an expository-prose argument," "integrating it in an enveloping expository discourse" (198–99). However, McHale's claim that this technique represents a "determinate framing" (199) of this material is complicated by his observation—consistent with my argument here—that Andrews "resolves

the conflict of interest . . . between literary and extraliterary discourse . . . by the simple expedient of devaluing literary discourse across the board" (183).

7. As for passing comments on the visual components of Andrews's work, DuPlessis notes in Andrews the "drift, as there is in all writing which faces the materiality of the signifier, to visual texts and to musical texts. Some of the poems are even well served by being seen as grids, along the lines of minimalist visual canvases" ("Surface Tension" 49). For John Taggart, "the pages of *Film Noir* have a specifically Mondrian look . . . about them," and "the visual design of the page is important beyond usual concern for layout appearance" as part of Andrews's effort "to have the reader come to a heightened experience of language" (*Songs* 67). Ron Silliman reviews the page space of *Wobbling* as something "which Andrews explores (exploits) through design, at moments to the point of seeming painterly (even the prose is double-spaced so as to appear striped)" ("[Review]" 158). In the 1999 *Aerial* special issue on Andrews, a number of responses match his own typographical and spatial experimentation in various ways: see Lang; Brown; Debrot; Retallack, "Con Verse"; Mark Wallace, "From BOYS."

8. For a related perspective on the conceptualism-materiality-Language writing nexus, see Gerald Bruns: "Poetry, or at least some modern and contemporary versions of it, is a species of conceptual art, meaning that in order to understand or even experience a piece of language (or a sound or a typographical arrangement on a page) as a poem at all, one has to be able to follow a line of thinking . . . that argues in favor of the text or event in question in spite of (or, more likely, because of) its failure to live up to the criteria or degrees of familiarity that usually help us to pick out things as poems" (*Material* 103). See also Barrett Watten's brief but importantly prescient discussion of overlaps between conceptual art and Language writing, in which he draws an analogy between "Robert Morris's card file or Joseph Kosuth's billboards using *Roget's Thesaurus*" and "the work of a number of poets now working—Ron Silliman, Bruce Andrews, and myself particularly" (*Total Syntax* 212). While arguing—in a firmly stated position with clear implications for the present moment—that "there can be no 'conceptual' poetry" (217), Watten goes on to suggest, with reference to Silliman's *Ketjak*, that "many of the sentences in the text could have analogues in the kinds of art propositions contained in [Lucy Lippard's] *Six Years* [: *The Dematerialization of the Art Object*]" (221).

9. Compare Steve McCaffery's remark from an influential early essay, "The Death of the Subject," that "the cipheral [or graphic] text involves a replacement in readerly function from a reading of words to an experiencing of graphemes, for conventional reading involves the use of referential vectors and it is such vectors that are here removed" (np). Reissued in a 1980 supplement to *L=A=N=G=U=A=G=E*, the essay first appeared in *Open Letter* 3 no. 7 (Summer 1977): 61–77. McCaffery changes the phrasing and title (to "Diminished Reference and the Model Reader") but preserves the point when he reprints a significantly revised version in *North of Intention* (13–29).

10. *0 to 9* is most easily available in the Ugly Duckling Presse reprint (2006). In a 1999 interview, Andrews says that as a beginning writer looking around for kindred spirits "extending radical modernist traditions," "I remember getting ahold of *0 to 9*" (qtd. in Kane 197). "I sent stuff to editor Acconci right when *0 to 9* ended" (198), perhaps just too late, since the work never appeared in the magazine.

11. "Language-based sculptor" is Roberta Smith's phrase from her review of the Whitney Museum's 2007 Weiner retrospective, "The Well-Shaped Phrase as Art," *New York Times*, November 16, 2007.

12. Only one of these pieces, "The Politics of Scoring," is reprinted in *Paradise and Method* (176–77). The others appeared as follows: "Layout," *L=A=N=G=U=A=G=E*

3 (June 1978): np; "Line Sites," *L=A=N=G=U=A=G=E* 4 (August 1978): np; "And for Anything That I Could Call My Own Thinking," *L=A=N=G=U=A=G=E* 13 (December 1980): np; "Articles," *L=A=N=G,=U=A=G=E* 3 (June 1978): np; "Articles, Part Two," *L=A=N=G=U=A=G=E* 4 (August 1978): np.

13. Both periodicals are most easily available on the Eclipse Archive website: for *L=A=N=G=U=A=G=E*, http://eclipsearchive.org, and for *Toothpick*, http://eclipsearchive.org. For a hard copy reprint of *L=A=N=G=U=A=G=E*, see *Bruce Andrews and Charles Bernstein's L=A=N=G=U=A=G=E: The Complete Facsimile*, ed. Matthew Hofer and Michael Golston (Albuquerque: University of New Mexico Press, 2020). Craig Dworkin writes of *Toothpick* that Andrews "edited [it] on the model of *0 to 9*" ("Delay" xviii n16), as well as including Acconci's work, and that beyond the example of *0 to 9*, "in the early 1970s, a few of Acconci's published poems" (xvi) were a significant spur to Andrews's early work. While Acconci describes his view of the page partly in terms derived from Olson and Duncan ("my involvement with poetry was with movement on a page, the page as a field for action"), he also stresses his "use of the page as a model space, a performance area in miniature or abstract form," "a system of flows and stopping places," and turns to the language of Fluxus: "Use this page as the start of an event that keeps going, off the page; use the page to fix the boundaries of an event, or a series of events, that take place in outside space" (4). For Acconci's poems, see *Language to Cover a Page: The Early Writings of Vito Acconci*, ed. Dworkin (Cambridge: Massachusetts Institute of Technology Press, 2006).

14. Like Robert Grenier's "JOE JOE" in *Sentences*, the card raises the question of whether the two words, "boom boom," are the "same"—a trope that by now has its own minitradition in American innovative writing, from Stein's distinction between repetition and insistence to Bob Perelman's play on the beginning of "The Waste Land": "I learned // that there are two *l*'s in / *cruellest*, neither one the same" (*Virtual Reality* 55).

15. William Howe points out how a number of the individual cards reflect on their own materiality: the "WHITE PULP" from which the cards are made, their "SHEET NESS," the "STIFF" quality of "EACH" (np).

16. The previously discussed essays on Susan Howe, "Suture—and Absence of the Social" and "Beyond Suture," in *Paradise and Method* (227–34) involve a "nod toward the treatments of 'suture' in film studies and post-structuralist political theory" (227). The term also forms part of Andrews's analytical framework for the essays on Michael Davidson (219–26) and Barrett Watten (235–45).

17. On reading the "unreadable," see Dworkin, *Reading the Illegible*. Andrews pays renewed attention to the act of reading in his 2007 essay "Reading Notes" (197–207).

18. Elsewhere Drucker is careful to separate her use of the term "trace" from its Derridean associations: "The concept of *écriture*, of writing as trace . . . does not contain a condition for the apprehension of materiality" (*Visible Word* 39). Steve McCaffery cites this distinction and goes on to develop a useful, materially centered minihistory of nonnormative typographies and alternative writing systems in his essay "Between Verbi Voco and Visual, Some Precursors of Grammatology" (*Prior to Meaning* 105–21).

19. See UBU, Contemporary, Bruce Andrews, "Love Song No 38," December 12, 2021, http://www.ubu.com.

20. See McCaffery, *Seven Pages Missing* (15–20) for selections from *Transitions to the Beast*. The full "post-semiotic" collection *Transitions* appeared as an issue of the Canadian little magazine *grOnk*, series 6, 2–3 (1970), and is available as a pdf at Loriemersondotnet, Archives, June 2012, https://loriemersondotnet.files.wordpress.com.

21. Compare Taggart's reservations about what he sees as the "small range of pos-

sibility" available in a visual writing even of such "bravery and sophistication" as Andrews's: "It can force or encourage a more conscious experience of language; it can produce varieties of irony in the process. It is not clear that it can do anything else" (*Song* 68–69).

22. Another underdiscussed aspect of Andrews's work is precisely this element of self-questioning or self-critique. See, as one example among many, the beginning of "Confidence Trick," which ventriloquizes a view of his work as merely trendy disjunctiveness in the imperative to "recite catatonia chic" and which sets its antiauthoritarianism ("Intentionally leaderless") next to an aggressively skeptical question about notions of community or network: "how s your ambient buddy system?" (*Give Em Enough Rope* 142).

23. *Edge* is most readily available at Eclipse, Complete Title List, http://eclipsearchive.org. In editing his issue of *Toothpick, Lisbon, and the Orcas Islands*, Andrews included handwritten work by Barbara Baracks, Philip Corner, Bern Porter, and Jim Rosenberg, and his own transcription of notes by Clark Coolidge, "(editor's excerpts from) NOTES ON C, W & Z." In the later mock sonnet sequence "Verbal Sallies," written over fourteen days in 1988 and framed as letters to the loved one (the title page features "dear Sally" and "love, Bruce" at its top left and bottom right corners), Andrews plays on the paradoxes produced by the intimacy of the handwritten letter-poem (with all possible puns on "letter" intended, I suspect) as published social critique. Originally published in *Hot Bird Mfg* 1, no. 3 (November 1990), it is reprinted in *Designated Heartbeat* (Cambridge: Salt, 2006) in typeset form, so that much of the point of the handwritten original is lost.

In the conceptualist context, compare On Kawara's stencil-like but actually hand-drawn and hand-painted date paintings.

24. At the same time, *Divestiture—E* illustrates some of Andrews's reservations about conceptual art and minimalism: "Something overwhelmingly *New York*ish about the 'tone' of conceptual art—very stylized, yet artificial, grim, obsessive" (np).

25. The grid made of letters, letter-clusters, words, or parts of words is a form running through much of Andrews's early work. See *BothBoth*; in *Love Songs*, see "No 114."

26. Gilbert Adair also captures nicely how Andrews uses typography to elicit competing modes of attention: "That every word in 'Swaps Ego' begins with a capital and is set off by two spaces on either side makes a happily fluent reading impossible; but to stop and ponder each word-unit in the 40 pages is, of course, to peter out in mystified exhaustion and complete loss of the rhythm/sense-shifts" (108). McCaffery frames what he too calls the "iconicity" of Andrews's early work more positively than Inman in praising the "strong object quality" of Andrews's "lettristic clusters" and their function "as pure space-time arrestments" ("Death of the Subject" np).

27. Andrews and Cobbing's use of the term "seriality" here differs significantly, I take it, from my own use of it throughout this project.

28. See Mallarmé, *Mallarmé in Prose* 125–33.

29. Having chosen what I still think is a fitting quotation, I discovered that McCaffery uses it to conclude his essay "Between Verbi Voco and Visual." So much for originality, once again.

## Chapter 12

1. I have chosen to key citations from *Spring and All* and *Kora in Hell* to the reprinting of those texts in *Imaginations* (New York: New Directions, 1970) as that is

the edition in which many of the writers discussed in this chapter encountered them in their complete (or completely incomplete) versions.

2. Regarding the increasingly vague term "experimental," Williams himself disavowed it in favor of "pure": "It is a mistake to speak of experimental writing. The distinction is not deep enough. There is pure writing and writing which is made to be the horse of anyone who has a burden to carry" (*Embodiment* 117), writing as an instrumental vehicle for subject matter.

3. Critics have discussed the idea of the "two Williamses" from various perspectives relevant to my argument here. As it is for Lazer, for John Lowney "the question of Williams's legacy . . . is a question of *which* Williams should be remembered" (189), and that question drives his overview of Williams's importance for a range of Objectivist and post-Objectivist poetries. Donald Wellman connects the "complex realism" and "hybrid forms" (297, 302) of *Spring and All* to the strain of material textuality within postmodernism, and specifically to Silliman's *What,* but flatly designates approaches that emphasize a more photographic realism as "modes of misreading" (301). Both Lisa Steinman and Burton Hatlen take the view, however, that the same Williams work, or even the same poem, can readily validate these different "misreadings." Steinman argues "that Williams's diverse *legacies* are not simply a matter of different contemporary poets looking to Williams's different stylistic experiments" but that "even a single Williams poem or style can authorize multiple different contemporary practices" (37). Hatlen proposes "two—*at least* two—Williamses: the creator of avant-garde, 'open,' radically experimental texts, and the maker of shapely, immensely evocative lyrics," and asserts that "both these Williamses are present within *Spring and All*" ("Openness and Closure" 27). For Michael Golston, Williams's twin legacy can be traced back to his bifurcated view of measure: a linguistic concept of measure that leads to a speech-based poetics and eventually "a verse of more or less transparent reportage," and an "allegorical" concept of measure, leading to a constructivist poetics that holds "measure as an allegorical structure for whatever object is under scrutiny" (252, 258). Using this second concept of measure, Golston argues that "[Clark] Coolidge's work is a crucial hinge between Williams' practice of the first half of the century and the experimental poetry of the second" (262); he develops an "allegorical" reading of Coolidge in greater detail in his essay "At Clark Coolidge: Allegory and the Early Works," *American Literary History* 13, no. 2 (Summer 2001): 294–316.

4. Linda Kinnahan, *Poetics of the Feminine: Authority and Tradition in William Carlos Williams, Mina Loy, Denise Levertov, and Kathleen Fraser* (New York: Cambridge University Press, 1994); John Lowney, *The American Avant-garde Tradition: William Carlos Williams, Postmodern Poetry, and the Politics of Cultural Memory* (Lewisburg, PA: Bucknell University Press, 1997). Lowney moves toward a general overview of Williams in relation to post–New American poetries (among others), however, in his later essay "Williams: The New Poetries." For more targeted discussions, see the two chapters in *The Legacy of William Carlos Williams: Points of Contact,* ed. Ian Copestake (Newcastle: Cambridge Scholars, 2007), by David Arnold, "Williams without Words: A Dialogue with Michael Palmer," 164–80, and Robert Stanton, "Close to Williams's House: Williams to Armantrout via Niedecker," 181–98.

5. Barrett Watten is right to argue that "the [1970] pirate edition [of *Spring and All*] had an immediate effect of canonical revision" (*Questions* 255n18) in that the paperback *Imaginations,* containing *Spring and All,* did not become available to fiscally challenged young poets until 1971, one year after the hardcover *Imaginations.*

6. While it does not affect Silliman's larger point, regarding his term "composed" Bruce Holsapple argues for late 1916/early 1917–September 1918 as the composition dates for *Kora in Hell*, published as a book in 1920 but with sections appearing earlier in *The Little Review* (81–82): see Holsapple, "Williams on Form: *Kora in Hell*," *Sagetrieb* 18, nos. 2–3 (Fall–Winter 1999): 79–126. As Silliman acknowledges, the writers associated with the New American poetry would mostly not have had access to the texts reprinted in *Imaginations*, except perhaps for the 1957 City Lights edition of *Kora* (by which time their poetics were largely formed).

7. Watten and Grenier coedited the first three issues of the magazine; Watten edited the subsequent issues.

8. The allusion is to Williams's widely cited aphorism that "all sonnets say the same thing of no importance" (*Selected Essays* 257).

9. Before its appearance as the prefatory poem in Silliman's anthology, "In the American Tree" was published in Robinson's *Down and Back* (Berkeley: The Figures, 1978). For a discussion of the poem, see Watten, *Total Syntax* (62–64). Watten concludes with the key remark that "distance, rather than absorption, is the intended effect" (64).

10. In "I Wanted to Write Sentences" (a play on Williams's *I Wanted to Write a Poem*), Silliman notes "the experimental prose of Willliam Carlos Williams" (13) as part of the reading that helped him break through the impasse of projectivist poetics, with its breath- and speech-based line, into his first work with the new sentence in *Ketjak*.

11. Compare Perelman's summary in a 2007 essay: "[Williams] has become an honored predecessor for an uncomfortably wide range of contemporary poets. Heterogeneous in itself, his work has had unmistakable influence on a contradictory set of heirs, leading to the polemical plainness of Levine and Rich as much as to O'Hara's erotic wit, Ginsberg's prophetic politics, and the textual activism of Language writing. *Just about any poem not in regular meter could claim Williams as a precursor*" ("Doctor Williams's Position" 74, my emphasis).

12. For an earlier, much briefer version of Silliman's argument, see his column "The Williams Influence," with its claim that "the question 'Do you read Williams?' so fundamental to the '50s has been supplanted with 'Which is the Williams you think you read?'" ("Williams Influence" 42).

13. In *The Grand Piano* Part 4, Silliman writes "To this day, *Spring & All* is the single act of critical writing that inspires me most," "show[ing] Williams to be a more accomplished theoretician than Ezra Pound" ("IX" 128).

14. Donald Wellman observes that "in opposition to the ringing cry of 'I am a poet' . . . Silliman weakly submits 'I'm not a poet' (*What* 49), a sardonic near-quotation" (315). It is possible, however, especially given Silliman's long-term scrutiny of the categories "poet" and "poetry," to read these words more in the spirit of David Antin's strong demurral: "'If robert lowell is a poet i dont want to be a poet if robert frost was a poet i dont want to be a poet if socrates was a poet ill consider it'" (1).

15. In this paragraph, I am quoting and paraphrasing Silliman's remarks from an October 12, 2000, reading and talk that focused on his relationship to Williams's work (University of Pennsylvania, Penn Sound, Authors, Silliman, https://www.upenn.edu). Earlier that afternoon, he had delivered a conference talk on *The Desert Music* and Williams at midcentury, later published as "The Desert Modernism," *Electronic Poetry Review* 4 (October 2002), http://www.epoetry.org. Regarding the "I": for a valuable discussion of how Silliman's (sometimes autobiographical) use of the first person coexists with "indeterminacy of agent and referent" and "obsessive attention to particular

'realistic' detail," see Perloff, *Differentials* (129–54), 138. For an example of autobiographical commentary within Silliman's own canon, see *Under Albany* (Cambridge, UK: Salt, 2004).

16. In "Z-sited Path" Silliman cites this phrase to illustrate the "identification of method with content" that constitutes Williams's oppositionality, glossing it through what became a standard defense of early Language writing's social formalism: "Opposition to the horrors of daily life in the twentieth century, whether or not these are equated with any given social and economic system, is expressed through opposition to the normative or inherited practices of that literature which embodies the status quo" (*New Sentence* 132). For the coinage "social formalism," see Barrett Watten, "Social Formalism: Zukofsky, Andrews, and Habitus in Contemporary Poetry," *North Dakota Quarterly* 55 (1987): 365–82.

17. For instance, "ras / pberries" (*Crow* 21), which uses the line break to draw attention to the silent "p" and to defamiliarize the word momentarily. Compare Williams's breaking of words across lines to draw attention to their component parts, most famously with "wheel / barrow" and "rain / water" in "The Red Wheelbarrow." The use of double and triple repetition in *Crow* may also be traceable to Williams's use of that trope in *Spring and All* (reissued the year before *Crow*'s publication)—in "I: clean / clean / clean" or "Not I // beds, beds, beds" (*Imaginations* 113, 114.) I am not sure what to make of the striking fact that both these repetitions occur in juxtaposition with the first-person pronoun.

18. On Russian Formalism's presence within Language poetics, see, for instance, Watten's essay "Russian Formalism and the Present" (*Total Syntax* 1–30) and the omnipresence of the movement's foundational concepts and theorists in Lyn Hejinian's *The Language of Inquiry*. Using as an epigraph the first stanza of Watten's *Progress*, Hejinian contributed a cotranslation of the beginning of Shklovsky's memoir "Once Upon a Time" to the 1995 special *Aerial* issue on Watten, remarking that "Watten's early and prominent interest in Shklovsky's writings had a major impact on the character of literary work in our community"; see Hejinian, "Introduction," 73. Watten and Hejinian begin the first issue of their influential *Poetics Journal* with Shklovsky's "Plotless Literature."

19. *Progress* detourns both Williams and his readers. It begins "Relax, / stand at attention, and. / Purple snake stands out on / Porcelain tiles. The idea / *Is* the thing. Skewed by design. . . ." (1), and the closing pages vary Grenier's influential adaptation of Williams: "Even all speeches say the same / Begins with, / *hate I* speech" (109). Watten's own "To Elsie" appears in *Bad History* (Berkeley, CA: Atelos, 1998), 35–37. For more recent examples of Watten's ongoing engagement with Williams, see his work-in-progress "Zone," a procedurally based re-reading-in-poetry of Williams's "immanent meditation on the relation of poetics to democracy" in *Paterson*: "What results is a work of transcoding seen as present politics—granting the intensity and limits of previous work, but reinterpreting them within a horizon that it could not anticipate" ("Note to *Zone*"). In a different register, see his critical defense of Williams as a "more philosophically profound poet" than Stevens for his capacity to connect "a poetics of material life" to capaciously (including politically) defined questions of "value" ("Poetics" 85).

20. It seems entirely possible that Williams's worrying over the problem of narrative "progress" in *The Great American Novel* partly underlies Watten's book-length poem by that title.

21. Watten proposes *Kora in Hell* as one model for the "'prosoid'" forms of "Smith-

sonian Depositions": "an extended, dense, lyric prose form" (*Total Syntax* 98). The baby Robert Smithson was actually delivered by Dr. Williams.

22. Commenting on this same passage, Michael Golston draws an analogy between the Cubist "designs" that "shatter[ed]" "the tyranny of the image" and Williams's variable measure as parallel examples of "an allegorical medium" in which form itself signifies, anticipating a later "disposition in American writing radically different from anything that has gone before" (261–62).

23. Compare Watten's analysis of *Spring and All* as a "hybrid object" staging "a primal scene of the modernist poet/critic" in its "dissociation of the poetry/prose dyad" and its anticipation of "Language writing's elision of the poetry/prose divide as 'writing'" (*Questions* 208–10). Watten enacts this dissociation in the form of his own book chapter, itself a hybrid in its sustained self-exegesis, its violation of academic norms of self-reference.

24. The title of the poem in the table of contents of *Electronic Poetry Review* is "Between Minsk and Pinsk." The title on the (digital) page is the ungrammatical, but more interesting, "Between Minsk to Pinsk." Williams is a crucial presence throughout Perelman's *Modernism the Morning After*, where one chapter begins explicitly, "Williams has remained a foundational poet for me" (156). For one more recent example of Perelman working in this Williams-influenced hybrid mode, see "Copying Whitman" (*Modernism* 24–31). He also returns to Williams in the essay "Doctor Williams's Position, Updated."

25. Though plausibility is hardly an issue in this text, the ventriloquizing of O'Hara on Williams gains a certain amount of it when we remember O'Hara's comment that "only Whitman and Crane and Williams, of the American poets, are better than the movies" (*Collected Poems* 498).

26. For Perelman's critical commentary not on *Kora* per se but on disjunct prose in Stendhal, Michael Gottlieb, and Clark Coolidge, see his essay "Plotless Prose," *Poetics Journal* 1 (January 1982): 25–34 (echoing the title of the essay that precedes it, Shklovsky's "Plotless Literature"). It is worth noticing that Williams's genre-bending improvisations do not get discussed as prose poems in two major studies of the genre, Jonathan Monroe's *A Poverty of Objects: The Prose Poem and the Politics of Genre* (Ithaca, NY: Cornell University Press, 1987), and Michel Delville's *The American Prose Poem: Poetic Form and the Boundaries of Genre* (Gainesville: University Press of Florida, 1998). Nor are they collected in the 1986 revised edition of his *Collected Poems, vol. 1, 1909–1939*.

27. Perelman's essay "Doctor Williams's Position" is an extended meditation on the implications of the well-known Williams passage cited here.

28. DuPlessis writes of her graduate work, "During my Columbia PhD oral examination in—was it 1966—I spoke about Williams's *Spring and All*, a work no one (I ever knew) except me had read in toto, written by a poet almost totally discounted" (*Blue Studios* 219).

29. These statements occur in *Imaginations* (120).

30. Regarding "a good form to be in a hurry in," compare Notley's quoting of Ted Berrigan's remark that Williams "helped you [Notley] to be as fast as you are" (*Doctor Williams' Heiresses* np). Elsewhere in the letter that Notley cites, Mayer writes "I associate ["The Red Wheelbarrow"] with all my ideas and instigations and inspirations to write poetry"—"from Williams I could deduct that the wonderful capacity for the world to exist without an I was good for me."

31. Email to the author, December 6, 2000. Quoted with permission.

32. Perelman summarizes the text, the context, and the complexities of that context

usefully: "Though the talk is rarely explicit about these groups, *Heiresses* now reads as an articulation of a fundamental opposition between a poetics foregrounding the poet writing in real time versus writing that foregrounds textuality. The boundary between the second-generation New York School and the Language scene was far from ironclad and many crossover figures could be cited. Nevertheless, in those days it was an easily felt difference" (*Modernism* 173). Notley's emphasis on various forms of "poetic authenticity was an antithetical gesture to some of the practices of the Language scene. Williams was as a crucial figure for Language writers as for Notley, but the admiration was for a more textual poet" (179). In Perelman's view, however, what may have seemed like a stable distinction in 1980, between two kinds of post–New American reading of Williams—"Notley's insistence on locating poetic history in her body" as against writing "where the transpersonal social composition of language was foregrounded" (180)—later seems much less so. As literary history post-1980 has evolved, "to contrast Notley's embodied poetics with the social textuality of Language writing has become a blurred shorthand. There are many examples of foregrounded language or foregrounded embodiment on either side. . . . Without the example of Williams there would have been neither Language writing nor the second-generation New York School" (182–83). The "blurred shorthand" retains its explanatory and descriptive relevance for the 1980 moment, however. For Perelman's full treatment of Notley's talk and related work, see the chapter "Alice Notley and Poetic Inheritance" in his *Modernism* (171–83).

33. Notley sandwiches these observations around an early-career rejection of any feminist recovery project: "I thought we didn't need to read women—I mean find the hidden in the woodwork ones—so much as find the poems among whatever sex that made you feel free to say whatever you liked" (*Doctor Williams' Heiresses*). Years later, however, she acknowledges that a central part of her "lifelong project, as it seems today, August 3, 2001, has been . . . to be a woman poet taking up as much literary space as any male poet" (*Coming After* vi). For a valuable reading of the gender positionings in Notley's Williams talk in relation to her later work, specifically *The Descent of Alette*, see Julia Bloch, "Alice Notley's Descent: Modernist Genealogies and Gendered Literary Inheritance," *Journal of Modern Literature* 35, no. 3 (Spring 2012): 1–24.

34. For Notley's own comments on the poem, see *Coming After* (161–63).

35. Armantrout discusses this poem in *Collected Prose* (58–59); it appears in her *Made to Seem* (Los Angeles: Sun and Moon, 1995), 13–14.

36. Since internal evidence in *True* seems to date this gift around 1959–60, the anthology in question was probably Untermeyer's midcentury edition (1950), which contained eighteen Williams poems. Williams has two early poems called "Metric Figure." "Metric Figure (There is a bird in the poplars—)" is the one that appears in the Untermeyer anthology. The other "Metric Figure," however, with its internally contradictory central image of "veils of clarity" (Williams, *Collected Poems* 1:51), has equal resonance for Armantrout's work (including the title of her 2001 volume *Veil: New and Selected Poems*)—though see chapter 9 for Armantrout's locating of that title in her reading of Dickinson.

37. See the end of chapter 9 for my comments on this poem.

38. In "The Descent of Winter," written in 1927 as Williams returned across the Atlantic from Europe, the "oceanic" becomes a metaphor for his disillusionment with his own writing: "There are no perfect waves— / Your writings are a sea / full of misspellings and / faulty sentences. . . . This is the sadness of the sea— / waves like words, all broken— / a sameness of lifting and falling mood" (*Imaginations* 235).

39. Such are the vagaries of poetic transmission, one could speculate that Denise Levertov, with whom Armantrout studied at Berkeley and who was no friend of what eventually became Language writing, may also have been important in fostering an interest in Williams.

40. "Literature is the social organization of writing" (*New Sentence* 129). See also Silliman's remark that "the process of public canonization, that which socially converts the broad horizon of writing into the simplified and hierarchic topography of Literature, capital L, is a disease" ("Canons" 152).

## Chapter 13

1. As one example among many possible, see Lennon: "Poets and visual artists working from a tradition of typographic experimentation that reaches back to futurism and Dada, and includes twentieth-century visual and Concrete poetry, are using networked, heterogenetic writing spaces to create and distribute a new electronic visual poetry" (64). For histories of digital poetics, see Loss Pequeño Glazier, *Digital Poetics: The Making of E-Poetries* (Tuscaloosa: University of Alabama Press, 2002); C. T. Funkhouser, *Prehistoric Digital Poetry: An Archaeology of Forms, 1959–1995* (Tuscaloosa: University of Alabama Press, 2007); Lori Emerson, *Reading Writing Interfaces: From the Digital to the Bookbound* (Minneapolis: University of Minnesota Press, 2014). For a recent book-length treatment of work and writers at the cusp of old and new media, anticipating or resisting that "convergence" (to use Henry Jenkins's term), see Daniel Morris, *Not Born Digital: Poetics, Print Literacy, New Media* (New York: Bloomsbury, 2016).

2. For a useful overview of debates around the term in new media studies, see Bill Brown's chapter on "materiality" in *Critical Terms for Media Studies*, ed. W. J. T. Mitchell and Mark B. N. Hansen (Chicago: University of Chicago Press, 2010), 49–63.

3. On "transparency," see also Lennon: "As the new writing technology of the computer nears ubiquity in the developed West, the task of an electronic poetics will be to operate on, to alter, the computer's instrumental teleology—its design for informational transparency and functionality—as other poetics have resisted the transparencies of discourse and media in their time" (77). For Bernstein on the antiabsorptive, see his verse essay "Artifice of Absorption," *A Poetics* (Cambridge, MA: Harvard University Press, 1992), 9–89.

4. My term "transitional materialities" has a family relationship to what Jessica Pressman calls "digital modernism": electronic works that "are text based, aesthetically difficult, and ambivalent in their relationship to mass media and popular culture" (2). Pressman defines "modernism" as "a strategy of innovation that employs the media of its time to reform and refashion older literary practices in ways that produce new art" (3–4)—making it new as media archaeology.

5. Subsequent to the drafting of this chapter, the full online publication of *Carnival* on the Coach House Books website that I describe in what follows has become unavailable. A partial version remains available at Penn Sound, https://www.writing.upenn.edu. According to McCaffery, a new digital version of *Carnival* is currently under construction, to be issued from London's Veer Books (email to the author, November 30, 2020). A full version of *Carnival*'s Panel 1 assembled can be found at Penn Sound, https://www.writing.upenn.edu. This image does not provide the panoptic view of the whole that the "map" of fig. 13.1 does but provides a much higher level of close-up detail and the option for moving around in the assembled whole.

6. Recordings of McCaffery performing some of the *Carnival* panels are available at University of Pennsylvania, Penn Sound, http://writing.upenn.edu.

7. Access Stefans's work online at Arras Publications, http://www.arras.net, https://ie10.ieonchrome.com.

8. The 2001 reprint edition of Ron Silliman's germinal anthology of Language writing, *In the American Tree*, features two of Grenier's drawing poems on the cover, "hello / to you," the first two pages of his small handwritten and digitally circulated book GREETING—a welcoming gesture, and implicitly a retrospective reading of Language writing as anticipating the digital revolution.

9. For a useful discussion of the "line" (poetic, prosodic, visual) in Grenier, see Ondrea E. Ackerman, "Wandering Lines: Robert Grenier's Drawing Poems," *Journal of Modern Literature* 36, no. 4 (Summer 2013): 133–53. See also, more briefly, Leslie Scalapino: "Robert Grenier's drawn superimpositions of a drawn phrase in one color on another phrase in some other color (so it's only its visual being) are the actual horizon line on the edge/meaning of the written poetic-line. Which may not 'exist' itself in the writing (line breaks of poems not existing, where there's only the physical line of drawing). // Nature has no line either" ( *Front Matter* 57).

10. See Charles Olson, *Selected Writings of Charles Olson*, edited by Robert Creeley (New York: New Directions, 1966), 13–14.

11. Other presentations on a larger scale than the limited edition include a 2004 exhibit at the Marianne Boesky Gallery in New York; the sixty-four prints exhibited at New York's Greene Naftali Gallery (both at University of Pennsylvania, Electronic Poetry Center, Authors, Robert Grenier, Notice of Marianne Boesky September 2004 Collection, and 64 / Robert Grenier Drawing Poem Prints from Greene Naftali Gallery in New York, http://writing.upenn.edu); seventy-one images made available for a 2009 University of Pennsylvania talk (http://www.whalecloth.org); and the 2013 exhibit at Brooklyn's Southfirst Gallery, "Language Objects: Letters in Space, 1970–2013" (University of Pennsylvania, Electronic Poetry Center, Authors, Robert Grenier, Southfirst Galley, NY, (2013), http://writing.upenn.edu). In a 2011 essay, Stephen Ratcliffe asserts that between 1989 and 2011 Grenier "completed some 130-plus 'notebooks' of these poems, each notebook measuring 8 3/4" high by 5 3/4" wide, each with 110 pages, which comes to a total of some 14,300-plus pages of 'drawn poems' by my count"; see Ratcliffe, "Words as 'Things.'" In 2016, Paul Stephens puts the number of notebooks at "177 notebooks (and counting)" (88).

12. "An Mosaic for Convergence" originally appeared in the *Electronic Book Review* 6 (Winter 1997–98). It is currently recirculated in a variant archival or "legacy" version, with a brief introductory essay, on the *Electronic Book Review* website, at https://electronicbookreview.com. In a 1994 interview, Bernstein uses the term "mosaic" to describe both his own writing and his friend/collaborator Henry Hills's filmmaking [*My Way* 25, 28]. For more on the mosaic as a metaphor for the structure of the digital environment, see Steven Holtzman (who in turn derives the figure from McLuhan's *Understanding Media*), *Digital Mosaics: The Aesthetics of Cyberspace* (New York: Simon and Schuster, 1997). Holtzman runs into a contradiction characteristic of much writing on new media, however: he validates the digital as the "other" of a writing conceived as monolithically linear at the same time as he is forced to acknowledge a strong tradition of nonlinear writing.

13. Bernstein's comments on his print essays and on his sense of the paragraph are relevant here: "One thing that I am proposing is a modular essay that allows for big jumps from paragraph to paragraph and section to section. In such essays, it becomes possible to recombine the paragraphs to get another version of the essay—since the 'argument' is not dependent on the linear sequence." He adds, "I think of paragraphs

as a series of extended remarks or improvisations on aphoristic cores" (*My Way* 7). For more detail on the provenance and form of "An Mosaic for Convergence," see Bernstein's account of the essay, which first appeared in *Electronic Book Review* 6 (Winter 1997–98), at https://electronicbookreview.com.

14. "Punic" is no longer available in a single-screen format but the text still comprises part of the current version of "Mosaic." Its original title derives from the final sentence of the text: "Just as likely, the ideological fixation on linear and expository discourse will be imported into this new medium—Roman gods in a Punic land."

15. Alan Filreis, "Kinetic Is As Kinetic Does: On the Institutionalization of Digital Poetry," *New Media Poetry: Contexts, Technotexts, and Theories*, ed. Adalaide Morris and Thom Swiss (Cambridge: Massachusetts Institute of Technology Press), 123–40.

16. These digital rematerializations of the 1976 *Veil* can be accessed at University of Pennsylvania, Electronic Poetry Center, Authors, http://writing.upenn.edu. A pdf of the print *Veil* is available at https://xexoxial.org and offers the best way to view/read the work outside of owning a physical copy. For Drucker's full discussion of the relationship between the print and the digital *Veil*, see "Intimations" (165–69).

17. Duguid offers a compelling critique of the allied rhetorics of "supersession (the separation of the past from the future[)]" and "liberation (the separation of information from technology[)]" (89) within new media theory.

18. Bernstein is probably alluding to Tom Raworth's one-line poem, "University Days," which reads "This poem removed for further study."

19. A distinction between "rematerialization" and "revision" is relevant here. After producing the 1997 "Alphabeta" out of the essay "I Don't Take Voice Mail," Bernstein writes on the essay's reprinting in 1999 that "I have resisted the tendency to revise this essay in the light of the often oppressively (or possibly exhilaratingly) fast changes in computer technology and the formats for using it" (*My Way* 318).

20. A far more explicit adaptation of the Shakespearean line occurs in the "Mosaic" screen that features twenty-one iterations of the line "The defaults are not in the stars but in ourselves."

21. See "Politics," University of Pennsylvania, Electronic Poetry Center, Authors, http://writing.upenn.edu, and "Politics2," UbuWeb, Contemporary, http://www.ubu.com.

22. Since the electronic "This Us" dates from 1996, its appearance in the 2001 *With Strings* may constitute a rematerialization from digital to print format. For one extension of "Alphabetica," see the work of Eric Zboya, who constructs, as asemic visual texts, "algorithmic translations of Charles Bernstein's *Alphabetica*." Zboya "utilizes the algorithmic computations found within graphic editors to translate and transform an already existing text into a work of visual art": http://www.theadirondackreview.com. For critical commentary on this work, see Rita Raley, "Algorithmic Translations," *CR: The New Centennial Review* 16, no. 1 (Spring 2016): 115–37.

# Works Cited


Acconci, Vito. "Early Work: Movement over a Page." *Avalanche* 6 (Fall 1972): 4–5.

Ackroyd, Peter. *T. S. Eliot: A Life*. New York: Simon and Schuster, 1984.

Adair, Gilbert. Review of *Give Em Enough Rope*, by Bruce Andrews. *Reality Studios* 10 (1988): 101–9.

Allen, Donald M. "Don Allen: Grove's First Editor." Interview with S. E. Gontarski. *Review of Contemporary Fiction* 10, no. 3 (September 1990): 132–36.

———. "Editor's Note." *One Night Stand and Other Poems*, by Jack Spicer. San Francisco: Grey Fox, 1980, xxix–xxxv.

———, ed. *The New American Poetry 1945–1960*. New York: Grove, 1960.

Allen, Donald M., and George F. Butterick, eds. *The Postmoderns: The New American Poetry Revised*. New York: Grove, 1982.

Altieri, Charles. "From Symbolist Thought to Immanence: The Ground of Postmodern American Poetics," *boundary 2* 1.3 (Spring 1973): 605–42.

———. "The Unsure Egoist: Robert Creeley and the Theme of Nothingness." *Contemporary Literature* 13, no. 2 (Spring 1972): 162–85.

Anderson, Margaret. *My Thirty Years' War*. New York: Covici, Friede, 1930.

Andrews, Bruce. "Bruce Andrews Interview May 1990, Vancouver." With Kevin Davies and Jeff Derksen. *Aerial* 9 (1999): 5–17.

———. *Designated Heartbeat*. Cambridge, UK: Salt, 2006.

———. *Divestiture—E*. Buffalo: Leave Books, 1993.

———. *Edge*. Washington, DC: Some of Us, 1973.

———. *Ex Why Zee*. New York: Roof, 1995.

———. *Factura*. Madison, WI: Xexoxial Editions, 1987.

———. *Getting Ready to Have Been Frightened*. New York: Roof, 1988.

———. *Give Em Enough Rope*. Los Angeles: Sun and Moon Press, 1987.

———. "'How Poignant That Sounds, Even As You Read Back the Transcript.' An Interview with Bruce Andrews 10/3/95." With Charles Bernstein. *Chloroform: An Aesthetics of Critical Writing*, 1997, 185–206.

———. *Love Songs*. Baltimore: Pod, 1982.

———. *Paradise and Method: Poetics and Praxis*. Evanston, IL: Northwestern University Press, 1996.

———. *Poetics Talks*. Calgary: housepress, 2001.

———. "Pulsed Scale." *What Is the Inside, What Is Outside? O / Two An Anthology*. Edited by Leslie Scalapino. Oakland: O Books, 1991. 126.

———. "Reading Notes." In Armand, *Contemporary Poetics*, 197–210.

———. "Redaction." *Writing* 27 (1991): 37–38.

———. *StandPoint*. Oakland: Score, 1991.

———. "Verbal Sallies." *Hot Bird Mfg* 1, no. 3 (November 1990): np.

———. *Wobbling*. New York: Roof, 1981.

———. "W O R K (-Dated from Earliest Items Included-)." *Aerial* 9 (1999): 284–88.

Andrews, Bruce, and John Bennett. *Joint Words*. Columbus, OH: Luna Bisonte, 1979.

Andrews, Bruce, and Bob Cobbing. *BothBoth*. London: Writers Forum, 1987.
Antin, David. *Talking at the Boundaries*. New York: New Directions, 1976.
Armand, Louis, ed. *Contemporary Poetics*. Evanston, IL: Northwestern University Press, 2007.
Armantrout, Rae. *Collected Prose*. San Diego: Singing Horse, 2007.
———. *Extremities*. Berkeley, CA: Figures , 1978.
———. "An Interview with Rae Armantrout." With Lyn Hejinian. In Beckett, *Wild Salience*, 12–26.
———. "Looking for Trouble." *Emily Dickinson Journal* 15, no. 2 (2006): 4–5.
———. *Necromance*. Los Angeles: Sun and Moon Press, 1991.
———. *Precedence*. Providence: Burning Deck, 1985.
———. *True*. Berkeley, CA: Hips Road, 1998.
Arnold, Matthew. *The Complete Prose Works of Matthew Arnold*. 11 vols. Edited by R. H. Super. Ann Arbor: University of Michigan Press, 1960–77.
———. *Poetry and Criticism of Matthew Arnold*. Edited by A. Dwight Culler. Boston: Houghton Mifflin, 1961.
Ashbery, John. *Reported Sightings: Art Chronicles, 1957–1987*. Edited by David Bergman. New York: Knopf, 1989.
———. *Selected Prose*. Edited by Eugene Richie. Ann Arbor: University of Michigan Press, 2005.
Back, Rachel Tzvia. *Led by Language: The Poetry and Poetics of Susan Howe*. Tuscaloosa: University of Alabama Press, 2002.
Baker, Peter. *Obdurate Brilliance: Exteriority and the Modern Long Poem*. Gainesville: University Press of Florida, 1991.
Baraka, Amiri. *The Autobiography of LeRoi Jones*. New York: Freundlich, 1984.
———. *Raise Race Rays Raze: Essays Since 1965*. New York: Random House, 1971.
Barbiero, Daniel. "Avant-Garde without Agonism?" In *Telling It Slant: Avant-Garde Poetics of the 1990s*, edited by Mark Wallace and Steven Marks, 79–94. Tuscaloosa: University of Alabama Press, 2002.
———. "States of the Art." *Witz* 3, no. 2 (Spring 1995): 7–8, 13.
Barone, Dennis, and Peter Ganick, eds. *The Art of Practice: 45 Contemporary Poets*. Elmwood, CT: Potes and Poets, 1994.
Basinski, Michael. "Robert Grenier's Opems." *Witz* 7, no. 1 (Spring 1999): 32–34.
Beach, Christopher. *Poetic Culture: Contemporary American Poetry between Community and Institution*. Evanston, IL: Northwestern University Press, 1999.
Beckett, Tom, ed. *A Wild Salience: The Writing of Rae Armantrout*. Cleveland: Burning Press, 1999.
Bell, Marvin. "An Open Letter to Donald M. Allen." *Choice* 1 (1961): 122–24.
Benjamin, Walter. *Illuminations*. Edited by Hannah Arendt. Translated by Harry Zohn. New York: Schocken, 1969.
———. "Program for Literary Criticism." Translated by Rodney Livingstone. In *Selected Writings*. Vol. 2, Pt. 1, *1927–1930*, edited by Michael W. Jennings, Howard Eiland, and Gary Smith, 289–96. Cambridge, MA: Harvard University Press, 1999.
Bennett, James R. "The Essay in Recent Anthologies of Literary Criticism." *SubStance* 60 (1989): 105–11.
Berg, Stephen, ed. *Singular Voices: American Poetry Today*. New York: Avon, 1985.
Berg, Stephen, and Robert Mezey, eds. *Naked Poetry: Recent American Poetry in Open Forms*. Indianapolis: Bobbs-Merrill, 1969.

——. *The New Naked Poetry: Recent American Poetry in Open Forms*. Indianapolis: Bobbs-Merrill, 1976.

Bernstein, Charles. "Access." University of Pennsylvania, Electronic Poetry Center, Authors. 1997. http://writing.upenn.edu.

——. "Alphabeta." Accessed January 20, 2020. https://www.ubu.com.

——. *Attack of the Difficult Poems: Essays and Inventions*. Chicago: University of Chicago Press, 2011.

——. "An Autobiographical Interview with Charles Bernstein." With Loss Pequeño Glazier. *Boundary 2* 23, no. 3 (Autumn 1996): 21–43.

——. "Avant." University of Pennsylvania, Electronic Poetry Center, Authors. Accessed January 20, 2020. http://writing.upenn.edu.

——. "Brooklyn Boy Makes Good: Charles Reznikoff, the Poet of New York." *Brooklyn Rail*, March 5, 2006. http://www.brooklynrail.org.

——. *Content's Dream: Essays 1975–1984*. Los Angeles: Sun and Moon Press, 1986.

——. "Defaults." University of Pennsylvania, Electronic Poetry Center, Authors. 1997. https://www.upenn.edu.

——. "Electronic Pies in the Poetry Skies." *Electronic Book Review*, January 31, 2012. https://electronicbookreview.com.

——. "Every Which Way but Loose." In Loiseaux and Fraistat, *Reimagining Textuality*, 178–85.

——. "Interview with Charles Bernstein." With Allison M. Cummings and Rocco Marinaccio. *Contemporary Literature* 41, no. 1 (Spring 2000): 1–21.

——. "Littoral." University of Pennsylvania, Electronic Poetry Center, Authors. 1996. https://www.upenn.edu.

——. "An Mosaic for Convergence." *Electronic Book Review* 6 (Winter 1997–98). https://electronicbookreview.com.

——. "My Veils." *Jacket 2*, June 28, 2011. https://jacket2.org.

——. *My Way: Speeches and Poems*. Chicago: University of Chicago Press, 1999.

——. *A Poetics*. Cambridge, MA: Harvard University Press, 1992.

——. "Realpolitick." Accessed July 20, 2020. Electronic Book Review. http://www.altx.com.

——. "Textuai." University of Pennsylvania, Electronic Poetry Center, Authors. 1997. https://www.upenn.edu.

——. *Veil*. University of Pennsylvania, Electronic Poetry Center, Authors. 1976. https://www.upenn.edu.

——. *Veil*. Madison, WI: Xexoxial Editions, 1987.

——. *With Strings*. Chicago: University of Chicago Press, 2001.

Bernstein, Michael André. *The Tale of the Tribe: Ezra Pound and the Modern Verse Epic*. Princeton, NJ: Princeton University Press, 1980.

Berry, Eleanor. "Language Made Fluid: The Grammetrics of George Oppen's Recent Poetry." *Contemporary Literature* 25, no. 3 (Autumn 1984): 305–22.

Bertholf, Robert J., and Dale M. Smith. *An Open Map: The Correspondence of Robert Duncan and Charles Olson*. Albuquerque: University of New Mexico Press, 2017.

Bervin, Jen. *Nets*. Brooklyn, NY: Ugly Duckling, 2004.

Blackmur, R. P. *Language as Gesture: Essays in Poetry*. New York: Columbia University Press, 1981.

Blaser, Robin. [Biographical note.] In Allen and Butterick, *Postmoderns*, 383.

——. [Untitled essay on Charles Olson]. *Minutes of the Charles Olson Society* 8 (1995): 5–14.

Bloomfield, Mandy. "'Aftershock of Iconoclasm': Ambivalence of the Visual Page in Susan Howe's *Eikon Basilike." Textual Practice* 23, no. 3 (2009): 417–37.

Blum, W. C. [James Sibley Watson]. "American Letter." *The Dial* 70, no. 5 (May 1921): 562–68.

Bolter, Jay David. *Writing Space: The Computer, Hypertext, and the History of Writing*. Hillsdale, NJ: Lawrence Erlbaum, 1991.

———. *Writing Space: Computers, Hypertext, and the Remediation of Print*. Mahwah, NJ: Lawrence Erlbaum, 2001.

Bolter, Jay David, and Richard Grusin. *Remediation: Understanding New Media*. Cambridge: Massachusetts Institute of Technology Press, 1999.

Brady, Taylor, Benjamin Friedlander, William Howe, and Nick Lawrence. "'Raiding the Vernacular': A Roundtable Discussion on Bruce Andrews 3/8/96." *Chloroform: An Aesthetics of Critical Writing*, 1997, 186–204.

Bremser, Ray. "Poem of Holy Madness, Part IV." In Allen, ed., *New American Poetry*, 352–56.

Breslin, James E. B. *From Modern to Contemporary: American Poetry, 1945–1965*. Chicago: University of Chicago Press, 1984.

Brooker, Peter, and Andrew Thacker, eds. *The Oxford Critical and Cultural History of Modernist Magazines*. Vol. 2, *North America 1894–1960*. Oxford: Oxford University Press, 2009.

Brown, Lee Ann. "Coptic b." *Aerial* 9 (1999): 124–25.

Bruns, Gerald L. *Interruptions: The Fragmentary Aesthetic in Modern Literature*. Tuscaloosa: University of Alabama Press, 2018.

———. *The Material of Poetry: Sketches for a Philosophical Poetics*. Athens: University of Georgia Press, 2005.

Bunting, Basil. *Collected Poems*. Oxford: Oxford University Press, 1977.

Butterick, George F. "The Mysterious Vision of Susan Howe." *North Dakota Quarterly* 55 (1987): 312–21.

Carbery, Matthew. *Phenomenology and the Late Twentieth-Century American Long Poem*. New York: Palgrave Macmillan, 2019.

Carroll, Paul. *The Poem in Its Skin*. Chicago: Big Table, 1968.

Chapin, Katherine Garrison. "Fifteen Years of New Writing." *New Republic*, January 9, 1961, 25–26.

Cohen, Milton A. "*The Dial*'s 'White-Haired Boy': E. E. Cummings as *Dial* Artist, Poet, and Essayist." *Spring: The Journal of the E. E. Cummings Society* 1, no. 1 (October 1992): 9–27.

Collier, Michael, ed. *The Wesleyan Tradition: Four Decades of American Poetry*. Hanover, NH: University Press of New England, 1993.

Colombo, John Robert. "*The New American Poetry: 1945–1960*." *Tamarack Review* 16 (1960): 85–86.

"Comment." *The Dial* 68, no. 3 (March 1920): 408–10.

Constanzo, Gerald, ed. *The Devins Award Poetry Anthology*. Columbia: University of Missouri Press, 1998.

Conte, Joseph. *Unending Design: The Forms of Postmodern Poetry*. Ithaca, NY: Cornell University Press, 1991.

Coolidge, Clark. *Smithsonian Depositions and Subject to a Film*. New York: Vehicle Editions, 1980.

Cope, Stephen. Introduction. "A Selection from 'Daybook One,' 'Daybook Two,' and

'Daybook Three' from *The Working Papers of George Oppen*." *Germ* 3 (1999): 192–201.

Crane, Hart. *The Letters of Hart Crane 1916–1932*. Edited by Brom Weber. Berkeley: University of California Press, 1965.

Creeley, Robert. [Biographical statement]. In Allen and Butterick, *Postmoderns*, 431.

———. *The Collected Poems of Robert Creeley, 1945–1975*. Berkeley: University of California Press, 1982.

———. Foreword to *The Holy Forest*, by Robin Blaser. Toronto: Coach House, 1993. xi–xvii.

———. "An Interview with Robert Creeley." With David L. Elliott. *Sagetrieb* 10, nos. 1 and 2 (1991): 45–65.

———. "Interview: Robert Creeley." With Ekbert Faas. *Towards a New American Poetics: Essays and Interviews*, edited by Ekbert Faas, 165–98. Santa Barbara: Black Sparrow, 1978.

———. "Olson and Others: Some Orts for the Sports." In Allen, *New American Poetry*, 408–11.

———. *Tales out of School: Selected Interviews*. Ann Arbor: University of Michigan Press, 1993.

———. *Was That a Real Poem and Other Essays*. Edited by Donald Allen. Bolinas, CA: Four Seasons Foundation, 1979.

Damon, Maria. *The Dark End of the Street: Margins in Vanguard American Poetry*. Minneapolis: University of Minnesota Press, 1993.

Darragh, Tina. "Howe." In Silliman, *In the American Tree*, 547–49.

Davidson, Michael. *Analogy of the Ion*. Great Barrington, MA: Figures, 1988.

———. *Ghostlier Demarcations: Modern Poetry and the Material Word*. Berkeley: University of California Press, 1997.

———. *Guys Like Us: Citing Masculinity in Cold War Poetics*. Chicago: University of Chicago Press, 2004. 1997.

———. *On the Outskirts of Form: Practicing Cultural Poetics*. Middletown, CT: Wesleyan University Press, 2011.

———. *The San Francisco Renaissance: Poetics and Community at Mid-century*. New York: Cambridge University Press, 1989.

Davie, Donald. "Notes on George Oppen's *Seascape: Needle's Eye*." In Hatlen, *George Oppen*, 407–12.

Debrot, Jacques. ":: BRUCE ANDREWS." *Aerial* 9 (1999): 144–45.

Deleuze, Gilles, and Felix Guattari. *Kafka: Toward a Minor Literature*. Translated by Dana Polan. Minneapolis: University of Minnesota Press, 1986.

———. *A Thousand Plateaus: Capitalism and Schizophrenia*. Vol. 2. Translated by Brian Massumi. Minneapolis: University of Minnesota Press, 1987.

Dembo, L. S. "The Existential World of George Oppen." *Iowa Review* 3, no. 1 (1972): 64–91.

Dickey, James. *Babel to Byzantium: Poets and Poetry Now*. New York: Ecco, 1981.

Dickie, Margaret. *On the Modernist Long Poem*. Iowa City: University of Iowa Press, 1986.

Di Prima, Diane. "In Conversation with David Hadbawnik." *Jacket* 18 (August 2002). http://jacket2.org.

———. *Recollections of My Life as a Woman*. New York: Viking Penguin, 2001.

Dorn, Edward. *Collected Poems*. Edited by Jennifer Dunbar Dorn. Manchester, UK: Carcanet Press, 2012.

Dove, Rita, ed. *The Penguin Anthology of Twentieth-Century American Poetry*. New York: Penguin, 2011.

Drucker, Johanna. *Figuring the Word: Essays on Books, Writing, and Visual Poetics*. New York: Granary, 1998.

——. "Graphical Readings and the Visual Aesthetics of Textuality." *Text* 16 (2006): 267–76.

——. "Intimations of Immateriality: Graphical Form, Textual Sense, and the Electronic Environment." In Loiseaux and Fraistat, *Reimagining Textuality*, 152–77.

——. "Not Sound." In *The Sound of Poetry/The Poetry of Sound*, edited by Marjorie Perloff and Craig Dworkin, 237–48. Chicago: University of Chicago Press, 2009.

——. *The Visible Word: Experimental Typography and Modern Art, 1909–23*. Chicago: University of Chicago Press, 1994.

Duguid, Paul. "Material Matters: The Past and Futurology of the Book." In Nunberg, *Future of the Book*, 63–101.

Duncan, Robert. [Biographical statement]. In Allen and Butterick, *Postmoderns*, 432–36.

——. "Eleven Letters to Charles Olson." *Sulfur* 35 (Fall 1994): 87–118.

——. "In Interview." With Michael McClure. *Conjunctions* 7 (1985): 69–86.

——. "Letters on Poetry and Poetics." *Ironwood* 11, no. 2 (1983): 96–133.

——. "Pages from a Notebook." Allen, ed., New American Poetry 400–407.

——. "A Partisan View." *Meanjin Quarterly* 35 (1976): 368–69.

DuPlessis, Rachel Blau. "Autobiography of a Practice." *Thresholds* 1. www.openthresholds.org.

——. "The Blazes of Poetry: Remarks on Segmentivity and Seriality with Special Reference to Blaser and Oppen." In *The Recovery of the Public World: Essays on Poetics in Honour of Robin Blaser*, edited by Charles Watts and Ted Byrne, 287–99. Burnaby, Can.: Talonbooks, 1999.

——. *Blue Studios: Poetry and Its Cultural Work*. Tuscaloosa: University of Alabama Press, 2006.

——. *The Collage Poems of Drafts*. London: Salt, 2011.

——. "Considering the Long Poem: Genre Problems." Unpublished paper, University of Sussex, May 2008.

——. "The Darkest Gush: Emily Dickinson and the Textual Mark." Dickinson Electronic Archives, Table of Contents, *Titanic Operas*. 1999. http://archive.emilydickinson.org.

——. *Drafts 1–38, Toll*. Middletown, CT: Wesleyan University Press, 2001.

——. *Drafts 39–57, Pledge, with Draft, Unnumbered: Precis*. Cambridge:, UK Salt, 2004.

——. "*f*-Words: An Essay on the Essay." *American Literature* 68, no. 1 (1996): 15–45.

——. *Genders, Races, and Religious Cultures in Modern American Poetry, 1908–1934*. New York: Cambridge University Press, 2001.

——. "George Oppen: 'What Do We Believe to Live With?'" *Ironwood* 3, no. 1 (1975): 62–77.

——. "An Interview with Rachel Blau DuPlessis." With Jeanne Heuving. *Contemporary Literature* 45, no. 3 (Fall 2004): 397–420.

——. "Introduction." In *The Selected Letters of George Oppen*, edited by DuPlessis, vii–xx.

———. "Lorine Niedecker's 'Paean to Place' and Its Reflective Fusions." In *Radical Vernacular: Lorine Niedecker and the Poetics of Place*, edited by Elizabeth Willis, 151–79. Iowa City: University of Iowa Press, 2008.
———. "Lyric and Experimental Long Poems: Intersections." In *Time in Time: Short Poems, Long Poems, and the Rhetoric of North American Avant-Gardism, 1963–2008*, edited by J. Mark Smith, 22–50. Toronto: McGill-Queens University Press, 2013.
———. "Objectivist Poetics and Political Vision: A Study of Oppen and Pound." In *George Oppen: Man and Poet*, edited by Burton Hatlen, 123–48. Orono, ME: National Poetry Foundation, 1981.
———. "Objectivist Poetry and Poetics." In *The Cambridge Companion to Modern American Poetry*, edited by Walter Kalaidjian, 89–101. New York: Cambridge University Press, 2015.
———. "On the Island." *Sagetrieb* 3, no.1 (Spring 1984): 113–18.
———. *The Pink Guitar: Writing as Feminist Practice*. New York: Routledge, 1990.
———. *Pitch: Drafts 77–95*. London: Salt, 2010.
———. *Purple Passages: Pound, Eliot, Zukofsky, Olson, Creeley, and the Ends of Patriarchal Poetry*. Iowa City: University of Iowa Press, 2012.
———. "Response: June 5, 1994." *Texture* 6 (1995): 4.
———. "Surface Tension: Thinking about Andrews." *Aerial* 9 (1999): 49–61.
———. *Surge: Drafts 96–114*. Cromer, UK: Salt, 2013.
———. "The Topos of the 'Thing': Some Thoughts on 'Objectivist' Poetics." In *The Idea and the Thing in Modernist American Poetry*, edited by Cristina Giorcelli, 31–51. Palermo, Italy: ILA Palma, 2001.
———. *Torques: Drafts 58–76*. Cambridge, UK: Salt, 2007.
———. "'A White Fiction': A Woman and a Page." *Temblor* 10 (1989): 168, 170.
DuPlessis, Rachel Blau, and Peter Quartermain. "Introduction." In *The Objectivist Nexus: Essays in Cultural Poetics*, edited by DuPlessis and Quartermain, 1–22. Tuscaloosa: University of Alabama Press, 1999.
Dworkin, Craig. "Delay in Verse." In *Language to Cover a Page: The Early Writings of Vito Acconci*, edited by Dworkin, xi–xviii. Cambridge: Massachusetts Institute of Technology Press, 2006.
———. *Reading the Illegible*. Evanston, IL: Northwestern University Press, 2003.
Eliot, T. S. "Tradition and the Individual Talent." In *The Sacred Wood: Essays on Poetry and Criticism*, 47–59. London: Methuen, 1960.
———. Untitled letter. In *The Little Review Anthology*, edited by Margaret Anderson, 380. New York: Horizon, 1953.
Ellingham, Lewis. "'The King's Two Bodies': From *Poet, Be Like God: Jack Spicer's Circle in San Francisco, 1956–1965*." *Line* 7/8 (1986): 57–89.
Ellingham, Lewis, and Kevin Killian. *Poet Be Like God: Jack Spicer and the San Francisco Renaissance*. Hanover, NH: University Press of New England/Wesleyan University Press, 1998.
Emerson, Lori. *Reading Writing Interfaces: From the Digital to the Bookbound*. Minneapolis: University of Minnesota Press, 2014.
Emerson, Ralph Waldo. *Selections from Ralph Waldo Emerson: An Organic Anthology*. Edited by Stephen F. Whicher. Boston: Houghton Mifflin, 1957.
Evans, George, ed. *Charles Olson and Cid Corman: Complete Correspondence 1950–1964*. Vol. 2. Orono, ME: National Poetry Foundation, 1991.
Evans, Steve. "The American Avant-Garde after 1989: Notes toward a History." In

*The World in Time and Space: Towards a History of Innovative American Poetry in Our Time*, edited by Edward Foster and Joseph Donahue, 646–73. Jersey City, NJ: Talisman House, 2002.

———. "Anthslide." Third Factory, Notes to Poetry, Archives. 1995. http://www.thirdfactory.net.

Ferlinghetti, Lawrence. "[Statement on Poetics]." In Allen, *New American Poetry*, 412–13.

Field, Edward, ed. *A Geography of Poets: An Anthology of the New Poetry*. New York: Bantam, 1979.

Finkelstein, Norman. "The Dialectic of *This in Which*." In Hatlen, *George Oppen*, 359–73.

Foster, Edward, ed. *Postmodern Poetry: The Talisman Interviews*. Hoboken, NJ: Talisman House, 1994.

Fraser, Kathleen. *Translating the Unspeakable: Poetry and the Innovative Necessity*. Tuscaloosa: University of Alabama Press, 1999.

Fredman, Stephen. *Poets' Prose: The Crisis in American Verse*. New York: Cambridge University Press, 1983.

Freitag, Kornelia. *Cultural Criticism in Women's Experimental Writing: The Poetry of Rosmarie Waldrop, Lyn Hejinian and Susan Howe*. Heidelberg: Universitätsverlag Winter, 2005.

Friebert, Stuart, and David Young, eds. *The Longman Anthology of Contemporary American Poetry 1950–1980*. New York: Longman, 1983.

Friedman, Susan Stanford. "Craving Stories: Narrative and Lyric in Contemporary Theory and Women's Long Poems." In *Feminist Measures: Soundings in Poetry and Theory*, edited by Lynn Keller and Cristanne Miller, 15–42. Ann Arbor: University of Michigan Press, 1994.

———. "Gender and Genre Anxiety: Elizabeth Barrett Browning and H.D. as Epic Poets." *Tulsa Studies in Women's Literature* 5, no. 2 (Autumn 1986): 203–28.

———. "When a 'Long' Poem Is a 'Big' Poem: Self-Authorizing Strategies in Women's Twentieth-Century 'Long Poems.'" In *Feminisms: An Anthology of Literary Theory and Criticism*, edited by Robyn R. Warhol and Diane Price Herndl, 721–38. New Brunswick, NJ: Rutgers University Press, 1997.

Frost, Elisabeth A. "Visual Poetics." In *A History of Twentieth-Century American Women's Poetry*, edited by Linda A. Kinnahan, 339–58. New York: Cambridge University Press, 2016.

Galassi, Jonathan. "Determined Forms." *Poetry* 129, no. 3 (December 1976): 164–70.

Gardner, Thomas. *Discovering Ourselves in Whitman: The Contemporary American Long Poem*. Urbana: University of Illinois Press, 1989.

Garrett, George. "Against the Grain: Poets Writing Today." In *American Poetry*, edited by Irvin Ehrenpreis, 221–39. New York: St. Martin's, 1965.

Géfin, Laszlo. *Ideogram: History of a Poetic Method*. Austin: University of Texas Press, 1982.

Gevirtz, Susan. "Errant Alphabet: Notes toward the Screen." In Sloan, *Moving Borders*, 655.

Ginsberg, Allen. *Allen Verbatim: Lectures on Poetry, Politics, Consciousness*. Edited by Gordon Ball. New York: McGraw, 1974.

———. *Journals Mid-Fifties 1954–1958*. Edited by Gordon Ball. New York: HarperCollins, 1995.

———. "Notes for *Howl* and Other Poems." In Allen, *New American Poetry*, 414–18.

Glazier, Loss Pequeño. *Digital Poetics: The Making of E-Poetries.* Tuscaloosa: University of Alabama Press, 2002.

Golding, Alan. *From Outlaw to Classic: Canons in American Poetry.* Madison: University of Wisconsin Press, 1995.

———. "From Pound to Olson: The Avant-Garde Poet as Pedagogue." *Journal of Modern Literature* 34, no. 1 (Fall 2010): 86–106.

Golston, Michael. "Weathered Measures and Measured Weathers: W. C. Williams and the Allegorical Ends of Rhythm." *Textual Practice* 18, no. 2 (2004): 251–64.

Gontarski, S. E. "Dionysus in Publishing: Barney Rossett, Grove Press, and the Making of a Countercanon." *Review of Contemporary Fiction* 10, no. 3 (1990): 7–18.

Gregory, Elizabeth, ed. *The Critical Response to Marianne Moore.* Westport, CT: Praeger, 2003.

Grenier, Robert. "For Larry Eigner." University of Pennsylvania, Electronic Poetry Center, Authors. August 16, 2009. https://www.upenn.edu.

———. "Greeting." University of Pennsylvania, Electronic Poetry Center, Authors. Accessed January 25, 2020. https://www.upenn.edu.

———. "Language/Site/World." In Perelman, *Writing/Talks*, 230–45.

———. "On Speech." In Silliman, *In the American Tree*, 496–97.

———. "A Packet for Robert Creeley." *Boundary 2* 6, no. 3/7, no. 1 (Spring–Autumn 1978): 422–41.

———. *Phantom Anthems.* Oakland, CA: O Books, 1986.

———. "*Pond I.*" University of Pennsylvania, Electronic Poetry Center, Authors. Accessed February 5, 2020. https://www.writing.upenn.edu.

———. "Realizing Things." State University of New York, Buffalo, October 28, 1998. Unpublished talk. University of Pennsylvania, Electronic Poetry Center, Authors. https://www.writing.upenn.edu.

———. "Review of *A Quick Graph*, by Robert Creeley." *This* 1 (1971): np.

———. "saplling." Accessed January 27, 2020. http://www.thing.net.

———. *Sentences.* Whale Cloth Press. Accessed January 27, 2020. http://www.whalecloth.org.

———. "10 Pages from RHYMMS." University of Pennsylvania, Electronic Poetry Center, Authors. 1996. https://www.writing.upenn.edu.

———. "Typewriter v Typeface: An Interview with Poet Robert Grenier." With Alastair Johnston. *Ampersand* 6, no. 2 (April 1986): 5–11.

———. [Untitled essay.] In Sanders and Bernstein, *Poetry Plastique*, 71–73.

Gunn, Thom. "Outside Faction." *Yale Review* 50 (1960–61): 585–96.

Gwynn, R. S. "What the Center Holds." *Hudson Review* 46, no. 4 (Winter 1994): 741–50.

Hall, Donald. "Ah, Love, Let Us Be True: Domesticity and History in Contemporary Poetry." *American Scholar* 28, no. 3 (Summer 1959): 310–19.

———. *Goatfoot Milktongue Twinbird: Interviews, Essays, and Notes on Poetry, 1970–76.* Ann Arbor: University of Michigan Press, 1978.

Hall, Donald, Robert Pack, and Louis Simpson, eds. *The New Poets of England and America.* New York: Meridian, 1957.

Halpern, Daniel, ed. *The American Poetry Anthology.* New York: Avon, 1975.

Harryman, Carla. "Reflections on the Incomplete Project of Poets Theater." In *The Grand Piano. An Experiment in Collective Autobiography, 1975–1980,* by

Kit Robinson, Carla Harryman, Lyn Hejinian, Ron Silliman, Bob Perelman, Barrett Watten, Ted Pearson, Tom Mandel, Steve Benson, Rae Armantrout, 28–50. Part 7. Detroit, MI: Mode A, 2008.

Hatlen, Burton, ed. *George Oppen: Man and Poet.* Orono, ME: National Poetry Foundation, 1981.

———. "Opening Up the Text: George Oppen's 'Of Being Numerous.'" *Ironwood* 13, no. 2 (Fall 1985): 263–95.

———. "Openness and Closure in Williams' *Spring and All.*" *William Carlos Williams Review* 20, no. 2 (Fall 1994): 15–29.

———. "Zukofsky, Wittgenstein, and the Poetics of Absence." *Sagetrieb* 1, no. 1 (Spring 1982): 63–93.

Hayles, N. Katherine. "'Materiality Has Always Been in Play': An Interview with N. Katherine Hayles." With Lisa Gitelman. *Iowa Journal of Cultural Studies* 2, no. 1 (Fall 2002): 7–12. Iowa University Libraries, Journals. https://pubs.lib.uiowa.edu.

———. "The Materiality of Informatics." *Configurations* 1, no. 1 (1992): 147–70.

———. *Writing Machines.* Cambridge: Massachusetts Institute of Technology Press, 2002.

Heap, Jane. "Full of Weapons!" *Little Review* 8, no. 2 (Spring 1922): 33.

———. "Loyalty: A Champion." *Little Review* 7, no. 3 (September–October 1920): 93.

———. "Notes." *Little Review* 9, no. 1 (Autumn 1922): 36–37.

Hejinian, Lyn. "An American Opener." *Poetics Journal* 1 (January 1982): 61–65.

———. "The Eternal Repository." Interview with Dodie Bellamy. *Chain* 2 (Spring 1995): 19–25.

———. "Hard Hearts." *Aerial* 9 (1999): 63–69.

———. "Introduction." *Aerial* 8 (1995): 73–74.

———. *The Language of Inquiry.* Berkeley: University of California Press, 2000.

———. *My Life.* Los Angeles: Sun and Moon, 1986.

Heller, Michael. *Speaking the Estranged: Essays on the Work of George Oppen.* Cambridge, UK: Salt, 2008.

Hemley, Cecil. "Within a Budding Grove." *Hudson Review* 13, no. 4 (Winter 1960–61): 626–30.

Herd, David. "By Catboat to New York." *Guardian,* November 8, 2003. https://www.theguardian.com.

———. "'In the Open of the Common Rubble': George Oppen's Process." *Textual Practice* 23, no. 1 (February 2009): 141–50.

———. *John Ashbery and American Poetry.* New York: Palgrave, 2000.

Heyen, William, ed. *The Generation of 2000: Contemporary American Poets.* Princeton, NJ: Ontario Review, 1984.

Hine, Daryl. *The Poetry Anthology 1912–1977: Sixty-Five Years of America's Most Distinguished Verse Magazine.* Edited by Daryl Hine and Joseph Parisi. Boston: Houghton Mifflin, 1978.

Hoffman, Daniel, ed. *Harvard Guide to Contemporary American Writing.*, Cambridge, MA: Belknap Press of Harvard University Press, 1979.

Hoffman, Eric. *Oppen: A Narrative.* Bristol, UK: Shearsman, 2013.

Hoffman, Frederick J., Charles Allen, and Carolyn F. Ulrich. *The Little Magazine: A History and a Bibliography.* Princeton, NJ: Princeton University Press, 1946.

Hokanson, Robert O'Brien. "'Projecting' Like a Man: Charles Olson and the Poetics of Gender." *Sagetrieb* 9, nos. 1–2 (Spring–Fall 1990): 169–83.

Holden, Jonathan. "American Poetry 1970–1990." In *A Profile of Twentieth-Century American Poetry*, edited by Jack Myers and David Wojahn, 254–74. Carbondale: Southern Illinois University Press, 1991.

——. *The Fate of American Poetry*. Athens: University of Georgia Press, 1991.

Homberger, Eric. *The Art of the Real: Poetry in England and America Since 1939*. London: Dent, 1977.

Hong, Cathy Park. "Delusions of Whiteness in the Avant-Garde." *Lana Turner Journal* 7 (2014): 248–53.

Hoover, Paul. "Cahiers de Corey/2." *Paul Hoover's Poetry Blog*, January 29, 2008. http://paulhooverpoetry.blogspot.com.

——. "Interview with Paul Hoover." By Vittorio Carli. May 11, 1995. http://www.artinterviews.org.

——, ed. *Postmodern American Poetry: A Norton Anthology*. New York: W. W. Norton, 1994.

——, ed. *Postmodern American Poetry*. 2nd ed. New York: W. W. Norton, 2013.

Horowitz, Stephen P. "An Investigation of Paul Goodman and Black Mountain." *American Poetry* 7, no. 1 (1989): 2–30.

Howe, Susan. *The Birth-mark: Unsettling the Wilderness in American Literary History*. Hanover, NH: University Press of New England, 1993.

——. "*The Difficulties* Interview." With Tom Beckett. *Difficulties* 3, no. 2 (1989): 17–27.

——. "The End of Art." *Archives of American Art Journal* 14, no. 4 (1974): 2–7.

——. *The Europe of Trusts*. Los Angeles: Sun and Moon, 1990.

——. *Frame Structures: Early Poems 1974–1979*. New York: New Directions, 1996.

——. "An Interview with Susan Howe." By Lynn Keller. *Contemporary Literature* 36, no. 1 (Spring 1995): 1–34.

——. "Interview with Susan Howe." By Jon Thompson. *Free Verse* 9 (Winter 2005). http://freeversethejournal.org.

——. *The Midnight*. New York: New Directions, 2008.

——. *My Emily Dickinson*. Berkeley, CA: North Atlantic Books, 1985.

——. *The Nonconformist's Memorial*. Hanover, NH: University Press of New England, 1993.

——. *The Quarry*. New York: New Directions, 2015.

——. "Robert Creeley and the Politics of the Person." *Poetics Journal* 9 (June 1991): 152–58.

——. "Since a Dialogue We Are." *Acts* 10 (1989): 166–73.

——. *Singularities*. Hanover, NH: University Press of New England, 1990.

——. "Speaking with Susan Howe." With Ruth Falon. *Difficulties* 3, no. 2 (1989): 28–42.

——. Untitled. In *The Line in Postmodern Poetry*, edited by Robert Frank and Henry Sayre, 209. Urbana: University of Illinois Press, 1988.

——. *The Western Borders*. Willits, CA: Tuumba, 1976.

——. "Women and Their Effect in the Distance." *Ironwood* 14, no. 2 (1986): 58–91.

Howe, William. "Remeaning: Sound, Text, Space, and Song." Master's thesis, University of Maine, Electronic Poetry Center, August 21, 2012.

Hunting, Constance. "'At Least Not Nowhere': George Oppen as Maine Poet." *Paideuma* 10, no. 1 (Spring 1981): 53–58.

Huyssen, Andreas. *After the Great Divide: Modernism, Mass Culture, Postmodernism*. Bloomington: Indiana University Press, 1986.

Inman, P. "Early/Later: 2 Scenarios For/On Bruce Andrews." *Aerial* 9 (1999): 88–90.
Izenberg, Oren. *Being Numerous: Poetry and the Ground of Social Life*. Princeton, NJ: Princeton University Press, 2011.
Jaeger, Peter. "Steve McCaffery's Visual Errata." Accessed January 27, 2020. http://www.ubu.com.
Jaffe, Aaron. "Adjectives and the Work of Modernism in an Age of Celebrity." *Yale Journal of Criticism* 16, no. 1 (Spring 2003): 1–37.
——. *Modernism and the Culture of Celebrity*. New York: Cambridge University Press, 2005.
Janssens, G. A. M. *The American Literary Review: A Critical History 1920–1950*. The Hague: Mouton, 1968.
Jarnot, Lisa. "Preface." In *An Anthology of New (American) Poets*, edited by Lisa Jarnot, Leonard Schwartz, and Chris Stroffolino, 1–2. Jersey City, NJ: Talisman House, 1998.
Jenkins, G. Matthew. *Poetic Obligation: Ethics in Experimental American Poetry after 1945*. Iowa City: University of Iowa Press, 2008.
Jepson, Edgar. "The Western School." *Little Review* 5, no. 5 (September 1918): 4–9.
Jewell, Megan Swihart. "Becoming Articulate: Kathleen Fraser and *The New American Poetry*." In *The New American Poetry Fifty Years Later*, edited by John R. Woznicki, 133–54. Bethlehem, PA: Lehigh University Press, 2014.
Jones, LeRoi. "'How You Sound??'" In Allen, *New American Poetry*, 424–25.
——. "An Interview on *Yugen*." With David Ossman. In *The Little Magazine in America: A Modern Documentary History*, edited by Elliott Anderson and Mary Kinzie, 317–23. Yonkers, NY: Pushcart, 1978.
Joost, Nicholas. *Scofield Thayer and The Dial: An Illustrated History*. Carbondale: Southern Illinois University Press, 1964.
——. *Years of Transition: The Dial 1912–1920*. Barre, MA: Barre, 1967.
Joost, Nicholas, and Alvin Sullivan, comps. *The Dial, Two Author Indexes: Anonymous and Pseudonymous Contributors; Contributors in Clipsheets*. Bibliographic Contributions 6. Edwardsville, IL: University Graphics and Publications, 1971.
Kac, Eduardo. "Holopoetry." *Visible Language* 30, no. 2 (1996): 184–213.
Kalaidjian, Walter. *Languages of Liberation: The Social Text in Contemporary American Poetry*. New York: Columbia University Press, 1989.
Kane, Daniel. *All Poets Welcome: The Lower East Side Poetry Scene in the 1960s*. Berkeley: University of California Press, 2003.
Keller, Lynn. *Forms of Expansion: Recent Women's Long Poems*. Chicago: University of Chicago Press, 1997.
——. "The Twentieth-Century Long Poem." In *Columbia History of American Poetry*, edited by Jay Parini, 534–63. New York: Columbia University Press, 1993.
Kelly, Robert. "Nothing but Doors: An Interview with Robert Kelly." With Dennis Barone. *Credences* n.s. 3, no. 3 (1985): 100–122.
——. "Postscript II." In Leary and Kelly, *Controversy of Poets*, 563–67.
——. "Spirit / Vanguard Art." In Schwartz, Donahue, and Foster, *Primary Trouble*, 450–51.
Kennedy, X. J. "The New American Poetry." *Poetry* 98 (1961): 242–44.
Kenner, Hugh. *A Homemade World: The American Modernist Writers*. New York: Knopf, 1975.

Khlebnikov, Velimir, and Alexei Kruchonykh. "The Letter as Such." *Collected Works of Velimir Khlebnikov*. Vol. 1, 257–58. Edited by Charlotte Douglas. Translated by Paul Schmidt. Cambridge, MA: Harvard University Press, 1987.

Kirschenbaum, Matthew. "Materiality and Matter and Stuff: What Electronic Texts Are Made Of." *Electronic Book Review*, October 1, 2001. www.electronicbookreview.com.

Koethe, John. "Contrary Impulses: The Tension between Poetry and Theory." *Critical Inquiry* 18, no. 1 (Autumn 1991): 64–75.

Kostelanetz, Richard. "Slight of Foot." *American Book Review* 16, no. 6 (March–May 1995): 17.

Kotz, Liz. *Words to Be Looked At: Language in 1960s Art*. Cambridge: Massachusetts Institute of Technology Press, 2007.

Landow, George P. *Hypertext: The Convergence of Contemporary Critical Theory and Technology*. Baltimore: Johns Hopkins University Press, 1992.

———. "Twenty Minutes into the Future, or How Are We Moving Beyond the Book?" In Nunberg, *Future of the Book*, 209–37.

Lang, Doug. "5 for B=R=U=C=E." *Aerial* 9 (1999): 112–17.

Lanham, Richard. *The Electronic Word: Democracy, Technology, and the Arts*. Chicago: University of Chicago Press, 1993.

Lauterbach, Ann. *The Night Sky: Writings on the Poetics of Experience*. New York: Viking, 2005.

Lazer, Hank. *Opposing Poetries*. Vol. 1: *Issues and Institutions*. Evanston, IL: Northwestern University Press, 1996.

———. *Opposing Poetries*. Vol. 2: *Readings*. Evanston, IL: Northwestern University Press, 1996.

Leary, Paris. "Postscript I." In Leary and Kelly, *Controversy of Poets*, 559–61.

Leary, Paris, and Robert Kelly, eds. *A Controversy of Poets*. Garden City, NY: Doubleday, 1965.

Lennon, Brian. "Screening a Digital Visual Poetics." *Configurations* 8 (2000): 63–85.

Levertov, Denise. "Poetry, Pure and Complex." *New Leader*, February 18, 1963, 26–27.

Lloyd, David. *Nationalism and Minor Literature: James Clarence Mangan and the Emergence of Irish Nationalism*. Berkeley: University of California Press, 1987.

Loiseaux, Elizabeth Bergmann, and Neil Fraistat, eds. *Reimagining Textuality: Textual Studies in the Late Age of Print*. Madison: University of Wisconsin Press, 2002.

Longenbach, James. "Ashbery and the Individual Talent." *American Literary History* 9, no. 1 (Spring 1997): 103–27.

Lowell, Amy. *Selected Poems*. Edited by Honor Moore. New York: Library of America, 2004.

Lowney, John. "Williams: The New Poetries and Legacy." In *The Cambridge Companion to William Carlos Williams*, edited by Christopher MacGowan, 188–205. New York: Cambridge University Press, 2016.

Loy, Mina. *The Lost Lunar Baedeker: Poems*. Edited by Roger L. Conover. New York: Farrar, Straus, Giroux, 1996.

Lukacs, Georg. *Soul and Form*. Translated by Anna Bostock. Cambridge: Massachusetts Institute of Technology Press, 1974.

Mackey, Nathaniel. *Discrepant Engagements: Dissonance, Cross-Culturality, and Experimental Writing*. New York: Cambridge University Press, 1993.

Magee, Michael. *Mainstream*. Buffalo, NY: BlazeVOX, 2006.

Mailhot, Lauren. "The Writing of the Essay." Translated by Jay Lutz. *Yale French Studies* 65 (1983): 74–89.

Mallarmé, Stephane. *Collected Poems*. Translated by and with a commentary by Henry Weinfield. Berkeley: University of California Press, 1994.

———. *Mallarmé in Prose*. Edited by Mary Ann Caws. New York: New Directions, 2001.

Marek, Jayne. *Women Editing Modernism: 'Little' Magazines and Literary History*. Lexington: University Press of Kentucky, 1995.

Mariani, Paul. *William Carlos Williams: A New World Naked*. New York: McGraw-Hill, 1981.

Marsh, Nicky. "'Note on My Writing': Poetics as Exegesis." *Postmodern Culture* 8, no. 3 (May 1998). https://muse.jhu.edu.

Maud, Ralph, ed. *Poet to Publisher: Charles Olson's Correspondence with Donald Allen*. Vancouver: Talonbooks, 2003.

Mayakovsky, Vladimir. *The Bedbug and Selected Poetry*. Edited by Patricia Blake. Translated by Max Hayward and George Reavey. Bloomington: Indiana University Press, 1975.

Mayer, Bernadette. *The Desires of Mothers to Please Others in Letters*. West Stockbridge, MA: Hard Press, 1994.

McAleavey, David. "Clarity and Process: Oppen's 'Of Being Numerous.'" In Hatlen, *George Oppen*, 381–404.

———. "Oppen on Oppen: Extracts from [1978] Interviews." *Sagetrieb* 5, no. 1 (Spring 1986): 59–93.

McCaffery, Steve. *Carnival Panel 1*. 1997. Penn Sound. https://www.writing.upenn.edu.

———. "*Carnival*." *L=A=N=G=U=A=G=E* 1, no. 1 (February 1978): np.

———. *Carnival: The First Panel 1967–70*. Toronto: Coach House, 1973.

———. *Carnival Panel 2*. 1999. Penn Sound. https://www.writing.upenn.edu.

———. "*Carnival* Panel 2 (1970–1975)." In Sanders and Bernstein, *Poetry Plastique*, 69–70.

———. *Carnival: The Second Panel 1971–75*. Toronto: Coach House, 1977.

———. "The Death of the Subject: The Implications of Counter-Communication in Recent Language-Centered Writing." *L=A=N=G=U=A=G=E* Supplement 1 (June 1980): np.

———. *North of Intention: Critical Writings 1973–1986*. New York: Roof, 1986.

———. *Prior to Meaning: The Protosemantic and Poetics*. Evanston, IL: Northwestern University Press, 2001.

———. *Seven Pages Missing*. Vol. 1: *Selected Texts 1969–1999*. Toronto: Coach House, 2000.

McCaffery, Steve, and bpNichol. *Rational Geomancy. The Kids of the Book-Machine. The Collected Research Reports of the Toronto Research Group 1973–1982*. Vancouver: Talonbooks, 1992.

McClatchy, J. D. "Introduction." In *The Vintage Book of Contemporary American Poetry*, edited by McClatchy, xxi–xxx. New York: Vintage, 1990.

———. "A Note on the Second Edition, 2003." In *The Vintage Book of Contemporary American Poetry*, edited by McClatchy, xxxiii–xxxiv. New York: Vintage, 2003.

McGann, Jerome. *Black Riders: The Visible Language of Modernism*. Princeton, NJ: Princeton University Press, 1993.

——. *The Textual Condition*. Princeton, NJ: Princeton University Press, 1991.
McHale, Brian. *The Obligation toward the Difficult Whole: Postmodernist Long Poems*. Tuscaloosa: University of Alabama Press, 2004.
McKible, Adam. *The Space and Place of Modernism: The Russian Revolution, Little Magazines, and New York*. New York: Routledge, 2002.
Melville, Herman. *Moby-Dick*. Edited by Hershel Parker. New York: W. W. Norton, 2018.
Melo e Castro, E. M. de. "Videopoetry." *Visible Language* 30, no. 2 (1996): 138–49.
Messerli, Douglas, ed. *From the Other Side of the Century: A New American Poetry 1960–1990*. Los Angeles: Sun and Moon, 1994.
Miller, James E., Jr. *The American Quest for a Supreme Fiction: Whitman's Legacy in the Personal Epic*. Chicago: University of Chicago Press, 1979.
Miller, Nolan, and Judson Jerome, eds. *New Campus Writing No. 2*. New York: G. P. Putnam's Sons, 1957.
Montgomery, Will. *The Poetry of Susan Howe: History, Theology, Authority*. New York: Palgrave Macmillan, 2010.
Monteiro, George. "George Oppen's Hudson River 'Night Scene.'" *Sagetrieb* 9, nos. 1–2 (Spring–Fall 1990): 225–27.
[Moore, Marianne]. "Announcement." *The Dial* 82, no. 1 (January 1927): 88–90.
——. *A Marianne Moore Reader*. New York: Viking, 1961
Morrisson, Mark S. *The Public Face of Modernism: Little Magazines, Audiences, and Reception, 1905–1920*. Madison: University of Wisconsin Press, 2000.
Mossin, Andrew. *Male Subjectivity and Poetic Form in "New American" Poetry*. New York: Palgrave Macmillan, 2010.
Mott, Frank Luther. *A History of American Magazines 1905–1930*. Vol. 5. Cambridge, MA: Belknap Press of Harvard University Press, 1968.
Mullen, Harryette. *Trimmings*. New York: Tender Buttons, 1991.
Munson, Gorham. "How to Run a Little Magazine." *Saturday Review of Literature* 15 (March 27, 1937): 3–4, 14, 16–17.
Murphy, Margueritte S. *A Tradition of Subversion: The Prose Poem in English from Wilde to Ashbery*. Amherst: University of Massachusetts Press, 1992.
Murphy, Michael. "'One Hundred Per Cent Bohemia': Pop Decadence and the Aestheticization of Commodity in the Rise of the Slicks." In *Marketing Modernisms: Self-Promotion, Canonization, Rereading*, edited by Kevin J. H. Dettmar and Stephen Watt, 61–89. Ann Arbor: University of Michigan Press, 1996.
Myers, D. G. *The Elephants Teach: Creative Writing Since 1880*. Englewood Cliffs, NJ: Prentice-Hall, 1996.
Myers, Jack, and Roger Weingarten. "Introduction." In *New American Poets of the 80's*, edited by Myers and Weingarten, xiv–xv. Green Harbor, MA: Wampeter, 1984.
——, eds. *New American Poets of the '90s*. Boston: David R. Godine, 1991.
Nash, Catherine. "Remapping the Body/Land: New Cartographies of Identity, Gender, and Landscape in Ireland." In *Writing Women and Space: Colonial and Postcolonial Geographies*, edited by Alison Blunt and Gillian Rose, 227–50. New York: Guilford, 1994.
Nelson, Cary. *Repression and Recovery: Modern American Poetry and the Politics of Cultural Memory, 1910–1945*. Madison: University of Wisconsin Press, 1989.
Newcomb, John Timberman. "*Others, Poetry,* and Wallace Stevens: Little Magazines as Agents of Reputation." *Essays in Literature* 16 (1989): 256–70.

——— *Wallace Stevens and Literary Canons*. Jackson: University Press of Mississippi, 1992.

Ngai, Sianne. *Ugly Feelings*. Cambridge, MA: Harvard University Press, 2005.

Nicholls, Peter. *George Oppen and the Fate of Modernism*. New York: Oxford University Press, 2007.

———. "Unsettling the Wilderness: Susan Howe and American History." *Contemporary Literature* 37, no. 4 (Winter 1996): 586–601.

Nielsen, Aldon Lynn. *Black Chant: Languages of African-American Postmodernism*. New York: Cambridge University Press, 1997.

Notley, Alice. *Coming After*. Ann Arbor: University of Michigan Press, 2005.

———. *Doctor Williams' Heiresses*. Willits, CA: Tuumba, 1980.

———. *Grave of Light: New and Selected Poems 1970–2005*. Middletown, CT: Wesleyan University Press, 2006.

———. "Interview." With Edward Foster. In *Poetry and Poetics in a New Millennium*, edited by Edward Foster, 64–78. Jersey City, NJ: Talisman House, 2000.

Nunberg, Geoffrey, ed. *The Future of the Book*. Berkeley: University of California Press, 1996.

O'Brien, Geoffrey. *Bardic Deadlines: Reviewing Poetry, 1984–95*. Ann Arbor: University of Michigan Press, 1998.

Ochester, Ed, and Peter Oresick, eds. *The Pittsburgh Anthology of Contemporary American Poetry*. Pittsburgh: University of Pittsburgh Press, 1993.

Oderman, Kevin. "Earth and Awe: The One Poetry of George Oppen." *Sagetrieb* 3, no. 1 (Spring 1984): 63–73.

O'Hara, Frank. *The Collected Poems of Frank O'Hara*. Edited by Donald Allen. Berkeley: University of California Press, 1999.

Olds, Sharon. "George and Mary Oppen: Poetry and Friendship." *Ironwood* 13, no. 2 (Fall 1985): 73–80.

Olson, Charles. *The Collected Poems of Charles Olson Excluding the Maximus Poems*. Berkeley: University of California Press, 1987.

Oppen, George. "An Adequate Vision: A George Oppen Daybook." Edited by Michael Davidson. *Ironwood* 13, no. 2 (Fall 1985): 5–31.

———. "The Anthropologist of Myself: A Selection from Working Papers." Edited by Rachel Blau DuPlessis. *Sulfur* 26 (Spring 1990): 135–64.

———. "The Circumstances: A Collection from George Oppen's Uncollected Writing." Edited by Rachel Blau DuPlessis. *Sulfur* 25 (Fall 1989): 10–43.

———. *The Collected Poems of George Oppen*. New York: New Directions, 1975.

———. "A Conversation with George Oppen." With Charles Amirkhanian and David Gitin. *Ironwood* 3, no. 1 (1975): 21–24.

———. "George Oppen." Interview with L. S. Dembo. In *The Contemporary Writer: Interviews with Sixteen Novelists and Poets*, edited by L. S. Dembo and Cyrena N. Pondrom, 172–90. Madison: University of Wisconsin Press, 1972.

———. "Interview with George Oppen [1975]." With Reinhold Schiffer. *Sagetrieb* 3, no. 3 (Winter 1984): 9–23.

———. [Letter to Shirley Kaufman.] University of Pennsylvania, Electronic Poetry Center, Authors. July 1970. https://www.writing.upenn.edu.

———. "Letters to Andy Meyer." *Ironwood* 13, no. 2 (Fall 1985): 104–10.

———. "Letters to June Oppen Degnan." *Ironwood* 13, no. 2 (Fall 1985): 215–36.

———. *New Collected Poems*. Edited by Michael Davidson. New York: New Directions, 2002.

———. "Oppen on His Poems: A Discussion." With L. S. Dembo. In Hatlen, *George Oppen*, 197–213.

———. "'The Philosophy of the Astonished': Selections from the Working Papers." Edited by Rachel Blau DuPlessis. *Sulfur* 27 (Fall 1990): 202–20.

———. "Poetry and Politics: A Conversation with George and Mary Oppen." With Burton Hatlen and Tom Mandel. In Hatlen, *George Oppen*, 23–50.

———. *Primitive*. Santa Barbara, CA: Black Sparrow, 1978.

———. *The Selected Letters of George Oppen*. Edited by Rachel Blau DuPlessis. Durham, NC: Duke University Press, 1990.

———. *Selected Prose, Daybooks, and Papers*. Edited by Stephen Cope. Berkeley: University of California Press, 2007.

———. "Selections from George Oppen's *Daybook*." Edited by Dennis Young. *Iowa Review* 18, no. 3 (Fall 1988): 1–17.

Oppen, George, and Mary Oppen. "Conversation with George and Mary Oppen, May 25, 1975." With Kevin Power. *Texas Quarterly* 21, no. 1 (1978): 35–52.

———. "Poetry and Politics: A Conversation with George and Mary Oppen." With Burton Hatlen and Tom Mandel. In Hatlen, *George Oppen*, 23–50 .

Oppen, Mary. "Conversation with Mary Oppen." With Dennis Young. *Iowa Review* 18, no. 3 (Fall 1988): 18–47.

Ossman, David. *The Sullen Art. Interviews by David Ossman with Modern American Poets*. New York: Corinth, 1963.

———. *The Sullen Art: Recording the Revolution in American Poetry*. Toledo, OH: University of Toledo Press, 2016.

Pack, Robert. "Introduction." In *New Poets of England and America*, edited by Donald Hall and Robert Pack, 177–83. New York: New American Library, 1962.

Pack, Robert, Sydney Lea, and Jay Parini, eds. *The Bread Loaf Anthology of Contemporary American Poetry*. Hanover, NH: University Press of New England, 1985.

Parini, Jay, ed. *The Columbia History of American Poetry*. New York: Columbia University Press, 1993.

Parkinson, Thomas. *Hart Crane and Yvor Winters: Their Literary Correspondence*. Berkeley: University of California Press, 1978.

Pearce, Roy Harvey. *The Continuity of American Poetry*. Princeton, NJ: Princeton University Press, 1961.

Perelman, Bob. "Between Minsk to Pinsk." *Electronic Poetry Review* 8 (January 2008). Penn Sound. https://www.writing.upenn.edu.

———. *Braille*. Ithaca, NY: Ithaca House, 1975.

———. *Captive Audience*. Great Barrington, MA: Figures, 1988.

———. "A Conversation with Bob Perelman." With Peter Nicholls. *Textual Practice* 12, no. 3 (1998): 525–43.

———. "Doctor Williams's Position, Updated." In Armand, *Contemporary Poetics*, 67–95.

———. "Exactly: The Poetry of Rae Armantrout." In Beckett, *Wild Salience*, 155–61.

———. "The First Person." *Hills* 6/7 (Spring 1980): 147–83.

———. *The Future of Memory*. New York: Roof, 1998.

———. *The Marginalization of Poetry: Language Writing and Literary History*. Princeton, NJ: Princeton University Press, 1996.

———. *Modernism the Morning After*. Tuscaloosa: University of Alabama Press, 2017.

——. *Ten to One: Selected Poems*. Hanover, NH: Wesleyan University Press/University Press of New England, 1999.
——. *Virtual Reality*. New York: Roof, 1993.
——, ed. *Writing/Talks*. Carbondale: Southern Illinois University Press, 1985.
Perloff, Marjorie. "The Avant-Garde Phase of American Modernism." In *The Cambridge Companion to American Modernism*, edited by Walter Kalaidjian, 195–217. New York: Cambridge University Press, 2005.
——. *Differentials: Poetry, Poetics, Pedagogy*. Tuscaloosa: University of Alabama Press, 2004.
——. [Letter to Ralph Maud, April 16, 1995] *Minutes of the Charles Olson Society* 8 (1995): 34–36.
——. *The Poetics of Indeterminacy: Rimbaud to Cage*. Princeton, NJ: Princeton University Press, 1981.
——. "Poetry on the Brink: Reinventing the Lyric." *Boston Review* 37, no. 3 (May/June 2012). http://bostonreview.net.
——. *Poetry On and Off the Page: Essays for Emergent Occasions*. Evanston, IL: Northwestern University Press, 1998.
——. "'The Shape of the Lines': Oppen and the Metric of Difference." In Hatlen, *George Oppen*, 215–29.
——. "The Shipwreck of the Singular: George Oppen's 'Of Being Numerous.'" *Ironwood* 13, no. 2 (Fall 1985): 193–204.
——. *21st-Century Modernism: The 'New' Poetics*. Malden, MA: Blackwell, 2002.
——. "Whose New American Poetry? Anthologizing in the Nineties." *Diacritics* 26, nos. 3–4 (Fall–Winter 1996): 104–23.
Phillips, J. J., Ishmael Reed, Gundars Strads, and Shawn Wong, eds. *The Before Columbus Foundation Poetry Anthology: Selections from the American Book Awards, 1980–1990*. New York: W. W. Norton, 1992.
Platt, Susan Noyes. "*The Little Review*: Early Years and Avant-Garde Ideas." In *The Old Guard and the Avant-Garde: Modernism in Chicago, 1910–1940*, edited by Sue Ann Prince, 139–54. Chicago: University of Chicago Press, 1990.
——. "Mysticism in the Machine Age: Jane Heap and *The Little Review*," *20/1: Twentieth-Century Art and Culture* 1, no. 1 (1989): 18–44.
Plumly, Stanley."[Review of *Seascape: Needle's Eye*]." *Ohio Review* 14, no. 2 (1973): 104.
Poster, Mark. *The Mode of Information: Poststructuralisms and Contexts*. Chicago: University of Chicago Press, 1990.
Pound, Ezra. *The Cantos*. London: Faber and Faber, 1975.
——. *Gaudier-Brzeska: A Memoir*. New York: New Directions, 1970.
——. *The Letters of Ezra Pound 1907–1941*. Edited by D. D. Paige. New York: Harcourt, Brace, and World, 1950.
——. *Literary Essays of Ezra Pound*. New York: New Directions, 1968.
——. *Pound/Joyce: The Letters of Ezra Pound to James Joyce with Pound's Essays on Joyce*. Edited by Forrest Read. New York: New Directions, 1970.
——. *Pound/The Little Review. The Letters of Ezra Pound to Margaret Anderson: The Little Review Correspondence*. Edited by Thomas Scott and Melvin J. Friedman, with the assistance of Jackson R. Bryer. New York: New Directions, 1988.
——. "Three Cantos: I." *Poetry* 10, no. 3 (June 1917): 115.
Pressman, Jessica. *Digital Modernism: Making It New in New Media*. New York: Oxford University Press, 2014.

Prinz, Jessica. *Art Discourse/Discourse in Art*. New Brunswick, NJ: Rutgers University Press, 1991.

Pritchett, Patrick. "Clarity or, Late Modernism (A Photological Midrash)." *Big Bridge* no. 14 (2009). http://www.bigbridge.org.

———. "*Drafts 1–38, Toll*, by Rachel Blau DuPlessis." *Jacket2*, May 2003. http://jacketmagazine.com.

Prunty, Wyatt. "Emaciated Poetry." *Sewanee Review* 93, no. 1 (Winter 1985): 78–94. Reprinted in *"Fallen from the Symboled World": Precedents for the New Formalism*. New York: Oxford University Press, 1990.

Quartermain, Peter. "Getting Ready to Have Been Frightened: How I Read Bruce Andrews." *Aerial* 9 (1999): 161–82.

Rainey, Lawrence. *Institutions of Modernism: Literary Elites and Public Culture*. New Haven, CT: Yale University Press, 1998.

Ramazani, Jahan. "Preface to the Third Edition." In *The Norton Anthology of Modern and Contemporary Poetry*, edited by Ramazani, Richard Ellmann, and Robert O'Clair, xxxiii–xxxvii. 3rd. ed. Vol. 2. New York: W. W. Norton, 2003.

Rasula, Jed. *The American Poetry Wax Museum: Reality Effects, 1940–1990*. Urbana, IL: National Council of Teachers of English, 1995.

———. *Syncopations: The Stress of Innovation in Contemporary American Poetry*. Tuscaloosa: University of Alabama Press, 2004.

Ratcliffe, Stephen. *Listening to Reading*. Albany: State University of New York Press, 2000.

———. "Words as 'Things' ('Actions'/'Events')." *Jacket2*, 2011. https://jacket2.org.

Reed, Brian M. *Phenomenal Reading: Essays on Modern and Contemporary Poetics*. Tuscaloosa: University of Alabama Press, 2012.

Retallack, Joan. "Con Verse Sing W/ Bruce Andrews Praxis." *Aerial* 9 (1999): 131–32.

———. *The Poethical Wager*. Berkeley: University of California Press, 2003.

———. "What Is Experimental Poetry and Why Do We Need It?" *Jacket* 32 (2007). http://jacketmagazine.com.

Rexroth, Kenneth. "Disengagement: The Art of the Beat Generation." In *A Casebook on the Beat*, edited by Thomas Parkinson, 179–93. New York: Crowell, 1961.

———. "San Francisco Letter." *Evergreen Review* 1 (1957): [5]–14.

Reznikoff, Charles. *The Poems of Charles Reznikoff 1918–1975*. Edited by Seamus Cooney. Boston: David R. Godine, 2005.

Richards, I. A. *Principles of Literary Criticism*. New York: Harcourt, Brace, and World, 1925.

Roberts, Andrew Michael. "The Rhetoric of Value in Recent British Poetry Anthologies," In *Poetry and Contemporary Culture: The Question of Value*, edited by Roberts and Jonathan Allison, 101–22. Edinburgh: Edinburgh University Press, 2002.

Robinson, Kit. "Song." In Perelman, *Writing/Talks*, 48–62.

Rosenthal, M. L., and Sally Gall. *The Modern Poetic Sequence: The Genius of Modern Poetry*. New York: Oxford University Press, 1983.

Ross, Andrew. *The Failure of Modernism: Symptoms of American Poetry*. New York: Columbia University Press, 1986.

Rothenberg, Jerome, ed. *A Big Jewish Book: Poems and Other Visions of the Jews from Tribal Times to the Present*. New York: Doubleday, 1978.

Rubin, Stan Sanvel. "Introduction." In *The Post-Confessionals: Conversations with American Poets of the Eighties*, edited by Earl G. Ingersoll, Judith Kitchen, and Stan Sanvel Rubin, 11–24. Rutherford, NJ: Fairleigh Dickinson University Press, 1989.

Russo, Linda. "Introduction: A Context for Reading Joanne Kyger." *Jacket* 11 (April 2000). http://jacketmagazine.com.

Ryan, Marie-Laure. "Cyberspace, Virtuality, and the Text." In *Cyberspace Textuality: Computer Technology and Literary Theory*, edited by Ryan, 78–107. Bloomington: Indiana University Press, 1999.

Sanders, Jay, and Charles Bernstein, curators. *Poetry Plastique*. New York: Marianne Boesky Gallery and Granary Books, 2001.

Scalapino, Leslie. *The Front Matter, Dead Souls*. Hanover, NH: University Press of New England, 1996.

———. *Objects in the Terrifying Tense Longing from Taking Place*. New York: Roof, 1993.

Schor, Naomi. *Reading in Detail: Aesthetics and the Feminine*. New York: Methuen, 1987.

Schuyler, James. "Poet and Painter Overture." In Allen, *New American Poetry*, 418–19.

Schwartz, Delmore. *Selected Essays of Delmore Schwartz*. Edited by Donald A. Dike and David H. Zucker. Chicago: University of Chicago Press, 1970.

Schwartz, Leonard. "Introduction." In Schwartz, Donahue, and Foster, *Primary Trouble*, 1–4.

Schwartz, Leonard, Joseph Donahue, and Edward Foster, eds. *Primary Trouble: An Anthology of Contemporary American Poetry*. Jersey City, NJ: Talisman House, 1996.

[Seldes, Gilbert]. "Comment," *The Dial* 74, no. 6 (June 1923): 637.

Shapiro, Karl. *In Defense of Ignorance*. New York: Vintage, 1965.

Shaw, Lytle. *Frank O'Hara: The Poetics of Coterie*. Iowa City: University of Iowa Press, 2006.

Shaner, Tim, and Michael Rozendal. "Introduction: 'The New Is the Old Made Known.'" *Verdure* 3–4 (February 2001): 47–48.

Shelley, Percy Bysshe. *The Complete Poetical Works of Percy Bysshe Shelley*. Edited by Edward Dowden. New York: Thomas Y. Crowell, 1900.

Shepherd, Reginald, ed. *Lyric Postmodernisms: An Anthology of Contemporary Innovative Poetries*. Denver: Counterpath, 2008.

Shetley, Vernon. *After the Death of Poetry: Poet and Audience in Contemporary America*. Durham, NC: Duke University Press, 1993.

———. "The Place of Poetry." *Yale Review* 75 (1986): 429–37.

Sieburth, Richard. "Pound's *Dial* Letters: Between Modernism and the Avant-Garde." *American Poetry* 6, no. 2 (1989): 3–10.

Silliman, Ron. *The Age of Huts*. New York: Roof, 1986.

———. "Berkeley." In *None of the Above: New Poets of the USA*, edited by Michael Lally, 63–66. Trumansburg, NY: Crossing Press, 1976.

———. "Canons and Institutions: New Hope for the Disappeared." In *The Politics of Poetic Form: Poetry and Public Policy*, edited by Charles Bernstein, 149–74. New York: Roof, 1990.

———. *Crow*. Ithaca, NY: Ithaca House, 1971.

———. "The Dysfunction of Criticism: Poets and the Critical Tradition of the Anti-Academy." *Poetics Journal* 10 (June 1998): 179–94.

———. [Interview]. With Manuel Brito. In *A Suite of Poetic Voices: Interviews with*

*Contemporary American Poets*, edited by Manuel Brito, 145–66. Santa Brigida, Spain: Kadle Books, 1992.

——, ed. *In the American Tree: Language, Realism, Poetry*. Orono, ME: National Poetry Foundation, 1986.

——. "I Wanted to Write Sentences: Decision Making in the American Longpoem." *Sagetrieb* 11, nos. 1–2 (Spring–Fall 1992): 11–20.

——. "IX." In *The Grand Piano: An Experiment in Collective Autobiography San Francisco 1975–80*, by Carla Harryman, Kit Robinson, Tom Mandel, Barrett Watten, Rae Armantrout, Ted Pearson, Lyn Hejinian, Bob Perelman, Ron Silliman, Steve Benson, 126–35. Part 4. Detroit, MI: Mode A, 2007.

——. "Language, Realism, Poetry." In Silliman, *In the American Tree*, xv–xxiii.

——. *Lit*. Elmwood, CT: Potes and Poets, 1987.

——. *The New Sentence*. New York: Roof, 1989.

——. "The Practice of Art." In Barone and Ganick, *Art of Practice*, 371–79.

——. [Review of *Wobbling*, by Bruce Andrews.] *Sagetrieb* 1, no. 1 (Spring 1982): 155–58.

——. Ron Silliman/William Carlos Williams Reading. University of Pennsylvania, Nine Contemporary Poets Read Themselves through Modernism. October 12, 2000. https://www.writing.upenn.edu.

——. "Third Phase Objectivism." *Paideuma* 10, no. 1 (Spring 1981): 85–89.

——. Untitled talk on William Carlos Williams. Modernist Studies Association. Kelly Writers House, Philadelphia. October 12, 2000.

——. *What*. Great Barrington, MA: Figures, 1988.

——. "The Williams Influence." *San Francisco Review of Books* 4, no. 1 (May 1978): 42–44.

Silliman, Ron, Carla Harryman, Lyn Hejinian, Steve Benson, Bob Perelman, and Barrett Watten. "Aesthetic Tendency and the Politics of Poetry: A Manifesto." *Social Text* 19/20 (Autumn 1988): 261–75.

Simpson, Louis. "Important and Unimportant Poems." *Hudson Review* 14, no. 3 (Autumn 1961): 461–70.

Sloan, Mary Margaret. "Of Experience to Experiment: Women's Innovative Writing, 1965–1995." In *The World in Time and Space: Towards a History of Innovative American Poetry in Our Time*, edited by Edward Foster and Joseph Donahue, 498–525. Jersey City, NJ: Talisman House, 2002.

——, ed. *Moving Borders: Three Decades of Innovative Writing by Women*. Jersey City, NJ: Talisman House, 1998.

Smith, Dave, and David Bottoms, eds. *The Morrow Anthology of Younger American Poets*. New York: Quill, 1985.

Snodgrass, W. D. "April Inventory." In Hall, Pack, and Simpson, *New Poets of England and America*, 297–99.

Spahr, Juliana. "Introduction." In *American Women Poets in the 21st Century: Where Lyric Meets Language*, edited by Claudia Rankine and Juliana Spahr, 1–17. Middletown, CT: Wesleyan University Press, 2002.

Spicer, Jack. *My Vocabulary Did This to Me: The Collected Poetry of Jack Spicer*. Edited by Peter Gizzi and Kevin Killian. Middletown, CT: Wesleyan University Press, 2008.

St. John, David. "Introduction." In Swensen and St. John, *American Hybrid*, xxvii–xxviii.

Stefans, Brian Kim. "Rational Geomancy: Ten Fables of the Reconstruction." Arras Publications. Accessed January 3, 2021. https://ie10.ieonchrome.com.

——. "Review: *Paradise and Method* and *The Language of Inquiry*." *Boston Review*, December 1, 2001. http://bostonreview.net.

Stein, Gertrude. "Composition as Explanation." In *Modernism: An Anthology*, edited by Lawrence Rainey, 407–11. Malden, MA: Blackwell, 2005.

Steinman, Lisa M. "Williams 'As Usual.'" In *Rigor of Beauty: Essays in Commemoration of William Carlos Williams*, edited by Ian D. Copestake, 35–56. Oxford: Peter Lang, 2004.

Stephens, Paul "At the Limits of Comprehension." *Art in America* 104, no. 4 (April 2016): 88.

Stevens, Wallace. *The Collected Poems*. New York: Vintage, 1982.

Strand, Mark, ed. *The Contemporary American Poets: American Poetry since 1940*. New York: Meridian, 1969.

Sutton, Walter, ed., *Pound, Thayer, Watson, and The Dial: A Story in Letters. Introducing New Letters from Ezra Pound's Dial Correspondence, The Sibley Watson Archive, and The Dial/Scofield Thayer Papers.* Gainesville: University of Florida Press, 1994.

Swensen, Cole. "Against the Limits of Language: The Geometries of Anne-Marie Albiach and Susan Howe." In Sloan, *Moving Borders*, 630–41.

——. "Introduction." In Swensen and St. John, *American Hybrid*, xvii–xxvi.

Swensen, Cole, and David St. John, eds. *American Hybrid: A Norton Anthology of New Poetry*. New York: W. W. Norton, 2009.

Taggart, John. "Deep Jewels: George Oppen's *Seascape: Needle's Eye*." *Ironwood* 13, no. 2 (Fall 1985): 159–68.

——. "George Oppen and the Anthologies." *Ironwood* 13, no. 2 (Fall 1985): 252–62.

——. *Songs of Degrees: Essays on Contemporary Poetry and Poetics*. Tuscaloosa: University of Alabama Press, 1994.

Thomas, Dylan. *The Collected Poems of Dylan Thomas 1934–1952*. New York: New Directions, 1957.

[Thayer, Scofield.] "Announcement." *The Dial* 79, no. 1 (January 1925): 89–90.

Thwaite, Anthony. "Good, Bad and Chaos." *Spectator*, September 1, 1961, 298–99.

True, Michael. "Modernism, *The Dial*, and the Way They Were." In *The Dial: Arts and Letters in the 1920s. An Anthology of Writings from The Dial Magazine, 1920–29*, edited by Gaye L. Brown, 5–13. Worcester, MA: Worcester Art Museum, 1981.

von Hallberg, Robert. "Poetry, Politics, and Intellectuals." In *Poetry and Criticism 1940–1995*, 9–260. Vol. 8 of *The Cambridge History of American Literature*. General Editor, Sacvan Bercovitch. New York: Cambridge University Press, 1996.

Vos, Eric. "New Media Poetry." *Visible Language* 30, no. 2 (1996): 214–33.

Waldman, Anne. "Feminafesto." In *Vow to Poetry: Essays, Interviews, and Manifestos*, 21–24. Minneapolis: Coffee House, 2001.

Waldrop, Bernard. "George Oppen." *Burning Deck* 1 (1962): 51.

Waldrop, Rosmarie. *Dissonance (If You Are Interested)*. Tuscaloosa: University of Alabama Press, 2005.

Walker, Jeffrey. *Bardic Ethos and the American Epic Poem: Whitman, Pound, Crane, Williams, Olson*. Baton Rouge: Louisiana State University Press, 1989.

Wallace, Mark. "From BOYS AT THE GUNS." *Aerial* 9 (1999): 149–50.

Wallace, Ronald, ed. *Vital Signs: Contemporary American Poetry from the University Presses*. Madison: University of Wisconsin Press, 1989.

Waltuch, Michael. Letter to Jessica Lowenthal. *Silliman's Blog*, March 12, 2003. http://ronsilliman.blogspot.com.

Wasserstrom, William. *The Time of The Dial*. Syracuse, NY: Syracuse University Press, 1963.

[Watson, James Sibley]. "Announcement." *The Dial* 84, no. 1 (January1928): 89–90.

——. "Comment." *The Dial* 69, no. 2 (August 1920): 216–18.

——. "Comment." *The Dial* 83, no. 3 (September 1927): 269–70.

Watten, Barrett. *The Constructivist Moment: From Material Text to Cultural Poetics*. Middletown, CT: Wesleyan University Press, 2003.

——. *Frame (1971–1990)*. Los Angeles: Sun and Moon, 1997.

——. "Note to *Zone*." *Armed Cell* no. 6 (2014). Scribd, Documents, Armed Cell 6. January 26, 2014. http://www.scribd.com.

——. "Poetics and the Question of Value; or, What Is a Philosophically Serious Poet?" *Wallace Stevens Journal* 39, no. 1 (Spring 2015): 84–101.

——. *Progress*. New York: Roof, 1985.

——. *Questions of Poetics: Language Writing and Consequences*. Iowa City: University of Iowa Press, 2016.

——. *Total Syntax*. Carbondale: Southern Illinois University Press, 1985.

Weinberger, Eliot, ed. *American Poetry since 1950: Innovators and Outsiders*. New York: Marsilio, 1993.

——. "Eliot Weinberger in Conversation with Kent Johnson." *Jacket* 16 (March 2002). http://jacketmagazine.com.

Weinfield, Henry. *The Music of Thought in the Poetry of George Oppen and William Bronk*. Iowa City: University of Iowa Press, 2010.

——. "'Of Being Numerous' by George Oppen." In Hatlen, *George Oppen*, 375–79.

——. "Oppen on Clarity, Opacity, and Prosody: Passages from the *Daybooks*." In *All This Strangeness: A Garland for George Oppen*, edited by Eric Hoffman. *Big Bridge* 14 (2009). https://bigbridge.org.

Wellman, Donald. "A Complex Realism: Reading *Spring and All* as Seminal for Postmodern Poetry." *Sagetrieb* 18, nos. 2–3 (Fall–Winter 1999): 297–317.

Whalen, Philip. "[Statement on Poetics]." In Allen, *New American Poetry*, 420.

Whitman, Walt. *An American Primer*. San Francisco: City Lights, 1970.

——. *Leaves of Grass and Other Writings*. Edited by Michael Moon. New York: W. W. Norton, 2002.

Whittemore, Reed. "A Treasure." In Hall, Pack, and Simpson, *New Poets of England and America*, 316.

——. "A Week of Doodle." In Hall, Pack, and Simpson, *New Poets of England and America*, 317–18.

Whitworth, John. "Out of the Ghetto." *Poetry Review* 81, no. 1 (Winter 1991/92): 46–47.

Williams, William Carlos. *The Autobiography of William Carlos Williams*. New York: Random House, 1951.

——. *The Collected Poems of William Carlos Williams*. Vol. 1, *1909–1939*. Edited by A. Walton Litz and Christopher McGowan. New York: New Directions, 1986.

——. *The Collected Poems of William Carlos Williams*. Vol. 2, *1939–1962*. Edited by Christopher MacGowan. New York: New Directions, 1988.

———. *The Embodiment of Knowledge*. Edited by Ron Loewinsohn. New York: New Directions, 1974.

———. *Imaginations*. New York: New Directions, 1970.

———. *Pictures from Brueghel and Other Poems*. New York: New Directions, 1962.

———. *Selected Essays of William Carlos Williams*. New York: New Directions, 1969.

———. *The Selected Letters of William Carlos Williams*. Edited by John C. Thirlwall. New York: New Directions, 1984.

———. *Spring and All*. New York: New Directions, 2011.

Williams, William Carlos, and Louis Zukofsky. *The Correspondence of William Carlos Williams and Louis Zukofsky*. Edited by Barry Ahearn. Middletown, CT: Wesleyan University Press, 2003.

Willis, Patricia C. "William Carlos Williams, Marianne Moore, and *The Dial*." *Sagetrieb* 3, no. 2 (Fall 1984): 49–59.

Winters, Yvor. *Uncollected Essays and Reviews*. Edited by Francis Murphy. Chicago: Swallow, 1973.

Woods, Tim. *The Poetics of the Limit: Ethics and Politics in Modern and Contemporary American Poetry*. New York: Palgrave Macmillan, 2002.

Wright, James. *Collected Prose*. Edited by Anne Wright. Ann Arbor: University of Michigan Press, 1983.

Young, Dennis. "Anthologies, Canonicity, and the Objectivist Imagination: The Case of George Oppen." In *No Small World: Visions and Revisions of World Literature*, edited by Michael Thomas Carroll. Urbana, IL: National Council of Teachers of English, 1996. 146–59.

Young, Karl. "Introductory Note: 10 Pages from *RHYMMS* by Robert Grenier." University of Pennsylvania, Electronic Poetry Center, Authors, Grenier. Accessed January 27, 2020. https://www.writing.upenn.edu.

Zahn, Curtis. "An Inch of Culture: The 'New' 'Poets'—1945–1960 As Defined by Evergreen." *Trace* 39 (1960): 40–44.

Zboya, Eric. ["Algorithmic Translations of Charles Bernstein's *Alphabetica*."] *Adirondack Review* 11, no. 4 (Spring 2011). https://www.theadirondackreview.com.

Zukofsky, Louis. *"A."* Berkeley: University of California Press, 1978.

———. *ALL: The Collected Short Poems 1923–1964*. New York: W. W. Norton, 1971.

———. *Prepositions +: The Collected Critical Essays*. Edited by Mark Scroggins. Middletown, CT: Wesleyan University Press, 2001.

# Index